Freud and Cocaine

THE FREUDIAN FALLACY

Freud and Cocaine

THE FREUDIAN FALLACY

E. M. Thornton

Blond
&
Briggs

First published in Great Britain in 1983 by Blond & Briggs
Limited, Dataday House, Alexandra Road, London SW19 7JZ.

British Library Cataloguing in Publication Data

Thornton, E. M.
　　Freud and Cocaine
　　1. Freud, Sigmund　　2. Psychoanalysis
　　3. Cocaine habit
　　I. Title
　　150.19'52　　BF173.F85

　　ISBN 0-85634-139-8

Every care has been taken to locate and acknowledge the sources of the illustrations used in this
book. If, however, any copyright has been un-
wittingly abused, the author and publisher
apologise and will gladly amend the inaccuracy
in future editions.

Printed in Great Britain by Billing & Sons Ltd., Worcester

Contents

Foreword

This book might well be called "The Demolition of Sigmund Freud". It is difficult to understand the strength of his influence over modern medicine for his teaching lacks any scientific support.

In my youth, six decades ago, I was vastly intrigued by his teaching, but enlightenment came when I began to see that no one in my admittedly small experience had been cured of his neurosis by psychoanalysis. One must be careful to avoid the *post hoc propter hoc* fallacy. A few people were better after spending what Noël Coward called "years and years of expensive humiliation". Many more were better after much shorter times spent in conversation with psychiatrists of widely different schools and with general practitioners, priests, favourite uncles or even myself.

I have heard Freud described as "the greatest con man in the history of medicine." This is unfair! He undoubtedly believed in the truth of his hypotheses when he first pronounced them, instanced by his ridiculous theory of infantile sexuality.

Then why has Freud held sway for so long? I think that all men faced with a mystery long for clarity. Mystery is a bugbear that physicians abhor. They have been led astray by other gurus than Freud, but this tendency they should resist. Of Sir William Osler, my old teacher Alexander George Gibson said, "I have never known any doctor say more often 'I don't know'." This is the beginning of wisdom.

Freud had a scientific training which should have protected him from the prevalent medical vice of explaining one mystery by the substitution of another. I think that Miss Thornton's view, so ably set forth in this book, that the answer lay in his addiction to cocaine has much to recommend it.

Raymond Greene
Harley Street, March 1982

Acknowledgements

It is with much sadness that I acknowledge the great assistance of the late Dr Raymond Greene, the eminent endocrinologist, who died on December 6, 1982. Dr Greene, as chairman of William Heinemann Medical Books, had published my previous work and read successive drafts of this book, giving generously and unstintingly of his time and wisdom both as physician and publisher in its preparation, and contributing the foreward as his final gesture.

I would like also to thank Professor Victor Wynn, Professor of Human Metabolism in the University of London, who read the final draft and made many valuable comments and helpful suggestions. Neither Professor Wynn nor Dr Greene, however, are responsible for any errors that may have crept in.

My thanks are due also to Dr C. Lill who made various stylistic suggestions and who contributed the greater part of the translations from the German used in the book, and Dr Ulrike Schauseil-Zipf of Cologne, whose additional translations were of very great help. I would also like to acknowledge the assistance of the staff of the library of the Royal Society of Medicine, London, who gave generously of their expertise, and that of the Librarian of the Psychology Section of the University of London Library whose patience and tolerance were always unfailing. Finally I gratefully acknowledge the expert secretarial assistance of Miss Patricia Dillon and Miss Stephanie Dodridge in the preparation of the final draft of the typescript.

E.M.T.

Acknowledgements of Illustrations

The photographs and illustrations in this book are reproduced by kind permission of the following:

The Mary Evans Picture Library: Frontispiece, 8, 28, 128, 159, 266, 305, 307

The Wellcome Institute Library, London: 18, 86

The Institute for the History of Medicine, Vienna: 26, 32, 44

The Austrian National Library, Vienna: 30, 125, 198

H. Roger-Viollet: 49

The Berlin State Library: 50

The illustrations on page 56 are from *The Neuro-Sciences and Behaviour* (Second Edition) by D. M. Atrens and I. F. Curthoys, Academic Press (Australia) Ltd. page 40

The illustrations on pages 67, 75, 76, 96, 100 and 102 are from *Iconographie Photographique de la Salpétrière (Service de M. Charcot)* by Bourneville and P. Regnard, Volume I, Bureaux du Progrés Medicale and V. Adrien Delahaye & Co. 1876–1877. Volume III, Bureaux du Progrés Medicale and V. A. Delahaye and Le Crosnier 1879–1880

The photograph on page 263 is from the article by Exonel E. published in *La Presse Medicale*, Volume 47 page 875, 1939 and is reproduced by kind permission of Masson S. A., Paris

Statue of Freud by Oscar Newman, 1970.

I

Overture

Probably no single individual has had a more profound effect on twentieth-century thought than Sigmund Freud. His works have influenced psychiatry, anthropology, social work, penology and education and provided a seemingly limitless source of material for novelists and dramatists. Freud has created "a whole new climate of opinion"; for better or worse he has changed the face of society. The vocabulary of psychoanalysis has passed into the language of everyday life. Freud himself has been described as a genius of the stature of Newton, Einstein, Darwin and Copernicus.

Yet this book makes the heretical claim that his central postulate, the "unconscious mind", does not exist, that his theories were baseless and aberrational and, greatest impiety of all, that Freud himself, when he formulated them, was under the influence of a toxic drug with specific effects on the brain. These are bold claims to make about one of the "latter-day saints" of the twentieth century. But they are amply substantiated in the chapters that follow.

Freud's early experiments with cocaine and his own use of the newly synthesised drug as a medication in the years 1884 to 1887 are known from his early papers and appear in all his biographies. But it has always been assumed that he ceased the practice in 1887, years before he began his major psychoanalytical work. This book presents evidence that Freud resumed his use of cocaine in the latter half of 1892, the year coinciding with the emergence of his revolutionary new theories, and asserts that these theories were the direct outcome of this usage. None of this is to be found in the definitive biography by Ernest Jones, yet all the clues are there, unnoticed in the thirty years since its publication.

This book could almost be termed "an alternative biography" in that most of the main facts covered by Jones' *Life and Work* appear. But the same facts are now shown to be elements of an entirely different story from that told by Jones, a story concealed from the world for over eighty years. Ernest Jones was Freud's close friend and most loyal disciple. His work received the blessing of the Freud family and letters and documents denied to others were placed at his disposal. The final word on Freud's life and work would seem to have been said in his official biography. But his book left many unresolved problems – Freud's inexplicable dependence on his strange friend Wilhelm Fliess, for instance, during the critical decade when he formulated his major theories. Why did Freud so uncritically embrace the fantastic theories of this friend? What was the nature of the "considerable psychoneurosis" he experienced during this period, and of the mysterious heart condition that appeared at about the same time? Why did Freud, arch apostle of sexual freedom, fail to put his own theories into practice and why did any proclivities in that direction cease entirely at the early age of forty one? These are only some of the many enigmatic features of the Freud story that have perplexed historians of psychoanalysis in recent years.

Freud's own *Autobiographical Study* (1925) was found by Jones to be at variance in important details with the facts as gleaned from the contemporary records. In the light of still later evidence, inconsistencies have emerged in Jones' own biography. Since its publication, historians of the psychoanalytic movement have been engaged in chipping away the massive edifice of the Freud legend, uncovering still further incompatible facts. The embargo by the Freud family on an important series of unpublished letters and the numerous deletions from those published has deepened the mystery; accusations of suppression and censorship have been levelled.

In this book, subjects discussed at length by Jones receive little attention. Conversely some of the events dismissed by him as unimportant and unrelated now stand out in vivid and significant relief. The "nasal reflex neurosis", for instance, appears frequently in Freud's correspondence during the nineties, the critical period of his "psychoneurosis", but is treated by Jones as a quaint anachronism. But its ubiquitous presence in the letters indicates that it must have been of considerable importance to Freud. The "neurosis" is here finally revealed to be the vital clue to the evidence that Freud resumed his use of cocaine in the eighteen-nineties and that whereas his earlier use of the drug had been sporadic and oral, he was now employing the far more formidable nasal route and in a much more regular usage.

The behavioural eccentricities displayed by Freud in the nineties and dismissed by Jones as the harmless peccadillos of a man of genius, must now be given a more sinister interpretation. Jones' dramatic picture of a tormented genius wrestling with the daemons of his unconscious mind, actually tells the story of a cocaine addiction following an almost classic course. Freud's rapid mood swings from exalted elation to profound depression, his episodes of clouded consciousness and periods of hyperactivity, interpreted by Jones as the manifestations of a "creative neurosis", are actually specific cocaine effects, as are the mysterious heart symptoms which appeared at about the same time. Freud's bitter complaints of ostracism and victimisation which Jones repeats, but which later biographers have shown to be groundless, were the paranoid delusions of persecution peculiar to the later stages of cocaine addiction; his suspicions and bitter denunciations of his disciples arose from the same cause. The unaccountable lapses in memory, the incompatabilities and discrepancies in his works which so taxed his editors and translators were also cocaine effects. Only deliberate mendacity, however, can explain some of these discrepancies and in this too Freud betrayed another symptom of his addiction.

Does Freud's cocaine usage completely invalidate his work? In the wake of the fashionable drug cult of recent years it has become almost sacrilegious to ascribe any harmful effect to any drug whatsoever. Critics of the cult have had to adopt an apologetic and deprecatory stance or remain silent altogether. This reticence is regrettable. There is ample evidence in the medical literature of cocaine's toxic and even lethal qualities. There is too an important difference between the "recreational" use of the drug fashionable today and that made by Freud ninety years ago. The amounts of the alkaloid currently present in street samples, adulterated as they are several times over, have been estimated as varying between seventeeen per cent and *none at all*. Freud used cocaine in its pure and unadulterated form and in strengths and dosages far exceeding those in use in later years even for strictly medical purposes.

Would not his use of cocaine have given Freud an increased capacity to explore the deeper levels of his unconscious mind, thus gaining fresh insights from an enhanced acquaintance with its mysterious depths? Many people today use drugs in the belief that these substances are "consciousness expanders", making possible access to the "hidden recesses of the mind". This is a fallacy. These drugs act not on the mind but on the *brain*. Their peculiar effects arise from their toxic action on highly sensitive nerve cells, the most vulnerable of which are in those brain centres where sense data are interpreted and memories stored. The false perceptions so vividly described in the drug literature which the deluded users interpret as emanations from the "deeper levels of the mind" are the distortions arising from poisoned brain cells. These drug-induced misperceptions were the daemons with which Freud wrestled when his "psychoneurosis" was at its height. Only when the sequestered portions of his correspondence are finally released will their true nature and extent become known.

The effects of cocaine on the human organism are little understood today. Ethical considerations prohibit prolonged experimental studies on human subjects and reliable information from known addicts is notoriously difficult to obtain. Animal experimentation, while helpful in elucidating the pathology in cells and tissues, can give little information on its effect on functions that are purely human. But there is one source of authentic information that has so far lain untapped – the long forgotten epidemic of cocainism that swept the United States in the eighties and nineties of the last century. Its earliest victims were medical men and those in allied professions, contemporaries of Freud, who used the drug unadulterated and in the same strengths and dosages as he would have employed. Many left fascinating and medically accurate records of their experiences. These accounts contain probably the most authentic descriptions of cocaine effects in the human organism we possess today.

The first significant fact obtained from the nineteenth-century data is that cocaine has highly specific effects on the sexual function, at first causing greatly increased sexual excitation as occurred with Freud. But with prolonged usage, sexual activity diminishes to the point of almost complete cessation and in this too Freud's addiction followed an almost classic course. Statements made today that cocaine has an anti-aphrodisiac effect or none at all probably derive from observations on seasoned addicts who usually come under the care of the physician in the later stages of their addiction.

The second significant finding is that, in common with other drugs, cocaine induces in its victims a peculiar messianic obsession. The addict is gripped by an exaggerated and pathological conviction that he alone has "the truth" and that he has an urgent mission to communicate this truth to all mankind. In many cases the "message" is that the whole world should enjoy the all-embracing benefits of the drug he himself uses and this results in the proselytising activities such as played so great a part in the drug cult of recent years. In Freud's case too this message played some part in his earlier use of cocaine when he pressed it on friends and family and wrote eulogistic papers in its praise. But in his second cocaine period the "message" was now the overriding supremacy of sexuality over all other facets of civilised existence and the urgent necessity that it should suffer no restraint or impediment if mankind were not to fall victim to mental illness of the gravest kind.

These two traits in combination, his own greatly increased libido and his messianic obsession with sexuality, must inevitably cast doubt on the validity of Freud's theories. The unavoidable conclusion is that they were the products of his cocaine usage and had no basis in fact. And with this realisation, how preposterous and pathological now appear the theories that have been accepted as truth for decades. That they have retained their hold on so many people of intellect and ability for so many years is one of the strangest aspects of the Freud story.

If Freud's main theoretical edifice was the result of his cocaine usage, its foundations were laid during his visit to Paris in 1885, where he spent some months under the aegis of the great French neurologist Charcot, then engaged in fascinating researches into "hypnotism" and "hysteria". Comparatively little space is devoted by Jones and Freud's other biographers to this important period in his life. Their works repeat the same legend – that at the Salpêt-rière Freud learned from Charcot that bodily disease could be caused by the agency of the mind alone, a fact that was in distinct contrast to the teaching he had received in Vienna. The conventional wisdom as expressed in these works is that this was a revolutionary new discovery which paved the way for Freud's further researches that were eventually to put psychiatry on a modern and enlightened footing. In fact, the attribution of physical disease to "the passions of the mind" is as old as medicine itself and, as will be demonstrated, was based on ignorance and superstition. Charcot's teaching was actually a regression to an earlier and less scientific era of medicine. The real revolution in psychiatry had taken place earlier in Vienna, when Freud's former chief, Meynert, discarding these old and unscientific beliefs, had begun systematically to seek out on the post-mortem table the brain pathology that was the real cause of so-called mental illness. Freud himself had participated in these studies and must have observed many times the massive cellular loss in the brains of cases of pre-senile dementia or the gross changes wrought in the tissues by the ravages of syphilis in those dying of "general paralysis of the insane".

In Paris, Freud was introduced to the mysteries of "hysteria" and "hypnotism", then Charcot's chief research interest. Both entities are paramount in the history of psychoanalysis; from patients diagnosed as suffering from hysteria and from subjects in the hypnotic trance, Freud built his entire theoretical edifice. Nearly a hundred years have passed since Charcot performed the experiments which so fascinated the young Freud and convinced him of the correctness of Charcot's teaching. Yet the validity of these experiments has never been questioned by any of Freud's biographers. Recreated for us in contemporary eyewitness accounts, Charcot's patients under "hypnosis" re-enact their strange performance and the dramatic spectacle of a patient in the convulsive crisis of "hysteria" is paraded anew. Recorded in minute detail in these old accounts, the clinical manifestations described make possible a modern reassessment in the light of the neurological advances that have taken place since those days. Significant errors are revealed both in Charcot's diagnoses of hysteria and in the inferences he drew when he placed patients so diagnosed into the hypnotic trance. These errors Freud incorporated uncritically into his own later work. The paper which signalled the start of his teaching on hidden mental trauma in the causation of hysteria was illustrated by case histories from Paris. His theoretical edifice was, in fact, built on flimsy foundations of error and ignorance. Ignorance because neither Charcot nor anyone else at that time knew what hypnotism actually was. In a later chapter the reader is introduced to what I hope to be able to demonstrate is the only possible explanation for the phenomena of hypnotism.

Somehow this *mélange* of ignorance, obsolete medicine and the products of a drugged brain became accepted as a revolutionary new science. In little more than a few decades psychoanalysis had become the dominating force in psychiatry. How was this possible? In Freud's lifetime, the most important factor was probably the same messianic trait conferred on him by cocaine. The false prophet of the drug world can propagate his message with as much conviction and authority as the true, and his manner will have the same burning fervour and sincerity. In common with other victims of brain pathology, Freud would still have been able to reason skilfully from his false premises and so to hide his psychotic traits from his followers. And yet, over the years, one by one, most of Freud's inner circle of early disciples left him. Jones, who remained loyal, attributed their desertion to motives of self-seeking, but his is only one side of the story.

With the shrewd calculation often displayed by the psychotic, Freud selected as disciples writers and other leaders of lay opinion. His appeal to the novelist or dramatist was obvious. The concept of hidden and unconscious motives had enthralling possibilities, suggesting compelling themes for plays and novels. Most of these intellectuals had had a philosophical rather than a scientific education and so were apt to value ideas for their own sake with little concern for their factual validation. The philosophical orientation as opposed to the scientific is illustrated by the writer who recently declared that it did not matter whether or not an idea was true as long as it was interesting. The philosopher himself is overvalued as a "great thinker" – an approach which places the onus for the validity of a concept solely on the pronouncements of a single individual who may be sick or even have a brain disease, like Nietzsche whose *folies de grandeur*, unrecognised for what they were, created the myth of the master race and paved the way for the emergence of Nazi Germany. Or the philosopher may have fallen into error because he lived in an era when insufficient knowledge existed for the formulation of valid scientific deductions, as in the cases of Aristotle and Plato, who, whatever their other merits, introduced innumerable absurdities into medicine and science.

But what they lacked in scientific judgement, Freud's intellectual disciples made up for in service to "the cause", propagating his theories to a lay public as proven fact over the heads of the medical profession, many being in an especially favoured position to do so, having, as writers and journalists, direct access to the popular press. From Freud they learnt his very effective methods of suppressing criticism. Opponents were ridiculed as old fashioned, too rigid or too inhibited to accept new ideas, and their reasonable objections given derogatory psychoanalytic motives – unscientific tactics, perhaps, but successful.

The climate of the times had also something to do with Freud's early success. In their lifetime many of Freud's contemporaries had seen the ground swept from beneath their feet by a succession of revolutionary movements in science and medicine. Darwin's evolutionary theory, Virchow's establishment of the cell as the fundamental unit of the animal organism, the discovery of the microbial origin of disease, all these had necessitated a fundamental rethinking of former concepts on a scale unrealised today. A climate of opinion had arisen in which no new theory, however bizarre or unlikely, could be entirely ruled out of court. Yet it was still a period of vast ignorance when there was in many cases simply too little information available to allow any reasonable discrimination between true and false.

Like all dubious nostrums and therapeutic regimes, Freud's theories were propagated by exaggerated claims of the innumerable "cures" allegedly obtained by psychoanalysis. The American edition of his early works carried a foreword by G. Stanley Hall testifying to the "thousands of cures" achieved by Freud with the method. This was a mathematically impossible figure. It was

Freud with his pet chow. Freud swore that the dog knew when the analytic hour was up, when it would rise and move about. It was seldom more than a few minutes out, he claimed, and then it was always at the expense of the patient.

Freud's practice to see every patient for an hour each day six days a week and their analyses often continued for years. In later life he saw few patients, devoting the greater part of his time to the now obligatory training analyses of aspiring psychoanalysts. The total number of patients analysed by him in his entire career could probably be numbered in tens rather than in thousands and few if any could have been cured by his treatment. It was pointed out by Professor Eysenck that a cure that takes years to achieve is not a cure. As we shall see, the most famous patient in the history of psychoanalysis – Anna O. – was still ill at the end of her treatment, a fact that was for decades one of the most closely guarded secrets in the entire Freud mythology.

The fact that psychoanalysis has no curative value is now generally conceded by analysts themselves. Anthony Storr, a practising psychoanalyst, admitted in his essay *The Concept of Cure* (1966) that "the evidence that psychoanalysis cures anybody of anything is so shaky as to be practically non-existent". The American Psychoanalytic Association, he revealed, had recently undertaken a survey to test the efficacy of psychoanalysis. The results were so disappointing they were withheld from publication. But the analysts, it seems, recovered undismayed from this blow. The relief of symptoms "tends to become less and less relevant" explained Storr, "the term 'cure' is in any case meaningless". "Who wants a cure anyway?" interpreted Cyril Connolly, who reviewed Storr's essay in the *Sunday Times*; "we are left with the feeling that cures are rather vulgar".

In the Freudian revival of the nineteen sixties other factors came into play. The centenary celebrations in 1956 of Freud's birth that had reawakened interest and paved the way for the revival had been the occasion of numerous lectures, broadcasts and articles in the press, most of them by leading psychoanalysts, in which his theories were described as "discoveries" and given the status of established fact. Freud was long-lived, and to the new generation introduced to his theories, his work might seem to have been of relatively recent origin, appearing new, modern and enlightened. But his major and fundamental theories were formulated in the last century. To be adequately assessed they should be replaced in their correct context in medical history. Few in the heady days of the Freud revival knew of the primitive state of knowledge in the nineties of the last century. The rapid advances in recent decades have masked the fact that modern medicine as we know it is barely a hundred years old. Freud entered medicine at a time when vast areas of ignorance existed, ignorance that was especially marked in the two areas most closely touched by psychoanalysis. Many readers will be surprised to learn that the brain was only finally identified as the organ of the mind in the early decades of the century of Freud's birth. The "ductless" (endocrine) glands maintained an enigmatic silence till the end of the century. Their rich supply of nerves and blood vessels pointed to important and even vital functions, yet what these functions were remained veiled in mystery. The secretions of the endocrine glands, the hormones, were still undiscovered. Through ignorance of the sex hormones, Freud made one of his major errors in deriving his theories of infantile sexuality from the condition now known as "precocious puberty".

"A writer can only regard himself as really famous", wrote John Rowan Wilson, "when people argue about his work without reading it." This could equally truly be said of Freud. Like other famous figures who have exerted such a profound influence on twentieth-century thought, he has been called "the great unread". No one in the first enthusiasm of the Freud revival appears to have gone back to the original writings he claimed contained the proofs of his theories. Had they done so, they would have discovered, as we shall, that they contain no such proofs – merely promises of later papers to follow in which the evidence for the truth of his theories would be fully set out. These papers *never materialised*. In citing his early papers as containing the proofs of his assertions, was Freud taking a calculated risk that no one would take the trouble to verify his claims by seeking out and reading these works? If he did, then the risk appears to have been fully justified. No one, at any rate in the sixties, appears to have taken this elementary precaution before adopting the invalid and aberrational theories of psychoanalysis and propagating these theories as established truth. Historians in the future will marvel at the credulity evinced in the Freud revival; they will find the whole Freud story an ironic commentary on human nature and the part played by imitation, fashion, and self-deception in its vagaries. But it is still a fascinating story, with elements that in a novel would seem contrived, and one which must continue to fascinate long after Freud's theories themselves have been consigned to oblivion.

PART I

The Seeds Are Sown

II

The Early Years

Sigmund Freud was born in 1856 in Freiburg, a small town in what is now Czechoslovakia. As might be expected, his early childhood has been the object of considerable psychoanalytical attention, from Ernest Jones, who, following Freud's own interpretation, described his somewhat boisterous play with a little girl relative as "infantile rape phantasies", to Fritz Wittels, who, quoting *The Interpretation of Dreams*, traced Freud's later disputes with his followers to the influence of early tussles with little playmates.

> "Freud, as he grows old, sees himself surrounded by members of the primitive horde, every one of whom is longing to get his teeth fixed in the progenitor's throat. But behind them all stands little Sigmund, defending himself, and saying 'Me slap him 'cos he slap me!'" (Wittels, 1924).

However, as these views are coloured by somewhat debatable theories, we should perhaps be on safer ground with the testimony of Freud's son Martin, who, in *Glory Reflected*, states that his father was a well-behaved, healthy and sturdy boy who was completely normal, who deeply loved his father and mother, and who romped in high spirits with his friends.

From the first, Freud was the object of the fond hopes of his parents, expectations engendered by an old woman's prophecy and the fact that he had been born in a caul, an event then popularly believed to presage future eminence. Their fond anticipations were soon reinforced by the boy's promise of unusual intellectual brilliance. His birth was followed by that of a boy who died in infancy and then five girls and two boys, so that for many years he was the only son of the marriage, the beloved Jewish first-born. He grew up confident in the expectation of future eminence. Years later, when he was only an aspiring young physician, he wrote to his fiancée that he had destroyed all his letters and papers. "As for the biographers, let them worry, we have no desire to make it too easy for them. Each one of them will be right in his opinion of 'The Development of the Hero', and I am already looking forward to seeing them go astray." (Jones, 1953).

In 1860, when Freud was four, the family moved to Vienna. Entering high school (Sperl Gymnasium) a year earlier than the normal age, he won many prizes and showed a special aptitude for languages which was later to win him recognition as a master of German prose. He passed out at the age of seventeen with the distinction of *summa cum laude*. On leaving school in 1873 he had not yet decided on a future career, wavering between politics, medicine and the law. It was hearing Goethe's romantic essay on *Nature* that decided him on a medical career. By his own admission he had never felt any special attraction to medicine – in later life he was to develop an aversion to it. Writing in his "The Question of Lay Analysis" (1926) he said, "I have no knowledge of having had in my early years any craving to help suffering humanity. My innate sadistic disposition was not a very strong one, so that I had no need to develop this one of its derivatives." The stirring events in the medical world at the time and the glamour surrounding the famous medical faculty of the University of Vienna, then at the height of its glory, must have played no small part in his decision. The popular press carried daily reports of the discoveries of its illustrious members, often in special editions, to satisfy a public avid for news of medical science. An admiring municipality named its city streets and squares after the distinguished physicians and surgeons of the faculty. Small wonder that the youthful Freud became captivated by the prospect of joining their ranks.

It was an exciting time to embark on a medical career when new and exciting discoveries were daily rendering obsolete the cherished concepts of centuries. Medicine had only recently emerged from a sleep that had lasted thousands of years, during which the canons of Galen and Hippocrates had dictated every facet of medical practice. Hippocrates (460–377 BC), the "Father of Medicine", is now mainly remembered for the code of ethics embodied in the famous Oath; his works are forgotten, but "this farrago of nonsense" – as they have been somewhat harshly, though not incorrectly, described by a modern physician – together with the works of Claudius Galen (130–circa 200 AD), who systematised the corpus of medical knowledge accumulated by his time, had been the physicians' Holy Writ for centuries. Medicine to the end of the eighteenth century had been based on the four humours of the ancients – blood, phlegm, black bile and yellow bile. Disease was allegedly caused by imbalance or superabundance of the humours, and treatment from Hippocrates until well into the nineteenth century consisted of bleeding and purging "to evacuate the morbific humours". The supposed activities of the humours – peccant, acrid or putrid – took up the greater part of lengthy dissertations of stupefying verbosity and, as succinctly described by R. Kerveran, "the Latin language was used to confer majesty on this rigmarole, and all this was punctuated with quotations from Galen and Hippocrates".

The beginning of the century in which Freud formulated his major theories saw the humoral theory still the basis of medical practice. Few but the most common diseases had a name or known pathology. A few specific remedies had been discovered by chance: digitalis from the foxglove for heart conditions, "Jesuit's bark" (quinine) for malaria. Jenner in 1798 had introduced vaccination; he had learnt from a milkmaid the fact well known to dairy workers that an attack of cowpox conferred immunity to small-pox. His introduction of vaccination was empirical – the science of immunology lay far ahead in the future. But it was the start of a process that was to lead to the World Health Organisation declaration in 1980 that smallpox had been eradicated from the entire world. But these limited advances were empiric discoveries made from a basis of almost complete ignorance.

The decisive break with Galenic authority occurred during the French Revolution. In 1794 the medical colleges and faculties were abolished by law. When they reopened under the Consulate in 1803, the break with tradition and authority was the determining factor in sweeping away the whole edifice of humoral medicine. But there was as yet nothing to take its place. The legacy of the past was an almost complete ignorance of the functioning of the human body and of its alterations in disease. A new beginning had to be made, and it was in the dead houses of the Paris hospitals that the early foundations of modern medicine were laid. There the causes of diseases were sought not in the Galenic texts, but on the post-mortem table. On it physicians saw for the first time the solidification of the lungs in pneumonia, the tubercles in "con-sumption", the diseased valves in rheumatic heart disease. Thus the true pathological substrate of many common diseases was at last identified. A process of the correlation of the signs and symptoms exhibited by the patient in his last illness with the necropsy findings after death (the famous *clinicopathological method*) made possible for the first time the diagnosis of these conditions during life. The early pioneers made their own errors, confusing the causes of diseases with their effects; the watery swelling of the tissues resulting from congestive cardiac failure, for instance, was thought to be the *cause* of the failure rather than its effect. The side effects of the drugs employed in some diseases were confused with their symptoms, thus the discoloration of the tissues produced by the sugar of lead then used in the treatment of epilepsy was thought to be part of the disease; syphilis was confused with the symptoms of poisoning by the mercury with which it was treated. Syphilis itself and gonorrhoea were thought to be one and the same disease as they frequently occurred in the same subject. Normal post-mortem findings were mistakenly described as pathological; the "chicken-fat" clots in the heart, for example, were thought to be warty growths. But despite these initial errors the early pathologists had chosen the right path, one that was eventually to establish medicine on a scientific foundation of fact in place of the unsupported theorising that had gone before. With the discovery of the stethoscope by Laënnec in 1816 following closely on Corvisart's introduction of the system of percussion of the chest, physical examination became part of medicine. About this time also physicians began to count the pulse rate. Although an esoteric pulse lore had existed from the time of Galen no one before this had thought of actually *counting* its rate. These innovations evoked some initial prejudice – Hildebrand of Vienna, commenting on the introduction of the stethoscope, declared that he had never been able to hear a pneumonia play the fiddle and called counting of the pulse rate "a ceremony best left to the quacks". But such objections were gradually overcome and within a decade physical examination, for the first time since Hippocrates, had become part of medical practice – this only half a century before Freud entered medical school.

The world of medicine was to be rocked by more revolutions as the century progressed. The establishment of the cell as the fundamental unit of the living organism by Virchow in 1858 changed the face of pathology. When Freud entered on his medical career in the autumn of 1873 the revolutionary work of Pasteur, Lister, Koch and others in establishing the microbial origin of the infectious diseases had barely taken effect, a fact that was reflected in the hospital conditions of the time. The Vienna General Hospital where Freud had his first confrontation with disease was then in a highly insanitary condition. It would, wrote a contemporary, John Plesch, "have been condemned by any government inspector of the keeping of pigs, but it housed hundreds of sick human beings". It was not unique in this respect. "In the Salpêtrière and the Hôtel Dieu in Paris" Plesch states, "patients lay on straw sacks in the overfilled wards, and to see fat canal rats scurrying over them was not an unusual sight. I can remember seeing these scurrying beasts when I was watching Dieulafoi using his famous apparatus to tap a pleurisy exudate." Frederick Treves tells a similar story of the London Hospital as it was in his youth (circa 1877). "I remember a whole ward being decimated by hospital gangrene" he wrote later. "Cleanliness was considered to be 'finnicking and affected' – an executioner might as well manicure his nails before chopping off a head." The rage for hygiene that followed the new discoveries in bacteriology had swept away these conditions long before Freud finished his studies, bringing in its train a dramatic decrease in mortality and morbidity.

But the deficiencies of hygiene that obtained when Freud entered the university were balanced by the brilliance of the Vienna medical faculty, then at the height of its glory. Up to the eighteen-forties, Paris had led the medical world. For decades the German-speaking universities had been steeped in the mysticism of

Karl Freiherr von Rokitansky.

Joseph Skoda

the *Philosophy of Nature*, the vague and esoteric creation of Schelling, which claimed that all the phenomena of nature could be deduced by reason alone and that all human life was a participation in a cosmic movement within nature. "Animal magnetism", the theory invented by Mesmer to explain the phenomena of hypnotism, had played a large part in the inception of this philosophical system, hence concepts of polarity and opposites figured prominently in its theories. These polarities often involved hypotheses of a dynamic interplay of antagonistic forces, all nature being seen as a struggle between positive and negative forces. As we shall see, some of Freud's theories were a regression to this obsolete and mystical pseudoscience.

Its founders defunct and the original impetus of its creation run down, the Philosophy of Nature had by the eighteen-forties revealed itself in all its fossilised sterility. A revolution such as that carried out in the Paris hospitals earlier in the century was urgently required. In Vienna this was achieved largely through the work of Carl von Rokitansky and Joseph Skoda. The eighteen-forties saw the emergence of a new school, its centre at Rokitansky's necropsy table in the mortuary of the Vienna General Hospital. The great pathologist's goal was to base German medicine on a solid foundation of material facts in place of the humoral medicine and the natural-philosophical theorising that had gone before. His chief collaborator, Joseph Skoda, the clinician, introduced the stethoscope to Vienna, achieving such acumen in its use that his diagnoses were invariably confirmed at autopsy. In doing so, he corrected the errors of the French; Laënnec, for example, had pronounced crepitation as being "pathognomonic" of pneumonia when in fact this sign is found in many other conditions. The value of the stethoscope in heart conditions had been limited by the fact that the meaning of the *normal* heart sounds was not established, thus it was hardly possible to distinguish abnormalities. Skoda's elucidation of their true meaning opened up a new approach to the study of cardiac pathology. But the greater part of the work of the two men was anonymous, passing into the corpus of medical knowledge now taken for granted but then a series of daily revelations.

A similar revolution was effected by the dermatologist, Ferdinand von Hebra. Humoral teaching had held that these diseases represented the discharge of corrupt humours in the body and that to cure them might be dangerous as the morbific humours might be driven back into the body. This belief was evidently still current as late as 1869 – we find in the *British Medical Journal* of that year an article on eczema asserting that its cure was fraught with danger, citing cases in which the cure of skin diseases had allegedly been followed by insanity. Setting out to disprove the humoral theory, Hebra chose scabies, then practically endemic among the poor, as the most suitable vehicle. The disease was till then believed to be the product of morbific humours. It is actually caused by a minute insect, the female of which burrows under the skin to lay her eggs, thus causing intense itching. Inserting a live scab insect into a finger, Hebra was soon plagued with a strong itch and the burrows spread over his entire body. After two months of this heroic effort he was able to state with authority, "without sarcoptes there is no scabies". Soon the humoral treatment of skin diseases – treatments aimed at "driving out acrimonies" and "purifying the blood" – was swept aside and those treatments only used which had proved effective in experiment.

The work of these men rapidly gained the attention of the medical world. To Vienna for postgraduate study under them

Ferdinand von Hebra.

came many famous men, Bright, Lister, Osler, to name but a few. Generations of foreign students were later to recall the silent figure of Rokitansky in his small, ill-equipped morgue dissecting rapidly, speaking only to dictate his findings in the terse manner habitual to him which accentuated all the more his rare and sudden outbursts of enthusiasm at the discovery of some curious anomaly or rare pathological condition. After a day spent in the wards and clinics of the *Allgemeine Krankenhaus* these foreign students would congregate in the little *Gasthof zum Goldenen Hirschen* in the Alserstrasse close to the hospital and discuss the day's happenings, the acute diagnoses of Skoda and the keen observation of Hebra which rivalled that of Joseph Bell, the Edinburgh surgeon on whom Conan Doyle modelled his Sherlock Holmes stories. "He [Hebra] rarely asked his patient any questions, but a hasty glance would usually enable him to tell more about the case than any of his students could elicit by a lengthy catechism," wrote George Fox in his *Reminiscences*. "He would say, 'This man is a tailor', and we soon found that he discovered this fact by feeling the needle pricks on the roughened forefinger. A hatter he recognized by some peculiar callus on the ball of the thumb. He could always guess the age and weight of a patient with unerring accuracy and tell us what province of Austria he came from."

But it was not for the sake of learning from these three great men alone that visitors flocked to Vienna in their hundreds from every part of the globe, but for the opportunity to learn something of the growing number of specialities developed there. After Czermak and Türck had in 1858 borrowed the laryngoscope for medicine from the singing teacher Garcia, who had invented it to obtain a view of the vocal cords of his pupils, Vienna led the world in diseases of the ear, nose and throat. Oesophagoscopy followed soon after, pioneered by Friedrich Semeleder in the sixties. "I turned to the best trained and most willing subject," he wrote of his discovery, "and experimented on myself" (Lesky, 1976). Soon a veritable arsenal of laryngeal instruments was developed in Vienna and difficult and delicate operations performed, operations very necessary for the relief of the stenoses and strictures that were the unfortunate sequelae of the ravages of syphilis, typhoid and diphtheria then endemic.

At the time of Freud's entry into the University in November 1873 the medical faculty was the most distinguished in Europe. Rokitansky was still in harness, though he now performed his necropsies in the sumptuous new Institute of Pathology in surroundings vastly different from the small, poorly equipped, tworoomed morgue in the *Allgemeine Krankenhaus* where he had done his greatest work. Early in the next year university and students combined to celebrate his seventieth birthday. The festivities culminated in a grand torchlight procession round the Ringestrasse in which nearly two thousand students paraded carrying torches, many wearing the fantastic uniforms of their societies, a parade in which the young Freud might well have taken part. The professor of anatomy was Joseph Hyrtl whose famous textbook of anatomy had run through twenty-two editions. As a young prosector he had perfected the techniques of injecting wax and resins into blood vessels. At the height of his career he had provided injection preparations for the museums of the whole world "from Kazan to Philadelphia, from Stockholm to Rio de Janeiro" (Lesky, 1976). Arlt, who had put diseases of the eyes on a clinicopathological basis as Hebra had done in dermatology, and Jaeger, whose test types for assessing visual acuity are still in use today, staffed the ophthalmology departments. Schnitzler, von Schrötter, Gruber and Politzer worked and taught in the departments for diseases of the ear, nose and throat. From them foreign postgraduate students learnt techniques never seen in their own countries, taught by Politzer, a superb linguist, in their own languages. They saw everything that could be observed in the larynx demonstrated by Schrötter, who often used his own larynx for the purpose. The talents of a living model kept by Schrötter in his department for demonstration purposes were vividly described by one of the winter semester group of 1877–78:

"This good woman had, in the course of time, become so insensitive to the introduction of the nasal and laryngeal mirror, that even the most clumsy beginner could move his mirror about in her pharynx without hindrance until he had learned the correct adjustment. His subject could also be used for learning to touch all separate parts of the larynx with the tip of the probe. She always indicated correctly whether the probe touched the left or right vocal cord, the left or right false vocal cord or the epiglottis, etc. In addition, this walking clinical museum had an old, healed iritis, which was a most suitable object for ophthalmological examinations. Furthermore, she was always willing to subject herself to introduction of a gastric tube for the sake of training, and to let her stomach be washed; she had a very evident and easily palpable floating kidney, and finally a myoma of the uterus which she was always willing to allow to be palpated by ambitious young physicians." (Lesky, 1976).

In striking contrast is the account of Sir St Clair Thomson who graduated from King's College Hospital, London, in 1881 and who states that when he gained his degree in medicine he had never seen the vocal cords or the drum of the ear in the living person. He recalled how, when it was necessary to operate for adenoids in the outpatient department in the eighties, the struggling child was held by the porter while the surgeon, whose only instrument was his fingernail, inserted his finger up behind the palate and scratched out as much of the adenoids as the yelling child would permit.

Thus the picture of a fossilised and reactionary faculty, hostile to any new idea, painted by Freud's biographers, is totally false. "Being a rebel," says one of his biographers, Max Schur, "Freud was contemptuous of the 'Old Guard' at the medical school of the University of Vienna – the *Hofräte* – who had been awarded honorary titles either because they were chairmen of departments, or were noted for some special achievement, or had merely arrived at a certain seniority and 'knew the right people'."

From the beginning, Freud appears to have been oblivious to the stirring events going on around him and to the fact that he was living in an historic epoch. He evidently had little historic perspective or appreciation of the struggles of the past that had overthrown ignorance and mysticism and created a budding science of medicine where none had before existed. Attracted to the study of medicine from a vague concept of penetrating the secrets of nature, he may have received his first disillusionment in the reality of the dissecting room. Its conditions, vastly different from those of today, have been evocatively described by Freud's contemporary Carl Schleich – "the uncleanliness . . . the bits of dead bodies lying about everywhere, the brutality of the attendants . . . the vile stench, and the business of rummaging in parts of the body which I had never seen before, viscera, the eyeless skulls, the glistening brains, the opened hearts . . ." By the time Freud entered the university the very numbers of students from all parts of the empire and abroad had led to overcrowded lecture halls, dissecting rooms and laboratories. There were only three hundred and fifty places in lecture halls for five hundred and eight students in 1869, and only twenty badly illuminated dissection tables for over six hundred and fifty students. In the Department of Internal Medicine where lectures were given in the wards as they had been since the introduction of Boerhaave's method of bedside teaching in the previous century, it was possible for only thirty out of the two hundred students present to actually see and hear the demonstration. The end result was that the classical Viennese bedside teaching, the special pride of the faculty, had to be abandoned. From 1872 onwards the patients were seen and lectured on in the amphitheatre. When Freud qualified he had never seen a patient in bed, let alone examined one.

Freud actually took eight years instead of the usual five to qualify, pursuing in negligent fashion the studies proper to a medical career and seizing every opportunity to drift into fields outside the strict medical curriculum, switching from "zoology for medical students" to zoology proper and taking courses in Darwinism and philosophy. Letters from this period demonstrate that Freud found philosophy far more congenial than his medical studies (Clark, 1981). By his third year he was spending most of his time in the Zoological Experimental Station at Trieste. By this time Freud had come to realise that "the peculiarities and limitations" of his character did not qualify him for a career in general medicine and he decided on a life of pure research. Accordingly in

Ernst Wilhelm Ritter von Brücke.

the autumn of 1876, at the age of twenty, he entered the physiological laboratory of Ernest Wilhelm Ritter von Brücke as a *famulus* (research student). Here at the microscope he felt he had found his true milieu and "men whom I could respect and take as my models". These men were the great Brücke himself and his assistants Exner and Ernst von Fleischl-Marxow, who was to figure so tragically in the events of the future. Freud's philosophical inclinations were now completely expunged by the strictly scientific orientation of his new chief. Brücke had come to Vienna from Königsberg in 1849, having there already participated in the revolution that had overthrown the Philosophy of Nature in Germany. With a handful of colleagues who included men of the stature of Helmholtz, famous for his invention of the ophthalmoscope which marked the beginnings of modern ophthalmology, he had dedicated his future life to the establishment of scientific objectivity in place of the vague speculation and airy theorising that had gone before. With this background, Brücke tolerated neither speculation nor faulty methodology. A student who had written in an essay the phrase "Superficial observation reveals", was reproved. "One is not to observe superficially", declared Brücke.

Physiology was then a new discipline. The clinicopathological school which had contributed so much to medicine nevertheless had its limitations. In many cases, pathological findings could not be interpreted because of the complete ignorance then existing about the functioning of the body in normal health. In the New World in 1822, an American army surgeon, William Beaumont, stationed at the frontier trading post of Fort Mackinac, had made the first observations in the physiology of human digestion. He had nursed back to health a Canadian hunter, Alexis St Martin, whose stomach had been permanently opened by an accidental gunshot wound. Through the open fistula he carried out experiments *in vivo* which, published in 1833, became the first comprehensive study of the digestive processes. But it was an isolated study. Little else had been discovered. The need for more information on the normal functioning of the organism now became urgent and, led by the French physiologists, Magendie and Claude Bernard, a new physiological school with the object of linking physiology to pathology and clinical medicine had become established. Its centre gradually moved to Germany and Brücke was one of the famous group, all pupils of Johannes Müller, who had taken medicine out of the mysticism of the *Philosophy of Nature* and established it on a firm physiological footing.

One of the immediate achievements of the school was the development of new instruments of investigation. The clinical thermometer was one of the first such aids to emerge. Guy's Hospital in London got its first thermometer only in 1870 – it was nearly a foot long. Writing in the *British Medical Journal* of 1866, a Dr Gibson declared, "The day is not, I think, far distant, when the physician will consider the thermometer not less indispensable to him than the stethoscope." As a novelty, it was shown at a meeting of the South-Eastern Division of the British Medical Association, and Sir Samuel Wilkes recalls that it excited much curiosity and interest among the members present, and, from one or two, ridicule. Other clinical aids followed. Crude instruments for measuring blood pressure came into use. The first reliable apparatus to appear, in 1880, evoked some disapproval – "by such methods we pauperise our senses and weaken clinical acuity," thundered the *British Medical Journal* at its introduction. Other instruments followed. The first ophthalmoscope invented by Helmholtz in 1851 depended on light reflected from an oil lamp by a mirror, yet many important observations were made by these crude means. Microscopy improved and for the first time the existence of the white blood cells was established (the larger red cells had been observed from the previous century). Methods of counting these cells developed, after which it became possible to diagnose many hitherto unrecognised blood diseases.

Brücke had inaugurated laboratory medicine in Vienna and become the founder of the Austrian physiological school. On his arrival in Vienna he found in the Institute only a microscope, an incubator and a dynamometer, but by the autumn of 1880 he had transformed it into a functioning and well-equipped laboratory. The Institute at the time of Freud's entry was housed in the first floor and basement of a disused gun factory, with neither gas nor electricity. Water was brought up from a well in the yard and all heating had to be done over a spirit lamp. Here too the monstrous growth of the student body had had its effect. Brücke had to sacrifice his own room to provide work space for forty-six more students. The lecture hall, where nearly five hundred students fought for the three hundred odd seats available, had to be transformed into a laboratory after each lecture. But in spite of

Brucke's laboratory in the Institute of Physiology.

these difficulties the famous Institute was a Mecca for foreign visitors and postgraduate students. When many years later it was replaced by an imposing new edifice, the state secretary von Hartl expressed at its inauguration the sentimental veneration felt by generations of former students towards the old buildings: "Let us never forget that Brücke and Hyrtl worked in that old and decaying building which you see, and that it was in a barn that Rokitansky produced his world famous preparations."

In the six years spent in the Institute, Freud came into closer contact than usual with Brücke and his assistants Exner and von Fleischl-Marxow, that tragic figure who eventually joined the ranks of the casualties of the post-mortem room and who plays an important part in the Freud story. He had been described by Dr Bernfeld as "young, handsome, enthusiastic, a brilliant speaker and an attractive teacher. He had the charming and amiable manners of the old Viennese society, ever ready to discuss scientific and literary problems with a flow of challenging ideas." At the age of twenty-five, while performing an autopsy, he had contracted an infection. Amputation of the right thumb saved him from death, but the continual growth of neuromas required repeated operations. His recourse to morphia for the pain eventually became an addiction, yet, says Bernfeld, "This mutilated and aching hand performed experimental work of technical perfection" (Bernfeld, 1944).

In Brücke's laboratory Freud was set to work on the problems of comparative anatomy posed by Darwin's evolutionary theory, involving in his case the nervous system of the lower vertebrates. He appears to have carried out his researches to the full satisfaction of the exacting Brücke, becoming a master of microscopic technique, and later even inventing a new staining method.

During this period he had also managed to put in the requisite number of lectures necessary for his medical degree. But he was in no hurry to take the examinations. "My acquaintances regarded me as a loafer and doubted whether I would get through," he later wrote in his *Autobiographical Study* (1925). He was by now set in his determination on a life of pure research. His decision to take the final examinations was based on the realisation that such leading physiologists as Helmholtz, du Bois-Reymond and Brücke himself had qualified for the degree of MD and some·had even practised medicine. His medical degree itself made no interruption to his work in Brücke's laboratory though it resulted in his promotion to the rank of demonstrator, a post which, in addition to his research, involved some teaching responsibility. Though carrying no salary, it would have led by slow progression to the

Freud at the age of twenty-nine with Martha Bernays, his fiancée.

post of assistant professor and eventually to the chair occupied by Brücke. His future was decided when in 1882 he met and fell in love with Martha Bernays, one of the decisive turning points in his career. Their engagement lasted four years, most of which time they were separated, she living with her family in Germany, he continuing his work in Vienna. The letters Freud wrote to his fiancée during their separation were preserved and provided valuable information for Freud's biographer, Ernest Jones, who considered them to be a "not unworthy contribution to the great love literature of the world."

Now Freud's plans had to undergo drastic revision. Brücke's assistants were both young. It would have been many years before he could step into the shoes of either. His father had lost his capital in the crash of 1873 and he had a family of seven children to care for. Freud decided that if he were to marry, he must abandon a career in research and earn his living as a practising physician. Owing to the system of instruction prevailing at the time, which consisted only of case presentations and lectures in the amphitheatre, he had qualified without any of the practical skills required of the general physician, skills ranging from the ability to set a fracture to that of the delivery of a baby. To gain this practical experience it was necessary to spend some time in voluntary residence in the General Hospital. Accordingly in July 1882, at the age of 26, Freud exchanged the laboratory benches of the Institute for the wards and clinics of the *Allgemeine Krankenhaus.*

Built in 1780 by Joseph II, the old, grey, musty buildings of the hospital covered nearly twenty-five acres near the centre of the city. Over its baroque entrance was carved the device *Saluti et Solatio Aegrorum* (for the care and consolation of the sick). To this great hospital with its three thousand beds came patients not only from the capital but from all provinces of the Empire. Many more came from other countries; in fact, rare cases seen elsewhere only once in a lifetime could be observed almost daily in Vienna. Because of this, the Viennese clinicians achieved a diagnostic mastery unsurpassed anywhere. "When Isidor Neumann, the syphilologist," wrote Fritz Wittels, "put on his pince-nez and after a short look at the patient pronounced 'this is syphilis' there was no appeal from the sentence." By this time both Skoda and Rokitansky were dead. Their spirit lived on, however; the physicians still worked in the traditions of those great forbears and used their methods – the correlation of the clinical findings with those of the morbid anatomy. Fritz Wittels describes the unvarying procedure adopted on the death of a patient. The entire medical

The Vienna General Hospital. A courtyard outside the
psychiatric ward.

team, chief, assistants and younger doctors, crossed over to the
Institute of Pathological Anatomy to attend the necropsy. Often
the diagnosis was confirmed; sometimes an unexpected condition
was revealed which had been overlooked. Back in the ward,
another post-mortem took place in the chief's sanctum. What
mistakes had occurred and why? How could they be avoided in
the future? Skoda's spirit of therapeutic nihilism was still alive –
careful nursing and reliance upon the defensive powers of nature,
powers that were beginning to be revealed by the immunological
discoveries of Pasteur and Metchnikoff, were producing results
superior to those achieved by the reckless drug therapy carried out
elsewhere. In obstetrics Chrobak carried on the traditions of Boër.
Prominently displayed in his anteroom was the sign *Primum est
non nocere* (the first thing is to do no harm) – a timely warning
when in other countries the indiscriminate use of the high forceps
for normal as well as abnormal deliveries was causing a whole
crop of children crippled by the injuries received at their birth.

Freud began his hospital career under the aegis of the great surgeon Christian Billroth (1829–1894). It was a time of excitement and adventure in surgery. The introduction of anaesthesia in the middle of the century had rendered surgery painless; now antiseptic techniques were making it safe. The old-type operator with frock coat stiff and green with dried blood, his sutures threaded for convenience through his button-holes, still existed, but was growing rarer. Surgeons were now venturing where they had not dared trespass before, inside the chest, the abdomen, even inside the skull. These operations were then embarked on with trepidation, an attitude that was all too soon to give way to overconfidence and to the excesses of the Arbuthnot Lane period described by Sir Geoffrey Jefferson as "a riot of operating by and on neurotics either to divide bands, to remove colons or to fix organs" that would have delighted a Voltaire. (It was said of Lane himself, an ardent evolutionist who believed the large intestine to be a vestigial organ, that if a patient came to him with a sore throat he would remove his colon. He also professed to have discovered a pathological kinking in the ileum – this somewhat ambiguously named by colleagues as "Lane's kink". Lane was believed by many to be the origin of Shaw's character Cutler Walpole in *The Doctor's Dilemma*, a surgeon specialising in the wholesale removal of the "nuciform sac"; however, in 1948, Shaw revealed that Walpole was based on a laryngologist who specialised in extirpating uvulas.)

The year before Freud entered the surgical ward, Billroth had made medical history in performing the first successful gastrectomy on man. In 1885, while operating on a patient with pyloric cancer, he anastomosed the stomach to the small intestine to bypass the lesion. These two procedures have gone down in medical history and the Billroth I and Billroth II operations still figure in the operation lists of today.

But the stirring events of those pioneering days failed to inspire Freud. He found the surgical wards physically tiring and remained in them only a little over two months. From there he progressed to the division of internal medicine under the great Nothnagel, recently come from Germany to occupy the chair of medicine. Professor Nothnagel represented the purest type of idealistic nineteenth-century physician. His work united the traditions of Skoda and Rokitansky with the findings of experimental physiology. He believed "the physician is merely the servant of nature and not its master". But he was no therapeutic nihilist and was quick to incorporate new discoveries such as those of Pasteur in immunology. He observed nature to the end; when he died of a heart attack in 1915, a page of his handwriting was left describing his symptoms up to the very last moment.

Freud admired Nothnagel but felt he could not emulate his ideals. It was, in fact, on Nothnagel's wards that he finally became convinced that the life of a general physician was not for him. He must have found the stark reality of medical practice in those days vastly different from the romantic notions inspired by Goethe's essay. Improved hygiene and nutrition, immunotherapy and anti-biotics have changed the face of medicine out of all recognition in the last hundred years. The cases of typhoid, cholera, diphtheria, scarlet fever, and mastoiditis which filled the wards in Freud's time are now rarities. Then children died in thousands of "scurvy rickets" (Barlow's disease) and others became deformed and crippled, because vitamins had not been discovered. Tuberculosis was known as "the Viennese disease", killing twenty a day in Vienna alone. Disease today, according to Sir Robert Hutchison (1950) who joined the staff of the London Hospital in 1900, is only a pallid shadow of what it then was. "What young physi-

Theodore Herman Maynert.

cian," he asked, "has seen an advanced case of pyloric stenosis with gastric fermentation in which the patient belched marsh gas so that sometimes when lighting his pipe the gas took fire and he seemed like a dragon breathing flame?" The course of pneumonia in the days before antibiotics was evidently very different to that of today: "When does one now see an old-fashioned case of lobar pneumonia ending dramatically by crisis in seven or nine days?" continued Hutchison, "Most cases of pneumonia in these degenerate times end not with a bang but a whimper."

Convinced he would never become a general physician, Freud, in May 1883, transferred to the quieter waters of the psychiatric department under Professor Theodor Meynert, a man as distinguished in his field as Brücke had been in his. A protégé of Rokitansky, he had applied the basic tenets of the clinicopathological school to the practice of psychiatry – his goal being to establish psychiatry on a scientific basis by the well tried methods of the school in determining the anatomical basis in the brain after death of the various psychiatric disorders exhibited during life. His orientation is summarised in the preface to his book *Psychiatry* published in 1884:

> "The reader will find no other definition of 'Psychiatry' in this book but the one given on the title page: 'Clinical Treatise on Diseases of the Fore-Brain'. The historical term psychiatry, i.e. 'treatment of the soul', implies more than we can accomplish, and transcends the bounds of accurate scientific investigation" (Meynert, 1884).

Already the clinicopathological method was accumulating an increasing volume of evidence correlating insanity with brain pathology, notably in the advanced stages of neurosyphilis, where the disease took the form of "general paralysis of the insane". An additional factor was the absence of mental functioning in early infancy and the declining mental powers of extreme old age, facts which seemed to correlate intellectual processes with the early development and later degeneration of the brain. It was in pursuit of this lead that Meynert began the investigation of the development of myelination in the human brain. At birth, large tracts of the nervous system are unmyelinated; the nerves are without their outer insulating sheath which makes conduction possible. Meynert demonstrated that in the newborn, myelination of the medulla, the area of the brain responsible for the control of respiration and other vital functions, precedes that of the cerebral hemispheres themselves. His basic idea, since amply vindicated, was to establish the correlation between the maturation of the brain centres and the commencement of mental functioning.

Joining Meynert's team in 1883 as his first introduction to psychiatry, Freud became exposed to this revolution in psychiatric thinking. He witnessed for himself the pathological manifestations of amentia, paranoia and the "delusions of grandeur" which marked the neurosyphilitic, and helped in the care of the large numbers of in-patients, fourteen to sixteen hundred annually being received into the division. His evenings were spent at the bench in Meynert's laboratory, using the microscope to discover the discrete lesions that might account for the mental derangement exhibited by the patient during life, working alongside perhaps many of Meynert's famous pupils, who included Carl Wernicke, later to discover the brain disease caused by severe vitamin deficiency, now known as Wernicke's encephalopathy. Wernicke's discovery of another speech area in the brain cleared up many obstacles to the understanding of the more subtle clinical manifestations of aphasia. August Forel, Carl Meyer and Franz Chvostek were among other pupils later to achieve fame in their own right. Here at the microscope Freud was as happy as he had been in Brücke's institute; the work was actually very similar – he was merely exchanging the nervous system of the lower vertebrates for that of the human being. Though his work carried him to other divisions of the hospital he continued to devote his spare hours to work in Meynert's laboratory, often till midnight, until he finally left the hospital in the summer of 1885. From his researches there he published many creditable papers in neuroanatomy which were later to further his career as a neurologist, the speciality for which he now felt best fitted; it was a compromise between the life of pure research he would have preferred and general practice for which he had no aptitude.

Neurology had only recently emerged as a speciality. In Paris the great neurologist Jean-Martin Charcot had recently been appointed to the first chair of neurology in the world. In London the National Hospital for the Paralysed and Epileptic (now the National Hospital for Nervous Diseases) had been established in 1859 with Hughlings Jackson, Gowers and Brown-Séquard as its shining lights. But in Vienna, for so long the seat of specialised medicine, there was no department of neurology, though Nothnagel had a special interest in the subject, having made important contributions to its elucidation and may have infected Freud with his enthusiasm. It was at this point that Freud conceived the ambition to go to Paris to study under Charcot at the famous hospital La Salpêtrière. Meanwhile from Meynert's wards he moved to the syphilis clinic under von Zeissl where he was able to study the numerous neurological manifestations of the disease of which there was a high incidence in Vienna. In December 1885 he joined the Fourth Medical Division whose chief, Dr Franz Scholz, had also a special interest in neurology and where the greatest number and variety of these cases could be found. Given a free hand by the ageing Scholz, Freud actively pursued his interest in the subject. From this period date his three clinical papers of 1884–1885.

Thus by January 1885, Freud had proved himself a competent neurologist according to the knowledge of the day, with several papers to his credit in which he had shown expertise in research techniques, a command of the existing known facts of the nervous system and of the literature in French and English as well as in German. He was already achieving a reputation in neurology; his new histological staining method had been noticed in the British journal *Brain* and the American *Journal of Nervous and Mental Diseases*, the two famous journals of neurology which had recently begun publication. In the spring of 1885 he was appointed lecturer in "neuropathology" (now known as neurology) and in this capacity attained the rank of *Privatdozent*, holders of which constituted an élite from which were chosen the professors of the future. Up to this time his career had been unexceptional; he presents a picture of a talented and hardworking young physician well regarded by professors and colleagues. There was one episode, however, which was to cast its shadows into the future – the cocaine episode.

III

First Encounter With Cocaine

From the time of the Spanish conquest of Peru, returning travellers from South America had brought back to Europe stories of a magical plant with mysterious properties growing on the slopes and high plateaux of the Andes. Legend had it that the plant was a gift to mortals from the children of the sun god, given to them to satisfy the hungry, renew the strength of the weary and give peace to the troubled in spirit. To the Incas it was a sacred emblem, for many centuries reserved exclusively for religious ceremonies; the fields whereon it grew were regarded as holy ground. This was the coca plant, a shrub growing to "about the height of a man"; it was in the leaves of this plant that the magic substance resided.

In the course of time, its use spread gradually to the greater part of the Indian populace and many reports reached Europe of prodigious feats of labour and endurance performed by the natives on chewing the leaves of the coca plant. It was reported that by its use the Indians were able to travel on foot for hundreds of hours, fleeter than horses and without fatigue. With it they performed prodigious excavations in the mines without food or sleep and were, moreover, reputed to live to ripe old age in perfect health and vigour.

In 1749 the plant was brought to Europe. It appeared in Lamarck's botanical encyclopaedia in 1786 under the name of *Erythroxylon coca*. Interest was reawakened and intensified in the nineteenth century with the publication in 1859 of a pamphlet by the Italian physician Paolo Mantegazza, who, following a long stay among the Peruvian Indians, extensively publicised the plant, declaring that a great new remedy for disease had been discovered. Thus began the chain of events that was to have such momentous consequences for mankind. In 1858 the Austrian government sent the frigate *Novarra* on an expedition round the world. A Dr Scherzer, a trade expert accompanying the expedition brought back with him a quantity of the leaves and sent them for analysis to the eminent chemist Wöhler, who entrusted this task to his assistant Albert Niemann. In 1860 Niemann succeeded in isolating the active principle of the leaves, an alkaloid, to which he gave the name "cocaine".

After this the substance was investigated by many others, including Professor Schroff of Vienna and von Anrep of Würzburg; both noted the numbing effects of cocaine on the lips and tongue when swallowed and the dilation of the pupils which accompanied its use, effects observed from the earliest times. No one, however, took the decisive step forward of investigating the drug's properties as a local anaesthetic. Freud himself, when he too investigated cocaine, missed this important and eventually only medical application of the drug. Like so many other medical discoveries the essential information was available decades and indeed centuries before, but the necessary correlation failed to be made until the fortuitous intervention of chance.

A spell of initial enthusiasm for the new drug rapidly gave way to disinterest. Many investigators could find no detectable properties of the drug, physiological or otherwise, and pronounced it inert. This, as Freud pointed out later, was probably due to the deterioration of the leaves during the drying and storing process and in the long journey from South America to the European centres. There were too, manufacturing difficulties as it was found that cocaine decomposed rapidly in solution, especially after heating. However, these difficulties appear to have been overcome by the firm of Merck of Darmstadt (now Merck, Sharpe and Dohme) and by the eighties they had succeeded in producing a stable (though very costly) product.

In the spring of 1884 an ambitious young Freud was casting around for some brilliant discovery which would bring his name to prominence in the competitive medical world of Vienna. But in Freud's case the most pressing motivation was the furtherance of his marriage plans to Martha Bernays as soon as he could reasonably expect to be able to support a wife and family. He was then still only an impecunious house officer in the hospital, his appointment to the rank of *Privatdozent* still in the future. At this crucial time in his life he came across a paper by a German army surgeon, Theodor Aschenbrandt, reporting his experiences with cocaine. Aschenbrandt had been an assistant at the Pharmacological Institute at Würzburg soon after von Anrep's term of office. Von Anrep's experiments had been performed on animals; he had intended to extend them to human beings but had neither the time nor the material suitable for his purpose. Such human material would consist of strong healthy subjects exposed to the greatest possible exertion, hunger, thirst and privation. Aschenbrandt determined to carry on the work of von Anrep but he too was handicapped by lack of such subjects. However, in the course of his career when he became surgeon to the Bavarian Artillery he eventually found the exact experimental conditions he needed. In the autumn manoeuvres of 1883 he encountered previously healthy men in various stages of exhaustion from arduous route marches performed during a period of unseasonably hot weather. Through the local pharmacist he obtained a supply of cocaine from the firm of Merck of Darmstadt, using the drug when a suitable occasion arose. Six cases are reported in his paper, of which the following is an example:

> "Case L.T., volunteer of one year, collapsed of exhaustion directly upon leaving W. on the second day of a march; the weather was extremely hot, I gave him approximately one tablespoon of water with twenty drops of a cocaine solution (0.5/10). A few minutes later (approximately five), he stood up of his own accord and travelled the distance to H., several kilometers, easily and cheerfully and with a pack on his back."

Searching for previous references in the medical literature to cocaine, Freud's attention was drawn to a paper by W. H. Bentley in an obscure journal, *The Therapeutic Gazette* of Detroit, reporting the author's success in weaning opium addicts and alcoholics from their habituation by the use of a preparation of the coca plant produced by the American firm of Parke, Davis and Co. This was of special interest to Freud in view of the condition of his friend and colleague von Fleischl-Marxow (see page 27) who had resorted to morphine for the intolerable pain he suffered and was now experiencing the most extreme consequences of addiction. Freud determined to investigate the substance for himself. "Perhaps others are working at it; perhaps nothing will come of it," he wrote to his fiancée. "But I shall certainly try it, and you know that when one perseveres, sooner or later one succeeds. We do not need more than one such lucky hit to be able to think of setting up house" (Jones 1953).

The cost of the drug was prohibitive but nevertheless Freud ordered some from the house of Merck. He immediately tested it on himself, taking a twentieth of a gramme, and was pleased to find that it turned his bad mood into cheerfulness and gave him a feeling of having dined well. From its action in obliterating all sense of hunger he deduced that cocaine acted as a gastric anaesthetic, suggesting its use in various gastric conditions and as an anti-emetic. In the hope of weaning Fleischl from his addiction he gave him a quantity. Clutching at the new drug "like a drunken man", within a few days Fleischl was taking it regularly. Freud himself, convinced of the harmlessness of this "magical drug", began to take small doses regularly "against depression and against indigestion" (Jones, 1953). He sent some to Martha to make her strong and give her rosy cheeks. He pressed the drug on friends and colleagues both for themselves and their patients, and gave it to his sisters. "In short," wrote Jones, "looked at from the vantage point of our present knowledge, he was rapidly becoming a public menace."

The result of these sporadic and scientifically uncontrolled researches was the paper *Über Coca* which appeared in the July 1884 issue of *Centralblatt für die Gesammte Therapie*. As aptly commented by D. F. Musto (1974), "papers about cocaine assert that everyone should try it, but also impatiently question the motives of those who disagree". Freud's paper is a good example of the genre. He describes his own self-experimentation and the sudden exhilaration experienced a few minutes after taking cocaine, with first a slackening, then an increase in pulse rate. He goes on to describe "the effects of cocaine in others, mostly people my own age" and describes their exhilaration and euphoria which he considered "the normal euphoria of a healthy person", and increased capacity for work. "Long-lasting intensive mental or physical work can be performed without fatigue", he said, "it is as though the need for food and sleep, which otherwise makes itself felt peremptorily at certain times of the day, were completely banished." A meal, though eaten without revulsion, was clearly felt to be superfluous under the effects of cocaine. During the first hours of the coca effect it was not possible to sleep, he continued, but this sleeplessness was in no way distressing.

Ernest Jones comments that the essay was written as if Freud was in love with the content itself. "He used expressions uncommon in a scientific paper", wrote Jones (1953), "such as 'the most gorgeous excitement' that animals display after an injection of cocaine, and administered an 'offering' of it rather than a 'dose'; he heatedly rebuffed the 'slander' that had been published about this precious drug." Jones' translations in this passage have been disputed, but reading the paper one must agree that the presentation is unusual. Freud himself referred to it in a letter to his fiancée as "a song of praise to this magical substance". Viewed objectively as a scientific paper *Über Coca* has many deficiencies. Though the review of the previous literature is comprehensive and appears accurate, the remainder of the paper is vague and disorganised. No information is given on the number of subjects treated, the dosages employed and the duration of the treatment. Beyond a brief mention of the variations in pulse rate, Freud omits reference to other important measurements such as blood pressure readings, temperature recordings and so on. He makes no mention of the dilation of the pupils probably present in those treated. In the section listing the effects of the drug he goes back and forth between his own subjects and those reported in the previous literature in a disorganised fashion. One must agree with Jones' unspoken inference that much of Freud's enthusiasm for cocaine arose from the euphoria engendered by the drug itself.

Freud's list of indications for the drug were, in this paper, comparatively few. But he was always seeking new applications for it, and before long was recommending it for everything from diabetes to seasickness – a truly universal panacea. Here he merely recommends cocaine as a stimulant especially useful in situations such as mountaineering, war conditions, etc., declaring it to be a "far more potent and far less harmful stimulant than alcohol": he recommends its use to psychiatrists in conditions such as neurasthenia; declares its benefits in various gastric and intestinal disorders and in cases of "cachexia" (state of general ill health and malnutrition). He states that it increased tolerance to mercury (then the only treatment for syphilis) and was therefore of value in this disease. Discussing the use of the drug in the treatment of morphine addiction he refers to cocaine as an "antidote" to morphine, mentioning the case of a man – almost certainly Fleischl – in whom morphine was successfully withdrawn without any of the symptoms experienced when this was attempted before, adding that "after ten days he was able to dispense with the coca treatment altogether". He further recommends the drug as an aphrodisiac, saying that the natives of South America represented their goddess of love with coca in her hand and that three of the people to whom he had given cocaine reported "violent sexual excitement". Finally, he mentions briefly the marked anaesthetising effect of the drug when brought into contact with the skin or mucous membranes – but only in connection with diseases of these organs. The use of cocaine as a local anaesthetic as an adjunct to surgery he missed altogether and the discovery was made by another.

The account of the discovery of the local anaesthetic properties of cocaine by Carl Koller in the summer of 1884 that Freud gave many years later in one of his lectures was slightly short of the facts. Both Hans Sachs and Ernest Jones repeat this version: Freud was standing in the courtyard one day with a group of colleagues, of whom Koller was one, when another intern passed by showing signs of great pain. Freud told him that he thought he could help him and they all went to his room where he applied a few drops of the substance which made the pain disappear instantly. "I explained to my friends that this drug was the extract of a South American plant, the coca, which seemed to have powerful qualities for relieving pain and about which I was preparing a publicaton," he said. "The man with the permanent interest in the eye, whose name was Koller, did not say anything, but a few months later I learned that he had begun to revolutionise eye surgery by the use of cocaine, making operations easy which till then had been impossible" (Jones, 1953).

In fact, the testimony of Koller's daughter decades later sheds a rather different light on the affair. Going through her father's effects soon after his death, Hortense Koller Becker, cutting open the strings of the neatly tied parcels that filled a dog-eared carton, found "fresh as the day they were written" letters, documents and manuscripts from over seventy-five years before. Slipped into the manuscript of her father's communication giving the world the first local anaesthetic was a tissue thin envelope containing the very grains of cocaine that her father used in his historic experiment. Koller was no mere chance bystander who had happened on the scene at the crucial moment and snatched the glory from Freud. Letters found by Mrs Becker showed that the two men had been close friends from their student days, part of a wider circle who enjoyed excursions to the Vienna woods and who regularly played cards together in the Vienna cafés. "How articulate they all were", she writes, "how much they had to say which, I suppose, would today have found its way over the telephone and vanished forever." As young interns Freud and Koller lived on the same floor of the hospital and saw each other daily. They worked side by side in Stricker's laboratory and collaborated in various experiments and projects from time to time. Koller was one of those who had collaborated with Freud in the observations of the physiological effects of cocaine and Freud had commandeered his services in later experiments in which, as Koller wrote later, "We would take the alkaloid internally by mouth and after the proper lapse of time for its getting into the circulation, we would conduct experiments on our muscular strength, fatigue and the like (measured by the dynamometer)."

At the time of his discovery, Koller had already achieved distinction in the field of embryology but it was his ambition to become an eye-specialist. While still at the university, the great ophthalmologist Arlt had inspired him with the need for a local anaesthetic in eye surgery. Ether and chloroform which had proved of inestimable benefit in general surgery were less successfuly in ophthalmology. Retching and vomiting after the operations performed under these anaesthetics often undid in a minute the entire work of the surgeon of the previous hour. Some procedures required the active cooperation of the patient – to turn the eyes to right or left for example. These difficulties resulted in many operations being performed without *any* anaesthesia at all and the surgeons had to act with the same lightning speed used by the general surgeons in the early decades of the century. Koller, therefore, began to experiment with many different substances on animals, using chloral, bromide, morphine and other drugs without success, and eventually abandoned these attempts for the time being. "Although these experiments had been unsuccessful they had the good effect that my mind was prepared to grasp the opportunity whenever I should encounter a real anaesthetic", he wrote later (Becker, 1963). Later, in Stricker's laboratory, he made extensive studies in pharmacology, studying the effects on circulation and respiration of many different poisons, so he was no stranger to the study of the action of powerful drugs.

Freud had already left Vienna on the journey to Martha in Germany when Koller made his great discovery. He had given some cocaine to a colleague, Dr Engel, who remarked on its numbing effect on the tongue. "Yes," answered Koller, "that has been noticed by everyone that has eaten it." As Koller related later, "And in the moment it flashed upon me that I was carrying in my pocket the local anaesthetic for which I searched some years earlier" (Becker, 1963). The story is taken up by Dr Gaertner (1919), a young assistant in Professor Stricker's laboratory on the fateful day, the sole witness of the birth of local anaesthesia.

"One summer day in 1884, Dr Koller, at that time a very young man, was engaged in a piece of embryological research. He stepped into Professor Stricker's laboratory, drew a small flask in which there was a trace of white powder from his pocket, and addressed me, Professor Stricker's assistant, in approximately the following words:

'I hope, indeed I expect, that this powder will anaesthetise the eye.' 'We'll find out about that right away,' I replied. A few grains of the substance were thereupon dissolved in a small quantity of distilled water, a large, lively frog was selected from the aquarium and held immobile in a cloth, and now a drop of the solution was trickled into one of the protruding eyes .... After about a minute came the great historic moment, I do not hesitate to designate it as such. The frog permitted his cornea to be touched and even injured without a trace of reflex action or attempt to protect himself – whereas the other eye responded with the usual reflex action to the slightest touch . . . The same tests were performed on a rabbit and a dog with equally good results."

Further experiments on their own eyes produced the same results. The discovery of local anaesthesia was complete.

In haste Koller wrote a short preliminary communication taking up barely two sides of a sheet of paper. Too poor to go himself to the ophthalmological congress in Heidelberg, he entrusted his paper to his friend Dr Josef Brettauer of Trieste, who read the paper and demonstrated the experiments before the many distinguished specialists gathered there. It must have been a moving occasion for Arlt, one of the participants. The effect on the assembly was electric. Within a few weeks reports of the successful use of the new local anaesthetic were being made from all over the world. When Freud returned from Germany, the name of Koller was on all lips. In the few weeks of his absence, his friend had achieved world fame.

At first, Freud's main reaction seems to have been one of proprietary pride – it was *his* remedy, cocaine, which had revealed yet a further indication for its use. But to Freud, who at this time was thinking of the magical drug as a universal panacea for every ill, and expecting new applications of even greater importance to be discovered in the near future, its local anaesthetic properties were a mere side issue. So for some time he looked with benevolent approval on Koller's activities and was especially gratified when his own father underwent an eye operation for glaucoma under the new anaesthetic. It was only much later when the bitter truth dawned on him that local anaesthesia was the *only* indication for the use of the drug that he realised how narrowly he himself had missed the glory now being accorded to Koller. Later, he admitted that he had not been thorough enough to pursue the matter further, and, in conversation, would ascribe the omission to his "laziness" (Jones, 1953).

By early 1885, the condition of his friend Fleischl was giving cause for concern. Fleischl had, it was true, been successfully weaned from morphia, but was now in the grip of a far more formidable allegiance to cocaine. By April 1885 he was consuming enormous doses of the drug; Freud noted that he had spent 1,800 marks on it in the past three months, a figure indicating a dosage of a full gramme a day, a hundred times that which Freud was accustomed to take, and then only occasionally (Jones, 1953). Fleischl had evidently also resumed his use of morphine and was

Ernst von Fleischl-Marxow.

taking both drugs concurrently, a usage that was to emerge as a very characteristic pattern whenever cocaine was used to wean morphine addicts from their former allegiance. By April, Freud had had to sit up all one night with his friend Fleischl lying in a warm bath by his side – "Every note of the profoundest despair was sounded," he wrote to Martha (Jones, 1953). On June 8 Freud was telling Martha that the frightful doses had harmed Fleischl greatly, and although he continued to send her cocaine, he warned her against acquiring the habit.

Yet knowing that Fleischl was taking these large doses of cocaine when he was supposed to have ceased its use, Freud read a paper on March 3 at the Physiological Club, and two days later at the Psychiatric Society in which he described what must certainly have been Fleischl's case, as one of "rapid withdrawal from morphine under cocaine"; the habit, he said, had been overcome in twenty days by the use of the latter drug. "No cocaine habituation set in," he claimed, "on the contrary, an increasing antipathy to the use of cocaine was unmistakably evident." He had no hesitation, he continued, in recommending the administration of cocaine for such withdrawal cures in *subcutaneous injections*. This paper was published in the *Medico-Chirurgische Centralblatt* on August 7, 1885. Between its original delivery and its publication, Fleischl's condition had deteriorated still further. By June he had begun to exhibit the classic symptoms of severe cocaine intoxication – attacks of fainting and convulsions, insomnia and behavioural eccentricities, culminating in the characteristic hallucinations of small animals, in this case white snakes, crawling over his skin. On June 4, Freud had found him in such a condition – Brücke and Schenk were also present – that he went to fetch his physician Breuer, and then stayed the night there – "the most frightful night he had ever spent," he wrote to Martha (Jones, 1953). In this sorry, broken-down state, the once gifted, brilliant, handsome and aristocratic Fleischl lingered for another six painful years before being released by death from his wretched existence. Yet, having been witness to these terrible scenes, knowing that Fleischl was still taking morphine as well as cocaine and having warned his fiancée of acquiring the habit, Freud allowed the 1885 paper to go forward for publication in August. Not only that, but Jones, failing to notice Freud's mendacity, reports that Freud was "gratified" when the *Lancet* subsequently abstracted it.

Freud was to regret this paper two years later when reports of addiction and its frightful consequences had begun to flow in from all parts of the globe and he was having to defend himself against the accusations of the psychiatrist Erlenmeyer that he had unleashed on the world the third scourge of humanity, the first two being alcohol and morphine. His defence, set out in a paper published in the *Wiener Medizinische Wochenschrift* of July 1887, was somewhat tendentious, laying the chief blame on others – "The new use of cocaine was first brought to the general attention of physicians and also, unfortunately, of morphine addicts – through the pamphlets of E. Merck Co., Darmstadt, and an extravagant article by Walle in the *Deutsche Medizinalzeitung*". Freud now conceded the fact of addiction to cocaine – a far more dangerous one than that to morphine, he admitted. He cited the rapid physical and moral deterioration, hallucinatory states of agitation similar to delirium tremens, and the "chronic persecution mania", as well as the characteristic hallucinations of small animals moving on the skin, effects which must have been only too familiar to him from the case of his friend. He compared its use in the treatment of morphine addiction to "the sad results of trying to cast out the devil by Beelzebub". Many morphine addicts who had until that time held their own in life now succumbed to cocaine, he admitted. But these terrible results were only found in morphine addicts, "persons who, already in the grip of one demon are so weak in will power, so susceptible, that they would misuse, and indeed have misused, any stimulant held out to them". Cocaine, he asserted, "has claimed no other, no victim on its own". It was a rash statement to make without supporting evidence. Reports from all over the world were soon to prove him tragically wrong.

Freud's second line of defence was that the harmful effects of the drug were due to its having been *injected subcutaneously* instead of taken by mouth, as he had recommended. Unfortunately, *he had*, in the 1885 paper, recommended these injections. This paper, as Jones relates, was subsequently suppressed by Freud. It appeared neither in his list of publications submitted with his application for the title of Professor in 1897, nor was it found among his collection of reprints after his death. Yet there were those whose memories must have gone back to this paper – Brücke, for instance, Freud's former chief and Fleischl's present one, who would, as a physiologist, almost certainly have attended the meeting of the Physiology Club at which it was first read and who was witness to the terrible scenes with Fleischl when he was supposed to have been cured. Was it for this reason that Freud wrote later in the *Interpretation of Dreams* of the "terrible gaze of his eyes", eyes of steely blue that were to haunt him for years to come?

Interestingly, the 1887 paper gives us some information on Freud's own experience with cocaine. He claims to have taken the drug himself "for some months" without ill effect or any desire for its continued use. "On the contrary, there occurred more frequently than I should have liked, an aversion to the drug, which was sufficient cause for curtailing its use." This would indicate that by 1887 Freud had ceased to use the drug himself. For Jones and Freud's other biographers, the story of his personal involvement with cocaine ends here. But as we shall see, an involvement with far greater consequences was yet to come.

However, all of this was still in the future. In 1885 the outcry against cocaine was still a year away and Freud was basking in the glory of having introduced into therapeutics a drug of enormous potential value to mankind. With his appointment to the ranks of *Privatdozent*, his fortunes had taken an upward turn and on June 20, 1885 he was, amid stiff competition, awarded a postgraduate travelling grant which involved six months leave of absence and the magnificent sum of 600 gulden. He had decided to use it to fulfil his long cherished ambition to visit Paris where the famous neurologist Charcot was then engaged in new and somewhat controversial research. On his return, an appointment awaited him at the children's out-patient clinic, where the director Max Kassowitz had asked him to take charge of the neurology department. In the autumn of 1885 when he left for Paris, there was no cloud on the horizon, only the brightest hopes which included the possibility of an early marriage to his beloved Martha, faithfully waiting for him.

IV

Charcot and the Salpêtrière

Famous in the history of medicine as in the history of Paris, the hospital of La Salpêtrière is situated on the left bank of the Seine at the east end of the city. Inscribed over its arched entrances are the names of the four illustrious men whose lives were intimately bound up in its history – Vincent de Paul, Mazarin, Pinel and Charcot. Its name – literally a saltpetre factory – betrays its original use in the thirteenth century as an arsenal, in this respect resembling Brücke's institute in Vienna.

Shortly after his ordination as priest in 1600, Vincent de Paul had been captured by Barbary pirates on a voyage in the Mediterranean. Escaping in 1607 after several years as a galley slave, he had worked his way back to Paris. Adjuring his followers to make their cloister the gutter, he began a life's work among the sick, the crippled and the poor. Towards the middle of the fifteenth century the buildings of the Salpêtrière were put at his disposal by Cardinal Mazarin for the establishment of a women's asylum for the aged, the crippled and the insane. By the end of the eighteenth century the Salpêtrière was the largest hospice in Europe. A contemporary physician reported that he saw there at one time "as many as eight thousand inmates, consisting of old and decrepit women, dissolute and criminal women in the prisons, pauper children, furious maniacs, imbeciles, epileptics, paralytics, the blind, the crippled and those afflicted with scurvy and a variety of incurable diseases". This was the Salpêtrière found by the famous alienist Philippe Pinel when he was appointed Physician-in-Chief to the hospital in the late eighteenth century. There, in cells that received neither light nor air, manacled to their beds, were confined the more maniacal of the hospital's patients. In winter, when the waters of the Seine rose, the lower cells situated at the level of the sewers were invaded by rats and many patients succumbed to their bites. It was in these cells that the famous episode of the freeing of the insane from their chains by Pinel took place in 1795.

La Salpêtriée.

But when Freud entered the Salpêtrière on October 21, 1885, there was nothing to suggest its grim past. The scene of Pinel's liberation of the insane from their chains was now the corridor, lined with neatly labelled and numbered brains and spinal cords preserved in alcohol, leading to Charcot's clinic. The clinic itself and the adjoining consulting room where he first met Charcot were hung with old prints depicting biblical occurrences, and scenes in demonology and witchcraft of which – because of the association with epilepsy – Charcot was an avid collector. In contrast, the room devoted to electrotherapy contained representations of "the modern possessed" – photographs and crayon drawings of Charcot's patients, victims also of epilepsy and the diseases which it accompanies.

Freud's sojourn started auspiciously. On his arrival the out-patient clinic was already in progress, being conducted by Pierre Marie, then Charcot's *Chef de Clinique*, later to achieve fame in his own right for, among other things, his discovery of acromegaly. At ten a.m. Charcot arrived and began to examine the patients. After the clinic Freud produced his letters of introduction and was received kindly by Charcot who showed him round the wards, taking in the laboratory and lecture hall, explaining the arrangements and usages as they proceeded. "I soon felt very much at ease," Freud wrote to Martha, "and I realised that in the most inconspicuous fashion he was showing me a great deal of consideration" (Freud, Ernst, 1961). Freud described Charcot to Martha as

"... a tall man of 58, wearing a top hat, with dark, strangely soft eyes (or rather one is, the other is expressionless and has an inward cast), long wisps of hair stuck behind his ears, clean shaven very expressive features with full protruding lips – in short, like a worldly priest from whom one expects a ready wit and an appreciation of good living" (Freud, Ernst, 1961).

Jean-Martin Charcot was born in Paris in 1825, the son of a carriage builder. His medical studies began in 1844; four years later he was an *interne* in the Paris hospital system, beginning his service at the Salpêtrière. There he early recognised the potential of the venerable institution for the investigation of diseases of the

Jean-Martin Charcot.

nervous system by the method of such proven value in the past – the correlation of the signs and symptoms exhibited by the patient during life with the pathology found after death. In the wards of this vast hospice were to be found collections of old patients in the later and terminal stages of neural disease, "a sort of living pathological museum" as he was later to describe it. Previous physicians had attempted to use the vast amount of clinical and pathological material available in the institution but had been defeated by the system then prevalent among the Paris *médecins des hôpitaux* of frequently changing hospitals and at the same time the speciality they were studying, until their career took them to the great clinical hospital of the Hôtel-Dieu. Charcot determined to return to the Salpêtrière as *médecin des hôpitaux* and thereafter never to leave it. His intention he did in fact carry out, returning to the Salpêtrière to take over the medical service in 1862. He was afterwards to declare that his only merit lay in carrying out this plan. Though he later attained high office, becoming Professor of Pathological Anatomy at the Collège de France, he continued his work at the Salpêtrière, delivering courses of clinical lectures on a voluntary basis for seventeen years though holding no official position in the institution. During this time Charcot distinguished many previously unknown neural conditions. Under his direction the ancient buildings of the hospice were converted into a centre for research and teaching on diseases of the nervous system. The course of lectures he gave in the institution rapidly became famous. His work was eventually crowned in 1881 by the recognition by the government of his great service to medicine with the establishment at the Salpêtrière of a professorial chair in diseases of the nervous system, Charcot its first incumbent.

It has been said that Charcot entered neurology in its infancy and left at its coming of age. To the physician practising at the beginning of the nineteenth century the nervous system was a perplexing enigma. The central nervous system, shielded from investigation by its bony encasements of skull and spine, had been slow to yield up its secrets and neurology too had participated in the long sleep of medicine. Though Galen in the second century AD had established the nervous system as a functional unit, tracing a continuity between brain, spinal cord and peripheral nerves, after his death knowledge remained static for nearly sixteen hundred years. His teaching that nervous function depended on the activities of the "animal spirits", the instruments and messengers of the soul (the word "animal" derived from the Latin "anima" – the soul) and that the nerves were merely channels for the flow of the spirits to different parts of the body, survived until the end of the eighteenth century. The concept of nerves as a network of inter-communicating channels lingered still longer, lasting almost to the twentieth century, a fact that has important bearings on Freud's later theory of "conversion hysteria".

The location of intellect and consciousness had, throughout the centuries, been placed in almost every organ of the body. Hippocrates, from his observations in epilepsy, had assigned the seat of the soul to the brain, but Aristotle later placed it in the heart, dismissing the brain as a mere organ for "cooling the blood" (the term "heart strings" derives from his belief that the heart was attached to the windpipe by cartilaginous strings which violent emotion might rupture). After Harvey's demonstration in 1628 of the circulation of the blood which showed the heart to be a mere muscular pump, Aristotle's doctrines declined and Galen's teaching on the supremacy of the brain gradually became universally accepted, though almost every site apart from the grey matter itself was favoured as the seat of the soul, the hollow spaces within the cerebrum (the ventricles), the meninges (the outer covering membranes) and the pineal gland (named by Descartes) being those most often chosen. As late as 1819, William Lawrence, lecturing on the brain, expressed the uncertainty still prevalent.

> "This large and curious structure which in the human subject receives one fifth of all the blood sent out from the heart, which is so peculiarly and delicately organised, nicely enveloped in successive membranes and securely lodged in a solid bony case, is left almost without an office, being barely allowed to be capable of sensation. It has indeed the easiest lot in the animal economy; it is better fed, clothed and lodged than any other part and has less to do."

It was Franz Joseph Gall (1758–1828) who definitely established the brain itself as the organ of the mind, in so doing transferring attention to the outer mantle of grey matter with its many convolutions, the cerebral cortex. Gall is today chiefly remembered as the founder of the pseudo-science of phrenology. But though his doctrines degenerated into quackery, their original impulse had sprung from valid researches in brain anatomy and it was these researches that definitely established the brain itself as the organ of mind. A brilliant neuroanatomist, Gall established the division between the grey and white matter of the brain, no small feat when one remembers that he was working with unfixed brains in their semi-fluid natural state. He recognised the fibrous nature of the white matter and its conductor function. Most important, he realised the supremacy of the cerebral cortex, and, in its grey matter, traced the origins of the nerves. It was only when these findings became widely known that the brain attained the pre-eminent place it holds today. Anyone doubting this fundamental fact should read John Elliotson's paper on Gall in the *Lancet* of 1837–8.

> "The first great principle is, that the brain is the organ of the mind. Although no rational being now doubts this, and it is admitted by the *British Association*, it was denied by a large number of writers, and by an immense number of persons at the time Gall wrote. Hippocrates and many able writers acknowledged the brain to be the organ of the mind, but Gall had a host of adversaries when he maintained this opinion. On account of it he was called a deist, an atheist, a materialist, and other opprobrious names."

The old theory demanded hollow nerves through which flowed the "animal spirits". Consequently anatomists "saw" hollow nerves even through their microscopes until well into the nineteenth century; it was only after the introduction of the achromatic microscope in the eighteen-thirties that the true nature of the nerve fibre was established. The doctrine of the spirits had by then fallen into abeyance and was replaced by the terms "nervous fluid" or "vis nervosa". Its vestigial traces persist in our language when we use the term "high-spirited" or talk about being in low spirits. The newer theories are illustrated by J. F. Blumenbach in his *Elements of Physiology* (1828) when he referred to the nervous fluid as "by some called animal spirits . . . by others conceived to be a matter analogous to fire, to light, to a peculiar ether, to oxygen, to electricity, or to magnetism, etc." Long after the electrical nature of nervous activity became generally accepted, however, the theory of the function of the nervous system remained the same in its essentials, being still regarded as a circulatory system fed by some kind of power or energy from the brain. This power still coursed through hollow nerves, travelling back and forth in either direction, the brain itself still being regarded as having little separate function beyond its generation of such power or energy and being the seat of the *sensorum commune* (the origin of our term "common sense").

The second break with the old theories came with the discovery by Bell and Magendie in the early decades of the nineteenth century of separate motor and sensory nerves, i.e. of the fact that different nervous pathways existed for motion and sensation. When Marshall Hall gave his first account to the Royal Society in 1833 of his studies on the nervous system, which eventually led to the establishment of reflex action as one of its chief phenomena, it was the first intimation of another major break with the old theories. Reflex action – the blinking of eyelids when the eyes are threatened, the instantaneous withdrawal of the hand from a hot surface, the contraction of the pupil in the presence of bright light – was a phenomenon with which it was impossible to associate any activity of mind or soul and so was difficult to accommodate in the old theories; it was accordingly explained as a "reflection" by the animal spirits of sensorial into motor impressions, hence the term "reflex". This theory was also postulated to account for the growing number of investigations in the eighteenth century with decapitated frogs, snakes and other creatures in which movement had been produced by stimulation of the spine even after the head had been removed. The startling results obtained by Aldini in 1804 who experimented with electrical stimulation on the head of a beheaded criminal and obtained muscle contractions resembling facial expressions led to the prohibition by law of such demonstrations in Prussia. When reflex action in the nervous system was, after much controversy, eventually accepted, inevitably many physicians went to the opposite extreme, postulating reflex activity where none existed. The *"paraplegia urinaria"* of those days, cited as a phenomenon of reflex action, was, for example, a misconception arising from the fact that cases of paralysis when brought to the post-mortem table sometimes showed no lesion in brain or cord, the only pathology present being in the kidneys; death in these cases was probably due to unrecognised uraemia (an excess of urea in the blood). The old theory that infantile paralysis, now known as poliomyelitis, was caused by teething, as it occurred so often in infants of the appropriate age, was now given a pseudoscientific rationale by the assertion that there was a reflex action between teeth and legs. Later in the century, a similar fallacy led to the theory of the "nasal reflex neurosis" which led Freud into error and which plays a large part in the story that is to follow.

The discovery by the Weber brothers in 1846 that stimulation of the vagus nerve slowed the heart and actually caused it to stop was a paradox that in the light of the knowledge of the day, evoked disbelief. It was actually the first inkling of any *inhibitory* effect of nervous action. The full explanation of the phenomenon, however, had to wait till Sherrington's great synthesis at the turn of the century, when he demonstrated that the discharge of even a single nerve cell could at one and the same time put one group of cells out of action and another group *into* action – the principle of Sherrington's law of the reciprocal inhibition of antagonistic muscles. But in 1846 the Webers' discovery was just one of many isolated facts that were being uncovered in piecemeal fashion and as yet not integrated with other data. When Helmholtz in 1850 succeeded in measuring the velocity of nerve conduction and found it to be only 25–40 metres a second, far slower than an electric current passing along a wire, he rendered untenable the simple analogy to such conduction that had previously been used to explain nerve conduction. These isolated facts could not yet be fitted into any integrated system. The result was that in practice they tended to be ignored and men continued to be tied to the old ways of thought, i.e. to the concept of the nervous system as a communicating network analogous to the circulation of the blood. This has important implications for some of Freud's theories which we shall come to in a later chapter.

The experimental results reported from the physiology laboratories added further to the confusion. Extensive efforts were now in progress to discover the function of individual nerves by compression or electrical stimulation of exposed nerves in animals. (The function of the motor branch of the fifth cranial nerve was strikingly demonstrated to Alexander Shaw when its stimulation at the spheno-palantine junction of a newly killed ass resulted in the jaws closing with a snap that crushed his fingers.) Faulty technology often led to conflicting results since attributed to the spread of the intense electrical current to adjoining areas to the experimental site. Ablation experiments, the removal of some part of the brain or spinal cord to observe consequent loss of function, produced results since attributed to haemorrhage into adjoining parts or spread of infection in pre-aseptic days. In addition, errors arose from the uncritical extrapolation of animal experiments to man. When Pierre Flourens established the respiratory centre, the *noeud vital*, in the medulla oblongata of the brain, the French physiologist Brown-Séquard vigorously contested the finding. He had kept frogs and toads alive for months without a *noeud vital*, he protested. These cold-blooded animals had, of course, obtained sufficient oxygen through their moist skins to maintain life. Flourens had himself with his experiments on pigeons brought confusion to the scientific scene. In an experiment in 1823 designed to disprove Gall's theories, he had removed both the cerebral lobes of a pigeon; the results verified Gall's choice of the brain as the seat of the mind – "it no longer judges," Flourens wrote, "it strikes itself twenty times of the same object without learning to avoid it" – but he denied Gall's teaching that the brain was made up of multiple organs, and declared from the results of his experiments that the brain acted as a whole. Flourens' views

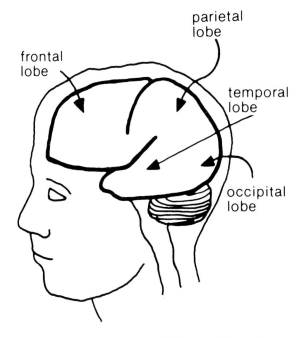

The lobes of the brain.

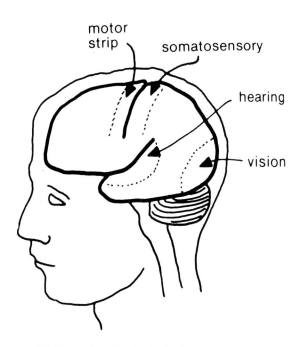

The location of different faculties in the brain.

dominated theories of brain function for several decades even though, as the microscopic anatomy of the brain progressed, evidence was accumulating through the work of Meynert and others that there was a considerable morphological difference in the arrangement and structure of the cells in different parts of the brain and in particular those of the cortex.

Clinical evidence in favour of the location of different functions in different areas of the brain was also building up. As early as 1825 Jean-Baptiste Bouillaud had pointed out how frequently loss of speech was associated with a lesion of the frontal lobes of the brain; but he had been writing in support of Gall, who had assigned the faculty of speech to these lobes, and his paper received little recognition, largely due to the swing of the tide against the unscientific excesses of Gall's followers, and the influence of Flourens' experiments. It was not until 1861 when Bouillaud's son-in-law Simon Auburtin took up his discarded work that the question was reopened. In a famous series of meetings of the *Société d'Anthropologie de Paris* in 1861, Auburtin argued in favour of cerebral localisation of function and in particular that of speech, which he allocated to the anterior lobes of the brain. Reporting a dramatic experiment carried out on a patient with a frontal cranial defect resulting from a head injury he stated: "During the interrogation the blade of a large spatula was placed on the anterior lobes; by means of light pressure, speech was suddenly stopped; a word that had been commenced was cut in two. The faculty of speech reappeared as soon as the compression ceased."

One of the participants in the discussion which followed Auburtin's paper was Pierre-Paul Broca, anatomist and anthropologist, whose name is now irrevocably associated with the localisation of the function of speech in the left frontal lobe of the brain. Soon after the discussion he came across a patient who proved to be the test case for Auburtin's theory – the famous "Tan", so called because this was the only syllable he could utter, though fully understanding the spoken word. Tan died on April 17, 1861. Necropsy revealed the lesions of the frontal convolutions of the brain anticipated by Auburtin. Broca's pathological demonstration before the *Académie de Médecine* of Paris demonstrating the astonishing fact that a local lesion in the brain could destroy the power of speech produced tremendous excitement in medical circles and provided the impetus for many new investigations into the whole tremendously complicated subject of speech and language disorders. Clinicians everywhere now observed their cases with greater interest as many new and often strange syndromes began to emerge. There were patients who, though able to write, could not read, even the words written by their own hand a moment before, or who retained the capacity for "serial speech" (in the form of the recital of prayers, etc.); jargon aphasia, when speech itself was unimpaired but only jargon emerged – though the intellectual faculties were intact – was another frequent manifestation. Some syndromes were so strange as to invite disbelief, as, for instance, in patients able to read aloud but unable to speak spontaneously and these cases tended to invite a diagnosis of "hysteria". We shall meet such a patient later – the famous "Anna O" of psychoanalytic renown. Many years were to pass before these syndromes were explained on an anatomical basis by the many investigators now researching speech and language. One of these was Carl Wernicke, Meynert's pupil, who in 1874 discovered another speech area in the left temporal lobe, destruction of which resulted in sensory, or receptive aphasia with the patient unable to *understand* the spoken word. When Broca in 1864 arrived at the correlation of speech loss with lesions of the *left* hemisphere of the brain, he made a discovery that had virtually escaped notice in the thousands of years since Hippocrates, during which innumerable patients with stroke were affected with speech loss and paralysis of the *right* side of the body, though the fact that paralyses supervening on a head injury occurred in the limbs on the side *opposite* to that of the lesion, had been known from the time of Aretaeus in the second century AD.

The establishment of recognisable landmarks in the topography of the brain that could be identified and named gave renewed impetus to the study of cerebral localisation of function. The convolutions of the surface of the brain had been neglected by the anatomists. Due to the lack of fixing and hardening agents, they had believed them to be as inconstant and variable as the loops of the intestines. The seventeenth-century anatomist Thomas Bartholin had ascribed their function to one of protection of the cerebral vessels from the danger of rupture from violent movement "especially during the full moon, when the brain swells in the skull". The constant and unchanging pattern of the convolutions was only established in the middle of the nineteenth century by the studies of Leurat and Gratiolet in the years 1839–1857. These convolutions did not even receive their anatomical names until 1869, a fact which demonstrates the ignorance still extant only a decade or so before Freud embarked on the study of neurology. Yet as the century progressed it became evident that each convolution was an organ, or part of one, each with distinct and individual functions.

In 1870, two young Germans, Hitzig and Fritsch, published their experiments on electrical stimulation of the cerebral cortex of a dog. Using a pair of blunted electrodes from a galvanic pile applied directly to the surface of the brain they obtained muscular contractions of the opposite half of the body – movements which enabled them to roughly map out the motor area of the cortex. The question of cerebral localisation now became the most important neurological issue of the day. Other cerebral centres for the control of function were eagerly sought.

Investigations into the sensory system had lagged far behind that of the motor, and had hardly progressed beyond the findings of Magendie, who had differentiated the spinal nerves subscribing sensation from those concerned with motor function. The difficulties of experimental testing on animals unable to report their sensations are evident from the morass of conflicting reports emanating from this era. Ignorance of the fact that pain, temperature and touch were transmitted along different nervous pathways led to many errors in diagnosis. Eventually in 1878, in a classic paper, Gowers, in a case of suicidal gunshot injury, demonstrated the dissociation of pain and touch sensations. These findings were not incorporated into clinical practice until much later, however.

Since the discovery of the motor area in the brain by Fritsch and Hitzig, investigators now sought a similar cerebral region governing sensation. But here again the scene was obscured by the difficulties of animal experimentation. David Ferrier had placed the area in the hippocampus, a region of the temporal lobe, but later retracted this erroneous view and eventually, in common with many others, denied such an area in the cortex at all. Finally in 1884, the American neurologist Alan Starr found that a direct anatomical connection could be traced from the surface of the body to the parietal cortex of the brain, a finding subsequently confirmed by succeeding investigators. The confusion on the role of the sensory system, persisting long after 1884, was the reason why Charcot and his contemporaries so often fell into error in ascribing disturbances of sensation to "hysteria", errors later incorporated into his own work by Freud. These discoveries of the cerebral localisation of different functions had important bearings on the clinical situation. From the disturbances of such functions it now became possible to diagnose gross brain lesions such as tumours or abscesses *during life*, rendering feasible the attempt to remove them by surgery, and in fact the first brain tumour to be successfully excised was removed by A. H. Bennett in 1884.

It was a far cry from the state of clinical neurology at the start of the century. "Nervous distempers" had been ascribed to the

obstruction of the "animal spirits" by a "gross phlegmatic humour" or a "hot vapour" from the ventricles, or obstruction of the
arteries carrying the "vital spirits" to the brain by a "cold
pituitous matter". They were known by their symptoms alone,
and a symptom constituted a disease – headache, frenzy (a relic of
the early belief that the seat of the mind was in the diaphragm),
"lethargy" (coma), palsy, etc., and were treated with such homely
remedies as that recommended by Gilbert of putting a sow into
bed with the patient in cases of "lethargy".

Though haemorrhage had been recognised as a cause of
"apoplexy" or stroke for over a century, thrombosis was unknown until Virchow's epoch-making paper in 1847 in which he
advanced the hypothesis, since amply vindicated, that the clots
responsible for the obstruction of the vessels had not originated in
the local circulation but had been carried in the bloodstream from
some distant part. Tumours and abscesses of the brain had, as we
have seen, been observed on the post-mortem table since the
inauguration of the clinicopathological method, but only late in
the century was it possible to diagnose them during life. In 1817
James Parkinson, a general practitioner in Shoreditch, then a small
village on the outskirts of London, published his famous *Essay on
the Shaking Palsy*, so called because of the tremor and rigidity
characteristic of the condition now known as Parkinson's disease.
The "falling sickness" (epilepsy) had been known from ancient
times. Hippocrates had assigned its cause to an excess of solid
phlegm from the brain passing into the blood, making it congeal
and stand still, an explanation that had lasted for nearly two
thousand years. Other causes favoured up to the mid-nineteenth
century were worms, teething, and the various "passions of the
mind". The influence of the moon was a strongly held belief. A
legacy from the ancients, it is to be found in the literature until the
middle of the nineteenth century. Romberg wrote in his *Diseases
of the Nervous System* (1853)

> "The planetary influence of the moon (especially of the new and
> full moon) upon the courses of epilepsy, was known to the
> ancients and although here and there doubts have been raised
> against this view, the accurate observations of others have
> established its correctness."

It was not until the statistical studies of Moreau of the Bicêtre
based on observations of a hundred patients with epilepsy over a
five-year period showed no correlation of their attacks with the
phases of the moon that belief in lunar influence began to die out.
But otherwise little more was known about the condition than

existed in ancient Greece. Many attacks with differing phenomena from those of the well-known major fits of the "falling sickness" were unrecognised as epileptic in nature until well after the discoveries in cerebral localisation later in the century. These fits, beginning in different areas of the brain from the former, presented a different range of phenomena, their symptomatology depending on the particular area of the brain from which they had originated. In some attacks the patient might not even convulse, might still be capable of walking and talking, but would nevertheless be undergoing an epileptic seizure. We shall encounter such patients later in the Freud story, where they play an important role. These conditions represent the sum of the common neural diseases known by the middle of the nineteenth century. Modern neurology, as stated by Fielding Garrison in his *History of Medicine*, is mainly of French extraction and derives from Duchenne de Boulogne, through Charcot and his famous pupils Marie, Déjerine and Babinski.

Duchenne de Boulogne was a familiar figure during the middle decades of the nineteenth century in the great Paris hospitals where he haunted the wards in search of cases of neurological interest. Holding no position in the hospital service of the city he only gained access to patients through the goodwill of the official physicians. Shy and awkward, he was at first barely tolerated, but gradually gained the respect and acceptance of the leading medical figures in Paris, who trusted his diagnostic judgement better than their own and who marvelled at the ease and confidence with which he threw the great muscles into contraction with the electric currents from his famous Faradic apparatus. Duchenne is remembered today for the first clinical description of glossolabiolaryngeal paralysis (bulbar palsy) now known as a form of motor neurone disease where the condition is limited to tongue, lips and throat. Duchenne's biographer Victor Robinson's evocative description of the disease conveys the formidable quality of the malady.

"One by one the dreaded symptoms develop until he is unable to talk, or close his mouth or swallow his food or expectorate his saliva or prevent its constant drooling – and all the time the mind remains clear so that the patient can watch the disgusting part he plays in his own tragedy."

Duchenne's monograph of 1858 delineated *tabes dorsalis*, then one of the commonest diseases of the nervous system. It is a late result of syphilis "ambushed for years in the neurones until the posterior columns of the spinal cord collapse", in Robinson's apt description.

> "Thus another of the endless victims of *spirocheta pallida* joins the army of incoordination, complaining he cannot button his collar or walk in the dark; the physician notes Romberg's sign and the Argyle-Robertson pupil; then drugs and massage and electricity occupy practitioner and patient; advice about avoidance of any excitement and injections of morphine for the tabetic crisis, attempting to relieve the symptoms as they occur, and the curtain falls on an unbrained, blinded, bed-ridden paralytic, lower than any beast" (Robinson, 1936).

This progression was the fate of many famous men who have left accounts of their illness, Alphonse Daudet and Guy de Maupassant among others. Daudet's description of the lightning pains of tabes and the strange disorders of sensation he experienced are considered medically valid accounts of this terrible malady, now happily curable. Duchenne also described the wasting palsy of adult males – progressive spinal muscular atrophy, still known as Duchenne-Aran disease; he described and gave his name to the pseudohypertrophic paralysis of Duchenne, a hereditary condition in which, as in haemophilia, the mother, herself unaffected, passes on the disease to her sons. "With strange incongruity the muscles enlarge while weakness increases", Robinson describes it; "then wasting ensues, and the boy is unable to stand: the knee jerks are abolished, and only the moving hands are left to protest against an inexplicable fate."

Duchenne held no high office, nor did he receive any honours or distinctions in his lifetime, but he laid the foundations of French neurology, foundations on which Charcot later was to build with such brilliance. He had met Duchenne, whom he always acknowledged as his "master in neurology", as a young *interne*, and now gave him the freedom of his wards, learning from the older man while in return offering him the facilities of his pathological laboratory. Within a short time he was building on this knowledge, proving by pathological evidence, for instance, the existence of the lesion of poliomyelitis in the anterior horn cells of the spinal cord which Duchenne from his clinical experience felt convinced must be there.

The story of how Charcot transformed the venerable institution of the Salpêtrière, hitherto regarded as the graveyard of professional aspirations, into a great teaching hospital has been told many times and has passed into medical legend. The clinical material available in the aged pauper population, so suitable for the clinicopathological method, he exploited to the full, supervising every post-mortem and examining the brain microscopically himself in the improvised laboratory in the old kitchen off the cancer ward. By its use he established many neurological conditions hitherto unknown. He was the first to diagnose multiple sclerosis in life. This is one of the commonest diseases of the nervous system in which the fatty myelin insulating sheaths of the nerves are attacked by disease, so impairing conduction function and giving rise to various paralyses, double vision and other symptoms.

Every year was a year of new discovery on which his pupils would reminisce in later years – the year of intermittent claudication – the year of amyotrophic lateral sclerosis – the year of poliomyelitis – the year of Charcot-Marie-Tooth Disease – the year of tabetic arthropathies – the year of cerebral localisation – a truly triumphant progress. A superb teacher, Charcot's lectures were enlivened with all the accoutrements of visual aids, slides, sculptures and photographs, now routine but then entirely novel, and hence greatly appreciated. No mean artist himself, he enlivened his words with admirable blackboard sketches using different coloured chalks for greater clarity. His gift of mimicry was utilised in demonstrating the various pathological gaits characteristic of different diseases, the broad-based stamping gait of the tabetic, the "scissors" gait of the spastic, the steppage gait of polyneuritis, when the patient, unable to lift his feet normally, has to adopt a high stepping walk to clear the foot off the ground. His famous Tuesday clinics were held in a large amphitheatre containing a stage illuminated by footlights and sometimes still further illuminated by a spotlight from a calcium burner at the back to light up some interesting detail while Charcot performed the examinations, demonstrating the various postures, deformities, and sensory disorders and mimicking the tics and spasms resulting from loss of nerve function. To emphasise the different forms of tremor he would sometimes have a procession of patients file across the stage with tall plumes attached to their head-dresses. This and many other devices rendered his lectures memorable to an ever widening body of students from many different parts of the world; Freud himself, one of this large clan, early succumbed to the fascination of the master and his teaching.

When his work at the Salpêtrière, carried out without reward or official recognition for many years, was finally recognised by the establishment of a chair, together with a new out-patient department, amphitheatre and laboratories to replace the old makeshift facilities, Charcot at his inaugural lecture spoke movingly of his emotion at the manner in which his ambitions for the institution had been fulfilled "beyond my wildest dreams".

Here is a glimpse of the great man at his best from his famous *Leçons du Mardi* which gives some insight into the fascination he exercised over Freud and his generation.

TABES DORSALIS

Charcot: The patient complains of facial insensibility on the left side, or rather of a kind of painless anaesthesia on that side: It is not painful is it?

Patient: No, but it pulls and half the tongue burns like fire.

Charcot: And the face?

Patient: That tugs as if the skin were pulled with pincers. The other day I had a swelling with stinging pains in the eye, the nose and the gums on the left side.

Charcot: She has lost her teeth on the left side, and without pain was it not?

Patient: Yes, sir.

Charcot: And these teeth were very sound. She plucked them, so to speak. Did you save them?

Patient: I did not bring them with me.

Charcot: Please bring them next time, we will put them in our museum. Here is a strange adventure. But there is something else. She has, from time to time, pains of an extremely acute and special character in the left shoulder.

Patient: They are sharp pains.

Charcot: Do they make you cry?

Patient: They go down the arm. Sometimes my hand swells.

Charcot: Any pains in the legs?

Patient: None at all.

Charcot: Not even a little pricking, jumpy pains?

Patient: Yes, at night.

After further questions Charcot announces his verdict.

Charcot: You are probably asking: What the devil is he after? Well, I am after nothing further, for I have already made my diagnosis, but it is out of the ordinary. I will tell you in a minute. Naturally, we have examined the pupils. They present a sign which is, in this case, very interesting, that of Argyll-Robertson. Let us see about the reflexes. The patellar reflexes are absent. Now then, I have my diagnosis, strange as it may seem to those of you who have, as yet, only studied noso-graphy and not clinical medicine. Clinical medicine is made up of anomalies, while nosography is the description of phenomena that occur regularly. What we look for in the clinics is almost always excep-tional; what we study in nosography is the rule. It is well to know that, in the practice of medicine, a nosographer is not always a clinician. Well then, this woman is a tabetic. She has, it is true, neither incoordination of movement nor shooting pains in the legs. But she presents certain phenomena in the tabetic series, namely, loss of teeth without any gingivitis, and a peculiar anaesthesia of the jaw, phases of the tabetic picture described by Vallin . . . Then the Argyll-Robertson pupil, the absent patellar reflex and perhaps pains in the legs . . . .

V

The hystériques of the Salpêtrière

By the end of the seventies, Charcot felt his work in neurology was finished, that he had exhausted the rich vein of the organic diseases of the nervous system and that there was nothing new to be discovered, a delusion shared by many in the long history of medicine. Accordingly he turned his attention to what he thought to be the psychologically determined conditions of "hysteria" and "hypnotism", conditions he hoped would shed light on the age-old problem of the mysterious gulf between mind and body. Evidently fascinated by the many strange phenomena revealed by the two conditions, Charcot had, by the time of Freud's arrival in 1885, made their study his major research interest. It was from the *hystériques* at the Salpêtrière and from Charcot's lectures and demonstrations on them that Freud received his first intimation of the concepts that were to form the basis of his own theory of "hysteria" on which the whole doctrine of psychoanalysis was founded. It was a shaky foundation on which to base such far-reaching theories – because these patients *were not hysterics*. The "hysterical fits" that Freud witnessed so often at the Salpêtrière have now been authoritatively identified by modern French neurologists as temporal lobe attacks, i.e. attacks originating in a lesion in the temporal lobes of the brain, from which the epileptic discharge may either spread to other areas of the brain or remain confined to the temporal lobes themselves. Writing in 1953 the prominent French authority Henri Gastaut stated, "It is now an established fact, well recognised by a large number of epileptologists that the 'hystero-epileptics' of the last century almost certainly consisted of patients with lesions in the perifalciform region, the hippocampal gyrus or the inferior surface of the temporal lobe."

The long train of error that led to Charcot's diagnoses of hysteria in cases of temporal lobe epilepsy begins in ancient Greece and Egypt and ends with the cerebral localisation of function in the late nineteenth century. The layman associates the term "hysteria" with excitable or emotional behaviour. To a physician

Patient and staff at the Salpêtriére.

the word expresses a rather different meaning. The name "hysteria" is itself misleading. It is derived from the Greek word "hystera" – uterus or womb – and is a relic of the strange belief held by the ancients that the womb wandered about the body and, in its upward passage to the head, caused a morbid condition that had a strong affinity to the "falling sickness" (epilepsy). The belief originated with the victims themselves. A woman afflicted with the condition would complain of attacks when she would suddenly become aware that her womb had left its station in the lower abdomen and was rising up through the body. As it travelled upwards it caused tightness and constriction of the chest. On its arrival at the throat, choking ensued, with the sensation of a ball in the throat – the classic *globus hystericus*. Finally, its arrival at the head caused the patient to fall down in a violent fit.

The women probably did experience just such a sensation. The above is an unmistakable description of the aura of temporal lobe epilepsy. In the major (*grand mal*) fit, the attack originates in the vital central core of the brain, immediately and simultaneously involving both hemispheres and the victim falls with a suddenness that underlines the name "the falling sickness". In contrast, in "focal attacks", i.e. attacks originating in a particular area of the cortex, consciousness is not immediately lost and then only if the epileptic discharge spreads to the rest of the brain. Before this happens the patient becomes aware of the initial symptoms of the attack and these will depend on the area of the brain from which the epileptic discharge emanates. A vivid sensation of tingling or heat or cold may begin in a foot and travel upwards until the fit becomes generalised and the patient falls unconscious, indicating that the fit has originated in a lesion in the "foot area" of the sensory cortex, spreading from there to the remainder of the brain. The sensations travelling upwards from the foot are the aura of this particular kind of fit. Such sensations or other manifestations preceding a seizure were defined by the famous epileptologist William Lennox as "that part of the fit for which the patient has memory", i.e. before consciousness is lost. The aura can be a valuable diagnostic pointer to the site of the lesion in the brain which is causing the attacks, but before the discovery of the cerebral localisation of function it was not possible to draw from it any diagnostic inferences and its value was unrecognised. The temporal lobe attack is another such "focal fit", the discharging lesion being situated in one of these lobes. The aura in such an attack, because of the connections between the temporal lobes and the limbic system containing the "visceral brain", frequently begins in the abdomen and travels upwards, giving rise to sensations identical to those described in the literature of the ancient Greek physicians. Profoundly ignorant, however, of the basic facts of anatomy, these physicians fully subscribed to the belief in the ability of the uterus to wander about the body. A discussion of the alleged peregrinations of the womb is even to be found in Plato's *Timaeus*.

Temporal lobe epilepsy was not finally defined until after the advent of the electroencephalogram (EEG) in the nineteen-forties. Meanwhile the characteristic fits were, since ancient times, known by the names "hysteria" in women and "hypochondria" in men, whose ascending aura had been referred to this region of the abdomen. (The use of "hypochondria" to describe the condition in men eventually died out and the term was applied to either sex indiscriminately.) When, in the sixteenth century it was demonstrated by the anatomists that the womb was too firmly bound by ligaments to be able to ascend anywhere in the body, noxious vapours from corrupt humours in the uterus were implicated. It was the seventeenth-century physician Thomas Sydenham who first rejected the influence of the uterus. The fits were, he declared, produced by the "animal spirits" suffering some disorder in their passage through the nerves. As the spirits were the emissaries of the soul, the inference was that the fits had no basis in reality but were produced entirely through the agency of the mind, though the theory precluded any conscious and deliberate deception on the part of the patient. The modern theory of hysteria, i.e. that it is a condition originating in the mind in which epilepsy and other diseases are simulated, originated with Sydenham and it was this theory that Freud, via Charcot, assimilated at the Salpêtrière.

There are many features in temporal lobe attacks which would have appeared to Sydenham to favour the simulation hypothesis. Apart from the distinctive aura with its spurious sensations of movement in the abdomen, these fits differ in many ways from the major epileptic attack. Unlike the random jerking of the *grand mal* seizure, the convulsive movements of temporal lobe epilepsy often appear to have some coordination and therefore to be semi-purposeful, similar to those that might be made by one feigning an attack. When this form of epilepsy came under investigation in the middle decades of the present century, the French authority Henri Gastaut found, by simultaneous cinematographic and electroencephalographic recordings during temporal lobe fits, that the semi-purposeful movements of the limbs were actually part of the fit pattern. But no such methods of clinical investigation existed in Sydenham's day. His warnings of the extremely accurate imitation of epilepsy in "hysteria", calling for watchfulness and sagacity on the part of the physician lest he mistake the spurious for the genuine attack, were given due recognisance by his own and future generations.

By the end of the eighteenth century Sydenham's theories had fallen into abeyance. Probably because of the sensations of the aura, the uterine theory once more became dominant, though by now tubes and ovaries were also implicated. Yet another rationale for the theory was acquired with the discovery by Marshall Hall of the reflex action of the nervous system, hysteria being defined by Romberg in 1853 as "a reflex neurosis dependent upon sexual irritation". This theory was to last almost to the end of the nineteenth century and, after anaesthesia and antiseptics had rendered safe and painless the opening of the abdomen, women in their hundreds were needlessly deprived of ovaries and womb as a result. As we have seen, before the discovery of cerebral localisation of function, the phenomena of the aura were deceptive, and many patients whose attacks began in a limb, similarly suffered amputation before it was realised that the sensations complained of were actually taking place in the brain.

Side by side with the uterine theory there existed, from ancient times, its corollary – that sexual factors, and particularly sexual frustration – could also be responsible for the attacks. Plato had tried to ascribe the peregrinations of the wandering womb to its longing to generate children and its distress at remaining barren for too long after puberty. This had led logically to the conclusion that sexual abstinence itself was harmful and the cause of the distempers emanating from the womb, and this view persisted down the centuries – the seventeenth-century physician Jorden, for instance, implicating "the want of the benefit of marriage, in such as have been accustomed or are apt thereunto" which he claimed "breeds a congestion of humours about that part" and thus "maidens and widows are most subject thereunto". Robert Burton writing on hysteria in *The Anatomy of Melancholy* prescribed marriage to good husbands. Still more explicit was Harvey: "How many incurable diseases also are brought about by unhealthy menstrual discharges", he wrote, "or from over-abstinence from sexual intercourse when the passions are strong." This implicit corollary to the uterine theory persisted till the latter decades of the nineteenth century. Thus when Freud later postulated a sexual cause of "hysteria" he was reverting to these old beliefs, which already after the publication of Briquet's 1859 treatise, *Traité Clinique et Thérapeutique de l'Hystérie*, were in decline. Pointing out that nuns rarely suffered from "hysteria" while prostitutes frequently did, Briquet had rejected both aspects of the uterine theory. Charcot, following his lead, and from his own wide experience, on several occasions specifically repudiated any sexual aetiology for the condition, a view which Freud heartily endorsed. Yet many years later he was to name Charcot as one of those people who had steered his mind in the direction of his sexual theories.

With little appreciation of their historical context in the primitive era of seventeenth-century medicine, Briquet had reverted to the naive theories of the humoral physician Thomas Sydenham. His book initiated a revival of Sydenham's concept of hysteria as a simulator of "genuine", i.e. *grand mal* epilepsy. When Charcot assumed the care of epileptic patients in 1870 he took over the concept of hysteria from Briquet, quoting with approval Sydenham's precepts, in so doing displaying as little historic perspective as had the former. It was an unfortunate choice which was to lead to the diagnostic errors later perpetuated by Freud.

Charcot had first become involved in the problems of the convulsive diseases in 1870 when the ancient buildings of the *Bâtiment Sainte-Laure* housing the patients of the alienist Delasiauve, were condemned as unsafe. Here patients suffering from epilepsy and "the graver forms of 'hysteria'" had been hospitalised indiscriminately with the insane. They were now rehoused and placed under Charcot's care. So Charcot came late to the study of epilepsy, hence his dependence on Briquet. He was also at a disadvantage in having at the time no out-patient clinic where the many varieties of epilepsy could be seen in their milder and more atypical forms. When he took over their care, there were only five so-called *hystériques*; these five formed the nucleus around which, with later additions, he built up the small coterie of permanent research and demonstration subjects on which all his later investigations were based.

We meet one of the original *hystériques* in the first volume of Charcot's published lectures; she is described as "an example of the hemiplegic form of hysterical contracture". A former hospital nurse, Etch—, aged forty, still carried the scars from her first fit when she had fallen into the fire, burning her face. Fourteen years later she had been admitted to the Salpêtrière with a left-sided hemiplegia (paralysis of one side of the body) which had supervened on one of her fits, and crippled with a contracture of the left leg which, declared Charcot, "ceased neither during natural sleep, nor sleep induced by chloroform". Another fit a year later left her with a contracture of the left arm. So rigid was she that if one foot were grasped it was possible to raise in one piece the whole of the lower half of her body. Her case was thus one of spastic paralysis with epilepsy, obviously dependent on severe intracranial disease. But she had two features which seemed to Charcot irrefutable confirmation of the original diagnosis of hysteria. "Although the hemiplegic contracture by which our patient is affected is, I repeat, of nearly two years standing," he states, "you perceive that the nutrition of the muscles has not sensibly suffered. I should also add that the electrical contractility has remained nearly normal." Here Charcot betrayed ignorance of a fundamental fact common to a generation who had learnt their neurology before the establishment of the neurone theory in 1891. An *upper motor neurone* lesion, i.e. a lesion lying in the motor pathways between the cerebral cortex and the spinal column, does *not* cause muscle wasting. Nor are the electrical reactions diminished. This is in contrast to the effects of more peripherally based (lower motor neurone) disorders, after which both wasting and degeneration of the electrical reactions occur. This fundamental error coloured all Charcot's teachings on "hysteria". From the fact, as he believed it, that the patient's hemiplegia was hysterical, it followed logically that her other signs and symptoms were of a similar nature. For example, when the patient later developed retention of urine, this was described in a succeeding lecture as "hysterical ischuria". Her characteristic aura was, for Charcot, the *aura hysterica* of tradition. He gives a detailed description of what was almost certainly a temporal lobe aura.

> "These sensations, springing from the ovarian region, successively attain: 1°. the epigastrium; 2°. the neck or throat – manifesting themselves in these regions by a more or less considerable oppression, the well-known sensation of a ball or globe (*globus hystericus*); −3°. the head, where the irradiation is characterised by buzzing and whistling in the left ear, by cephalgia with throbbings, which the patient compares to so many hammer-strokes on the left temple, and finally to an obnubliation of sight in the corresponding eye" (Charcot, 1877).

Compare the above with the following description of a temporal lobe aura written in 1954 by the distinguished neurosurgeon Murray Falconer.

> "A very common one [aura] is an epigastric sensation which may be likened to 'the stomach turning over' or some similar feeling. Sometimes the sensation may be situated instead in the lower chest or even in the umbilical and rectal regions. A common sequence, however, is for the epigastric sensation to

rise up quickly to the throat where a choking feeling ensues. The alimentary representation in the insular and Sylvian regions is presumably concerned with these auras" (Falconer, 1954).

By the same stepwise reasoning from the original misdiagnosis of his patient's hemiplegia to that of her retention of urine, Charcot now began to build up criteria for the general diagnosis of hysteria. Contractures that failed to relax during sleep were diagnosed as hysterical because that of Etch— had not done so. Over a decade later we find him giving the diagnosis to a thirty-four-year-old blacksmith whose hand had, following an injury, become rigidly deformed into a permanent fist by a contracture. So great was the pain from the penetration of the growing fingernails into the flesh of his palm that the patient pleaded for amputation. It was, said Charcot, "a contracture so pronounced that it resists every attempt at reduction, and which for three months has not ceased to exist, not only during the day, but also, and on this point I lay much stress, during the night" (Charcot, 1889). An operation on the median nerve eventually ended the blacksmith's suffering.

When Charcot, from the nucleus of the original five *hystériques* he had inherited, began to build up a larger group for purposes of observation and experiment, the presence of the characteristic aura evidently played a large part in the selection. When Professor Gamgee and his party visited the Salpêtrière in 1878, every one of the five *hystériques* demonstrated to them had this identical aura. This accounts for the similarity of their fit pattern which lent an apparently stereotyped quality to these attacks, suggesting an element of artificiality, thus giving credence to Charcot's designation of hysteria as a simulator of organic disease.

But Freud evidently found no flaw in Charcot's teaching. He had fallen completely under the spell of the master. By November 24 he was writing to Martha, "I sometimes come out of his lectures as from out of Notre Dame, with an entirely new idea about perfection". He no longer had any desire to work at his "own silly things" – it was three days since he had done any work – his brain was sated as after an evening at the theatre – "no human being has ever affected me in the same way," he declared (Freud, Ernst, 1961). On the day of his arrival in the clinic Charcot had written to a colleague for some children's brains which Freud, perhaps with an eye to his future appointment at the Kassowitz clinic, perhaps in pursuance of a lead suggested by Meynert, had intended as the object of his research while at the Salpêtrière. He soon abandoned this work, blaming inadequate laboratory facilities for the decision, and passed his time almost exclusively in the company of Charcot and the brilliant circle who formed his staff, which included besides Pierre Marie, Charles Richet and Joseph Babinski, then a twenty-nine-year-old junior assistant, later to achieve fame in his own right for the discovery of the reflex that still bears his name. After working with him on a case, Freud contemptuously dismissed him as "a novice". Gilles de la Tourette, who discovered a disease we shall encounter later, had moved to another hospital, but Freud met him socially during his stay. Freud also attended the demonstrations of the forensic pathologist P. C. H. Brouardel, who seems to have had the same special acumen with the dead as Hebra had displayed with the living, being able to judge the rank, character and origin of an unidentified body by the same subtle indications as those employed by the latter. One of his sayings, later quoted by Freud (SE 12, 1913) "*Les genoux sales sont le signe d'une fille honnête*" ("Dirty knees are the sign of a respectable girl") is a sad commentary on the social conditions of the times.

At first Freud was only one of many foreign visitors but after he had offered to translate Charcot's lectures into German, he was singled out from the others and admitted into the intimate circle around the master, being invited to the famous Tuesday soirées given in the *Fauburg St Germain*, where Charcot was accustomed to entertain the leaders of the medical profession as well as distinguished writers, philosophers and politicians. Here Freud met Alphonse Daudet and other famous literary figures. Nervous of these grand occasions, he boosted his confidence with cocaine "to loosen my tongue – I was quite calm with the help of a small dose of cocaine," he wrote to Martha (Freud, Ernst, 1961) after one such occasion.

Freud never did complete the work on children's brains he had selected for his research project. There were far more fascinating things to be seen on the wards. Many physicians rarely, if ever, see a complete epileptic fit. By the time they arrive on the scene the patient has recovered. A strange phenomenon of reflex pathology enabled Charcot and his assistants to see these fits at will and observe their minutest particulars, recording them for posterity, these records losing none of their fascination by the attacks being labelled hysterical rather than epileptic. Charcot had learnt the secret from one of his *hystériques*. "This cures me," she had explained to Charcot at the first warning of an attack, while at the same time forcibly exerting pressure over the region of an ovary (Yellowlees, 1880). It was the reverse of what Charcot had previously discovered, that by pressure over an ovary or other part of the body which he termed "the hysterogenic zones", a fit could, in a susceptible patient, be reflexly provoked by an external stimulus. He had, in fact, discovered *reflex epilepsy* long before it became generally known in the present century, though he himself did not recognise it as such. The discovery that, in this particular patient, pressure on an ovary could conversely *abort* an attack rather than provoke it, led to the invention by Charcot of the famous appliance worn by the patient when experiencing the initial prodromal symptoms of an impending fit. It was thanks to this device that the many visitors to the Salpêtrière, including perhaps Freud himself, were able to see the dramatic spectacle of the patient *en pleine crise* as often as they wished and for as long as it was necessary to capture every minute detail.

Perhaps the best eyewitness account is that contributed by an American visitor, W. J. Morton, to the New York *Medical Record* of 1880. After the out-patient cases in the clinic had been disposed of, he had accompanied Charcot to one of the wards where a patient named Dorizon was undergoing a series of attacks which were being held in abeyance with the aid of a strong elliptical band of steel encircling her body and penetrated by a screw attached to

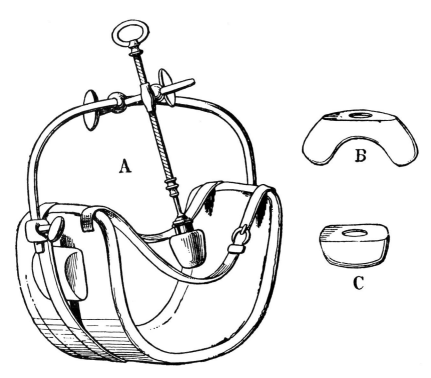

Charcot's ovarian compressor.

a pad which, placed over the ovarian region, could exert any required degree of pressure. Ignoring the protests of the patient, apparently well aware of what was to happen, Charcot requested the attendants to remove the apparatus. "The effect was instantaneous," Morton wrote, "like taking the brakes off a machine wound up to go at a certain time."

> "First a pallor of the face, momentary, however, and straightway changing to a congested red; then a slight gasp, showing a constriction of the larynx; then a slow upward movement of the globes of the eyes, until the pupils disappear beneath the upper lid, and already the patient has completely lost consciousness.
>
> At the same moment the head stiffens backward, throwing out into marked contrast the now swollen neck, the respiration has ceased or occurs in gasps, the facial muscles are contorted into a variety of fixed grimaces, the shoulders are raised and drawn forward, while the arms proceed to perform a peculiar rotatory movement, first rigidly and slowly flexing, then pronating, and again extending to their extremest limits, with the dorsum of the hand and the whole arm stiff, like a bar of wood, and held rigidly alongside of the body.
>
> And simultaneously with the occurrence of these phenomena in the upper part of the body, tetanic movements are taking

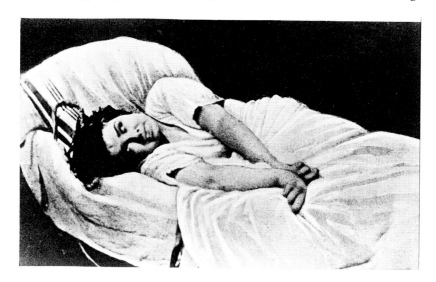

La grande Hysterie. The patient is in the early, tonic phase of the attack. Head and eyes are deviated to the right. The jaws are clenched and foam appears on the lips. The facial muscles are contracted and rigid. The arms are held in extension and pronation, the wrists bent. This is a characteristic epileptic appearance.

place in the legs. These latter are rigidly extended, though the ankles, like the wrists, are flexed. The patient's whole body is now in a state of perfect tetanic rigidity."

This was the tonic phase, quickly followed by the clonic – rapid jerking movements of the whole body, shaking the patient back and forth violently and increasing in force up to a "certain acme", after which followed complete resolution with muscles relaxed and body flaccid, the face congested and the respirations stertorous with foam at the mouth. So far, continued Morton, the attack had taken the form of "an ordinary epileptic fit" – hence the description "epileptoid phase". But the attack was by no means ended.

"... all at once she begins a series of violent bounding movements of the body, executed by suddenly arching the back upward until she rested on the vertex and the balls of the feet, and then dropping back on the bed and flexing her body in the opposite direction, to gain a start for a new opisthotonos. The scene, what with these bounding movements, becomes a very violent one, until she suddenly remains fixed, bent like a bow, resting now only on her head and toes, in the position called *l'arc de ciel*. Soon the body again falls to the bed, and Dorizon goes through with various contortions, uttering at the same time cries, and struggling to escape, as it afterwards appeared, snakes, which she believed were trying to bite her. Her appearance was maniacal."

This was the third phase, that of the *"grandes mouvements"*. Then followed the phase of the *"attitudes passionelles"* in which the patient appeared to be a prey to a succession of swiftly changing emotions often accompanied by hallucinations. These "passionate attitudes" were probably the result of the epileptic discharge passing through the limbic system, which contains the seat of the physical expression of the emotions in the brain. At that time, however, they were interpreted as confirmation of the psychogenic origin of "hysteria". The final phase was that of "terminal delirium" in which the patient returned to her senses, looking about her intelligently, but was still to some extent under the influence of the hallucinations, imagining that snakes were trying to bite her and so on.

This was *la grande hystérie* in its most florid form, illustrating vividly the four periods into which Charcot divided the attacks. But this was not all. The patient had no sooner come out of the first seizure than she immediately fell into another and so on, repeating in one attack after another all the features of the first until the scene became "as monotonous as it was distressing". Then followed the most interesting aspect of Dorizon's case. The attack could be arrested at any period or phase of a period, by strong pressure upon the ovary.

> "It is sufficiently remarkable to see violent contortions and the hallucinations of delirium vanish as if by magic, but it is still more remarkable to see the lost consciousness instantly return. This was what was demonstrated to us again and again in Dorizon's case. Taking the moment of the tonic stage (abolition of consciousness, suspended or jerking respiration, rigidity of the body, cyanotic face, etc.) Professor Charcot pressed both hands firmly down into the iliac fossa upon the ovary. Dorizon was at once herself, capable of answering questions intelligently, looking about naturally, and her body without any rigidity. But suddenly the pressure is remitted, and again the poor girl goes on through all the now familiar periods, to use a simile already made use of, like a piece of wound up automatism, stopped for a moment by the hand, and again moving on when the arresting power is removed."

It is difficult to discover why this obvious epileptic fit, with its loss of consciousness, cyanosis, foaming at the mouth and phase of tonic rigidity (far exceeding that which could be induced by voluntary stiffening of the muscles) followed by clonic jerking, was called hysteria. It was conceded that the first, or epileptoid phase, presented the typical picture of an ordinary epileptic fit, for which reason Charcot at first coined the term "hystero-epilepsy" though he later abandoned the name and declared the entire attack hysterical. It was the succeeding phases, the period of the "great movements" and the hallucinatory delirium, which invited suspicion. These coordinated movements, in contrast to the uncoordinated jerking of the clonic phase must have seemed, as they had done to his forbears, semi-purposeful and therefore capable of being feigned. This was the type of epilepsy which in more primitive times had been interpreted as demonic possession, hence Charcot's interest in the literature of witchcraft and demonology. In those days, the cry, the strangulation, the convulsive struggles and the confused post-seizure behaviour appeared to the onlooker as a struggle with an invading entity attempting possession of the victim's body.

That the convulsions seen at the Salpêtrière were far more severe than many seen today is unquestioned, but epileptic attacks before the advent of effective anticonvulsant therapy were often of far greater violence and frequency than those of today. Bromide was then the only anticonvulsant in use, but Charcot had found his patient refractory to this drug and did not use it. Even today ordinary anticonvulsants are often ineffective in temporal lobe attacks which require different medication, a fact which emphasises the importance of correct diagnosis. But to suppose as implied by the label "hysteria" that after the severe neuronal exhaustion left by the tonic/clonic phases the patient would, without regaining consciousness, be still capable of acting out an elaborate charade, is nonsensical. This is the view of modern French authorities.

The regularity of the attacks, so vividly demonstrated in the case of Dorizon, was a feature seeming to lend to them an element of artificiality. Even Charcot's biographer Georges Guillain takes this view. The stereotyped nature of Dorizon's fits was the result of the constant demonstrations which provided such a dramatic spectacle for the foreign visitors who thronged the wards of the Salpêtrière. Once Charcot had discovered the secret of provoking and aborting the attacks at will, that is, of manipulating the reflex aspects of the epileptic events, Dorizon and others like her must have been the subject of daily demonstrations. These would have exerted a facilitatory effect, the epileptic discharge taking the neuronal pathways of lowered resistance breached by previous attacks. It was the special environment of the Salpêtrière, in fact, with its long-term patients, and Charcot's renown, which had led to the development of the severe and prolonged temporal lobe seizure which he named *la grande hystérie*. The four phases were rarely seen in other centres and thus were claimed by many to be a peculiarly French condition, or, as Guillain unjustly states, "coloured by artificiality".

The process that had begun with Etch— and her colleagues continued. From incidental findings and further developments common to their type of epilepsy, Charcot proceeded to formulate still further criteria for the diagnosis of hysteria and its differentiation from "genuine epilepsy". The most important of these were the various transient anaesthesias supervening on fits, some of which would, in the course of time, become permanent. The most constant of these was hemianaesthesia – absence of sensation in one half of the body. Next ranked the pharyngeal and corneal anaesthesias. These for Charcot became the most important of the "stigmata" of hysteria, a word derived from the old books on witchcraft of which he was an avid reader, in which such areas were described as the *stigmata diaboli* – the marks of the devil. During the witch-hunting mania of the sixteenth and seventeenth centuries, official "witchfinders" armed with long pins travelled the country seeking out areas of anaesthesia in harmless old women suspects. As we saw in Chapter IV, the area subserving sensation is localised in the parietal lobe of the brain. The sensory disturbances of temporal lobe epilepsy are the result of the spread of the abnormal discharge to the adjacent parietal lobes. Such spread was the probable cause of the hemianaesthesia of Charcot's patients. So great was his belief in the symptoms of hemianaesthesia as one of the "stigmata" of "hysteria", however, that we find Charcot, in the third volume of his published lectures (that covering the period of Freud's sojourn at the Salpêtrière), diagnosing hysteria in Gil—, a young metal gilder who had actually been stabbed in the *right parietal region* with subsequent infection, and who suffered from *left* hemianaesthesia as a result.

Confusion also arose because the knowledge that different modalities of sensation, touch, pain, temperature, etc. take different nervous pathways, had not yet percolated into neurological practice; the fact that a patient showed some signs of having *felt* a pinch or other painful stimulus, for instance, was interpreted as a sign that her claim to have no sensation of *pain* was false. Janet, for instance (1925), describes a common test applied in Charcot's time. A sleeping patient would receive a painful pinch. If this caused her to *wake*, then the diagnosis of hysterical hemianaesthesia was confirmed. Other so-called "stigmata" included restriction of the visual fields, certain abnormalities of colour vision, and diplopia (double vision). "Peculiar to the condition", according to Charcot, were the curious visual disturbances of macropsia and micropsia, when objects in the visual field appear either abnormally enlarged or greatly diminished in size respectively; these symptoms are now regarded as pathognomonic of temporal lobe pathology.

The process of enlarging the symptomatology of "hysteria" did not end there. Joseph Babinski, Charcot's chief assistant for many years, who was to spend almost as many after Charcot's death correcting the teachings of the master, in 1914 described from his own experience the train of error that had arisen from the primary diagnosis of hysteria in cases of epileptic hemiplegia. The diagnosis had led logically to the false deduction that the tendon reflexes, involuntary manifestations, were invariably exaggerated in "hysteria". Such exaggeration is now regarded as a sign of upper motor neurone pathology. Ignorance of the significance of changes in different diseases of these reflexes was then almost universal.

The same situation applied to the pupillary and pharyngeal reflexes. But the train of error did not end with the reflex phenomena. As Babinski describes it:

"It is not uncommon indeed to find vaso-motor phenomena and hypothermia on the paralysed side in organic hemiplegia; in such a case with an erroneous diagnosis of hysterical hemiplegia one was inevitably bound to conclude that hysteria has the faculty of producing circulatory disorders, hence to the conclusion that it could give rise to haemorrhages and other lesions in the skin there was only a step, so why should there not be visceral haemorrhages also due to hysteria? Hysterical fever likewise appeared to some to be quite a natural occurrence, for if hysteria was able to exercise a disturbing influence on the centres of the tendon reflexes and the vaso-motor centres, there were grounds for supposing that it might also disturb the working of the centres which regulated the temperature. As all these deductions were logical and were apparently corroborated by actual cases, they were accepted by men of the keenest intelligence, but as they originated in error they were absolutely vain and worthless."

By following this line of reasoning, Charcot had been led into the gravest error. As Babinski described it, "this eminent neurologist believed in the existence of hysterical haemorrhages and skin lesions and he gave the name of blue oedema to a circulatory disorder which he attributed to hysteria".

Charcot's concept, the *oedème bleu* of hysteria, had been announced at a lecture reported in *Progrès Médicale* of October 1890. He had first observed the condition in a hysterical patient at the Salpêtrière, he said, and had seen several cases since. With as little historic perspective as Briquet, he took as his authority for the existence of hysterical oedema (watery swelling of the tissues) Sydenham's *Epistolatory Dissertation*, quoting with approval the latter's criteria for its differentiation from dropsy: that the swelling was greatest in the morning, did not pit under pressure, and generally occurred in only one of the legs. A patient with the alleged condition, Marguérite F., aged twenty-two, was demonstrated. The fingers and wrist of her right arm were swollen, not pitting on pressure. The general tint was blue, with a little irregular marbling of shades of red and violet; the surface temperature was 76°F., of the other hand 85°. No voluntary motion was present in the hand and forearm and complete anaesthesia extended to the shoulder.

Charcot's prestige and influence at this time were great. Soon the concept of blue oedema began to appear in the textbooks, as well as a whole variety of other complaints now recognised as being under the control of the autonomic nervous system and hence outside the control of the mind. Babinski, writing in 1914, describes the absurdities that followed.

> "To sum up, in former times hysteria was credited with the faculty of producing vesicles, ulceration, superficial gangrene, cutaneous or visceral haemorrhages and fever; it was also supposed to be able to produce albuminuria and anuria. All this was to be found in the text-books, and there were numerous cases of the kind reported."

This was no exaggeration. George Ormerod's monograph of 1893, for instance, contains the following:

> "Lastly, I may be permitted to allude briefly to trophic disturbances in hysteria. The possible association of the two has only been recognised in recent times. Most of these troubles take the form of cutaneous disorders. There may be pemphigus, vesicular erythema, gangrene of the skin, haemorrhage . . ."

Highly sceptical on the issue, Babinski began to challenge colleagues to produce examples of the cases they had so glibly diagnosed as hysteria. None survived a searching examination. As he recounted in 1914, it was a repetition of what had happened in "hysterical exaggeration of the reflexes" – sometimes a case of "hysterical oedema" would afterwards be shown to be tuberculous synovitis; sometimes vesicles would be found to have been produced deliberately by the patient by artificial irritation.

It was a time when the whole classification of diseases was in the melting pot. When in 1880 Pasteur announced that he had found the same bacterium to be the cause of both the furuncle and of acute osteomyelitis, he was greeted with polite disbelief, so absurd did it seem. But it was only the prelude to many such discoveries. Koch's classic work on tuberculosis which appeared in 1881 established as a single entity the different stages of the disease formerly thought of as separate and unrelated conditions, as well as tuberculosis of bones, joints, glands, kidneys and other organs. A similar reappraisal occurred in diphtheria when Klebs discovered the bacillus in 1883, and croup, malignant angina and pharyngeal diphtheria were established as different forms of the same disease. When the specific microbe of syphilis was discovered in 1905 by the German zoologist Schaudinn, a strangely assorted collection of affections of the heart, nervous system and aorta (the last being the characteristic aortic aneurysms which had given the vessel the name "girdle of Venus") were found to be different manifestations of the same condition.

In seeking to establish diagnostic criteria for a disease entity that did not exist, Charcot inevitably began to draw his boundaries wider and wider. His pronouncement that the existence of convulsions was not necessary for the diagnosis of hysteria extended these still further. Yet so great was his authority that these criteria were seldom questioned in his lifetime. When, probably on the grounds of the similarity of the symptoms, he declared that the chronic intoxications of lead poisoning, alcoholism, etc., were hysterical phenomena, we find in the *Lancet* of January 3, 1891 a paper by R. Saundry on "toxic hysteria" describing the case of a house painter complaining of pain in the chest, with his left hand firmly clenched and cyanosed, and with a pathognomonic sign of lead intoxication, a strong blue line on his gums.

To Charcot must be attributed the major share of the blame for the rage that rapidly spread throughout the medical profession in the later decades of the century for the detection and hunting down of cases of "hysteria", a chase entered into with as much zeal as that of the witchfinders of previous times. Cases of paralysis were diagnosed as hysterical because of ignorance of the distinction between upper and lower motor neurone lesions. Patients with cortical blindness, i.e. blindness due to lesions of the occipital cortex (containing the visual area of the brain), were similarly diagnosed because the pupillary reactions were intact and no abnormality was found in the eyes themselves. The more subtle forms of aphasia were prone to invite the diagnosis because it was not appreciated, for instance, that a patient might be able to repeat, but could not utter spontaneously. Often some small deviation from the classic text-book description was the deciding factor. Charcot's teaching opened up a veritable Pandora's box of reports of hysteria covering every conceivable disease, even to death itself. "Can hysteria cause death?" was a question frequently asked after the misdiagnosis of some fatal condition. The answer was always in the affirmative. The obvious comment was made in 1912 by Professor Chauffard: "We too, under the influence of Charcot", he admitted, "went through a great period of hysteria." Sad to relate, Freud proved no more critical than these colleagues. It was from Charcot's erroneous concepts that he was to develop his major theories in the next decade.

VI

Experiments In Hypnosis

In Paris, Freud was introduced to the mysteries of hypnotism, then the object of intense interest and investigation at the Salpêtrière. Deeply impressed by the fascinating experiments he witnessed daily, Freud's report to the Faculty of Medicine in Vienna conveys something of his awe at the strange manifestations of the condition. "I found to my astonishment", he said, "that here were occurrences plain before one's eyes, which it was quite impossible to doubt, but which were nevertheless strange enough not to be believed unless they were experienced at first hand" (Freud, 1886). These experiments had a profound effect on Freud's future theories. To him, they afforded irrefutable proof of the power of the mind to cause bodily disease; from the spectacle of hypnotised patients who spoke, answered questions, performed complex actions, albeit drowsily and automatically, the first seeds of his later theory of the unconscious mind were sown. Yet though seemingly scientifically impeccable, there was a major flaw in Charcot's experiments, and, as we shall see in a later chapter, contrary to what was then believed, these patients were not unconscious.

The conventional accounts relate that hypnotism was discovered by Franz Anton Mesmer (1734–1815), a Viennese physician who practised in Paris in the second half of the eighteenth century. By a series of manipulations, the most important of which were the "passes" made by waving his hands over the faces of his subjects, Mesmer found that he could induce in them the state now know as hypnosis and in so doing, brought help and succour to innumerable patients. There are many inaccuracies in this story; that the process was *not* curative was established by the investigations of the so-called cures by the French Royal Commission of 1784 which included the most eminent scientists of the day.

But the most important omission is the fact that Mesmer formed his theories from patients suffering from epilepsy (Thornton, 1976), in this respect resembling Charcot, whose experiments we are about to encounter. There was, in fact, a strong association between hypnotism and epilepsy throughout the nineteenth century. Hypnotism (or, as it was previously called, "animal magnetism") was thought to be only effective in the sick and especially so in those suffering from epilepsy. For many decades it was held to be harmful to use the method on healthy people – in them, it was believed, the process could actually *cause* epilepsy. In this the old physicians were correct. From the time of Mesmer to the present day, the literature of hypnotism contains clear descriptions of epileptic events. The various spasms, shocks and starts produced by the process were then regarded as its normal accompaniments; Mesmer had postulated a mysterious invisible fluid analogous to electricity to account for the phenomena he produced (hence the name "animal magnetism"). Even the convulsions that accompanied the process were explained by analogy to the manner in which a strong electric current could produce twitching, jerking and other nervous system effects. Convulsions were indeed a frequent accompaniment to the process throughout the nineteenth century and the old instruction manuals contain many vivid descriptions of the cessation of respiration, the cyanosis, the protracted comas which followed, and even the prolonged fit, *status epilepticus*, and there is much advice on dealing with these emergencies should they occur. When the convulsions Mesmer produced are mentioned at all in the conventional modern accounts of his work, they are glossed over or treated as emotional outbursts although the contemporary literature leaves no doubt that they occurred. How did Mesmer produce these fits?

It is not difficult to produce fits in susceptible patients; they can be reflexly precipitated by a variety of sensory stimuli. The most effective of these is an interrupted light stimulus such as that produced by a flickering television set, or by driving along a tree-lined avenue with the sun low in the sky, when its light is interrupted at regular intervals by the trees. This finding has been exploited for diagnostic purposes in EEG departments when a flashing light is used as a provocative test to discover abnormal brain waves in persons suspected of a tendency to epilepsy. The fits, fainting attacks and behavioural aberrations that occurred when stroboscopic lighting began to be used at concerts and in dance halls in the sixties is an example of the action of this precipitant; the phenomena were interpreted at the time as the effects of the emotions produced by the singers and many an indifferent performer achieved undeserved acclaim on this account. The use of stroboscopic lighting at certain frequencies is

ANIMAL MAGNETISM — *The Operator putting his Patient into a crisis*

Animal Magnetism. The operator putting his patient into a trance.

now prohibited by many public authorities in the United Kingdom and the phenomena have declined.

Mesmer's famous "passes", the rhythmic waving of the out-stretched hands over the patient's eyes, were, in fact, highly effective interrupted light stimuli. In an article entitled "Photo-genic Epilepsy: self-precipitated attacks" E. G. Robertson in *Brain* (1954) reported a series of patients, mainly children, who, for reasons never elucidated, precipitated their attacks by gazing at the sun or other bright light and passing an outstretched hand in rhythmical fashion between it and their eyes. One of these patients was placed in the sun and EEG electrodes were applied to her head. After an interval she began to glance at the sun and wave her hand rhythmically before her eyes in such a way that the light was interrupted by each finger in turn. In this way about fifteen fluctuations of light per second were produced. Soon the tell-tale spikes signifying epileptic activity appeared on the record, while the patient passed into a trance-like state. The manoeuvres of Robertson's patients in waving their hands over their eyes were identical to the "passes" used by Mesmer. Mesmer only treated patients with neurological disease, as he believed the magnetic fluid to act more powerfully in such persons. Of these, as now, a large number would have been suffering from epilepsy; it was only in these patients that the "fluid" produced any effect and these effects, as testified by the Royal Commission of 1784, took the form of undoubted epileptic fits. What he produced, was, in fact, reflex epilepsy but nearly a century was to pass before the reflex action of the nervous system became an accepted fact and Mesmer interpreted the phenomena he produced in his own way. This then was the secret of his methods. There was no mysterious fluid – he was merely employing a now well recognised method of provoking seizures in susceptible patients.

Many other stimuli capable of provoking reflex epileptic attacks in susceptible people have now been discovered, some of which were also employed by Mesmer. Nearly all have been exploited by his successors in the long history of hypnotism. Visual precipitants include the play of light on water or snow with constantly changing patterns of light and shade, television screens and stroboscopic lights, and even some patterned or striped fabrics.

Auditory stimuli include loud, sudden repetitive noises such as those made by drums (the trances and other effects induced in Shamanism and other primitive rites are most probably induced by the beating of drums which invariably form part of the ritual – probably also an additional factor in the production of the phenomena already mentioned in the concerts and dance-halls of the sixties). Hissing and scraping sounds and the ringing of bells can also be epileptogenic to susceptible patients. Music of every kind can be a potent precipitant, displaying an extraordinary selectiveness in its effects – only one type of music can affect some people and the type in question varies from person to person. Tactile stimuli include unexpected touching or repetitive stroking. All these different stimuli are also used in hypnotism.

The mechanism for all these triggering factors is a reflex one.

The stimulus or activity acts on the appropriate area of the cerebral cortex in which the stimulus is perceived or the activity controlled. Instability in the region of the cortex in question can generate an abnormal electrical discharge which, spreading to adjoining areas, will result in a seizure. By an analogous process many patients with epilepsy discover for themselves that they can *arrest* an attack by some simple action such as grasping the limb in which the seizure begins, or even trying to concentrate on some problem. One recent hospital patient, for instance, was able to abort his attacks by getting some one to talk to him, suggesting that the attacks originated in Wernicke's speech area. If he could not find anyone at the first warning he sat down; the fit was then confined to the upper part of his body instead of spreading to the whole of it. Such patients are, in fact, without knowing it, reflexly manipulating the abnormal discharge.

In the middle decades of the present century, an epileptic variant previously almost unknown was distinguished by the newly discovered techniques of recording the electrical activity of the brain. This form of epilepsy was called "psychomotor" and was identified as one of the complex of temporal lobe epilepsies. Psychomotor attacks are focal fits, the discharging lesion being in one of the temporal lobes of the brain. In such attacks the epileptic discharge is confined to these lobes and their immediate environs without spread to the rest of the cerebral hemispheres; hence *consciousness is retained*. As the motor area is not involved the patient does not, as in the seizures described in the last chapter, pass into convulsions, though there might be slight twitching around the mouth or eyes. There will often be little to indicate that the patient is undergoing a seizure. The phenomena present consist of a trance-like state, the patient being capable of speech and accessible to communication, though the eyes may appear glazed and staring, the movements automatic, and there will be loss of memory, total or partial, for the events occurring during the attack. Spread to the adjoining parietal lobes will result in insensibility to pain. If the discharge reaches the area of alimentary representation in the limbic system of the brain, there may be crude gustatory manifestations like swallowing or chewing, or an excess of salivation. The phenomena are, in fact, identical to those occurring in hypnotism.

Long before the positive identification by the EEG in the present century, the British neurologist John Hughlings Jackson (1835–1911), physician to the National Hospital for the Paralysed and Epileptic, had recognised the epileptic nature of these episodes. A contemporary of Charcot, he too was fascinated with the phenomena of epilepsy. But he had an important advantage over the former in that from the beginning the National Hospital had an out-patient department where the milder and more atypical cases could be found, a benefit Jackson was well aware of. "If we work in the wards of a hospital only where we find patients who are admitted for *severe* intracranial disease", he wrote in 1870, "we shall be misled. We must work also in the out-patient room where we see patients year after year with fits of the kind above mentioned." These fits were the focal attacks already discussed. Slight local twitchings which would not even send the patient to the doctor spelt epilepsy to Jackson as surely as did the major fit. He described a workman who used to display his twitching forearm as a curiosity to his fellow workmen. One day, however, the twitching spread to the rest of his body and the man fell down in a generalised fit. From his observations that a seizure might begin in a thumb or great toe and spread up the limb before becoming generalised, Jackson had arrived at the concept of the cerebral localisation of motor function even before the experiments of Hitzig and Fritsch and he realised that the localisation of other functions was the only possible explanation for many epileptic variants he was encountering daily in the clinic. Thus, in contrast to Charcot, he rejected all references to "genuine epilepsy", stating in 1879:

> "There are numerous epilepsies, under the definition that any epilepsy is, on its anatomical side, a 'discharging lesion' of some region of the *cortex cerebri*. The kind of paroxysm differs according to the particular region of the cortex affected; and since many regions, if not any region, of it may be affected, the number of different epilepsies, scientifically regarded, is great".

Jackson always paid careful attention to the accounts of his patients, recording them no matter how trivial they might at first appear, and instructed his assistants to do the same. Physicians who spoke of "just another epilepsy" aroused his scorn. Numerous case reports published in these years document his patients' attacks in their own simple language. Not recognising them as seizures they described "turns", "spells", "thinkings", "faints", "stupidities". They spoke of having heard, during attacks, "voices without any sound" or of having a "tasteless taste" in the mouth. One patient complained of dropping off to sleep "in the most extraordinary way". Many manifestations of epilepsy are quite outside the range of ordinary experience – the oculogyric crises when the eyes may be forcibly and involuntarily rolled upwards, or twisted sideways and held there, for instance, or the myoclonic twitchings that may cause a cup raised to the lips to appear to be dashed out of the hand by an invisible power. Small wonder that in former times victims of the disease considered themselves bewitched. Today patients experiencing such phenomena for the first time fear for their sanity and many of the more bizarre events of the seizure are withheld from even a trusted physician. Unfortunately too, in the hurried conditions of the average neurological clinic the doctor often has no time to probe for these interesting details; sadly in some cases he is just not interested – regarding his patient as "just another epilepsy" – the type of physician Hughlings Jackson was so impatient of. But his patients' confidences received Jackson's close attention when they would have been dismissed as nonsense by his colleagues. Consequently his works are rich in the symptomatology of the "intellectual aura", minutely documented by him long before its epileptic nature was confirmed in the present century by the EEG. "There is a feeling of being somewhere else; there is the feeling of having seen things then present as they were seen in former times", Jackson wrote in 1879, describing the strange states of depersonalisation and *déjà vu* that could usher in the attacks. "Occasionally there is a definite vision, one more elaborate than a spectral face". He was fortunate in having as a patient an epileptic physician and thus enjoying the benefit of a trained mind accustomed to making accurate observations. Initially the seizures of his doctor patient consisted of trance-like episodes for which he afterwards had no memory. On one such occasion he had felt an attack coming on while he was examining a patient in the clinic. After coming to himself he discovered the patient in a bed in the ward; he had examined him and admitted him in the meantime. Examination of the case-notes he had written during the trance showed that he had made the correct diagnosis but there were numerous linguistic errors, showing that he had not been in an entirely normal state at the time. The attacks progressed to overt convulsive fits and after the doctor's suicide Jackson was able to make the final diagnosis at necropsy of a lesion in the temporal lobe of the brain. By the end of the century Jackson had collected over fifty similar cases of what he called "epileptic somnambulism" or the "epileptic dream" or just simply "the dreamy state".

Jackson does not reveal whether he deduced any conclusions about the localisation of the faculty of memory from his physician patient who had always had amnesia for his attacks. But his prophecy that epilepsy would one day provide the key to the mystery surrounding the higher functions of the brain was fulfilled in the middle decades of the present century in the newly opened

Neurological Institute of Montreal, where the great neurosurgeon Wilder Penfield had been attacking the problem of severe and intractable epilepsy by removal of the contracted scar tissue or other lesion responsible for generating the abnormal discharge. The brain itself feels no pain and Penfield performed the operations under local anaesthesia only, leaving a conscious and cooperative patient able to speak and guide the surgeon in his work. In order that the speech area or other vital centre was not removed with the diseased tissue, he used electrical stimulation directly on the exposed brain cortex to guide his scalpel. It was a dramatic occasion when, one day in the thirties, he made the "awesome discovery" that underneath his probing electrode were the living records of past events in the lives of his patient. Stimulation with the electrode had produced a complete reliving of previous happenings, trivial in themselves, complete with neighbourhood noises in the background and snatches of conversation, all clear and vivid as if actually taking place then and there. The area of the brain from which these memories were evoked was that part of the temporal lobe called the hippocampus. Penfield's discovery of the faculty of memory in the temporal lobes of the brain provides the final experimental clarification of the amnesia that occurs in the psychomotor seizure. This amnesia is now explicable on the basis of an epileptic discharge passing through those areas in the temporal lobes where the records of past events are deposited, and the neuronal exhaustion left behind when the discharge has passed. This has important bearings on Freud's later theory of repression, developed from this amnesia.

A constant feature of the hypnotic trance is that the patient behaves like an automaton, hence the seeming ability of the hypnotiser to impose his will on the subject. Automatic behaviour also characterises the psychomotor seizure. Penfield produced identical automatisms when he stimulated the amygdala, an important nerve centre in the temporal lobe. The chief phenomena in both hypnotism and the psychomotor seizure – automatisms, hallucinations, sensory disturbances and amnesia – are, in fact, identical. Other facts also point to the similar identity of both conditions – the induction processes in hypnotism which are the same as those known to produce reflex epilepsy, and the strong association already mentioned between hypnotism and epilepsy. The inevitable conclusion is that, when the hypnotic trance is genuine, the patient is actually undergoing a psychomotor seizure. This will become evident from the many clinical details contributed by the eyewitnesses to Charcot's experiments.

In using his *hystériques* for his experiments in hypnosis, Charcot was, as we have seen, actually operating on epileptic subjects.

How did it happen that in the middle decades of the present century, when the clinical features of psychomotor epilepsy were being minutely documented, it was not immediately apparent that here was the solution to the age-old mystery of the nature of hypnosis? In the next chapter we shall meet the man largely responsible for clouding the issue and masking the true identity of hypnosis. Publishing, in opposition to Charcot, erroneous statistics, he declared that the capability of being hypnotised was practically universal, being possessed by ninety-five per cent of the normal population. Most importantly, his declaration that hypnotism was no different from normal sleep considerably widened the criteria by which a subject was judged to be hypnotised and accounted for his apparent success in inducing hypnosis in such large numbers of people. Throughout the nineteenth century the hypnotic trance had been a rare phenomenon. When not associated with overt epilepsy, those possessed of the faculty of entering into it were called "sensitives" and were chosen because of special characteristics that distinguished them from other people. They had, perhaps, walked in their sleep as children, a fact now known to be frequently associated with the later development of temporal lobe epilepsy. Many people have a low convulsive threshold without ever having an overt fit. Often in these cases there is a past history of head injury, or a family history of epilepsy in a near relative. One of Robertson's epileptic patients, for example, had an aunt who had only one overt fit in her life, at the time of the delivery of her baby, but she had a mild attack after standing for some time under the flashing neon light of a shop sign. In many such cases some hereditary metabolic condition may raise the vulnerability of the brain to electrical disturbance. Drugs, exposure to intoxicating fumes, or a heavy alcohol intake after a prolonged fast can precipitate an attack in a normal subject without any family history of epilepsy. In such cases the temporal lobes may be selectively affected as they have a lower seizure threshold than other parts of the brain and prolonged exposure to the stimuli discussed earlier may induce a psychomotor fit.

I would like, at this stage, to anticipate a point raised by a reviewer of my previous book (1976) in which I first equated the hypnotic trance with the psychomotor seizure. The classic EEG experiments on hypnotised subjects, which mostly revealed a normal waking state, date from a time when older and more primitive machines were in use, which had many fewer leads than those of today. In more recent EEG studies, where admittedly temporal lobe lesions were not being sought, few leads were also used, this time for convenience, and those were not placed over the temporal lobes. Even today in cases of undoubted epilepsy when such foci *are* sought, insufficient leads over the temporal lobes, as used in the routine recording, can result in foci being missed. Moreover, scalp electrodes can only record potentials from the *convexities* of the brain, thus a large area of the cortex contained in the fissures is inaccessible to the EEG. Additionally, for anatomical reasons, much of the temporal lobe is especially inaccessible to the scalp electrodes, most of the surfaces being folded in underneath the main mass of the brain. Where a focus is suspected, a "sphenoidal recording" has therefore to be made. This involves the insertion of needle electrodes under the sphenoidal ridge of the skull, a minor invasive procedure, now mainly used when surgery is contemplated. Until the development of more sophisticated methods, the proof that the hypnotic trance is a psychomotor seizure must reside in the clinical evidence. As stated by Dr Sutherland and Professor Eadie (1980), "A normal EEG does not exclude a diagnosis of epilepsy when there is a clear description of an epileptic event from an observer."

Such clear descriptions were recorded in detail in the days of "animal magnetism" when they accorded with the current theory of the subject. When magnetism was superseded by the new psychological concepts, these epileptic manifestations were ignored or glossed over. Those reported in the modern literature are given psychoanalytic explanations. The convulsions are described as "severe abreactions" with "intense somatic concomitants". The paroxysmal facial contractions appearing at the onset of the trance are said to have a "symbolic significance". The techniques used to induce the trance are explained by the hypothesis that "a gesture or touching may have deep symbolic meaning". The tonic rigidity sometimes encountered is interpreted as "tensing as from a blow from a parent". Evidently the hazard that beset the magnetisers – the failure to rouse the patient at the end of the session – still occurs; it has been interpreted as "the patient's wish to remain in a trance to perpetuate the archaic rapport with the hypnotiser" or conversely as an unconscious desire on the part of the patient to punish him. Thus the vagaries of medical fashion have helped to obscure the epileptic nature of hypnotism. Interestingly, however, one practitioner has suggested the use of hypnotically induced convulsions as a substitute for electroconvulsive therapy in the treatment of psychiatric disorders.

Clear epileptic events are readily discernible in the records of Charcot's experiments. It was because this fact was not recognized that his work in hypnotism was so cursorily dealt with by Guillain, his own biographer, and by the many biographers of Freud. Without the assumption that Charcot's hypnotism was actually the production by reflex methods in epileptic subjects of actual psychomotor seizures, the whole of his work is unintelligible. I hope to show that his work is still valuable, affording fascinating insights into the intricacies of the human brain and its functioning.

Charcot's interest in hypnotism was a natural outgrowth of his investigations into *la grande hystérie*. He had observed that his *hystériques* frequently lapsed into spontaneous somnambulism and that this event had been preceded by a definite external stimulus. One patient, for instance, was rendered cataleptic by the brass instruments of a military band; another by the bark of a dog; a third became entranced in the act of pulling on her stockings. In other words, they were subject to reflexly produced psychomotor seizures. When he began his experiments in about the year 1878, Charcot had thus a ready-made caucus of ideal trance subjects in his *hystériques*. This small coterie of a dozen or so permanent inmates of the Salpêtrière, or, as they were sometimes irreverently called, "Charcot's circus", were carefully nurtured by the great neurologist. If in the course of time their attacks remitted, he retained them on the wards as attendants. Their faces gaze out from the faded photographs of the publications emanating from the Salpêtrière at this time – Witt—, Bar—, Gl— and others, some possessing more than average good looks, a small section of the anonymous band of experimental subjects who have helped to create medical history.

After the great neurologist of the Salpêtrière had led the way, others followed and the phenomena of hypnotism became the object of legitimate scientific enquiry. Soon his wards and clinics were thronged with distinguished physicians from abroad to whom Charcot with his unfailing courtesy demonstrated the mysteries of hysteria and hypnotism; in addition, postgraduate students from many lands were given the freedom of the wards to carry out their own experiments.

One of these latter, Axel Munthe, in *The Story of San Michele*, gives a vivid glimpse of Charcot's *hystériques*.

> "Hypnotised right and left, dozens of times a day, by doctors and students, many of these unfortunate girls spent their days in a state of semi-trance, and certainly not responsible for their doings, sooner or later doomed to end their days in the *salle des agités* if not in a lunatic asylum."

(However, he adds, "I myself was just then by the permission of the *Chef de Clinique* carrying out some interesting experiments in post-hypnotic suggestion and telepathy with one of these girls, one of the best somnambulists I have ever met.") This subject was Geneviève and evidently there were compensations in life at the Salpêtrière; Munthe draws a lively picture of his subject as the prima donna of the Tuesday clinics, "spoiled and petted by everybody, very pleased with herself and her surroundings".

> "Geneviève was sitting dangling her silk-stockinged legs from the long table in the middle of the ward with a copy of '*Le Rire*' in her lap with her own portrait on the title page. At her side sat Lisette, another of the leading stars of the company. Geneviève's coquettishly arranged hair was adorned with blue silk ribbon, a row of false pearls hung round her neck, her pale face was made up with rouge, her lips painted. To all appearances she looked more like an enterprising midinette off for a stroll on the boulevards than the inmate of a hospital."

Munthe was later ignominiously ejected from the Salpêtrière by Charcot for attempting to lure the same Geneviève to his rooms by means of post hypnotic suggestion, which may account for his somewhat harsh descriptions of Charcot and his methods.

Geneviève's portrait on the front cover of *Le Rire* highlights the intense interest taken by the lay press and the general public in the experiments being conducted at the Salpêtrière. The interest of the medical profession was scarcely less and it is to the foreign visitors who journeyed to Paris to see the strange events for themselves that we owe some of the best eyewitness accounts of Charcot's experiments. The fact that the phenomena were labelled "hysteria" and "hypnotism" does not detract from their fascination or diminish their value in the glimpses they afford of the complexities of the human brain. Freud was one of the numerous foreign visitors to witness the strange phenomenon of patients suddenly rendered cataleptic by the sound of a gong, body and limbs statue-like in their immobility and the contrasting state when the condition was terminated, "giving one very vividly the impression of a statue coming to life". The peculiar neuromuscular hyperexcitability" of the deeper states and the extraordinary hallucinations induced by suggestion in the lighter ones afforded dramatic experimental situations which Charcot exploited to the full.

Freud saw the curious spectacle of the rigid body of a girl under hypnosis stretched between two chairs supported only by head and heels. This was a variant of a favourite music hall trick when the hypnotist was able to stretch the rigid body of his subject between two chairs, then proceeding to sit on the subject's abdomen supported entirely by the iron-like tonicity of the

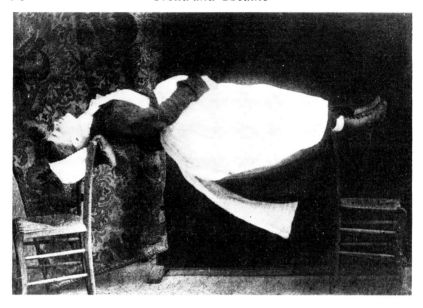

One of Charcot's patients in hypnosis. The body is extended in tonic spasm balanced between two chairs. A weight of up to forty kilogrammes could be placed on her rigid abdomen without producing sagging.

muscles. The trick exploited the tonic spasm engendered by the epileptic event. That the rigidity was totally unlike anything produced by the voluntary stiffening of the muscles can be seen by the account of D. Hack Tuke writing about this time.

> "I remember a gentleman witnessing for the first time the intense rigidity of the muscles in a boy, which allowed of his being placed in a horizontal position, only supported by his head and heels on chairs, while a heavy man sat on the abdomen. It was maintained by this gentleman that the feat was accomplished by strong wires secreted in the boy's clothes, and he was only convinced of the genuineness of the phenomenon when the boy was stripped" (Tuke, 1881).

Hughlings Jackson, writing from his unrivalled experience, had stated that the "dreamy state" could often be a *post* seizure phenomenon. Often the preceding fit could be so slight and transitory as to pass unnoticed by the patient and those around him. As he described it in 1881,

> "We may occasionally be consulted because a person suddenly acts strangely, violently, or passes into a state which resembles somnambulism, and nothing will be volunteered as to epileptic

attacks. Unless we have very carefully studied the phenomena of
very slight seizures of epilepsy we shall misinterpret these cases;
we shall dwell with exaggeration on the striking, and neglect the
essential; the thing is to ferret out the quasi-trifling signs of a
transitory fit."

The "quasi-trifling signs" he enumerated were transient pallor,
movements of mastication and turning up of the eyes. Many
others are scattered throughout Jackson's works – the fixed, vacant stare, the slight spasms of face, hands or eyes, spasm of the
glottis, ejaculation of saliva, rapid blinking of the eyelids – all
signs that demonstrated to him that a slight fit had taken place.
Such signs appear throughout the reports of hypnotic experiments
emanating from the Salpêtrière.

An early account which demonstrates many of them was
contributed to the *British Medical Journal* of October 12, 1878 by
Professor Gamgee of Manchester University, who, with a party of
distinguished medical and scientific observers, visited Charcot in
1878. A young patient aged twenty, suffering from "hystero-
epilepsy" was hypnotised by the eye-fixation method. She was at
first refractory to the process, but finally succumbed.

> "At 10.6, the eyelids dropped, and, at the same time, began *to
> wink in a rapid tremulous manner*; this phenomenon continued
> throughout the whole duration of the induced sleep, and being,
> Professor Charcot remarked, constant; at the same time *a tonic
> contraction of the flexors of both forearms occurred*, the fists
> becoming temporarily clenched." (my italics)

After demonstrating the patient's ability to perform simple tasks
like writing and sewing in the trance state with complete coordination Charcot blew into the patient's eyes, and she awoke.

> "The act of awakening, in her case and that of all hystero-
> epileptics who have been thrown into the mesmeric sleep, is
> accompanied by *a peculiar reflex; there is an automatic and
> sudden act of expulsion of saliva – as if it were a slight effort to
> spit.*"

An anonymous account of Charcot's hypnotism at the Salpêtrière appears in the *St Louis Courier of Medicine* of March 1879.
The subject, "a hysterical woman of twenty-one", was hypnotised
by fixing her eyes on a bright light. "In a few seconds she became
cataleptic and completely anaesthetic. The limbs were flexible, and
assumed any position in which they were placed by the operator."
If the light was removed the condition of "lethargy" was pro-

duced. (Here the word is used in its old connotation of a comatose or semi-comatose condition.) "If the patient were standing (in the cataleptic state) she would fall backward, the head thrown back, the neck arched prominently. The eyes are closed, and *a whistling inspiration is heard, accompanied by noisy movements of degluti-tion.*" In this condition the phenomenon of "muscular hyperexci-tability" occurred, and slight friction on the skin produced a contraction of the underlying muscles. "Another feature of this condition is *a constant motion of the upper eyelid, convulsions of the globe of the eye in various directions, and persisting anaesthe-sia.*" The patient was restored to normal by breathing or blowing on the face, or pressing on an ovary and had no recollection whatever of what had occurred.

The essentially epileptic nature of the hypnotic state induced by Charcot is strikingly demonstrated in the report of a Dr Yellowlees to the Medico-Psychological Association of Edinburgh printed in the *Journal of Mental Science* the following year (1881). One of the assistants on the ward, now well, had been afflicted with fits before the age of ten. Though they had now ceased she continued to be "very sensitive to mesmerism".

"She was very quickly thrown into sleep, merely by Dr Char-cot's fixing his eyes on her, and she went over again with equal readiness subsequently when I regarded her the same way. At the moment of falling over there was invariably, as Dr Charcot pointed out, *a slight spasm of the glottis, and often a very slight moistening of the lips, suggesting the faintest possible approach to an epileptoid seizure.* While asleep she was quite uncon-scious, and any muscle, when excited to action by rubbing, contracted readily and strongly, so that by this means, any contortion, such as extreme flexion or extension of the arm could be produced; and by irritating the facial nerve at the front of the ear, the angle of the mouth was twitched and retracted. If awakened by blowing sharply in her face, or by a sharp, sudden push over the ovaries, she recovered consciousness at once, but the arm remained contorted, and she could not straighten it. When again put to sleep the arm remained rigid until the eyelid of the corresponding side was raised, and the eyeball exposed to the light, when with *another scarcely observable spasm of the glottis,* such as occurred when she went over, the contracted muscles relaxed at once, and the arm regained its usual mobility. This result was, of course, also obtainable by excitation of the opposing muscles so as to cause them to act, and to undo the contortion or rigidity. But the mere opening of the eye, as above, seemed at once to relax the rigid muscles; they no longer acted when rubbed, nor did the angle of the mouth respond to irritation of the facial nerve. Dr Charcot does not know, nor profess to know, why the raising of the eyelid should have this singular effect."

Modern neurophysiologists could probably explain the mystery. Opening and shutting the eyes has a profound effect on the EEG tracing, resulting in a marked change in the brain rhythms. A subject such as Charcot's, whose brain was already the seat of an abnormal fluctuating and unstable epileptic discharge, would be especially vulnerable to this manoeuvre. Spread of the abnormal discharge to the subcortical areas governing muscle tone would be a likely consequence. Charcot, though he did not realise it himself, was, by simple reflex mechanisms, actually manipulating a highly unstable epileptic discharge to produce the effects which his visitors found so inexplicable. As with *la grande hystérie* the repeated experimental sessions carried on in his wards would tend to encourage facilitatory neuronal mechanisms, the discharge tending to use as preferred pathways those already taken in previous experiments.

As Charcot's experiments proceeded he found that by the use of different reflex stimuli, he was able to produce at will the three distinct stages of hypnotism briefly touched on in Yellowlees' account. A slight pressure on the eyeballs induced the *lethargic* state (used in its old meaning of comatose), and the patient became motionless, passive and unobservant. By opening the eyes to the light the *cataleptic* state was induced in which the patient was also motionless and unobservant with eyes fixed and expression vacant, but in the state of waxy rigidity described earlier. "A slight sound and movement of deglutition announces the transition, and perhaps a little foam in the corner of the mouth," wrote W. J. Morton in 1880. An altogether different condition had supervened, "body and limbs now maintain any position in which they are placed; in short, we have the condition familiarly known as catalepsy. If the arm is raised to a right angle with the body, it remains so; if the leg is placed in a similar position it does not fall. The patient may be moulded at will, like a waxen figure, into any pose one pleases, and the position will be retained."

The state was equally simply resolved by rubbing the forehead or closing the eyes. "The arms, for instance, a second before raised and fixed like a statue in a given attitude, fall, at first slowly, then more quickly and heavily, downward." This manoeuvre induced the *somnambulistic* state that is now normally associated with

Hemicatalepsy. On opening the patient's left eye, one half of the body becomes cataleptic. The left arm is raised and remains so while the right is still in spastic contraction.

hypnotism. The patient's expression instantaneously altered, the effect being compared by Robertson (1892) to a statue coming to life. "Instead of the fixed vacant stare, and the stolid expression, the face suddenly became lit up with animation and intelligence"; she began to look around her, notice things and answer questions; there was, as Robertson described it, "considerable mental activity, though of a peculiar kind". Tests showed a marked diminution of mental capacity and memory, the patient being unable to perform simple arithmetical calculations or give the names of her parents or of her former school.

It was in the lethargic state that the phenomenon of neuromuscular hyperexcitability was elicited. This, compared by eyewitnesses to the action of the faradic current on the muscles, demonstrates more effectively than anything else that hypnotism was a pathological process as opposed to a psychological one. In this state, whatever nerve was pressed on, a muscular contraction resulted exactly corresponding to the contraction produced by electrical stimulation. This contracture persisted after the pressure was stopped and was removed by stimulation of the opposing muscles. "One cannot help agreeing with Charcot," wrote Robertson in 1892, "that here there was a very strange nervous state which could not possibly have been simulated, for not only were the anatomy and physiology of the nerves unknown to these women, but contraction of muscles could be caused, which are, as a rule, more or less involuntary, such as the superior muscle of the ear." Moreover, the onset and degree of the contracture was regular and gradual, corresponding exactly to the amount and timing of the pressure. "I was impressed with the involuntary nature of the phenomenon," he commented. W. J. Morton (1880) describes the way in which each muscle of the body could be made to exert its normal action. "Taking for convenience a penholder, its blunt end was pressed upon the *attollens auriculae*, at once the ear was elevated; or upon the *retrahens*, and the ear moved correspondingly. I satisfied myself of this again and again."

But if the patient was woken with the contracture in place, it could not be removed, as Morton continues.

"We will suppose that, having produced a strong contracture of flexion at the wrist and at the elbow, one blows quickly in the face of the subject and wakes her up. She blinks her eyes, stares about her a few seconds to get her bearings, and then suddenly discovers that her arm is rigid; she tries in vain to move it; it seems as firm as metal, and thus it will remain for several days if left to itself. The physician cannot now, as previously, resolve this contracture by rubbing the antagonistic extensors. True, a very strong faradic current applied to the extensors will over-come the contracture, but the moment the current is remitted the arm flies back to its contractured state almost as if it were a steel spring put on the stretch and suddenly let loose."

There was but one means of resolving this state of affairs and that was to rehypnotise the patient, whereupon the contracture could be made to yield by the usual process of exciting the

Contracture. Rigid deformity of the right limbs resulting from an hypnotic experiment. The right arm is in a state of extension and pronation while the right leg is in extension and adduction and cannot be bent.

antagonistic muscles. Morton was alive to the significance of this, commenting that for instance, a torticollis (wry neck) could be produced in this manner. The resolving of these contractures is probably the only way in which hypnotism could ever have produced a cure; a few such cases, however, would have been enough to ensure its reputation. Very occasionally an overt epileptic fit has been known to produce the same result.

As we have seen, it was in the somnambulistic stage that the manifestations usually associated with hypnotism, especially those seen in stage performances, occurred. The most remarkable symptom of the somnambulistic stage was the complete "credivity" of the subject and the extreme willingness to receive suggestions. Anything suggested to the patient was implicitly believed no matter how absurd; it was possible to alter the patient's personality in the most ridiculous way and to place the subject in the most imaginary surroundings and he or she would act in as consistent a manner as if "accustomed to it from birth". A curious phenomenon associated with these hallucinations was that they often persisted for some time *after the patient had awakened*. This was one of the post-hypnotic phenomena which gave rise to the concept of post-hypnotic suggestion which later became such a feature of stage hypnotism. Exhaustion of inhibitory neurones is a likely explanation for the phenomenon of post-hypnotic suggestion. Its occurrence has probably been greatly exaggerated; nevertheless it exists.

This then was the hypnotism of the Salpêtrière that was to start Freud off on the tortuous path he was later to follow and change the course of pyschiatry. It will be seen that physical and automatic mechanisms predominated and that in only one stage (the somnambulistic phase) in which a lighter stage of trance was obtained, were purely psychological mechanisms elicited. Of the physical phenomena, perhaps the most striking were the cataleptic postures which presented such a dramatic spectacle to Charcot's visitors. Catalepsy is a *physical* condition. The statue-like posturing is dependent on alteration in muscle tone, producing the characteristic waxy rigidity. This alteration implies spread of the epileptic discharge to the subcortical regions governing tone. A similar, but more severe alteration is responsible for the tonic rigidity which enabled patients to be stretched out unsupported between two chairs. Lennox (1961) with his unrivalled experience in epilepsy, subsumed catalepsy under the "akinetic seizures" of temporal lobe epilepsy. De Jong (1945) listed a number of drugs with which he was able to produce the condition experimentally in animals and his book contains a photograph of a cat and mouse confronting each other in a state of cataleptic immobility. W. Feldberg in 1963 describes experiments when, after injection with anticholinesterases and other substances into the ventricles of a cat, catalepsy was a late reaction.

"When, after a period of increased reflex hyperexcitability and tremor, catatonic stupour developed, the cat could be put in abnormal positions which it would retain for some minutes. For instance, when its forepaw was abducted or placed across its back, it made no attempt to remove it . . . when placed with the groin across the lower rung of an inverted stool; or when placed in an erect posture with its front paws on the upper rung; or when placed across the rungs or across two stools, the cat remained in these positions for many minutes. Nevertheless, its movements were not impaired because when pushed from behind it jumped in a well coordinated manner."

These experiments would appear to associate the condition with definite brain pathology. Stronger evidence, however, emerges from the study by Engel *et al.* reported in *Neurology*, 1978. The patient, a case of temporal lobe epilepsy observed over three years, had four episodes of psychomotor *status epilepticus*, (i.e. unusually prolonged attacks) lasting for days, and which afforded a unique opportunity for the study of this form of epilepsy. EEG recordings from the sphenoidal lobes showed paroxysmal activity, greatest in the temporo-occipital regions. Under observation the patient demonstrated a fluctuating level of consciousness, ranging from the comatose to the more common trance-like state. The authors do not say at which of these stages it occurred, but state definitely that "passively positioned extremities were maintained in unusual postures".

The "automatic obedience" that was such a feature of stage hypnotism occurred in the lighter stages of hypnosis. The phenomenon was probably the response of a brain in an abnormal state, unable to interpret sense data or make judgments. It was a feature around which many myths had grown, which Charcot was at pains to dissemble. Many times he demonstrated that no effort of will was exerted and that the patient responded to the manipulations of one person as easily as to another. Professor Gamgee (1878) for instance, relates "That the instantaneous production of the mesmeric state was not due to any special influence of M. Charcot was evidenced by his allowing me to repeat his procedure [of staring fixedly into the eyes], when instantly the same result followed".

Unlike contemporaries who rushed into print with premature

theories based on scanty evidence, Charcot made no attempt to explain the nature of the astonishing phenomena of hypnotism. "Facts first, theories afterwards" was his invariable response to eager questioners (Morton, 1880). But though he declined to say what it was, he had something to say about what it was *not*. He held steadfastly to the belief that hypnotism could only be induced in patients suffering from "hysteria", and if for this word we substitute temporal lobe epilepsy he was not far wrong. Though Charcot, as we shall see, appeared to imply that both hypnotism and "hysteria" were psychogenic in nature, one must remember that he believed that the psychogenic aspects of both were mediated through the *brain*. For that reason, he always laid great stress on the physical phenomena, insisting that these phenomena, especially the muscular hyperexcitability, accompanied *true* hypnosis.

Precisely because of this belief, Charcot never used hypnotism for therapeutic purposes. "Of the therapeutic uses of hypnotism Charcot did not say a single word to me," wrote Robertson (1892). What then were the uses of hypnotism according to Charcot? "The question has been concisely answered by M. Féré (one of Charcot's assistants)," Robertson continued, "that the hypnotised hysterical woman is to be regarded as 'the psychological frog', and that what the frog had done for physiology, the hysterical woman is to do for psychology." Regarded in this light, Charcot's experiments are well worth studying today when ethical considerations would probably prohibit repetition of, for instance, the production of contractures by these means. Charcot's work has been denigrated since his death. Those actually present at his experiments had no doubt of their authenticity and validity, though many expressed their awe at the bizarre and completely inexplicable nature of the phenomena. Those who had never seen them found them difficult to accept, precisely because of this bizarre content. After Charcot's death this attitude increased and disbelief is plainly evident in the only biography of Charcot in existence, that by Guillain, who writes quite erroneously that "Charcot personally never hypnotised a single patient himself" and that he left this and the setting up of the experiments to interns and other assistants not of the calibre of the master. The reports given in this chapter amply refute this allegation.

The key to the understanding of Charcot's work both in "hypnotism" and "hysteria" is to regard them as two different faces of temporal lobe epilepsy, both representing seizures of the different types found in this condition. As they did not have this key, Charcot's work was quite unintelligible to his detractors both during his life and after his death. But to imply that a man of his calibre spent years of his life in pursuit of a chimera is to do an injustice to a very great neurologist. As the British neurologist S. A. K. Wilson remarked, (*Brain*, 1910) "no one who has known the wards of that famous Hospice as they used to be will deny the reality of the phenomena that once drew the whole medical world to Paris".

VII

Traumatic Hysteria and The Nancy School of Hypnotism

By the time of Freud's visit to the Salpêtrière in 1885 there had been many changes in Charcot's service since he had first become involved with the problems of the convulsive diseases. With the establishment in 1882 of an out-patient department and wards for the short term admission of both men and women, the somewhat cloistered atmosphere of the hospice had been enlivened by a succession of male patients – most of them artisans and labourers from the surrounding districts of Paris. The *hystériques* were now augmented by cases of "male hysteria" admitted from the out-patient clinics, a subject of special interest to Charcot during Freud's sojourn at the Salpêtrière. "Male hysteria", a concept almost forgotten since the days of Sydenham, Charcot, following Briquet, was now in the process of reviving. These patients suffered from symptoms identical to those of the *hystériques*, had similar auras and convulsive crises, and exhibited some or even all of the famous "stigmata". Thus they received the same diagnosis of "hysteria". As with the former, the characteristic aura played the most important part in the diagnosis. Typical examples of the ascending visceral aura are described in the third volume of Charcot's lectures covering this period, under the classification *aura hystericus*; for example, that of the mason Ly—:

"All that day he had suffered from epigastric pain, the sensation of a *globus*, and from buzzing noises in the ear."

The fit which ensued is described by Charcot;

"At the moment when the attack commenced, he tells us that he felt his tongue retracted in his mouth towards the left side by a kind of involuntary and irresistible action. Then he lost consciousness, and when he came to himself he was told that his face was drawn towards the left, that his extremities were agitated by tremors, and that when the convulsions ceased he spoke in a loud voice without awakening."

Many of the cases of "male hysteria" sent into Charcot's service from the streets of Paris suffered from fits supervening on fights or injuries resulting from accidents at work. They were probably examples of what would now be classed as "closed head injury" but which Charcot called "traumatic hysteria". "Traumatic hysteria" was a topic of considerable practical interest at the time. With the growth of the railway systems and the high incidence of accidents, apparently far greater than that of today, the railway companies were faced with a great deal of litigation, and questions of liability and compensation frequently involved medical men appearing in court on opposite sides as expert witnesses. There was often no external injury to account for the symptoms of the victim and this naturally led to the suspicion of malingering. Charcot for his part came out strongly in favour of the diagnosis of "hysteria" and this involved him in controversy with the German neurologists led by Oppenheim and Thomsen who, basing their views on a series of seven stokers and engine drivers, victims of railway accidents, assigned the symptoms to some hitherto undescribed organic pathology. In this debate, Charcot threw the whole weight of his great authority on the side of "hysteria". The areas of anaesthesia described in their patients by Oppenheim and Thomsen were, he declared, identical to those found in his own hysterical patients. The existence of male hysteria was a fact, he affirmed, though sometimes difficult to believe. "That a vigorous artisan, well built, not enervated by high culture, the stoker of an engine for example, not previously emotional, at least to all appearance, should, after an accident to the train, by a collision or running off the rails, become hysterical for the same reason as a woman, is what surpasses our imagination" (Charcot, 1889). Freud's whole psychoanalytical edifice began with the cases of "traumatic hysteria" he witnessed on Charcot's wards.

One example from the many described in Charcot's published lectures from this period is sufficient to illustrate the epileptic nature of the attacks subsumed under the diagnosis of hysteria. Mar— was a baker's apprentice whose fits started fifteen days after an attack in the street when he was knocked unconscious.

"The attack, whether spontaneous or provoked, is always preceded by an aura: iliac pain at the level of the hysterogenic point, a sensation as of a ball rising from the epigastrium up to the throat, buzzing sounds in the ears, and beating of the temples. Then the attack commences; the eyes are turned upwards in their socket, the arms become stiff and extended, and the patient, if standing, falls to the ground with complete loss of consciousness" (Charcot, 1889).

Epileptic fits follow closed head injury in about a quarter of the cases, the proportion being greater in patients with a family history of epilepsy. The first fit often occurs some days after the trauma. The injuries are the result of the soft tissues of the brain being flung against the hard outer casing of the skull, with resultant contusion, injury to the tissues, swelling and ultimately scarring, these injuries often being on the opposite side of the brain to that receiving the blow (the *contrecoup* phenomenon). The temporal lobes of the brain are highly susceptible to these effects, the tissues being flung onto the sphenoidal ridges inside the skull with consequent bleeding and other trauma.

Gross injuries such as fractures of the base of the skull may also have been present in cases of "railway brain", as the reports of bleeding from ears, nose and mouth would suggest – a blunt impact over a wide surface area may cause linear fractures which can travel for many centimetres across the top of the skull cap and into the base which forms the floor on which the brain lies. The X-ray was, of course, not yet in use. These fractures produce bleeding inside the skull or infection, though no wound on the surface is visible, and cause symptoms after a deceptive period of normality. The case of Le Log—, admitted to Charcot's service after being in collision with a laundryman's van and remaining unconscious for five or six days after the accident, was probably of this nature. His recovery was complicated by frequent copious epistaxes (bleeding from the nose). His attacks did not proceed to the fully developed fit but were represented merely by pain in the pharynx, the sensation of a ball rising in the throat, a stifling sensation and beating in the temples. They were diagnosed as hysterical because of the absence of any external wound or other signs of injury.

The advantages of the Salpêtrière for the pursuit of the clinico-pathological method were less apparent in cases of closed head injury. Few such patients came to post-mortem examination, their condition following a comparatively benign course and the victims being mainly young men. On the rare occasions when they did succumb, the disease left no discernible trace in the brain. Though Charcot examined every brain himself, the microscopic techniques of his day were inadequate to reveal the subtle injuries to the cells exhibited by such cases. The carmine stain he used, at the time an innovation, failed to reveal the nervous system in the clarity and distinctness given by the later Golgi stain and its modification by

Ramon y Cajal. The difference between the old stain and the new is dramatically highlighted by Cajal in 1887:

> "All was sharp as a sketch with Chinese ink on transparent Japanese paper. And to think that that was the same tissue which, when stained with carmine or logwood, left the eye in a tangled thicket where sight may stare and grope forever fruitlessly, baffled in its effort to unravel confusion and lost forever in a twilight doubt. Here, on the contrary, all was clear and plain as a diagram. A look was enough. Dumbfounded, I could not take my eye from the microscope."

This vivid comparison demonstrates the hazards of accepting the findings of nineteenth-century pathology unsupported by later verification. Since then superior microscopic techniques, X-rays, and other investigative procedures have confirmed the existence of the minute and diffuse lesions responsible for the signs and symptoms of closed head injury. But these diagnostic aids were not available to Charcot and, in the absence of demonstrable pathology, and from the criteria drawn from his *hystériques*, he declared the whole symptom complex to be the result of the *mental and emotional* trauma caused by the accident.

It was in a discussion on the paralyses supervening in these cases that Charcot introduced his conception of "those remarkable paralyses, paralyses depending on idea, paralyses by imagination" which so captured the attention of Freud. "I do not say *imaginary paralyses*", Charcot continued, "for indeed these motor paralyses of psychical origin are as objectively real as those depending on an organic lesion; they simulate them, as you will see, by a number of identical clinical characters, which render their diagnosis very difficult." He drew the concept from an earlier work, that of the British physician, J. Russell Reynolds whose paper in the *British Medical Journal* of 1859 had presented three cases whose paralyses had been diagnosed as imaginary on the same erroneous grounds as those of Charcot's *hystériques*, i.e. that little or no muscle wasting was evident. In the first of these cases, that of a young girl, her father had some time previously suffered a paralytic stroke and according to Reynolds the thought had crossed his patient's mind that she too might become paralysed. Hence the concept of paralysis caused by an idea which Charcot so enthusiastically embraced and which so captured the imagination of the young Freud.

But Charcot was not content merely to advance his theory of "traumatic hysteria". He proceeded to furnish experimental "proof". In demonstrating a male patient with a paralysis resulting from some accident or other trauma, he would place in close juxtaposition with him one of his *hystériques* in a state of hypnosis and demonstrate that the paralysis produced in her by hypnotic suggestion was identical to that caused by the accident in his other patient. Thus, for example, in demonstrating two cases of "hysterical monoplegia" (paralysis of one limb only) he introduced into the lecture theatre one of his permanent inmates, Greuz—. Putting her into a state of hypnosis by means of light pressure on the eyeballs, he satisfied himself of the depth of her trance by obtaining rigidity of the limbs by light touches over their surfaces. He then induced paralysis of one arm by a sharp but not very forcible blow on the shoulder with the palm of his hand. Total paralysis of the limb rapidly supervened, comparable in every clinical detail to its "hysterical" counterpart. This was Charcot's experimental proof and it was apparently entirely convincing to Freud. He came away from the Salpêtrière a strong believer in the psychogenic origin of "hysteria". As his erstwhile disciple and earliest biographer Fritz Wittels wrote in 1924, "Charcot thus proved that ideas can induce bodily changes. But if an idea deliberately introduced from without into the subject's mind can have such an effect, does it not seem even more likely that the subject's own unconscious ideas work in like manner? Today, of course, we no longer hesitate to speak of 'unconscious ideas'."

But were these experiments valid? The patient in the hypnotic trance would have actually been undergoing a seizure, as evidenced by the fact that light touches on her arms produced rigidity of those limbs. The paralysis induced by the blow on the shoulder would have been caused by the spread of the epileptic discharge in the brain to the area of the motor cortex concerned with arm movements consequent on this reflex stimulus. It was not a psychic paralysis but an epileptic one.

Throughout the centuries there had been a great deal of loose thinking relating to the "influence of the mind on the body", from the time of the ancients who had, from the fact that strong emotions could cause the heart to beat faster and that a similar acceleration occurred in disease, made the simple correlation that such emotions were themselves responsible for illness. The correlation was made in ignorance of the autonomic nervous system of which little was known until the end of the nineteenth century. In the succeeding centuries many books were written on the agency of the mind in the causation of disease. The same second-hand hearsay instances such as the case Russell Reynolds quotes – "the well-known case of the butcher, who was agonised almost past endurance by the fact that a flesh hook had caught itself not in his skin, but only in his sleeve" – occur in book after book, copied one from the other, without supporting medical data or evidence to rule out coincidence.

Many such books repeat the old tale of the university students who captured an unpopular college servant and telling him they had sentenced him to death, pinioned him, covered his face and finally with appropriate accompaniments, drew a blade across his neck. When they removed the covering from his face the man was dead. This incident has been cited in book after book as proof of the power of the mind over the body. But there is no mention of the previous health of the victim, who must in any case have been well-versed in student caprices, and would have been unlikely to actually fear for his life. Here, coincidence must have played a part. Raised blood pressure in a man with advanced circulatory disease could have set in motion the events leading to the fatal outcome, perhaps dislodging an embolus into the blood-stream that would eventually block a major vessel.

The influence of the mind over the body was also a convenient concept to be invoked in the explanation of many matters not otherwise explicable in the light of the knowledge of the day. An example from the days before the germ theory occurs in the *British Medical Journal* of July 12, 1856.

> "Dr Gull at Guy's Hospital . . . cited several instances where emotional influence also, so allied but opposite in action to chloroform, had caused jaundice, most probably by the action of such nervous agency on the gall-ducts. He had known two candidates for examination at college both to be seized with jaundice from the excitement and apprehension of not succeeding; and several such cases are mentioned in medical works . . ."

The students of course must have had infectious hepatitis, caught one from another in the close proximity of their working conditions, or perhaps independently from a patient, the microbial origin of the disease being then unknown. If jaundice could be produced by emotions connected with approaching examinations, there would be a great many yellow faces amongst the student body.

The endocrine system – the last to be elucidated of the major bodily systems – was a fruitful area for mind-body theorising before its functions were known. A hen, for example, who developed spurs and a cockscomb was said by sixteenth-century physicians to have done so because she thought herself the equal of a cock. She was most probably suffering from masculinisation due to abnormal secretion of the male hormone caused by a tumour or other such pathology. Many of the cases of "hysterical pregnancy" in the old literature were undoubtedly cases of prolactinoma. The chief symptoms described were cessation of periods and spontaneous flow of milk from the breasts, though examination showed a normal, non-gravid uterus. Intense longing for a child in a barren woman was blamed for the condition. However, rising levels of the hormone prolactin from a prolactinoma, a pituitary tumour, would have produced all this symptomatology, including the previous infertility. Prolactin, like the other pituitary hormones, was not discovered until the present century.

By the end of the nineteenth century, the accelerated growth of medical knowledge and the increasing respect for statistical confirmation led to a reaction against mind-body theorising. The Viennese school of medicine had always had its feet firmly on the ground in this respect and to the young Freud much of Charcot's teaching must have seemed new and original. He appears to have accepted it uncritically – as Fritz Wittels wrote in 1924, "Charcot showed that in an hysterical subject it is possible, under hypnosis, to arouse ideas – with the aid, perhaps of some trifling physical impression, such as a tap on the skin – which lead to a paralysis of one of the limbs, ahysterical paralysis. This paralysis will last for some time after the awakening from hypnosis. Anaesthesia could be experimentally produced, as well as paralysis. Charcot thus proved that ideas can induce bodily changes." This was the message Freud took back to Vienna from the Salpêtrière.

By this time, following Charcot's courageous lead, hypnotism was being investigated in many other centres. Some, however, claimed they were unable to obtain the famous three stages and therefore asserted they did not exist. In addition, an increasing number of physicians were adopting hypnotism for *therapeutic* purposes, often with an enthusiasm that outran caution. Once again appeared the uncritical reports of the wondrous cures that had abounded in the days of Mesmer. To these enthusiasts Charcot's dictum that only "hysterical" patients could be truly hypnotised was unwelcome and hence disputed. This was the background to the challenge to Charcot's authority by the Nancy school that had arisen even by the time of Freud's sojourn in Paris.

It is to Hippolyte Bernheim, Professor of Medicine at the University of Nancy, that we owe our present concept of hypnotism, i.e., that it is a condition capable of being entered into by the great majority of people, that it is a purely psychological condition in which one mind can achieve domination over another and that its induction is entirely a matter of suggestion and nothing else. Suggestion too explained all the phenomena of the trance. Bernheim also maintained (though this is no longer believed today) that the hypnotic condition was no different from natural sleep. From this latter belief emerged all the appurtenances associated with hypnotism today, the dimmed lights, the quiet soundproofed rooms, and above all, the "patter" – ". . . you are getting sleepy, your eyes are feeling heavy, you can hardly keep them open . . ." etc. These accompaniments, an integral part of hypnotism today, *were unknown in the entire previous century since the time of Mesmer.*

The actual founder of the Nancy school was an obscure general practitioner, a Dr Liébeault, who for many years had practised the art among his humble patients on the outskirts of the town, long regarded as a crank and known to his colleagues as "the fool of the rue Bellevue". All this changed when Bernheim visited his practice. So impressed was he that he introduced Liébeault's methods into his own wards. The unknown doctor became instructor to the professor and it was his techniques and theories that Bernheim made his own. Liébeault's treatments are succinctly described by Professor Delboeuf of Liège University:

> "After having inquired of the patient what he is suffering from, without any further or closer examination, Liébeault places a hand on the patient's forearm and, scarcely looking at him, says, 'You are going to sleep.' Then, almost immediately, he closes the eyelids of the patient, and tells him that he *is* asleep. After that, Liébeault raises an arm of the patient and says: 'You cannot put your arms down.' If the patient does, Dr Liébeault appears hardly to notice it."

The suggestions were all-embracing – "You are going to be cured, your digestion will be good, your sleep quiet, your cough will stop, your circulation become free and regular, you are going to feel strong and well" . . . etc. "Thus he fires away at every disease at once, leaving the client to find out his own", continued Delboeuf, but "notwithstanding the inevitable monotony of his speeches, and the uniformity of both style and voice, the master's tone is so ardent, so penetrating and so sympathetic that I have never once listened to it without a feeling of admiration".

The rationale for Liébeault's approach was based on the phenomenon of "post-hypnotic suggestion" discussed on page 103. Such all-embracing suggestions of good health would have fallen well outside the category of the simple commands obeyed after awakening from the trance. Liébeault's treatments also implied that the mind had control over the vegetative functions of the body, a common error in the days before the delineation of the autonomic nervous system showed that these functions were outside the conscious control of the organism.

Bernheim's use of hypnotism was equally indiscriminate. George Robertson, who visited his wards in 1892, saw him use the method in cases of pneumonia, emphysema, phthisis (tuberculosis), mitral stenosis, hemiplegia and hypertrophic cirrhosis of the liver with jaundice. What then was the truth behind the reports of "miracle" cures from the Nancy school of hypnotism? Probably many of the diseases treated were self-limiting; other chronic diseases commonly follow a pattern of relapse and remission. A constant feature of the reports of cures emanating from this school was the absence of follow-up studies. Similar claims by Mesmer in the previous century had proved without foundation when the patients were followed up by the Royal Commission of 1784. Hearsay and rumour as in Mesmer's time would also have played a part. Robertson (1892) believed Bernheim's patients came to him in a state of abnormal tension and expectancy. "They feel that this man has some occult power over them, and that he is able to put them into a peculiar sleep," he wrote, "so that they fall a ready victim to his artful wiles and suggestions."

> "There is no doubt that this frame of mind exists in Nancy, for I questioned my cabman as he was showing me the town in an artless and innocent manner about hypnotism and its powers. He told me that he had never been treated, but that friends of his had, and that Bernheim had the most wonderful powers, their indefiniteness no doubt lending a useful mystery to them, and that he was able to cure all the lesser diseases." (Robertson, 1892).

A further factor was Bernheim's method of telling his patients positively and forcefully that they *were* cured, a procedure based on his belief in the value of suggestion. His method is described by George Robertson in the treatment of an elderly man suffering from sciatica.

> "The man settled himself comfortably in the chair and looked steadily in front of him. Bernheim stood at his left side and placed the palm of his hand on the man's forehead, and spoke to him, slowly, in a quiet and gentle tone of voice, much as follows: 'You are feeling calm; you are feeling comfortable; you are feeling at rest; my hand is soothing your brain; you are beginning to feel drowsy; your arms are feeling quite heavy.' Here he took up the patient's hand with his own disengaged hand, raised it slightly, and let it fall. He then said; 'your eyes

are beginning to ache; your eyelids are feeling heavy; you can scarcely keep them open; they are beginning to close; they have closed.' While he was saying the last few words he slowly brought his hand down over the patient's eyelids and gently closed the eyes."

The suggestions continued in this fashion until finally in a tone of positive assurance and authority Bernheim assured him, "You are sound asleep – perfectly sound asleep." Robertson saw no marked change in the patient's appearance during this period. Bernheim now told the man he was going to remove the pain, that it was going away, that his leg was feeling easier, passing his hand along the leg at the same time "to suggest that some active measures were being used". He then said suddenly and positively that the pain was gone, asking the patient if that was not so. The man replied that it was much easier but he still felt it. "Bernheim replied that he would not stop till he had entirely removed it," reported Robertson, and the same process was repeated again and again, ending with the positive assertion, "Your leg is quite cured now; you don't feel any pain in it, do you?" Finally the man agreed that he no longer felt any pain. It later transpired that many patients treated by the methods of the Nancy school had actually pretended to be cured because they dared not contradict their authoritarian physicians (Janet, 1925). Sciatica is generally caused by pressure on the sciatic nerve usually by protrusion of an intervertebral disc. There was no way that hypnotism could have cured this pathology.

Were Bernheim's patients ever really hypnotised? The question is important in view of Bernheim's claim that, far from being a rare condition, almost all sane people were capable of entering the state. This was in contrast to Charcot who maintained that it was only possible to induce the condition in patients with "hysteria", and then not in every such patient. He believed that when Bernheim actually *did* induce hypnotism he was dealing with an hysterical patient. Robertson, visiting Bernheim after leaving the Salpêtrière, had similar doubts. "At first one is sceptical and very doubtful if hypnosis has really occurred in the lesser degrees", he said, "as the patients look so natural and are so conscious of all that goes on around." He noted the absence of one of the characteristic signs of induction by Charcot's methods – the slight spasm or start of some of the facial muscles. There were no physical phenomena such as the neuromuscular hyperexcitability obtained by Charcot and the catalepsy Bernheim allegedly produced by suggestion "was not like true catalepsy, and was much more like voluntary posturing".

Bernheim's strongly authoritarian approach to his patients was recorded by Freud, who visited him in 1889, in his paper *Group Psychology and the Analysis of the Ego* (1921). "I can remember even then feeling a muffled hostility to this tyranny of suggestion," he wrote. "when a patient who showed himself unamenable was met with the shout: 'What are you doing? *Vous vous contresuggestionez!*'" In fact many patients of the Nancy school were subsequently found to have only feigned hypnosis. Benedikt relates that when he allowed students to hypnotise patients in his outpatient department they had at the time said they had been in hypnotic sleep but to senior physicians confessed they had only pretended to be hypnotised in order to please the young doctors. The same thing occurred with patients of Forel and Wetterstrand. Bernheim himself makes a revealing comment:

"We may see him laugh or try to smother a laugh. He may remark upon his condition. He sometimes pretends that he is cheating or that he is trying to be obliging. Behind the doctor's back he boasts in good faith that he has not slept but has only pretended to sleep" (Bernheim, 1885).

Bernheim's equation of hypnosis with natural sleep obviously opened the door to a wide range of criteria for trance induction. Any degree of drowsiness could have sufficed. If even this were not obtained, Bernheim took care to say that sleep was not essential.

"Others are more rebellious, preoccupied, unable to give themselves up: they analyse their own feelings, are anxious, and say they cannot sleep. I command them to be calm. I speak only of drowsiness, of sleepiness. 'That is sufficient,' I say, 'to gain a result. The suggestion alone may be beneficial without sleep. Keep perfectly quiet and do not worry'."

When this had no effect he found "it is better to be abrupt, to restrain with an authoritative voice the inclination to laugh, or the weak and involuntary resistance which this manoeuvre may provoke".

It was also Bernheim's custom to have new patients watch others being hypnotised before undergoing it themselves. Seeing the older patients fall asleep, obey the hypnotiser and admit the disappearance of their symptoms on waking brought them, he considered, into a condition of psychical preparedness. This casts doubt on the genuineness of the catalepsy, for instance, produced by Bernheim. "I raise the patient's arms; they remain uplifted," he demonstrated to Robertson. "We have induced cataleptic sleep."

In fact, as Bernheim later told Freud, his "great therapeutic successes" were only achieved with his hospital patients. He was unable to obtain the same results with private patients. Pierre Janet, a contemporary of Bernheim, writing in 1925, summed up the difficulties many would-be practitioners at this time experienced when dealing with such patients who differed from the hospital patients in a very important respect – they were paying.

> "A patient, and especially a paying patient, does not like to feel nothing at all when he is being treated," Janet (1925) writes. "The doctor would do his best to console the patient, saying: 'You were wrong to expect anything extraordinary. Hypnotism is a simple affair, nothing more than what you have been experiencing. Don't say you have experienced nothing. You seem rather bored, and that is already something; we learn from the great teachers of hypnotism that a sense of boredom is the first degree . . .'"

Suggestibility is a well demonstrated and well documented feature of hypnotism. A hypnotised subject will eat with enjoyment a raw potato on being told it is a delicious pear, for example. But this is a highly pathological type of suggestibility. It does not follow that hypnotism is *caused* by suggestion. The special suggestibility of hypnotism arises when the epileptic discharge spreads from the temporal lobes of the brain to the adjoining parietal lobes. The well-known insensibility to pain is one result of this spread. Patients with disorders of the parietal lobes are similarly open to suggestion, one of Macdonald Critchley's patients, for instance, on being shown a sponge was readily persuaded it was a brush (Critchley, 1953) though her visual apparatus was intact. It is thought that parietal disease interferes with the final stage of coordination and interpretation by the brain of sense data received from the outside world. That suggestion alone could explain phenomena as varied as the fact of a single muscle springing into rigidity, and moreover a muscle not normally under control of the mind or only in conjunction with other muscles as part of a willed movement, was a contention which Charcot rejected emphatically. In this he was, of course, correct as any reader can verify for himself. The upper motor neurons which initiate willed movement control *movements* rather than individual muscles. Hence it is impossible to produce voluntarily movement of a single muscle. However, Bernheim in making these extraordinary claims, carried most of his colleagues with him. "The air of Nancy is heavy with suggestion," reported Professor Wood of Philadelphia after a visit there around this time.

But the Nancy school flourished and Bernheim, increasing in confidence and assurance, began to take issue with every tenet emanating from the Salpêtrière. Though privately, as Axel Munthe tells us, the very mention of Bernheim's name was enough to make Charcot fly into a rage, publicly he defended his theories with dignity, citing in rebuttal of Bernheim's claims, the physical phenomena such as neuromuscular hyperexcitability. These dignified rejoinders were no match, however, for the vociferous contentions of the bombastic professor from the south. Moreover, Charcot was now at a disadvantage in that his reputation had suffered from his too dramatic demonstrations of hypnotism to non-medical audiences.

In a sincere effort to involve philosophers and writers with the psychological problems of hypnotism and hysteria, Charcot had opened his clinic to them as well as to dramatists, magistrates and other interested parties. What had probably started as a limited innovation, however, rapidly escalated and led to the scenes so vividly depicted by Axel Munthe in *The Story of San Michele*. He describes the huge amphitheatre "filled to the last place with a multicoloured audience drawn from *tout Paris*, authors, journalists, leading actors and actresses, fashionable demi-mondaines, all full of morbid curiosity to witness the startling phenomena of hypnotism almost forgotten since the days of Mesmer and Braid". These public demonstrations undoubtedly led to an element of sensationalism and the reputation of the great neurologist suffered accordingly. The premature death of Charcot in 1893 from a heart attack left Bernheim in undisputed possession of the field. His is the theory of hypnotism which has come down to us today, and which has led to such a false impression of the subject in the popular mind. Of the legacy of errors from Bernheim's teaching, perhaps the most important is that it is a condition capable of being entered into by ninety-five per cent of the *normal* population and that it can be brought about by suggestion alone.

After Bernheim one can never be certain of the validity of the hypnotic experiments reported in the literature as there is often nothing to suggest that the subjects of the experiments were truly in the trance state. Various "suggestibility scales" are employed which are claimed to prove that the patient is hypnotised, but no physical criteria are apparently used. This is another factor in assessing the value of the EEG studies previously mentioned. In the therapeutic situation, few patients are probably ever really hypnotised; they are merely put into a relaxed drowsy state which most people could probably achieve equally well in their own homes, and have a clear remembrance of the events that have taken place. Modern hypnotists discourage any greater expectations than this, one medical hypnotist for example complaining that his patients expect to "go under"and "yield up their symptoms" and that because of the stage demonstrations, they do not think they have been truly hypnotised unless they have been stretched out between two chairs and sat upon.

In fact the public stage is probably the only place today where it is possible to see hypnotism as Freud saw it at the Salpêtrière, though such demonstrations are now prohibited by many local authorities because of the untoward effects that have sometimes attended these displays – the spontaneous recurrence of the trance for days and even weeks, often in extremely unwelcome circumstances, or the failure after the performance to rouse the subject, for example. Genuine trance mediums too can exhibit the condition as it was in Charcot's day. These people have learnt the particular stimulus that can in their case, reflexly induce the trance state. Many of the signs enumerated by Jackson can be observed by the attentive watcher as they pass into this state.

Freud was later to follow fashion in using hypnosis for therapeutic purposes, thus abandoning the principles taught him by Charcot. He spent many weeks in Bernheim's department in 1889 learning his technique and from what he saw there, developed his later concept of repression. From Charcot he had gained an intimation of unconscious mental processes and the concept of traumatic hysteria. He had already been told of the "cathartic treatment" of the famous patient "Anna O." by his friend Breuer. He was therefore by 1889 possessed of all the ingredients for the development of his theories apart from one and that was the most important of all – cocaine.

VIII

The Famous Anna O. Case

Freud returned to Vienna agog with the wonders he had to reveal of Charcot and his work at the Salpêtrière. Eager to impart his newfound knowledge to his colleagues, on October 15, 1886 he delivered a paper before the Imperial and Royal Society of Physicians, an august body which had seen the first announcements of some of the most famous discoveries in the history of the faculty. To it Czermak had demonstrated the laryngoscope, Nitze and Leiter their cystoscope, Koller the local anaesthetic properties of cocaine; to it Semmelweiss had announced his discovery of the infectious nature of puerperal fever. It was a tradition of the society that the speakers should bring forward something new and original at the meetings. Imagining the subject to be unknown to his audience, Freud chose to speak on "male hysteria", introducing Charcot's concept of traumatic neurosis. As H. F. Ellenberger (1970) has pointed out, this meeting has passed into psychoanalytic legend.

> "The standard account of that event reads as follows; Freud presented a paper on male hysteria before the Society of Physicians on October 15, 1886. This paper was received with incredulity and hostility. Freud was challenged to present a case of male hysteria to the Society, and though he met this challenge on November 26 of the same year, the reception was cool, and this was the starting point of Freud's lifelong feud with the Viennese medical world."

Freud's paper on this occasion was never published, but from the records of the society and reports of the proceedings in contemporary journals Ellenberger has uncovered an entirely different picture of the event. What Freud had imagined to be a new and original concept had been a subject of controversy in the German-speaking medical faculties for some years, where the opposition to the neurosis theory of "railway brain" and "railway spine" was led by Thomsen and Oppenheim. The discussion of

Freud's paper revolved around the issue of the organic or non-organic nature of these conditions. The concept of male hysteria was one with which his audience was well acquainted. Charcot's work was well known in Vienna. He was a personal friend of Meynert and Benedikt visited him every year. By presenting problems of which his audience was already well aware, Freud had violated the traditions of the society that new and original work should be presented, hence the remark of Professor Bamberger, in the chair, that there was nothing new in Freud's interesting paper. Freud's later version says, "Persons of authority, such as the chairman (Bamberger, the physician), declared that what I said was incredible" (*Autobiographical Study*, 1925). Moreover, many of Freud's distinguished seniors had had victims of railway accidents under their care for long periods. Professor Leidesdorf stated that he had often examined patients who, following a railway accident or similar trauma, had developed organic symptoms that had nothing in common with hysteria, and warned that the true extent of the lesions could not be evaluated in the early stages.

Freud's account of Meynert's contribution also differs from the contemporary records; he implies that the latter challenged him to demonstrate such cases of male hysteria as he had described to the society, whereas Meynert's remarks were concerned with the validity of the diagnosis – he stated that he had repeatedly observed cases of epileptic seizures and disturbances of consciousness after trauma and that it would be interesting to check whether these cases also presented the symptoms depicted by Freud. The objections to Freud's paper were therefore mild and reasonable and in no way personal to Freud. The paper that followed received far more stringent criticism.

Evidently misunderstanding the point at issue, Freud felt challenged to present a case in which Charcot's "stigmata" could be observed in a clearly marked form. Accordingly on November 26 he presented such a case, published later under the title "Observations of a severe case of hemianaesthesia in a hysterical male". The case was undoubtedly one of epilepsy, in a patient with a strong family history, who had suffered from fits in childhood, with recurrence in the last few years. On this patient Freud demonstrated the "stigmata" – "I can introduce my finger and touch all the pharyngeal tissues on the left side without the result being retching . . . touching the left conjunctive palpebrarum and bulbi produces scarcely any closure of the lids." Finally hemianaesthesia of the entire left side was established. Unfortunately there was a heavy schedule that evening which left no time for discussion, so we shall never know what Meynert thought of all this. "The impression that the high authorities had rejected my innovations remained unshaken", Freud wrote in 1925, "and, with my hysteria in men and my production of hysterical paralyses by suggestion, I found myself forced into the opposition." After this experience he said, he withdrew from academic life. In 1925 he wrote, "It is a whole generation since I have visited the *Gesellschaft der Aerzte*'." Contemporary records prove this statement untrue. The following year he was elected to the society, sponsored by seven prominent members and did not cease to be a member till he left Vienna over fifty years later.

On his return from Paris, Freud took up his appointment as an honorary consultant at the Kassowitz Institute, the famous Vienna paediatric outpatient department. There, in charge of the neurology service he joined a team of ambitious young heads of department. The head of the institute, Max Kassowitz, was already famous as the discoverer of the first curative treatment for the universally prevalent rickets – cod liver oil, though to the day of his death he denied the effect of the oil. He had in 1879 begun to administer small doses of phosphorus to children with this condition, only later adding the oil as the most suitable solvent for the phosphorus. When this was done the effect was astonishing and the treatment became a worldwide success. The curative properties of the treatment actually lay in the vitamin D content of the cod liver oil, but the discovery of this and other vitamins had to await the early decades of the present century when they were shown to be the missing elements responsible for many non-infectious diseases.

From this institute where he attended three afternoons a week Freud published many papers and monographs on neurological conditions in children, though he began to find the work increasingly uncongenial as his interests became centred in psychoanalysis. He continued working on brain anatomy in Meynert's institute in the mornings and now felt ready to take rooms in Rathausstrasse 7 and set up in private practice as a specialist in diseases of the nervous system. He was referred patients by his former teachers at the university as well as his faithful friend, Joseph Breuer, a prominent general physician in the city. The modest success of his practice as well as gifts of money from his fiancée's family enabled him to fulfil at last his greatest ambition, and he married Martha Bernays on September 13, 1886. Five children were born to the marriage; Freud expressed his homage to Charcot by naming his first son Jean-Martin in his honour.

Freud found private practice where the responsibility for his patients' care was his alone very different from his hospital work where advice and help were always available. The fourteen months spent in Scholz's wards and the four months at the Salpêtrière, where only clear-cut advanced cases were seen, were scarcely adequate preparation for the burdens he now assumed. He judged most of his patients as neurotics, by which one gathers that they were cases of obscure aetiology differing markedly from the "classic" text-book cases he had seen in hospital. Apart from a case of sciatica mentioned in a letter to Martha, we only know of an Italian patient who was thrown into a convulsive attack every time she heard the words "*Apfel*" or "*poma*" (Jones, 1953). This must have been a fascinating case of reflex epilepsy, but Freud could scarcely have made this diagnosis in the eighteen-eighties. As he wrote to Martha he felt "ashamed of his ignorance, embarrassment and helplessness" (Jones, 1953).

By this time more and more adverse reports from all parts of the world were being published on cocaine, the drug on which his hopes for fame and fortune were founded. His lack of success with the conventional treatments of electro-therapy, baths and massage, the final realisation that cocaine was not going to bring him fame but rather the reverse, and no doubt the pressures of providing for his rapidly growing family eventually led him to succumb to the lure of hypnosis as a therapeutic agent and to join the rapidly expanding band of enthusiasts using hypnotic suggestion in the manner of Liébeault and Bernheim, thus abandoning the precepts of his erstwhile mentor, Charcot. A letter to his friend Fliess of December 28, 1887 dates the commencement of his use of hypnotism in his practice. "I have taken up hypnosis and have had all sorts of small but remarkable successes," he wrote. He found "there was something positively seductive in working with hypnotism. For the first time there was a sense of having overcome one's helplessness; and it was highly flattering to enjoy the reputation of being a miracle-worker." Before long he was translating Bernheim's book and adding a favourable preface. In his review of August Forel's book *Hypnotism* in 1889 he repeated with approval Bernheim's fundamental error that hypnotism was "nothing other than ordinary sleep".

But now he found that the confident assertion made by Bernheim that ninety-five per cent of normal people were capable of being hypnotised was simply not true. Assuming his technique to be at fault he travelled to Nancy in the summer of 1889, spending several weeks there in the clinics of Liébeault and Bernheim. "I witnessed the moving spectacle of old Liébeault working among the poor women and children of the labouring classes," he wrote later in his *Autobiographical Study*. "I was a spectator of Bernheim's astonishing experiments upon his hospital patients." He had persuaded one of his patients, "a highly gifted hysteric", to follow him to Nancy. All his attempts at a permanent cure by hypnotic suggestion had been unsuccessful, a failure he attributed to the fact that her hypnotism had never reached the stage of somnambulism and amnesia. Bernheim himself now made several attempts to achieve this but he too failed. It was then he admitted his lack of success in inducing hypnotic suggestion in his private patients.

While at the Salpêtrière and observing Charcot's cases of "traumatic hysteria" Freud was strongly reminded of a curious

Josef Breuer.

case treated some years before by his physician friend Breuer. He mentioned the case to Charcot but failed to arouse his interest and dismissed it from his mind. Now faced with the exigencies of his practice and his therapeutic helplessness, he again recalled the case.

He had first met Joseph Breuer, a man twelve years his senior, in the Institute of Physiology in the late seventies. Though having many scientific achievements to his credit, including his discovery of the control of respiration by the vagus nerve, and his later work on the functions of the semicircular canals in the inner ear, Breuer had renounced an academic career in favour of private practice. When Freud met him, he was one of the most highly regarded practitioners in Vienna and trusted physician to the families of prominent members of the medical faculty, including Brücke, Exner, Billroth, Chrobak, and many others. The two men had become close friends, sharing their scientific interests, and Breuer, taking a benevolent interest in the younger man, helped Freud over the many financial difficulties of his student years. For nearly two decades, therefore, Freud was on terms of the most intimate friendship with Breuer and his wife for whom he had a special admiration.

It was the end of November 1881 that Breuer was first called to the young woman whom psychoanalysts the world over know as Anna O., her case universally acknowledged as the first example of the "cathartic cure" with which psychoanalysis originated. The patient was a girl of 21 who had developed her illness in the course of her devoted attendance on her sick father. The emotional trauma connected with his illness and eventual death was, in Breuer's view, the precipitating cause of her symptoms. As such her case "agreed entirely with Charcot's theory of traumatic hysteria" (*Studies in Hysteria*, 1895), and he expressly rejected the alternative theory of hysteria – the sexual hypothesis – then still current; "the element of sexuality was astonishingly undeveloped in her," he wrote. She had never fallen in love and that element had never emerged in the numerous hallucinations which occurred during her illness.

When many years later, Freud, now firmly adhering to the sexual theory of hysteria, was reminded of the absence of this element in the case that had started it all, he was accustomed to counter with the following story as told by Jones (1953): Breuer had developed what Jones called a "strong counter-transference" to his interesting and attractive young patient, spending long hours at her bedside and becoming so engrossed that his wife became jealous. It was a long time before he divined the cause of her unhappiness, but eventually enlightened, Breuer saw the danger light and resolved to bring the treatment to a close. He said goodbye to the patient, now much better, but was that evening recalled to find her as bad as ever and moreover in the throes of a "hysterical childbirth", the "logical outcome of a phantom pregnancy that had been invisibly developing in response to Breuer's ministrations".

Freud enlarged on this story in a letter to the author Stefan Zweig of February 7, 1931 (Freud, Ernst, 1961). On the evening when Breuer was summoned back to the patient he "found her confused and writhing in abdominal cramps. Asked what was wrong with her, she replied: 'Now Dr B's child is coming!'" Later in the letter, however, Freud speaks of the episode being a "reconstruction". "I was so convinced of this reconstruction of mine that I published it somewhere," he said. He adds, however, that Breuer confirmed his surmise shortly before his death. The Jones version adds that Breuer, profoundly shocked by his patient's statement, hastily hypnotised her and left the house "in a cold sweat". The next day he and his wife left for Venice on a second honeymoon, which resulted in the conception of the daughter who was to commit suicide in New York sixty years later.

It was not until many years after her illness that inconsistencies in the story of Anna O. began to emerge. Firstly, in a seminar at Zurich in 1925, Jung revealed that this famous case, "so much spoken about as an example of brilliant therapeutic success, was in reality nothing of the kind .... There was no cure at all in the sense of which it was originally presented" (unpublished typescript quoted by Ellenberger (1972).) Then in 1953 Ernest Jones in his life of Freud revealed the real identity of the patient. She was no unknown girl, but Bertha Pappenheim, daughter of a prominent old family well known in the Jewish community, later to become famous in her own right as a pioneer social worker. The family was much displeased by Jones' indiscretion, but knowledge of the real name of the patient proved an important point of departure for future historians, foremost of whom is H. F. Ellenberger, author of *The Discovery of the Unconscious* (1970). Researching for this book in Vienna, Ellenberger found an important discrepancy. Breuer's last child Dora was registered as having been born on March 11, 1882 so could not possibly have been conceived during the "second honeymoon" in June 1882.

However, Jones' revelation of the patient's real name made his quest easier. She was no nonentity, and her death in 1936 had made available obituary material on which he was able to draw.

Freud and Cocaine

Anna O. – Bertha Pappenheim.

Moreover, a short biography was published by Mrs Dora Edinger in 1963. On the subject of a nervous illness in her youth these sources were, however, silent. She and her mother had eventually left Vienna and settled in Frankfurt. She had devoted the rest of her life to philanthropic activities, travelling in the Balkans, the Near East and Russia to investigate prostitution and white slavery. She founded the League of Jewish Women, and wrote many sociological and other works. So valuable were her philanthropic and other activities that after World War II a special commemorative postage stamp was issued by the government of West Germany.

Jones had recorded that after Breuer's withdrawal from the case she was sent to a sanatorium in Gross Enzersdorf, but Ellenberger discovered that there never had been a sanatorium there and his enquiries were brought to a halt. Now, however, he performed an ingenious feat of historical detection. The biography by Dora Edinger had contained a photograph of Bertha dated 1882 showing a "healthy-looking, sporting woman in riding habit, in sharp contrast to Breuer's portrait of a home-bound young lady who had no outlets for her physical and mental energies". From the author, Ellenberger succeeded in obtaining the original of the portrait. Embossed on it was a date, 1882, but the name and address of the photographer could no longer be deciphered. Examined under special light in the laboratory of the Montreal City Police, however, the name Constanz became visible, with part of the address. What was Bertha doing in Konstanz, Germany, at the time when she was supposed to be in a sanatorium near Vienna? There was, however, a famous sanatorium in the Swiss town of Kreuzlingen very near Konstanz and there, in the Bellevue Sanatorium, Ellenberger eventually traced the records of Bertha Pappenheim's admission from July 12, to October 29, 1882. Various documents were found in the case notes, including a copy of a case history written by Breuer in 1882 and a follow-up report written by one of the doctors of the sanatorium. Reporting his discovery in 1972, Ellenberger makes the trenchant comment that the newly found documents confirm that "the famed 'prototype of a cathartic cure' was neither a cure nor a catharsis". Recently the documents were published in full by Dr Albrecht Hirschmüller as appendices to his biography of Breuer, *Physiologie und Psychoanalyse in Leben und Werk Josef Breuers* (an English translation by Dr C. Lill is to be published this year by Princeton University Press), thus enabling a comparison between the actual case-notes written by Breuer during the patient's illness with the account he gave in the *Studies in Hysteria* written in 1895 after a lapse of thirteen years.

The two case histories are superficially similar but there are significant additional details in the earlier history which give an entirely different complexion to the case. The follow-up report by the sanatorium doctor contains definite proof that the symptoms which Breuer had claimed had been "permanently removed" by the "cathartic" treatment were still present long after he had ceased to have her in his care. The file also paints a somewhat different picture of the termination of Breuer's involvement with the case from that given by Freud. Both versions give little clinical data and describe the case as a hysterical illness, the presenting symptom of which was a "*tussis nervosa*" (hysterical cough), for

which Breuer was first called into consultation, with the implication that the illness was precipitated by her overwrought state and
long hours spent by the bedside of her sick father to whom she was
devotedly attached. Soon the full-blown picture of hysteria as
described by Charcot developed, with contractures, paralyses, fits,
anaesthesias, diplopia and other peculiarities of vision, as well as
many strange disturbances of speech. The case was actually an
illness with cough as the presenting symptom followed by the
development of focal neurological signs indicating lesions in
widely separated regions of the brain – displaying, in short, the
characteristic symptomatology of *tuberculous meningitis*. The
illness suffered by Bertha's father was a sub-pleuritic abscess, a
frequent complication of tuberculosis of the lungs then highly
prevalent in Vienna. Helping with the nursing, and spending many
hours at the bedside, Bertha would have been exposed to numerous occasions of infection. In addition, early in 1881 her father
had had an operation – probably incision of the abscess and
insertion of a drain; this was performed at home by a surgeon
from Vienna. The changing of dressings and the disposal of the
purulent secretions would have led to further dissemination of the
infecting organisms. The isolation of the bacillus by Koch had not
yet taken place and aseptic precautions would probably have been
minimal. The father's death in spite of every care would indicate a
virulent strain of the invading organism. Support for this aetiology
is also provided by the fact that Bertha's sister died in childhood of
tuberculosis.

The pathogenesis of tuberculous meningitis was established in
1933 by A. R. Rich and H. A. McCordock at the Johns Hopkins
Medical School in Baltimore. The condition invariably originates
from a focus of infection elsewhere in the body, most commonly
from the lungs (Bertha's illness, it will be remembered, began with
a cough). Meningitis develops when an older caseating tubercle on
the surface of the brain (Rich's focus) ruptures into the subarach-
noid space, injecting large numbers of bacilli into the cerebrospinal fluid. A massive tuberculin reaction is the immediate result.
Exudates and adhesions accumulate in the base of the brain and
spinal canal, constricting cranial and spinal nerves, producing
infarction in blood vessels and impeding the flow of the cerebrospinal fluid. Translated into clinical terms the injury to the cranial
nerves and infarction of vessels produces lesions in many different
parts of the brain, giving rise to squints, impairment of vision,
paralyses and other focal signs: obstruction to the flow of the
cerebrospinal fluid causes hydrocephalus with accumulation of
such fluid in and around the brain with impairment of conscious-

ness and mental dysfunction. Headache, contrary to the text-book descriptions, was not a prominent feature in recent papers.

Breuer, however, recounts the entire case history from an entirely psychogenic bias. We learn much about the previous character of his patient, her penetrating intelligence and poetic and imaginative gifts (the latter, however, well under control of "a sharp and critical common sense"). He dwells heavily on the lack of intellectual outlets in her restricted family life and her conse-quent habit of day-dreaming (her "private theatre", as she called it). The prodromal phase of her illness with early symptoms of cough, malaise, lethargy, nausea and anorexia are given a similar psychogenic interpretation:

"During the first months of the illness Anna devoted her whole energy to nursing her father and no one was much surprised when by degrees her own health greatly deteriorated. No one, perhaps not even the patient herself, knew what was happening to her; but eventually the state of weakness, anaemia and distaste for food became so bad that to her great sorrow she was no longer allowed to continue nursing the patient" (*Studies*).

When, after the prodromal symptoms of cough, anorexia and malaise, Bertha developed the characteristic pattern of sleep reversal often seen in cerebral infections, marked by a craving for rest in the afternoon followed in the evening by a "sleep-like state" succeeded by a "highly excited condition", Breuer again adopts a psychological explanation:

"During the nights she had watched by the patient's bedside or had been awake anxiously listening till the morning; in the afternoons she had lain down for a short rest, as is the usual habit of nurses."

In its subsequent course Bertha Pappenheim's illness, as regards symptomatology and time course, corresponds almost exactly to the progression described by Rich. At the beginning of December 1881 the first of the focal neurological signs appeared – a conver-gent squint. An ophthalmic surgeon called in "explained this (mistakenly) as being due to paresis of one abducens," wrote Breuer (*Studies*). No reason is advanced for his doubt of the diagnosis. The earlier case history of 1882 merely states, "An eye doctor explained it as paresis of the abducens which I am convinced it wasn't." The abducens is the sixth cranial nerve supplying the motor fibres of the external rectus muscle of the eye. A lesion of this nerve makes it impossible to turn the eye outward and the unopposed pull of the internal rectus causes the eye to turn in, producing squint. Since images then do not fall on the corresponding parts of the left and right retinae they cannot be fused and the result is diplopia or double vision, a symptom complained of by Bertha. There is no way that such a paralysis could be produced psychogenically, since the voluntary motor pathways operated by the upper motor neurones govern entire movements and not individual muscles. At some stage she developed a "conjugate deviation of both eyes to the right so that her hand always groped leftwards". This implies an upper motor neurone lesion of the corticomesencephalic tract. Following such a lesion both eyes are deviated to the same side as the lesion so that the patient "looks at his lesion".

About the same time the patient developed a whole range of subtle visual symptoms – Breuer described them as "disturbances of vision which it was hard to analyse" (*Studies*). She complained that the walls of the room seemed to be falling over; she was only able to see one flower at a time in a bouquet or only individual parts of a face (case history of 1882), though there was no impairment of actual vision. Such symptoms since the investigations of Macdonald Critchley, published in his *The Parietal Lobes* (1953), are now well recognised as resulting from parietal lobe lesions. Critchley's book actually contains the description of a similar patient who could only see one flower at a time in a bouquet. The symptom is a disorder of perception, an impairment of simultaneous surveying occurring when the visual apparatus itself is intact, but the patient is unable to see more than one object at a time in the visual field.

On December 11, Breuer writes (*Studies*), "the patient took to her bed", a pejorative statement with the implication of a voluntary decision on her part and connotations of malingering. She could, in fact, scarcely do otherwise. She had developed further and disabling neurological signs, the first of which was paresis of "the muscles of the front of the neck" (the earlier case history names the scaleni muscles which would indicate involvement of the spinal nerves). This progressed until "finally the patient could only move her head by pressing it backward between her raised shoulders and moving her whole back". A contracture of the right arm, then of the right leg, appeared. The latter was "fully extended, adducted, and rotated inwards". Later the left leg and finally the left arm became similarly affected but in this case the fingers to some extent retained the power of movement. "I at once recognised the seriousness of the psychical disturbance with which I had to deal," wrote Breuer (*Studies*). Further details, however, in the earlier case history definitely rule out a psychogenic aetiology – the affected limbs were cold and oedematous and the contractures failed to relax either during sleep or chloral sedation.

Concurrently with the development of the contractures which, it will be remembered, began on the right side, Bertha developed a curious form of aphasia, characteristically expressed by Breuer in psychological terms – "words failed her". The symptoms enumerated by Breuer, however, are an almost classic description of the "telegrammatism" encountered in the expressive dysphasias resulting from a lesion in Broca's area or its connections.

> "She lost her command of grammar and syntax; she no longer conjugated verbs, and eventually she used only infinitives, for the most part incorrectly formed from weak past participles; and she omitted both the definite and the indefinite article" (*Studies*).

When she tried to write (until prevented by the contractures) she employed the same telegrammatism.

A period of two weeks ensued when "she became completely dumb". With this period of complete aphasia, Breuer states in the *Studies*, "the psychical mechanism of the disorder became clear. As I knew, she had felt very much offended over something and had determined not to speak about it." (The earlier case history is more explicit – "having been offended by her father she had decided not to ask after him any more".) "When I guessed this and obliged her to talk about it," Breuer continues, "the inhibition, which had made any other kind of utterance impossible as well, disappeared." This was naive *post hoc, ergo propter hoc* reasoning. In fact, though she recovered her ability to speak, from then on she could do so only in English, with which, as a good linguist, she was already familiar. The recovery coincided with the return of the power of movement to the left side of the body and disappearance of her squint which from then on "only reappeared in moments of great excitement". She was once again able to support her head. She was actually already in the recovery stage of the earlier phase of her illness (March 1881) when her speech returned. Breuer's action in compelling her to speak about the incident with her father was probably nothing more than coincidence. In fact her recovery proceeded so rapidly that on the first of April she left her bed for the first time.

The peculiar speech disturbance persisted, however. She continued without realising it to speak only in English though still able to understand those about her speaking German. Only some months later was Breuer able to convince her that she was talking in English. Episodes of complete aphasia continued to recur however – characteristically interpreted by Breuer – "Only in moments of extreme anxiety did her power of speech desert her entirely" (*Studies*). Other episodes occurred when she would use a mixture of three different languages. At her best she spoke French and Italian and there was complete amnesia between these times and those in which she talked English. Still later she spoke only English and was then unable to understand German. Those about her were obliged to speak English and even her nurse learned to make herself understood to some extent in this language. She was, however, able to *read* French and Italian. If asked to read aloud a text in either of those languages what she produced was an "admirable extempore English translation read with extraordinary fluency". Thus she had an extremely interesting form of aphasia which takes us into a still esoteric area of neurology, that of polyglot aphasia.

Prior to 1978 it had been assumed that a lesion in the speech area of the brain causes loss of the mother tongue and subsequently acquired languages in an equal degree; in fact this is the usual finding. But more complex patterns with considerable variability in the language loss had been reported in other studies of polyglot aphasia. One language might recover, for instance, and then regress as a second language recovered. Or, as in the case of Bertha Pappenheim, a previously little used second language might persist while the mother tongue was lost. A particularly interesting case in many ways resembling hers was reported by Robert April and Peter Tse in the *Archives of Neurology* of 1977. In this case the patient, born in China, settled in the United States at the age of seven. Though he became fluent in English, Chinese continued to be spoken in the family circle. At the age of fifty-four he sustained a stroke, developing aphasia and hemiparesis. Word comprehension was relatively preserved but he spoke in short agrammatical incomplete phrases. Spontaneous utterances were made in English, not Chinese. When addressed in Chinese he first responded in English, though he later attempted to speak Chinese, and his final responses were usually mixtures of Chinese and English speech. His family had difficulty in understanding the Chinese he did speak. He laughed when told Chinese jokes but was unable to explain why or describe the humorous content. Computerised tomographic brain scans revealed encephalomalacia in the distribution of the middle cerebral artery.

It was cases such as these which prompted the Seattle neurosurgeon George Ojemann to wonder whether the same areas of the brain were utilised for the mother tongue and later acquired languages, or whether they did, in fact, occupy different areas of the language centre. He decided to further explore this aspect and his paper reports the results of the investigations on two bilingual patients undergoing craniotomy for the eradication of epileptogenic foci. Stimulation experiments during operation revealed that sites in the centre of the language area were involved in both languages, but peripheral to this were sites involved in only one of the languages. The strange vagaries of Bertha's aphasia, so incomprehensible to Breuer's generation, are thus explained on an anatomical basis.

Her father's death on April 5, produced no exacerbation in the patient's condition. In fact a quiet phase ensued. But the rapid changes of mood, altered states of consciousness and definite psychic symptoms which had set in soon after the onset of the focal neurological signs, persisted. Alternating with her normal state was an abnormal one in which she hallucinated, became aggressive, abusing those around her and throwing cushions at them, and tearing the bedclothes with such of her fingers as she could move. She had already had brief and hardly noticeable "absences" during the earlier phase of her illness – episodes resembling attacks of *petit mal* epilepsy when she would stop in the middle of a sentence, repeat her last words, pause, and then resume talking. These absences extended till they resembled long drawn out trance-like states replacing the previous pattern of afternoon somnolence, so that during the day she was almost never completely normal. This and the psychic symptoms probably arose from raised intracranial pressure due to obstruction of the circulating cerebrospinal fluid from the exudates and adhesions at the base of the brain. The earlier case history reveals that occasional hallucinations had actually preceded the focal signs and suggests that they were the accompaniments of slight fits. "As often as the hallucinations of black snakes occurred, called forth by increasing anxiety or by snake-like objects, her right arm became extended and completely stiff," Breuer states. This is a description of the partial tonic seizures common in epilepsy, especially in children, when one limb only becomes rigid and extended.

By the middle of April 1881 a new symptom had appeared – the loss of the ability to recognise faces. This rare condition is now known by the name of prosopagnosia (from the Greek for "face non-recognition") and indicates an occipital lesion. The name does not imply the common failure to remember the appropriate name for a recognised face, nor is it part of a general inability to recognise or remember other objects – this ability remains intact. It is the specific inability to recognise faces at all. A patient may for instance be unable to recognise his own wife by her face and only succeed in doing so by her voice. Such people rapidly develop a system of cues to aid their memory, telling themselves for instance that such-and-such a face must belong to so-and-so because of bushy eyebrows or a moustache, or by peculiarities of clothes or gait. Breuer gives an almost classical description of prosopagnosia, then unrecognised as a neurological entity. Normally, he states, Bertha had been able to recognise people without effort – "now she was obliged to do laborious 'recognising work' and had to say to herself 'this person's nose is such-and-such, his hair is such-and-such, so he must be so-and-so'". A curious variant was that all the people she saw now seemed like wax figures without any connection with her.

Subtle defects of colour vision have often been reported in these patients and these were present in Bertha's case, though interpreted by Breuer in his customary way. She had complained of "seeing colours wrong", and in a particular instance said she knew she was wearing a brown dress but saw it as a blue one, which Breuer attributed to the fact that the previous year she had been making a dressing gown for her father in the same material as her present dress but in blue instead of brown.

Ten days after her father's death a consultant was called in. The earlier case history reveals that he was none other than Richard von Krafft-Ebing, then occupying the chair of the First Department of Psychiatry at the Lower Austrian Asylum for the Insane, later to succeed Meynert at the General Hospital. During his visit Bertha experienced what Breuer described as a complete "negative hallucination" for Krafft-Ebing, though he joined in the conversation and examined her. He eventually succeeded in breaking through her trance by blowing smoke from a burning piece of paper in her face.

George Robertson (1892) described a similar "negative hallucination" in a hypnotic experiment he witnessed during his visit to Bernheim's wards. As the subject of the experiment was a "hysterical young woman", one may assume the phenomenon was genuine.

> "Bernheim hypnotised this woman and then suggested to her that on waking she was not to see himself, that he would be gone away. She was then wakened and soon after expressed surprise at Bernheim's absence. She then began to talk and to amuse herself with one of the assistants. Bernheim during this time walked up to her, and stood beside her, and touched her on the face and hands, and she took not the slightest notice of what

he did, and completely ignored his presence. He then called for a pin, and as one of the assistants came towards him with it, the patient ran away laughing and scolding, as she thought the assistant was going to prick her with it. The moment, however, he handed the pin to Bernheim she no longer saw the pin and took no further notice of it, though Bernheim bared her arm and stuck the pin right through the skin. Her total insensibility to all that related to Bernheim was most astonishing, considering that she appeared thoroughly awake and talked quite naturally."

Here Bernheim was probably exploiting a phenomenon presumably resulting from the spread of the epileptic discharge from the temporal lobes to the nearby parietal lobes. One of the peculiar syndromes of disease of these lobes is an inability in an affected patient to see and hear more than one person at a time. Macdonald Critchley has described similar phenomena in *The Parietal Lobes*, reporting the case, for instance, of a patient completely unaware of the presence of his wife sitting beside his bed. In his direction to the patient that she was not to see himself Bernheim assumes the role of magician, but the explanation is simple. Previous hypnotic or spontaneous trances had probably indicated her propensity to this perceptual disorder. He was thus able to give the order confidently, knowing that it would seem to be obeyed. She was already in conversation with his assistant when Bernheim walked up to her, therefore he was the *second* person present, hence the most likely to be ignored. Bertha Pappenheim's "negative hallucination" of Krafft-Ebing is likely to have been of the same variety, and would accord with her parietal lobe pathology.

The earlier case history of 1881 reveals that, during the predominantly somatic phase of her illness, Breuer did at one stage entertain the idea of "a tubercle in the pons, chronic meningitis or such like extending into the left sylvian fossa" but rejected the diagnoses on the grounds that the affectation had begun with "a clear *tussis nervosa*" and "a circumstance to be described". This circumstance was none other than the introduction of the famous cathartic method (and Breuer's confidence in its validity).

The "discovery" of the method was fortuitous. From a few chance words dropped by the patient, it became obvious that she was re-experiencing the same hallucinatory events in her evening trances, which Breuer called "autohypnosis" and she herself called "clouds", as in the earlier daytime absences. But there was an important difference in that in her evening trances Bertha was, to a limited extent at any rate, accessible to communication with the outside world, and thus able to make known to Breuer the content of the hallucinations she had experienced earlier in the day. The picture is a familiar one, resembling the phenomena encountered in temporal lobe epilepsy when a patient might, after a psychomotor seizure, have complete amnesia for the events of the trance but would be able to recall them again in a subsequent trance, whether spontaneous or hypnotically induced, an indication that the epileptic discharge was once again taking the same path as it had taken previously.

When someone around her accidentally uttered a phrase Bertha had used in an earlier hallucinatory episode, she had at once joined in and begun to depict a situation or story revolving around the phrase used, hesitatingly at first and in her paraphasic jargon (this was at the end of 1881 when she was still able to speak German) but becoming more fluent till at last she was speaking quite correct German. It was this fact that, according to the 1882 case history, confirmed for Breuer the diagnosis of hysteria. Today it would seem a very slender fact on which to base so important a diagnosis. The improvement in her speech could be equally interpreted as a result of her persistent efforts to speak correctly and their facilitatory effects on the neurones in the speech centres. Breuer, however, believed her language difficulties were caused by "the effect of the products of her imagination as psychical stimuli", and her improvement was therefore due to their removal "when she gave utterance to them in her hypnosis". Thus encouraged, he proceeded to inaugurate a systematic ritual, arranging to be present during the evening "auto-hypnosis" and drawing out from his patient the stories indicated in her day-time hallucinatory states. It would be noticed, for instance, that she would let fall the words "sandy desert" in her daytime absences. In the evening Breuer would give her the word "desert" whereupon she would at once embark on a story of wanderers lost in a sandy desert. These stories were the beginning of the "cathartic" treatment.

As H. F. Ellenberger (1972) has pointed out, there was in Vienna at the time of Breuer's treatment of his famous patient, a widespread interest in the concept of "catharsis". It had been engendered by the publication the previous year of a book by Jacob Bernays on the Aristotelian concept of catharsis. Interestingly, he was the uncle of Martha Bernays, Freud's future wife, who was in turn a friend of Bertha Pappenheim's. With its publication, catharsis had become a fashionable talking point in the intellectual circles of the day. So it is reasonable to suppose that Aristotle's concept was the motivating force behind Breuer's adoption of the cathartic treatment of his patient.

In the fourth century BC Aristotle had spoken of the psychic benefits to be derived from the drama. "Tragedy", he said, "by means of pity and terror, accomplishes the purging of such passions." Here one must replace these words in their historical context. The physiology of Aristotle's time was that of the four humours: blood, phlegm, black bile and yellow bile. Corresponding to these humours were the "temperaments", these dating from Galen who had stated (*De Humoribus*) that "blood makes one cheerful; yellow bile makes one irascible, bold or truculent; phlegm, slow and stupid; black bile fierce and shameless" (later this humour came to be predominantly associated with morbid depression or sadness). As the predominance of any of these humours was held to result in a particular cast of mind the terms sanguine, phlegmatic, choleric and melancholic came into use. Gradually the word humour itself came to be equated with emotion, hence the terms "good humoured" or "ill humoured" still extant. Conversely, the emotions themselves began to acquire the connotations of the humours – as having substance and occupying space. This dogma has survived through the ages. Though the doctrine has no place in modern physiology, we still use phrases referring to the emotions as solid entities. We speak (erroneously) of "pent up emotions", "letting off steam", "bottling up anger" in exactly the same way as did the Greeks of Aristotle's time. The latter phrases contain the kernel of the theory of the supposed cure of excess or harmful emotions. Just as in physical illness treatment was aimed at the removal of the excess of some particular humour by bleeding or, more often, by purging (catharsis), in his famous aphorism Aristotle recommends the tragedy as a means of effecting a similar purgation of passions that are too strong. Thus Breuer's cathartic cure was a regression to the obsolete humoral theory. It has no validity in the light of modern physiology. Emotions are reactions, not solid entities.

The Freud revival in the sixties of this century caused a considerable renewal of interest in the cathartic concept among dramatists, writers and other intellectuals. Catharsis was the philosophy behind the cult of violence and aggression which began in the sixties and was epitomised in the "theatre of cruelty" and the rehabilitation of writers such as de Sade in intellectual circles. Latterly, attention has focused on the cathartic effect of mourning as expressed in Freud's *Mourning and Melancholy* (Standard Edition *14*) when he returns to the concept of catharsis in connection with bereavement, emphasising the "work of mourning" when feelings of grief, loss and guilt had to be "worked through" if permanent psychological damage was not to ensue. This concept is also of Aristotelian vintage, grief being treated as a tangible solid entity that has to be "discharged" if lasting harm is not to result. The concept has, nevertheless, caught the imagination of psychiatrists and therapists. The rash of articles on death and mourning appearing recently in medical and other journals is about catharsis, Freud's "authority" being the only "evidence" quoted for the views expressed. All kinds of conditions have been traced to some bereavement in the near or distant past "not adequately mourned". Parents have been made to undergo "ritual mourning" for pregnancies that have miscarried. One girl was alleged to have been cured of her anorexia nervosa when her *parents* underwent such mourning for an aborted fetus. Counsellors to supervise mourning and special courses for health visitors and social workers on the subject of death have been arranged, with "field visits" to mortuaries and funeral parlours.

Whatever the validity of the theory, however, the telling of the stories became a regular therapeutic procedure which both Breuer and his patient saw as being of cathartic value. He writes in the *Studies* of "relieving" her of the stories, which he viewed as "psychic stimuli" and the "easing and removal of her state of stimulation when she gave utterance to them in her hypnosis". In her turn his patient enthusiastically endorsed the theory, referring to the process as her "talking cure" or "chimney sweeping".

But judged by the overall situation the stories appear to have been of short-term benefit at best. Breuer states the procedure started during "the early period before she began talking English only", which would date it to some time before March 1881. We learn from the *Studies*, however, that though her squint and contractures improved after that date, the patient's psychic condition deteriorated steadily. Strong suicidal impulses appeared, necessitating her removal to a villa in the grounds of an asylum at Inzersdorf under the care of the psychiatrists of that institution. There Breuer visited her every few days, when "he relieved her of the whole stock of imaginative products" which she had "accumulated" since his last visit. But several attempts at suicide occurred, which Breuer does not elaborate, and episodic violence when she smashed windows. She would fly from hallucinatory dangers, climbing trees in an effort to escape them. When she returned to Vienna in the autumn and the former regime of daily story-taking was resumed, Breuer was disappointed with her response. In fact a definite deterioration had occurred which he was unable to explain. She now began to experience a curious aberration of memory, hallucinating the old room she had had the previous year and re-living events from that year, events which Breuer confirmed from her mother's diary. The change-over from one state to another occurred spontaneously but could also be easily brought about by any sense-impression which vividly recalled the previous year. "One had only to hold up an orange before her eyes (oranges were what she had chiefly lived on during the first part of her illness) in order to carry her over from the year 1882 to 1881." This would seem to have been an interesting example of a psychomotor seizure reflexly precipitated by a memory cue.

It must have appeared to Breuer a vindication of his faith in the Aristotelian theory when what appeared to him as the first cathartic cure of an individual symptom occurred. It happened during the hot summer of 1881 when his patient developed symptoms suggestive of hydrophobia. Though suffering from intense thirst she was unable to drink. As soon as the glass touched her lips, Breuer recalls, she "would push it away like someone suffering from hydrophobia". As she did this, he continues, "she was obviously in an *absence* for a couple of minutes". To ease her thirst she lived almost exclusively on fruits such as melons. This had lasted for six weeks when one evening during her "autohypnosis" she mentioned to Breuer her disgust about the little dog of her English lady-companion whom she had seen drinking water from the glass of its mistress. She had said nothing at the time as she had wanted to be polite. "After giving further energetic expression to the anger she had held back," wrote Breuer, "she asked for something to drink, drank a large quantity of water without any difficulty and woke from her hypnosis with the glass on her lips; and thereupon the disturbance vanished, never to return."

This incident signalled the start of the "cathartic cure" proper, a systematic procedure aimed at the eradication of individual symptoms by causing the patient to describe under hypnosis the experiences which had first allegedly given rise to them. In this way, Breuer claimed, a number of "extremely obstinate whims" were removed. But the incident requires further examination. The sight of an animal eating or drinking from a vessel intended for human use is surely a frequent one. This commonplace incident was alleged to be responsible for an aversion to water so great as to give the patient a thirst described as "tormenting". Hydrophobia, as it occurs as the most prominent symptom of rabies, is caused by spasm of the pharynx and larynx precipitated by the attempt to take fluids. A similar spasm occurs in the rare form of reflex epilepsy which is precipitated by eating or drinking. It is probable that Bertha's hydrophobia was also of this variety. The fact that when the glass touched her lips she would fall into an *absence* for a couple of seconds would support this view. She was already in the recovery stage of the initial focal lesions when the symptom disappeared and its disappearance was probably nothing more than part of the same recovery process.

Encouraged by this incident, however, Breuer began to actively pursue this line of therapy. Physician and patient now began an intensive collaboration in which each individual symptom was investigated separately under hypnosis in an effort to discover the first provoking cause of the disability. In her waking state, Breuer claimed, Bertha had no knowledge of such causes. It is interesting too that it proved impossible to shorten the work by trying to elicit from her the first provoking cause straight away. "She was unable to find it, grew confused, and things proceeded even more slowly than if she was allowed quietly and steadily to follow back the thread of memories on which she had embarked." Thus she had to proceed in reverse chronological order and one is reminded of a patient described by the famous epileptologist W. A. Lennox (1960). For many years her convulsions had been precipitated by the same aura, a remembrance of a past event. This remembrance would be repeated in flashlike succession and the patient termed them "flashes" though afterwards could not recall what she had remembered.

> "Finally, one day, when reading in bed with a temperature of 102°, she encountered a picture of spools of thread. 'Immediately, the flashes started and kept on till they finally stopped (and what a strange feeling) to the memory of when I was a child and we would use a wooden spool with nails in one end to crochet with'."

By means of these "autohypnoses" supplemented by artificial hypnosis induced by methods arrived at empirically, a number of incidents alleged to have been precipitating causes of Bertha's symptoms were elucidated. Her visual disturbances were, for instance, traced to an occasion when

> "sitting by her father's bedside with tears in her eyes he suddenly asked her what time it was. She could not see clearly; she made a great effort, and brought her watch near to her eyes. The face of the watch now seemed very big – thus accounting for her macropsia and convergent squint. Or again, she tried hard to suppress her tears so that the sick man should not see them."

One is struck by Breuer's confidence in his patient's ability to discover under hypnosis the cause of her illness. Another remarkable feature is the extreme triviality of the events allegedly responsible for the onset of the patient's severe symptoms. This Breuer himself admitted. Their very insignificance, he claimed, argued in favour of their reality, i.e., not invented. But this does not validate them as actual precipitants. Nor does the fact that the incidents were remembered under hypnosis give them greater validity than if they had been recalled in the normal state. Here Breuer seems to have fallen victim to the superstitious beliefs surrounding the mysterious trance state which had existed since the time of the ancients who had attributed to trance subjects the gifts of prophecy and divination. Both he and his patient regarded her illness as a psychogenic one, and it was natural that the patient should direct her memory – enhanced in this case, under hypnosis – to a psychogenic cause. Such rationalisations were extremely common at the time. Even today patients will try to trace the onset of an undoubted physical illness to a previous stressful event in their lives, often for the reason that the milder symptoms of the disease may have passed unnoticed until the distressful event causes them to pay more attention to their bodily state. Often the time-scale will be inappropriate – an infectious disease with a long incubation period, for instance, will be attributed to an event of the same day as its onset, or the effects of a slowly growing tumour which would have been present for some years before the initial symptoms, to a stress incurred the day before.

A typical example from the nineteenth century is reported in *The Practitioner* of 1890 under the heading *Acromegaly following Fright* by a Professor Pel of Amsterdam. A twenty-five-year-old woman had been admitted under his care in October 1890 with enlargement of the hands, feet and face and with amenorrhoea (cessation of menstrual periods) dating from March the previous year. This date coincided with a fall down a flight of steps; missing her footing in the dark, the patient had been caught up by a passing man. "Thinking she was attacked by him she shook herself loose and ran home, where she fell on the floor weeping," reads the report. "From that moment she became ill." Acromegaly is caused by excessive secretion of the growth hormone produced by the pituitary gland. The hands and feet become massive and square, and there is thickening and coarsening of the features, especially of the eyebrows, nose, lips and jaw. The fact that the patient's periods had ceased indicates also hypersecretion of prolactin, another pituitary hormone. The most likely cause for both these conditions would be a pituitary tumour which must have been gradually enlarging long before its effects became manifest, as a quite high level of prolactin would be required to cause amenorrhoea. Both growth hormone and prolactin were unknown at that time. Pel's acceptance of his patient's interpretation was therefore highly uncritical; Breuer's acceptance of Bertha Pappenheim's explanations was equally so, with the same inherent fallacy.

At the beginning of June 1882, Bertha entered into the "talking cure" with the greatest energy as she was determined that the treatment should be finished on the anniversary of the day in which she moved into the country (June 7, 1881). On the last day, therefore, with the room rearranged so as to resemble her father's sick room, she reproduced the episode which according to Breuer "constituted the root of her whole illness". It had happened in July 1880, long before her illness became manifest and while she was still helping to nurse her father. Her mother had gone away to rest and Bertha was sitting at the bedside of her father, who was in a high fever. A surgeon from Vienna was expected, presumably to incise the abscess. Her right arm over the back of the chair had gone to sleep and had become anaesthetic and paretic; when she looked at it the fingers turned into little snakes with death's heads replacing the nails.

> "When the snake vanished, in her terror she tried to pray, but language failed her: she could find no tongue in which to speak, till at last she thought of some children's verses in English and then found herself able to think and pray in that language. The whistle of the train that was bringing the doctor whom she expected broke the spell."

This version is an interesting rationalisation of what must have been the patient's first seizure, manifested by aphasia with paralysis of the *right* arm and hallucinations, and an altered state of consciousness brought to an end by the stimulus of the train whistle. It had probably been precipitated by another whistle of the same train.

After the reproduction of this episode in her hypnosis, Breuer states, she was able to speak German and was freed from "the innumerable disturbances which she had previously exhibited". Furthermore, he claimed, each individual symptom, when it had been traced back to the event that had originally started it, was "permanently removed" when given verbal utterance in hypnosis. After this final episode, he says, Bertha "left Vienna and travelled for a while; but it was a considerable time before she regained her mental balance entirely. Since then she has enjoyed complete health."

In actual fact, Bertha was transferred to the Bellevue sanatorium. Her deplorable state of health at the time is evident from the sanatorium case-notes. A letter from Breuer to Dr Binswanger arranging the transfer states that his patient was in a state of "hysterical insanity". A preliminary report sent by Breuer at the end of June 1882 discloses that Bertha had been having severe fits which had begun with chorea minor and increased to the most severe "rolling convulsions" only controllable by heavy doses of morphine, in addition to the large doses of chloral she had already been receiving. She was evidently still having hallucinations and trances, since Breuer advocated cold showers or rubbing down as hot baths had the effect of producing these hallucinatory states. Weaning her from morphine and the danger of addiction was now an anxious preoccupation of her family.

Bertha had arrived at the sanatorium in a pitiable state from the effects of drugs and a most painful trigeminal neuralgia, still with her trances and hallucinations and still with the most prominent and persistent feature of her illness, her dysphasia – the report of the sanatorium doctor specifically mentions "the loss of her native language in the evening". This phenomenon occurred regularly every evening on laying down – "as soon as her head had touched the pillow, she neither spoke nor understood German". He adds an interesting detail. "If in laying down her head she was still speaking German she ended the sentence she had begun in English." Her morphine addiction presented the most acute problem of her management, since for a long time any attempt at withdrawal produced a renewal of the convulsions. It must have been thanks to her careful treatment at the sanatorium and a healthy regime which included outdoor exercise – hence her photograph in riding habit – that she gradually recovered and it was possible progressively to reduce the dosages of her drugs. On October 29, 1882 she became fit enough to be discharged to the care of relatives living close by in Carlsruhr. A letter from a cousin there to Dr Binswanger dated January 4, 1883 states that she was still occasionally lapsing into English in the evenings.

A poignant testimony to the fact that Breuer's treatment had *not* cured her of her main symptom exists in a document in English written by Bertha herself, and found in her case-notes at the sanatorium. It dates from September 1882.

"I, a native German girl, am now totally deprived of the faculty to speak, to understand or to read German. This symptom lasted during the time of a heavy nervous illness, I had to go through, in permanence longer than a year; since about 4 months it only returns regularly every evening. The physicians point it out as something very strange but rarely to be observed; therefore I will try to give, as well, as a person who never has made any medical studies, can do, a short account of my own observations and experiences considering this terrible estate.

It appears quite suddenly without the slightest transaction in the very moment I recline in my bed, independent from the hour, which I have varied already between 9 o'clock in the evening till 1 a.m. Two days I had once been obliged to stay in bed for some other little unease, and then the phase begun at 10 o'clock. For some hours then I am perfectly unable to communicate anything in German, whilst the other languages, which I have learned later, are present to my mind, and the English I can use nearly to perfection."

No symptoms accompanied the change – "The whole going on it not accompanied from the slightest physik sensation; no pain, no oppression or giddyness are to be felt" – the whole process would have passed unnoticed but for the fact that "I do not understand my servant nor am I understood". She herself confirms the fact that she was still having trance-like episodes when she arrived at the institution: "In the first 2 months of my sojourn here, I had shorter or longer absences, which I could observe myself by a strange feeling of 'timemissing' one told me that I used to speak with great vivacity during this absences, but since some weeks there have been none."

Freud's version of the termination of Breuer's involvement with the case as retold by Jones is completely negated by the correspondence found in the sanatorium case-notes. The letters present the picture of an orderly transfer planned ahead, the details of the patient's condition, drug dosages and special requirements being sent on ahead of her arrival. Why had Freud given such a deceptive account of the affair, and why had both he and Breuer concealed the fact that Bertha had not been cured by the cathartic method, a fact that, as amply documented by Dr Hirschmuller in his biography of Breuer, was well known to both men? The report of her case published six years later in the famous *Studies in Hysteria* omitted to disclose this fact. From its publication in 1895 till Jung's revelation in 1925, a period of thirty years, the case had been passed off as the perfect prototype of a cathartic cure.

The inconvenient fact of the persistence of the patient's symptoms, however, failed to deter Freud. Still under the influence of Charcot's teaching that emotional trauma could cause bodily disease, he began, in 1889, to use the cathartic method to bring these traumas to light, working in collaboration with Breuer on cases of "hysteria" referred by the latter. These cases, along with that of Bertha Pappenheim, were eventually reported in the *Studies in Hysteria*. As we shall see, in these patients too, no cure was effected.

PART 2

Strange Harvest

IX

The Nasal Reflex Neurosis

We come now to the watershed years of Freud's career, the period roughly spanning the last eight or nine years of the nineteenth century, when the major theories now associated with his name came to be formulated. During these years the theoretical foundations of psychoanalysis were laid and Freud's orientation underwent a radical change with the adoption of his theory of the sexual origins of the neuroses, culminating in the concept of the Oedipus complex in 1897.

The change was an abrupt one. At the end of the eighties, Freud was a respected member of the younger professional classes, a *Privatdozent* of the University of Vienna, honorary consultant to the Institute for Children's Diseases, and director of its neurology department. In his published papers he had made respectable contributions to the neurology of his day. An accomplished neuroanatomist, his technical mastery was said to be unsurpassed. A happily married man with a rapidly growing family to support, he was actively engaged in building up a private practice in diseases of the nervous system. In his personal life and outlook he conformed to the conventional morality of his day, if anything leaning towards conservatism and orthodoxy, a trait that first became evident during his student days with his censorship of the reading matter of his young sisters. As recently as 1885, when his fiancée announced her intention of visiting an old friend who had "married before her wedding", Freud had sternly forbidden such moral contamination. Now only eight years later he was advocating the complete overthrow of all conventional sexual morality.

From about 1893 onwards, a perceptible change is detectable in Freud's published papers. Up to the early nineties his scientific writings were lucid and concise. Though sometimes misled in their conclusions, they conformed to the state of knowledge then extant. Only a few years later we find papers of extraordinary prolixity, indefinite and inconsistent and containing a disproportionate amount of speculation and theory, much of it involved, strained and contrived. And yet with all their wordiness, it is a surprising fact that they contain no information whatever about what had induced Freud to adopt his sexual theory; though claiming sexual factors to be at the root of all neuroses, he provided no case histories or other evidence in support of this belief. After reading these papers one is still in ignorance as to what had caused Freud to formulate these views. Freud's later accounts are hardly more informative. His *Autobiographical Study* merely states:

> "I now learned from my rapidly increasing experience that it was not any kind of emotional excitation that was in action behind the phenomena of neurosis, but habitually one of a sexual nature, whether it was a current sexual conflict or the effect of earlier sexual experience. I was not prepared for this conclusion and my expectations played no part in it for I had begun my investigation of neurotics quite unsuspectingly."

In his *History of the Psychoanalytical Movement* (1914) Freud is still less informative, quoting chance remarks by Charcot, among others, as implanting the first seeds of the sexual theory in his mind. Here his memory had played him false. He himself had, on his return from Paris in 1886, read a paper specifically reiterating Charcot's often expressed opinion that there was no connection between hysteria and the genital organs and with the implication of his own tacit agreement. Freud had, too, in his paper *The Aetiology of Hysteria* of 1896 denied any preconceptions in singling out the sexual factor, declaring, "The two investigators as whose pupil I began my work on the subject, Charcot and Breuer, emphatically had no such presupposition; in face, they had a personal disinclination to it which I originally shared." On page 259 of the *Studies*, he explicitly states, "I had come fresh from the school of Charcot, and I regarded the linking of hysteria with the topic of sexuality as a sort of insult." Why then did he name Charcot as one of those who had implanted the idea of the theory in his mind? Charcot had been dead for many years by the time of Freud's attribution, but there is ample evidence in his published lectures of his rejection of a sexual aetiology for hysteria. Moreover, Freud's description of the occasion when Charcot allegedly made the remark which led him to the sexual theory seems highly uncharacteristic of the austere Charcot and altogether more reminiscent of the stock stage Frenchman.

> "For Charcot suddenly broke out with great animation: '*Mais, dans des cas pareils c'est toujours la chose genitale, toujours – toujours – toujours*'; and he crossed his arms over his stomach, hugging himself and jumping up and down on his toes several

times in his own characteristically lively way. I know that for a moment I was almost paralysed with amazement and said to myself: 'Well, but if he knows that, why does he never say so?' "

So, without case histories, or other corroborative evidence, we are left with the surprising fact that his published works contain no reliable information as to what had led Freud to adopt the sexual theory, or to explain the abruptness of his reorientation.

The mystery deepens when we learn from his biographer, Ernest Jones, that this period (1892–1900) coincided almost exactly with the time when Freud underwent a marked personality change and that during just these years he suffered from a "very considerable psychoneurosis, characterised by swings of mood from extreme exhilaration to profound depression and twilight states of consciousness;" that over the same period he developed unexplained cardiac symptoms with irregularity and rapidity of the heart's action; that he suffered from a strange entity called the "nasal reflex neurosis" and that he conceived a violent hatred for his old friend Breuer and concomitantly an intense admiration for and devotion to a rather strange man with even stranger theories. Finally, though by this time sex had become the cornerstone of his system he himself had, by the end of this period, virtually ceased any practice of it.

If Freud's own accounts and his published papers give no indication as to his reasons for the adoption of his sexual theories, we are fortunate in having another and contemporary source of information. By a strange stroke of fate, the whole of this period has been illuminated by a long-forgotten packet of letters which only came to light after Freud's death. Written by Freud to his closest friend and confidant, Wilhelm Fliess, over the years 1892 to 1902, this hitherto unknown correspondence forms a unique record of this critical period of Freud's life. The letters hold the vital missing pieces in the puzzle, explaining both the deterioration in his health and the abrupt reorientation in his thinking. Some time after Fliess' death, his widow sold Freud's letters to a Mr Stahl, a Berlin bookseller, on the express condition that they were not to pass to Freud himself. Jones surmised that, sharing her husband's hostility to Freud after the eventual estrangement of the two men, she shrewdly guessed that he would immediately destroy them if they passed into his hands. That her supposition was correct is evident from Freud's reactions when, in 1936, he was appraised of their reappearance by one of his most devoted disciples, Marie Bonaparte. An analyst in her own right and a Princess of Greece and Denmark, she had been offered the letters in Paris by the bookseller, who had fled there from the Nazis just before the war. Her correspondence with Freud on the subject was published by Max Schur in 1965. On December 30, 1936, she wrote about Stahl's offer. "He has obtained from Fliess's widow your letters and manuscripts belonging to Fliess's estate," she said. "At first the widow wanted to deposit the whole thing in the National Library of Prussia, but as your works have been burned in Germany, she gave up the idea and sold the manuscript in question to this Mr Stahl, a writer and art dealer, who makes a very favourable impression . . . I decided to buy them all from him." The news evidently caused Freud some perturbation. On January 3, 1937 he wrote;

> "The matter of the correspondence with Fliess has stirred me deeply. After his death the widow requested the return of his letters to me and I agreed without question, but was unable to find them. I don't know till this very day whether I destroyed them, or only hid them ingeniously . . . Our correspondence was of the most intimate nature, as you can surmise. It would have been most painful to have it fall into the hands of strangers. It is, therefore, an extraordinary labour of love that you have got hold of them and removed them from danger. I only regret the expense you've incurred. May I offer to share half of it with you? I would have had to acquire the letters myself if the man had approached me directly. I don't want any of them to become known to so-called posterity . . ."

But Freud had not reckoned with the obstinacy of his usually docile disciple. His offer was refused. "The letters and manuscripts have been offered to me on condition that I not sell them, either directly or indirectly, to the Freud family," she wrote, "for fear that this material, which is so important for the history of psychoanalysis, will be destroyed." She also reiterated her own aversion to the destruction of his letters and manuscripts. "Perhaps you yourself . . . do not perceive your full greatness," she said. "You belong to the history of human thought, like Plato, should we say, or Goethe." She was sure there could be nothing in the letters that could lower the stature of her mentor, and she reminded him that he himself had written "a beautiful paper opposing the idealisation at any cost of great men, mankind's great father figures". Some of the history of psychoanalysis which was "more important than Plato's theory of ideas" would be lost if the material were destroyed because of a few personal remarks contained in the letters.

The main body of the correspondence was still in Berlin and this news caused Freud some anxiety. "Naturally it's all right with me if you don't read the letters either," he replied, "but you should not assume that they contain no more than a good deal of indiscretion. In view of the intimate nature of our relationship these letters cover all kinds of things, factual as well as personal topics; and the factual ones, which indicate all the presentiments and blind alleys of the budding psychoanalysts, are also quite personal in this case . . . For these reasons, it would be so desirable for me to know that this material was in your hands . . ."

Arriving in Vienna with the letters, now all in her possession, Marie Bonaparte remained obdurate against Freud's insistence that they should be destroyed. Convinced that they must be preserved for posterity, she deposited the correspondence unread in the Rothschild Bank of Vienna during the winter of 1937–8 intending to study them fully on her return in the summer. Her plans were, however, disrupted by the Nazi invasion of Austria in March. The Rothschild Bank was a Jewish one and, as such, liable to confiscation. It became urgently necessary to retrieve the letters. Hurrying to Vienna, she used her rank as Princess of Greece and Denmark to obtain them and they were handed over to her in the presence of the Gestapo, who would surely have seized them if they had known whose they were. When she had to leave Paris, which was about to be invaded, in February 1941, she deposited the letters for safe keeping with the Danish legation in Paris. Fortunately, Paris escaped bombardment during the German invasion and, wrapped in waterproof and buoyant material, the letters eventually survived the perilous journey across the mine-filled English Channel. Thus this invaluable collection of source material survived.

In London, the letters were transcribed and a selection for publication was made by Anna Freud, Freud's youngest daughter, by then a considerable psychoanalyst in her own right, and another analyst, Ernst Kris. This selection was published in 1950 in Germany and in 1954 in England under the title *The Origins of Psycho-Analysis: Letters to Wilhelm Fliess, Drafts and Notes; 1887–1902* (hereinafter referred to as the *Origins*). The selection was made, according to the editor's note, "on the principle of making public everything relating to the writer's scientific work and everything bearing on the social and political conditions in which psychoanalysis originated; and of omitting or abbreviating everything, publication of which would be inconsistent with professional or personal confidence". It soon emerged that the selection printed in the *Origins* fell far short of the principles quoted above. Extracts of letters included in the biographies of

Ernest Jones and Max Schur (both of whom had access to the full correspondence) which had *not* been published in the *Origins* suggested that much relating to Freud's scientific work, some of it of vital importance, had been omitted from that book. Thereafter, the letters were impounded in the Freud Archive in Washington and a moratorium imposed which forbids access to them until the end of the century without the express permission of the Freud family. The embargo has been extended to serious researchers and historians. Writers of the calibre of Ellenberger, Roazen, Sulloway and Clark, authors of major works on Freud in the last decades have been denied access to the correspondence.

Not surprisingly, an aura of mystery has grown up around the letters. It has been pointed out that of the two hundred and eighty-four letters and drafts available, only one hundred and fifty-three were quoted and of these, one hundred and nineteen published with cuts, some of which, amplified in the biographies of Jones and Schur, are shown to have been important and significant. Accusations of censorship have been levelled. "What have the Freud family got to hide?" asked a recent reviewer. This kind of accusation will only be refuted by the lifting of the embargo to serious researchers and historians and those not of psychoanalytical persuasion alone. As it is, the complete correspondence has only been made available to two authors of published biographies, Jones and Schur, both friends and disciples of Freud, and friends of the Freud family, and it is from their accounts and from the *Origins* that the facts that follow have been gleaned. There are, however, enough clues in these sources to lead eventually to the complete solution to the many enigmatic aspects of the Freud story.

Ernest Jones was in a unique position to write his definitive biography of Freud. One of the inner circle of prominent analysts who surrounded Freud, and by far the greatest intellect amongst them, he was, of course, a personal friend of Freud and his family. Born in Wales in 1879, his medical career showed early promise of a brilliant future. Qualifying at twenty-one, he passed his membership examination of the Royal College of Physicians at the age of twenty-four. Honours, gold medals and coveted junior hospital appointments, in the first steps towards his chosen goal of becoming a consultant neurologist, fell easily into his lap. Everything seemed set fair for a brilliant future, but it was not to be. As he freely admits in his autobiography, *Free Associations*, youthful arrogance and tactlessness in his hospital work had offended important colleagues as well as ward sisters and the matron. A technical misdemeanour gave his enemies the opportunity to act and he was forced to resign his hospital appointment, now with a permanent label of being "difficult", which , in the small medical world of London in those days, followed him wherever he went. He earned his living as best he could, becoming a school medical officer, coaching, invigilating at examinations. He gave first aid lectures to the police, and even, having taught himself shorthand, reported medical conferences. In his spare time he studied statistics, publishing several papers on the subject. He began to slowly climb the ladder again, at last securing a part-time appointment at the West End Hospital for Nervous Diseases, London, which would have eventually led to promotion to the permanent staff. The future was beginning to look more hopeful when disaster again struck. A child at a school for mental defectives, which he attended in his capacity as school medical officer, made a complaint that he had behaved indecently with her. The magistrate dismissed the charge, but Jones resumed his professional life under no illusion that life would henceforth be the same. Two years later a further disaster occurred which signalled the end of his medical career in England. It happened at the West End Hospital for Nervous Diseases and coincided with his growing interest in Freud's theory of hysteria. A case in the wards diagnosed as hysterical paralysis of the arm seemed to resemble some of the cases described by Freud and Jones questioned the patient as to the origin of her symptoms. She told the other children in the ward that the doctor had been talking to her about sexual matters and her incensed father complained to the hospital board. For the second time in his life, Jones had to appear before the hospital committee and tender his resignation. The doors of orthodox medicine in London were now finally closed to him.

To Jones, psychoanalysis was a lifeline, bringing to the former pariah friendship, colleagues, approval. Hence his emotional involvement with Freud and his movement was great. With the help of patients referred to him by Freud, he was able to set up a successful psychoanalytic practice in London. Making frequent visits to Vienna, he rapidly became one of the influential inner circle surrounding Freud. Other psychoanalytic leaders defected one by one, first Adler, then Jung, then most of the other members of the circle, but Jones remained steadfastly loyal. His biography, highly biased towards Freud and his theories, appeared in three volumes in the years that spanned the Freudian centenary and introduced a new generation to psychoanalysis. It contributed more perhaps than any other influence to the Freudian revolution that followed. But whatever the effect of the final product, one must acknowledge the "dauntingly stupendous task" he undertook in compiling this definitive biography, a task which involved the examination of over five thousand letters, contemporary records, and a study of the entire three million words of Freud's published works.

Freud's other main biographer, Max Schur, had as a medical student attended the original introductory lectures in psychoanalysis given by Freud in Vienna in 1915. A fellow student at the course was Anna Freud. After qualifying he became a general practitioner in Vienna for a decade. In 1932 he underwent a personal analysis, by that time a requisite for the practice of psychoanalysis, and was accepted as a member of the Vienna Psychoanalytic Society. He had already, on the recommendation of Marie Bonaparte, become Freud's personal physician in 1928. Schur eventually came to England with Freud after the Nazi invasion of Austria, taking care of him during his last painful illness. After Freud's death, Schur emigrated to the United States and became a prominent figure in psychoanalytic circles. Having read the whole of the Fliess correspondence, his book *Freud: Living and Dying* (1972) contains extracts not previously published in the *Origins* or by Ernest Jones which are more illuminating than he had probably ever realised.

Reading the Fliess correspondence, Ernest Jones was confronted with an entirely different Freud from the man he had known in later years. Plainly amazed that his hero should have developed such a close friendship with a man "so intellectually his inferior" and had, moreover, for so long subordinated his own opinions to those of his friend, Jones contrived an elaborate psychoanalytical explanation which need not concern us here. Others have evinced equal mystification and remarked on the enigmatic features surrounding the friendship of the two men. Their reactions will be better understood when we learn more about Fliess and the opinions he held.

Wilhelm Fliess (1858–1928) was then an ambitious young nose-and-throat specialist practising in Berlin. Visiting Vienna in 1887 for postgraduate study, he attended a course of lectures given at the university by Freud on the anatomy and physiology of the nervous system. The two men became friends and corresponded occasionally on professional matters, but when Fliess married a Viennese girl in October, 1892, a circumstance leading to frequent visits to Vienna, the acquaintance deepened into closer friendship. The two had much in common, both were young, ambitious, professional men of the Jewish middle class in the early years of married life, both engaged in building up a practice and raising a family. By a strange coincidence both suffered severely

Freud and Fliess in the nineties.

from migraine. Both, and here coincidence ends, later developed severe nasal trouble and underwent frequent cauterisations and other surgical procedures.

The close friendship was continued by letter when Fliess later returned to Berlin with his bride in October 1892, a correspondence which was interspersed by frequent meetings in intermediate places to discuss each other's scientific interests – their "congresses" as they used to call them. The two men rapidly became close confidants, both being extremely receptive to each other's scientific ideas. As during these years both were producing theories that became increasingly bizarre, one might suppose that each had stretched the other's credulity to the utmost. Such, however, is not the case – each man received from the other the most extravagant praise. In particular, Freud's reception of Fliess's theories were a mixture of awed respect and wonder. What were these theories and why did Freud accept them so uncritically?

Though the correspondence reveals that Fliess had formulated these theories as early as 1892, their full exposition in print was not until 1897 when, in a monograph of extreme volubility, he announced the discovery of a new syndrome – the nasal reflex neurosis. He described how, on a dull winter's day in February, while sitting in his bath, a man entered the room to inspect the gas installation. As he bent forward the man appeared unsteady. Holding onto the wall he wiped the perspiration from his brow. Questioned by Fliess the plumber admitted to almost uninterrupted vertigo and on further interrogation confessed to back pain, aching in the right scapula and sternum, an oppressive sensation in the heart, digestive disturbances and insomnia with "anxious dreams". He also admitted to an intolerance of liquor or beer. So astonished was the plumber that Fliess had so accurately elucidated his symptoms, he asked for a professional consultation – all previous examinations had failed to disclose the cause of his troubles. "For me," wrote Fliess, "the diagnosis was clear." Seating the plumber under a lamp in his consulting room, he found a considerable swelling in the lower part of the septum of the nose near to the *tuberculum septum*. An application of cocaine to this spot caused the headache and vertigo immediately to vanish, breathing improved and the pressure around his heart disappeared. The diagnosis was confirmed. The man was clearly suffering from the "nasal reflex neurosis".

Fliess had, by this time, among his "thousands of patients" discovered over one hundred and thirty cases of the syndrome. The main features were headache, dizziness and vertigo, acceleration and irregularity of the action of the heart and respiratory difficulties. Neuralgic pains of shoulders, ribs and chest, together with sensations of pressure on the heart or lower chest, back or abdomen were also present. In addition there was an intolerance of all forms of alcohol. Later papers reiterated with increasing confidence Fliess' conviction that migraine, vertigo, asthma and hay fever were also associated with nasal pathology. But, with what was to have a much more far-reaching effect, he declared that symptoms relating to the uterus, such as dysmenorrhoea (painful menstruation) and repeated abortions, also had their origin in that organ. Examination of the nose in all these conditions, he claimed, invariably revealed swelling of the mucosa, though he admitted that this varied in intensity depending on the perfusion of blood so that sometimes no swelling was visible. The reflex-producing spot, he claimed, was abnormally sensitive, bleeding easily if examined with a probe. The most characteristic feature of the syndrome was the fact that all the symptoms could be temporarily diminished by anaesthetising the responsible areas of the nose with cocaine. The fact that they disappeared together,

Fliess claimed, proved that the symptoms were all part of the same complex. The most frequent cause of the neurosis was nasal swelling, but it could also originate in a polyp or bony deviation of the septum and could be cured by removal of these.

The "nasal reflex neurosis" is not to be found in the medical text-books today, but it looms large in the Fliess correspondence. It was evidently a subject of enormous importance to both Freud and Fliess, one which has never been adequately dealt with by Freud's biographers. Jones skates over the whole subject, dismissing it in a few sentences. Schur discusses it in more detail, though mistakenly adopting the view that Fliess was treating the nose as a "septic focus" – a focus of chronic infection which allegedly poisoned the whole body, leading to general ill-health and debility. The "septic focus" theory was fashionable in the early decades of the present century, many years after Fliess formulated the theory. Though not now considered tenable, it enjoyed an enormous vogue for some years. One of the foremost exponents of the theory was Sir William Wilcox of St Mary's Hospital, London, who believed that most illnesses derived from focal sepsis. As a result, hundreds of normal teeth were needlessly extracted. The young William Sargant, then one of his assistants, related that one of his jobs was to try to explain to patients why their good teeth had to come out when Sir William's own filthy teeth stayed in. The theory, however, made large fortunes for many physicians before it was eventually discredited. But Fliess's theories were formed long before the era of the septic focus vogue.

What, then, was the "nasal reflex neurosis"? The answer is simple. Fliess had omitted to ascertain the pharmocological properties of cocaine. In fact, at that time there were few data on the precise effect of the mode of action of the drug. Contrary to its action on the unbroken skin, the application of cocaine to *mucous membranes*, such as those inside the nose, results in extremely speedy absorption. Entering the bloodstream the drug reaches the brain rapidly and practically unchanged. The effects Fliess attributed to reflex action were thus, in reality, those of the action of cocaine on the brain. The dramatic amelioration of the pains of such conditions as dysmenorrhoea or migraine by nasal applications of cocaine, resulted from the action of the drug on specific brain centres and had no connection with the nose itself. No reflex mechanism was therefore involved.

This was the golden age of the reflex. The controversies over Marshall Hall's pronouncements on the reflex action of the nervous system had died with the discovery that many ascending nerve tracts in the spine did not actually extend to the brain. Now, after the descriptions by Erb and Westphal in 1875 of the tendon reflexes, clinicians were vying with each other in discovering new reflexes – often where none actually existed. A cynical writer once estimated that by this time more reflexes had been described than there were muscles and nerves in the body. Sometimes there was only a limited understanding of what was actually implied by reflex action. "Will the knee jerk divide typhoid fever from meningitis?" asked a Dr Money in the *Lancet* of May 21, 1887. So reflexes were very much to the forefront in the medical fashions of the day. Fliess had probably been introduced to cocaine anaesthesia for nasal procedures during his earlier visit to Vienna in 1887. In the course of time, he would have observed the dramatic effect of the anaesthetic on the patients' other ailments concomitantly, such as migraine or hay fever, and introduced these patients to the regular use of cocaine. He would then have encountered the more chronic effects of this usage; believing that they originated in the nose, he named these the "nasal reflex neurosis". The diagnosis is actually to be found in the old ear-nose-and-throat text-books of the period and appears to have been adopted by many specialists.

From the effects of cocaine in the nose on the pains of dysmenorrhoea, Fliess deduced that there was a special reflex connection between the nose and the sexual organs. In support of this contention he cited the rare phenomenon of vicarious menstrual nose-bleeding, and claimed that the swelling of the turbinate bone during the menstrual period could be observed with the naked eye. He also reported cases in which an application of cocaine to the nose had led to miscarriage. From these observations he postulated the existence of "genital spots" in the nose around the *tubercula septi* where, he claimed, the reflex effects were generated. The spots were, of course, nothing but the areas to which he had applied cocaine. Once having assumed their existence, however, any real or imagined swelling of the "genital spots" became a diagnostic indication for the presence of the "nasal reflex neurosis", leading to the logical deduction that this was the cause of the patient's other concurrent complaints. The corollary was that these complaints had a sexual aetiology. Using the criteria of the "genital spots" he reached the conclusion that the reflex connection between the nose and the genital organs was present also in men. "I will only mention a recent case," he stated, "in which in a typical neurasthenic episode associated with ophthalmic migraine caused by onanistic abuse [masturbation], the nasal mucous membranes were very much swollen." To Fliess this explained why "neurasthenic complaints, in other words the neuroses with a sexual aetiology, so frequently take the form of the nasal reflex neurosis". Thus he had arrived at the far-reaching deduction that "*neurasthenic*" complaints, in which he evidently included migraine, were of a sexual origin. As we shall see, this had important implications for Freud's theories.

In his later monograph *The Relations between the Nose and the Female Sex Organs from the Biological Aspect* (1902), Fliess had already left reality behind and the work embodies the mysticism which characterised the new direction of his ideas. From the starting point of the effects of cocaine on the "genital spots", he traced a relationship between the nose and every variety of neurotic symptom and sexual irregularity. The corollary that these conditions should be treated by the nasal use of cocaine was also made. He was already making grandiose generalisations from these conclusions, declaring that menstruation was the prototype of numerous phenomena in sexual life and parturition nothing but a transmutation of the menstrual process. From the 28 days of the menstrual cycle he developed a mystical numerological pseudoscience, postulating a 28 and a 23 day cycle in all human beings, the male component being keyed to the 23 day and the female to the 28 day cycles, though the presence of the cycles indicated that every person was really bisexual, a concept later taken over by Freud. The two cycles played a didactic role in all living things and were present in every living cell. Both cycles started at birth, the sex of the child being determined by the cycle first transmitted. The periods continued throughout life, manifesting themselves in all life's fluctuations, eventually determining the date of death. From these "facts" he generalised to the entire universe, postulating an astronomical connection between the 28 and 23 day periods:

> "A mother transmits her periods to her child and determines its sex by the period first transmitted. The periods then continue in the child, and are repeated with the same rhythm from generation to generation. They can no more be created anew than can energy, and their rhythm continues to survive as long as organised beings reproduce themselves sexually. These rhythms are not restricted to mankind, but extend into the animal world and probably throughout the organic world. The wonderful accuracy with which the period of 23, or as the case may be, 28 whole days is observed permits one to suspect a deeper connection between astronomical relations and the creation of organisms."

Fliess's writings, we are informed, have now been consigned to "the realms of psychopathology". But it was a very special kind of psychopathology of which the above type of writing is highly characteristic. His works would be quite forgotten today, but for what has been called the "unbelievable fact" that Fliess was Freud's closest friend and confidant over the period compassing the entire reorientation of Freud's ideas towards the sexual aetiology discussed earlier. What was so difficult for Jones and Schur to believe was that not only did Freud fully subscribe to these bizarre theories, but greeted them with awed respect and admiration; the evidence clearly emanating from the newly emergent correspondence was irrefutable. However much his biographers tried to explain it away, the unpalatable fact had to be accepted that for many years Freud enthusiastically embraced a fantastic series of hypotheses of a highly pathological nature.

Fliess's theories were certainly strange. But, looked at in the cold dispassionate light of a non-analytical approach, are not Freud's theories, with their emphasis on infantile incestuous desires, death wishes and the concept of an unconscious mind dominated by dark and horrid phantasies, equally bizarre? Was not his teaching that all civilisation and all manifestations of human endeavour are the result of sexual sublimation a similar grandiose generalisation?

Not only did Fliess's theories present no difficulty to Freud, but his letters to his friend show many points of similarity to the writings of the former. A similarly mystical vein is strikingly present, for instance, in the letter of October 20, 1897, when, discussing the draft of a projected paper he was sending to Fliess for his approval, Freud said:

> "One evening last week when I was hard at work, tormented with just that amount of pain that seems to be the best state to make my brain function, the barriers were suddenly lifted, the veil drawn aside, and I had a clear vision from the details of the neuroses to the conditions that make consciousness possible. Everything seemed to connect up . . ."

A month later, he was telling Fliess that he did not understand the state of mind in which he had produced the draft. "I cannot conceive how I came to inflict it on you," he said, "it seems to me to have been a kind of aberration."

Passages such as the above give a distinct sensation of *déjà vu*. Where does one most often find that characteristic mystical conviction that the riddles of life have suddenly become instantly comprehensible with the effect of the drawing aside of a veil? The illusion of sudden confrontation with ultimate truth appears in the literature of drug taking from De Quincey to Leary, from opium to LSD. It has unfortunately been the lure which has enticed many into bondage to one or other of these powerful drugs, a deceptive lure because the feeling is entirely subjective and spurious, one of the many false perceptions that can occur when the brain is subject to the action of a highly toxic substance. Perhaps the best example of the falsity of the "ultimate truth" revealed by these drugs is that found in the autobiography of Captain H. R. Robinson, who became addicted to opium in the years after the First World War.

A young ex-army officer, disbanded in 1921 after war-time service on the north-west frontier of India, he broke his journey home in Mandalay. It was a fateful decision. Moved by curiosity, he one night visited an opium den and partook of the forbidden drug. Two nights later he returned; soon he was a regular visitor. He cancelled his passage home and took a bungalow in the city. The months drifted by. He was now smoking nightly but it was always in the back of his mind that he could stop whenever he wished. But when the testing time came he realised too late that his bondage was complete. He had, out of curiosity, entered "a web as tangible as smoke, but stronger than any fetters forged by human hand". The final outcome was tragic. His funds running low, and creditors clamouring for settlement, every rupee he could scrape together went towards the purchase of opium. His Burmese friends deserted him. Appeals to friends and relatives in England, formerly fruitful, now brought no results. To raise the money for opium his furniture, Persian carpets, Japanese scrolls, anything saleable was sold. About to be arrested for non-payment of debts, he made a fateful decision. He was not going to prison. Too many times in the past had he heard the howls of imprisoned men deprived of opium. There was only one thing to do. Making an excuse to the police officers waiting to take him away, he went into the next room and shot himself through the head. He recovered consciousness to find he had only succeeded in blinding himself. But the shock of the experience had at last freed him from his bondage and he had no regrets.

It was the pursuit of an elusive opium "dream" which had lured him to the den night after night and ultimately sealed his fate.

"I dreamed that I was travelling through a vast unknown jungle. I was on a pilgrimage to some ancient and forgotten temple. The jungle and the path were not familiar to me, but for some unaccountable reason I thought it must be Malaya or Indo-China. As I neared the ancient temple I was met by a beautiful brown-skinned girl, the daughter of the old priest whom I had travelled so far to see. There was something that I was to receive from this old man, something very precious. The girl led me through the crumbling gates of the old city to the stone cell in which she and her father lived. As I entered the open door, I saw the old priest lying apparently asleep on the couch. But he was not asleep – he was dead. He had died, the girl explained, about two days previously, but he had known of my search and what it was for which I was searching. It was the key to the mystery of life, the final answer to the eternal 'Why'? He had written the secret on a slip of parchment which the girl was to remove from his dead hand and give to me on my arrival. I took the slip from the girl's hand and read. Of course, of course, why had man never thought of that before? Now I knew, but . . .

. . . When I woke next morning I had completely forgotten. Every detail of the dream was clear to me except the actual words which I had read on the parchment."

This recurrent dream continued to tantalise him for several weeks. It had only occurred to him after taking opium. Through its constant repetition every detail was familiar except the secret itself. One night he determined to make a supreme effort to wake himself before the memory of the words had faded and to write them down before falling asleep again. The difficulty was to rouse himself sufficiently from his stupour to do so. However, he placed a pencil and pad on a low table close to his head.

"The pleasant languor began to permeate my body until, very soon, I felt that I was no longer bound by any ties of the flesh. Then the dream began to form before my eyes: the jungle, the girl, the temple, the cell, the dead man, the parchment. I read, woke and with a superhuman effort of will-power, I forced my opium-soaked body to turn until my hand found the pencil and pad, and then, by the light of the moon, I wrote it down . . . My object achieved, I fell back and knew no more until I awoke in the morning. The dream was still vivid in my mind up to the point of reading the script, and it was a minute or two before I remembered the pad which I had placed by my bed the night before. Suddenly it all came back to me – my struggle during the night and my achievement. I grabbed the pad and read in a very clear, if a trifle shaky writing the following: THE BANANA IS GREAT, BUT THE SKIN IS GREATER."

Other substances, such as nitrous oxide – "laughing gas" – once a popular anaesthetic, can produce similar illusory intimations of ultimate truth. An anonymous account of a young student's experience in the dental chair reported in the *Psychologi-*

cal Review of 1898 very strikingly illustrates the phenomenon. As consciousness was receding he suddenly "became aware of, who shall relate! my God, *I knew everything*! A vast inrush of obvious and absolutely satisfying solutions to all possible problems overwhelmed my entire being, and an all-embracing unification of hitherto contending and apparently diverse aspects of truth took possession of my soul by force." His curiosity aroused by similar reports, the philosopher and psychologist, William James performed an experiment with nitrous oxide, writing down or indicating his own thoughts while undergoing anaesthesia with the gas. The subsequent "revelation" consisted of phrases such as the following:

"What's a mistake but a kind of take?"
"What's nausea but a kind of -ausea?"
"Emphasis, EMphasis; there must be some emphasis in order for there to be a phasis."
 "By George, nothing but othing!"
"That sounds like nonsense, but it is pure *on*sense!"

The most coherent and articulate sentence was: "There are no differences but differences of degree between different degrees of difference and no difference."

An anonymous correspondent of Christopher Mayhew after experiencing a "revelation of ultimate truth" under nitrous oxide wrote, "When I came round, I told the doctor I understood the meaning of everything. He said, 'Well what is it?' and I faltered out, 'Well, it's a sort of green light.'"

Not only do many drug takers develop the illusion that they are in possession of ultimate truth but they feel impelled to pass on the benefit of their new-found knowledge to all mankind. The previously mentioned undergraduate's visionary state in the dental chair was followed immediately by another when he was "seized with an immense yearning to take back this truth to the feeble, sorrowing, struggling world" in which he had lived.

"I pictured to myself with justifiable pride how they could not fail to recognise it as being the real truth when they heard it and I saw that previous prophets had been rejected only because the truths they brought were partial and on that account not convincing. I had a balm for all hurts and the prospect of how entire humanity would crowd around to bless the bringer nearly intoxicated me."

It is this conviction that he has a message for all mankind which gives the drug taker his special proselytising quality. And often his manner is so burningly sincere that there will be many who will believe him no matter how unlikely the message he has to convey. When the bearer of the "message" is a person of literary gifts, and clothes his intimations in language of aesthetic merit he will be sure to find adherents who fail to make the distinction between their content and the language in which they are expressed.

Was drug usage, then, the explanation for Freud's change of personality, his neurosis, his sudden conversion to the sexual theory, and the peculiar bond between himself and Fliess? There is nothing in Jones' biography to suggest that Freud continued to take cocaine orally after his early work in the years 1884–1887. But Freud too suffered from migraine, a "nasal reflex neurosis", a condition in which he fully subscribed to his friend's findings. What more natural than that he should use Fliess' remedy for the condition? That in fact he did so is confirmed by Schur.

> "During the 1890s, Freud frequently mentioned migraine attacks and colds. He was prone to relate his headaches to the nose, with the result that he not only made frequent local applications of cocaine, but also permitted Fliess to perform several cauterisations and perhaps some surgery of the turbinate bone in the course of their 'congresses'."

The practice probably started in the summer of 1892 when Fliess was a constant visitor to Vienna, and the two men became close friends. By this time, Fliess, 'having made the corollary that migraine attacks originated in the nose and could therefore be abolished by the nasal use of cocaine, would almost certainly have been using this treatment for his own severe migraine headaches. But Freud, also a sufferer, must at some stage during Fliess' prolonged visits to Vienna, have complained of a migraine attack. It it more than probable that at such a time Fliess would have introduced him to his own sovereign remedy for the condition. Freud's abrupt reorientation had, after all, begun just after the summer of 1892.

There is evidence, however, that what probably started as an occasional application progressed to chronic usage. A passage in Jones' biography gives a clear pointer to this progression.

> "Then, as was fitting in his relation to a rhinologist, Freud suffered badly from nasal infection in those years. In fact, they both did [Freud and Fliess] and an inordinate interest was taken on both sides in the state of each other's nose, an organ which, after all, had first aroused Fliess' interest in sexual processes. Fliess twice operated on Freud, probably cauterisation of the

turbinate bones; the second time was in the summer of 1895. Cocaine, in which Fliess was a great believer, was also constantly prescribed."

In fact, in due course both men developed considerable *real* nasal pathology. Such pathology is concomitant with chronic regular use of cocaine. Necrosis of the membranes, crusting, ulceration and frequent nose-bleeds with resultant infections are invariable sequelae of such usage. In fact, in the early years of this century when cocaine abuse was common among sailors and the drug was nearly always used by sniffing or snorting, such pathology was used by naval surgeons as confirmation of a suspected individual's addiction, being considered more reliable than the dilation of the pupils which could be inconstant. Infection of the ulcerated tissues leads to severe sinus infections from which, in fact, Freud suffered badly in the second half of the decade. This, then, was the reason for the "inordinate interest" in each other's noses which so amused Jones. That it occurred to neither man to wonder if the drug was not being absorbed from the nose and that the effects they thought local and reflex were, in fact, systemic, was probably due to the fact that both men had begun to suffer from the effects of cocaine on the brain. Hence the progressively bizarre quality of the theories of both men as the decade progressed.

X

The Great Cocaine Epidemic

In the aftermath of the drug culture of the last decade, there has been in recent years a move to rehabilitate cocaine and to "liberalise" the laws restricting its sale. Respected professors of psychiatry have claimed that it is a comparatively harmless euphoric and a useful antidepressant (while at the same time somewhat inconsistently advocating its use as a "model for the study of naturally occurring psychoses"); that as one of the first to experiment with it Freud was "one of the founders of psychopharmacology"; that the regulations against cocaine are based on a "moralistic view on the enjoyment of drugs", and that the passing of anticocaine legislation in America had been the work of fear-stricken white lawmakers concerned with the effect on the black indigent population and its potentiality to incite revolt. Paradoxically, it has at the same time been pointed out that little or no research has been done in recent years and that little is known about the effects of the drug on particularly human functions.

There are many obstacles today to the study of long-term cocaine use in the human organism. Its unlawful use in secret by addicts of unreliable witness, its purchase from illegal and irregular sources, the common practice by its illicit vendors of adulterating the pure substance with sugar, boric acid and other additives, and the fact that most addicts now use cocaine together with a variety of other drugs greatly complicate the assessment of the effects of isolated chronic usage.

Fortunately a more dependable reservoir of information is available to supplement the scanty gleanings from these dubious sources. The great American cocaine-taking epidemic in the eighties and nineties of the last century is a long forgotten chapter in medical history, but it is amply documented in the medical journals of the period. Cocaine was then a new substance. Hailed as a miracle drug, the intense interest in its effects, the detailed case reports in the medical press, the self-experimentation carried out by many medical men and, sadly, the large number of physicians, pharmacists and those in allied professions who became addicted to its use, and who subsequently on recovery gave frank accounts of their experiences, make the years 1884 to 1900 a unique source from which to supplement the sparse information available to us today.

The indiscriminate sale of cocaine was then perfectly legal. It could be bought from any pharmacist by anyone prepared to meet the high cost of its purchase. It was prescribed in good faith by reputable physicians who were able freely and openly to observe its effects on their patients, no guilt or stigma and therefore no secrecy being attached to its use. In fact, the climate of opinion prevailing at the time is most aptly illustrated by Conan Doyle, who depicts his hero Sherlock Holmes as a frequent user of cocaine, the practice eliciting from the faithful Watson no more than a mild rebuke such as would be bestowed today on someone smoking too much or indulging too freely in alcohol. Prescribed medicinally for specific medical ailments, there was then no confusion about the concurrent use of other addictive drugs which is today such an obstacle to the study of the effects of isolated cocaine usage in the human organism.

After Freud's early experiments, interest in cocaine shifted to the United States. The dry coca leaves which were the only ones supplied to Europe lost some of their activity through both the drying and storage processes and in transportation to Europe. The processes involved in the manufacture of the alkaloid required great care as the cocaine was found to decompose rapidly in solution especially after heating. Hence many preparations containing no active cocaine at all came into use. These factors, plus the high price of the drug, prevented its widespread use in Europe and in fact, soon after, in about 1885 Merck suspended the production of cocaine because of the poor quality of the leaves obtainable. In America the coca plant was native: the leaves could be obtained in fresh condition and Parke Davis & Co. began production there in 1885. Freud had been asked to evaluate their product and pronounced it to be fully the equal of the Merck preparation. In view of the greater availability of the leaves in America and the lower price because of reduced transportation costs, he foresaw a very great future for the preparation. The firm later added coca wines, cordials and even coca cigarettes to their repertoire. Other manufacturers followed suit and the magic substance was added to wines and soft drinks freely obtainable by the public. Mariani's wine, an infusion of coca leaves, evoked enthusiastic testimonials from many illustrious people, including the Czar and Czarina of Russia, the Prince and Princess of Wales,

US President McKinley, General Grant, Thomas Edison, the King of Norway and Sweden and Pope Leo XIII, who awarded Mariani a gold medal for the excellence of the wine! The original Coca Cola was an extract of coca leaves and caffeine-rich African kola nuts, and was advertised as an "intellectual beverage and temperance drink". However, coca was removed from the product in 1906 with the passing of the Food and Drug laws.

It was thus in the United States that cocaine's anaesthetic properties were first fully exploited. Koller's paper and the demonstration of the new local anaesthetic at the Heidelberg Congress in 1884 had electrified the medical world. Almost immediately, eye surgeons in the USA began using it in eye operations for squint, cataract and even enucleations, all performed completely without pain. With relief they realised that they were for ever free from the "smothering cone" on which ether, poured drop by drop, filled the theatre with fumes, half stupefying surgeons and nurses as well as patients. The cooperation of a conscious patient was now available throughout the operation; it was possible, for instance, to make a quick assessment of visual acuity. But the greatest benefit conferred by the drug was the elimination of the distressing and harmful post-operative vomiting. The heavy protective dressings, formerly obligatory, were now replaced by a simple strip of adhesive tape. It was no longer necessary in cataract operations to perform iridectomies concurrently. They had been necessitated by the tendency of post-operative vomiting to produce prolapse of the iris. Now it was possible to revert to the far simpler operation of Von Graefe. It was observed that during these operations the use of cocaine invariably produced dilatation of the pupil.

Soon gynaecologists were using the drug on operations to the cervix and other minor procedures. Its application spread to dentistry and to operations on the nose and throat where it was used with equal success. In general surgery it was found invaluable in small procedures such as the opening of cysts and abscesses, though unsuitable for major operations except in cases where a general anaesthetic was contraindicated. It was found to be more effective used on the mucous membranes than on the intact skin and had an added advantage in that it had the property of contracting blood vessels. Such vasoconstrictive effects were found helpful in rendering the operation field bloodless, though some surgeons questioned whether this action might not impair the nutrition of the tissues; operations for cataract under cocaine had been reported, which had been followed by sloughing of the flap, though this was thought possibly coincidental. Sometimes too, a rebound dilatation of the blood vessels ensued with attendant risk of haemorrhage. A valuable innovation was introduced by William Halstead, the distinguished surgeon and one of the brilliant quartet which included William Osler who founded the Johns Hopkins Medical School. He discovered in 1885 that injection of cocaine near a nerve produced anaesthesia in the entire area served by the nerve. But his introduction of nerve block anaesthesia brought a heavy price. Halstead was one of the first of numerous medical men to become addicted to the drug. His addiction was a closely guarded secret of the Johns Hopkins for many years. He disappeared from the world he had known. Months later he returned to the hospital. But the brilliant, gay and extrovert surgeon had vanished for ever; he was a different man. After his death in 1922 it was revealed that his trusted friend and co-founder of the Johns Hopkins, William Henry Welch, had hired a schooner and three reliable sailors and slowly sailed to the Windward Islands and back in an effort to break the connection with cocaine. Halstead's recovery was not without price, and was only achieved by the use of morphine, to which he ultimately became addicted also, thus reversing the usual process of treating morphine addiction with cocaine.

Meanwhile, physicians too were experimenting with the drug for a variety of medical conditions, vying with each other in discovering new indications for its use. Cocaine was advocated for hay fever, asthma, sciatica, tuberculosis, even for the common cold. In fact, declared the New York *Medical Record* of February 14, 1885, the more it was used in general practice, the wider its range of applicability. The ultimate was reached when a Dr J. E. Baker of Lancaster, Pa, wrote to that journal recommending cocaine for irritability in teething infants. He had used it rubbed on the gums in his own child with great success. The results, he suggested, indicated the use of cocaine in the diarrhoea due to the "reflex irritation from teething" and he proposed to try it at the earliest opportunity. The suggestion was evidently well received as the journal later reported the case of an eighteen-month child who drank the entire contents of a bottle containing eight grammes of cocaine in four drachms of syrup of marshmallow prescribed for teething pains, and developed serious symptoms of poisoning as a result.

Before very long, cocaine was being added to patent remedies of every description from cough mixtures to corn plasters, sometimes with rather odd results. A case was reported by a Dr D. D. Gilbert in the *Boston Medical and Surgical Journal* of 1898 of a patient who had sought relief from catarrh by the use of "Binney's Catarrh Snuff", containing two and a half per cent of cocaine.

When the patient came under his care he was using three to six bottles *daily* and was a confirmed victim of the cocaine habit. He had run up bills for $600 in various drug stores. He was now in a home.

Cocaine was widely used in the treatment of alcoholics and in weaning victims of the morphine and opium habits from their addictions. However, by September 1885 the New York *Medical Record* was reporting cases similar to that of Fleischl's, where cocaine had left the patient with a far more dangerous addiction. Moreover, morphine addicts usually continued using both drugs, as had Fleischl, and it was noted that the addition of cocaine caused hallucinations whereas the morphine alone had never done so. In contrast, however, when cocaine was prescribed for alcoholism the patient became addicted to the drug while now developing a *complete aversion to alcohol*. It will be remembered that an intolerance to alcohol was listed by Fliess as a symptom of the "nasal reflex neurosis".

Before long, reports of the untoward effects of cocaine use in surgery began to appear in the medical literature. What was thought to be the first fatal case was reported from St Petersburg where the eminent surgeon Professor Kolomnin had used the drug to cauterise a tuberculous ulcer of the rectum in a young girl otherwise healthy, giving, under the impression that it was harmless, a total of 23 grains in four injections. The patient died and the surgeon's subsequent suicide sent reverberations throughout the medical world. Minimal safe doses had not yet been established and over-confidence in the safety of the drug led to reports of unseemly incidents in consulting rooms with patients, who, after receiving injections of the drug, passed into a peculiar state with wild incoherent shouting, singing, declamation of poetry and wrecking of furniture, or who rising from the examination couch attacked their surgeon. A Dr Charles Chetwood reported in the New York *Medical Record* of 1889 a case of stricture of the urethra (a complication of the then common gonorrhoea) when cocaine was employed to ease the passage of bougies to dilate the opening. Within three minutes the patient became unruly, fighting and shouting like a patient in acute mania. Tonic spasms followed, his arms became rigid and spasm of the muscles of the throat led to impaired respiratory movements. The attack passed off in a quarter of an hour, leaving only dizziness and a vague recollection of having made a disturbance. Though Chetwood observed that the patient's pupils had become dilated within *three minutes* of the introduction of cocaine he failed to make the logical deduction that the drug must somehow have been absorbed through the mucous membranes.

Reports of deaths preceded by collapse, convulsions and coma began to appear, the heart being arrested in systole (contraction). These sometimes bore no relation to the dosage of cocaine used and it became obvious that many patients exhibited an idiosyncratic reaction to the drug. Sometimes a single administration caused long-term impairment, loss of speech, numbness of a limb or other focal deficits, probably the result of the constrictive action of the drug on small vessels, leading to interruption of the supply of blood to various areas of the brain, always especially vulnerable because of its heavy dependence on oxygen and glucose. Such incidents were reported more frequently after *nasal* operations. The pathology of these accidents was elucidated by Dr Zanchanski of St Petersburg, who had meantime been conducting animal experiments to determine the action of the drug on cells and tissues. A lethal dose of cocaine was administered to several dogs, while in another series, injections of smaller quantities were given to simulate the effect of chronic intake. In both series degenerative changes throughout the nervous system were found at post-mortem examination, most marked in the spinal cord, the medulla and in the heart ganglia. The changes were more advanced in the chronic cases, where minute cavities and simple atrophy were visible. These findings explained why recovery did not invariably follow cessation of the drug.

The untoward effects of cocaine anaesthesia were the subject of anxious discussion at the medical meetings of those years. A meeting of the Practitioners Society of New York, reported in the *Medical Record* of 1890, was called to discuss the growing number of reports of sudden collapse after the use of a spray in the nose. The consensus of the opinions expressed was that such cases were attributable to "hysteria" caused by "an impression on the nervous system" due to the sight of the instruments and the blood which under general anaesthesia they had been spared. The disturbances caused by railway accidents and Charcot's concept of "traumatic neurosis" were cited in support of this theory. A lone voice raised in opposition was that of Dr Chetwood, who protested that his patients had previously undergone the same procedures without any anaesthesia at all and had suffered no ill-effects. An alternative hypothesis was advanced by a Dr Dana, who believed the untoward effects were a reflex phenomenon. Though it was conceded that the drug might have got into the nasopharynx and been swallowed, the possibility of its having been absorbed through the membranes was evidently not entertained – the effects, it was maintained, had occurred too suddenly to be the result of absorption of the fluid into the circulation. And yet *only three minutes* had elapsed after the introduction of cocaine before the pupils of Chetwood's patient had begun to dilate. The following year, however, the obvious correlation of such observations were finally made by a Dr Andrew Fullerton of the Miller Hospital, Greenwich. Writing in the *Lancet* of September 19, 1891, he argued forcefully that a powerful drug like cocaine could hardly be applied to the mucous membrane without some absorption occurring. In his experience the drug was absorbed very rapidly from the Scheiderian membrane of the nose, immediately giving rise to systemic effects. He had deduced this from the simple observations of its effect on the pupil. Though no cocaine had been applied locally to the conjunctiva, the pupil dilated and accommodation was relaxed. This obvious and simple observation was apparently never made by Fliess, nor did Fullerton's receive the attention it deserved.

By November 1885, the New York *Medical Record*, which had played such a prominent part in the promotion of the drug, decided it was "time to sound a note of warning, positive and decided" to the profession. Several physicians had already fallen victim to the cocaine habit and a number of others had observed the pernicious effects on their patients. The warning was reiterated on December 5, 1885 when the journal reported the case of a Dr Charles Bradley, a Chicago physician who had become insane from the excessive use of the drug. He had made absurd claims about its powers, declaring that he was going to revolutionise medicine and become the benefactor of the world. In pursuit of his "wild imaginings" he had mortgaged all his property, leaving his sick wife and invalid children destitute. Two doctors who had attended him certified him insane and recommended his removal to an asylum. While before the judge he had acted in a most eccentric way, calling on God to convince the judge and physicians in general of the truth of his theory. A similar case was one of two reported by a Dr Brower in the *Journal of the American Medical Association* in 1886. Believing the drug to be a harmless stimulant his physician patient began using cocaine in one-eighth grain doses by hypodermic injection, increasing the dose until he was taking fifteen grains daily. He too considered himself possessed of a mission to revolutionise medicine by the use of cocaine, which he believed able to cure all known diseases, and went about brandishing a pistol in public places, threatening vengeance on all who ventured to doubt the correctness of his claims.

By this time it had become apparent that a large number of physicians and other medical personnel had become addicted, some having to be confined to asylums because of the violence of their conduct. From the first, doctors and their more affluent patients had been the chief victims. At two shillings a grain, cocaine was, according to the New York *Medical Record* of 1887, "dearer than gold itself". It was this high cost which prevented still greater abuse of the drug; it was beyond the reach of any indigent population, black or white.

At first it was difficult for the profession to accept that the new wonder drug was responsible for these tragedies. In this they had a champion in the famous neurologist, W. A. Hammond. It was in refutation of the disquieting reports circulating in the press that he rose to speak at the meeting of the New York Neurological Society of November 2, 1886. He had determined by self-experimentation, he said, to discover the truth or otherwise of these reports. He had begun with one grain injected subcutaneously. Within five minutes, the first symptoms appeared – acceleration of the pulse, a sensation of fullness in the head and heat in the face. These phenomena were accompanied by a sense of exhilaration similar to that following one or two glasses of champagne. He was writing at the time and felt that his thoughts flowed with increasing freedom and were unusually well expressed. The influence lasted two hours. Four hours after the injection, at midnight, he went to bed but lay awake till daylight, when he slept for two or three hours, waking the next morning with a severe frontal headache. The next night he injected two grains and experienced the same phenomena as on the previous night but to a more intense degree. He felt "an inordinate desire to write" and did so with a freedom and apparent clarity that astonished him. He thought it was the best he had ever written but the next morning found that it was the most extreme nonsense. Each sentence was complete in itself but no two sentences had any relation to each other. The first part was more incoherent that the latter. Four nights later he injected four grains of the hydrochlorate of cocaine. The effects were similar to those of the previous experiments though more intense.

"The mental activity was exceedingly great, and in writing, my thoughts as before appeared to be lucidly and logically expressed. I wrote page after page, throwing the sheets on the floor without stopping to gather them together. When, however, I came to look them over on the following morning, I found that I had written a series of high-flown sentences altogether different from my usual style, and bearing on matters in which I was not in the least interested . . . and yet it appeared to me at the time that what I was writing consisted of ideas of very superior character, and expressed with a beauty of diction of which I was in my normal condition altogether incapable."

Disturbed action of the heart was an early symptom. Three minutes after the injection his pulse had become so rapid as to be uncountable and this continued throughout the night, varied by periods when it would suddenly fall to below 60 per minute, every now and then dropping a beat. This was accompanied by respiratory difficulties and by a sense of oppression in the chest. On subsequent nights he took increasing doses of the drug. One night when nine grains were taken he was conscious of increased loquacity and as far as he could remember made a long speech, the subject of which he was unable to recall the next day. Severe cardiac irregularity caused him some alarm.

In a final experiment he decided to take twelve grains which he took in four portions within five minutes of each other. Before he had taken the last injection his pulse rate had risen to 140 and was "characteristically irregular". Within five minutes of the last injection he found his "mind passing beyond his control", though this caused no alarm; he felt elated and believed that nothing could harm him. Within half an hour he had no memory for subsequent events but next morning found the floor of his library strewn with books and overturned chairs.

He had, he surmised, taken a near-fatal dose. The cardiac symptoms had shown that the innervation of the heart had been seriously affected. There had been some muscle twitching especially of the face. The sharpness of his vision had been much diminished but in contrast his hearing had become more acute. But he had none of the horrible effects attributed to the drug, no disposition to murder or commit acts of violence. He had acquired no habit and was able to discontinue its use at once. He emphatically denied that cocaine was addictive; its use was similar to the tea and coffee habit and quite unlike that of opium.

In the discussion that followed, Dr J. B. Mattison, who was to become the foremost opponent of cocaine in the United States, declared he could not agree that there was not a cocaine habit. Within a few months he had had seven cases under his care, five physicians and two druggists. He cited a doctor, arrested in the street under its influence, and another who attempted to write a prescription, but instead wrote for the sheriff to come and take him to jail. In contrast, however, the next speaker, a Dr Leonard Cornung, stated that there was a morbid fear of cocaine spreading throughout the country and that the remarks of Dr Hammond were timely in allaying prejudice against a most useful remedy. This sentiment was echoed in the medical press. Hammond's reputation and prestige were high and sufficient for the time to assuage the fears of his fellow doctors.

Mattison, however, was not a man to be silenced. He returned to the attack in the *Lancet* of May 23, 1887, citing one case of cocainism, four deaths and forty-six less toxic cases. He dismissed the evidence from Hammond's self-experimentation as being both bad and insufficient, bad because reported by himself – "The testimony of an intoxicated person respecting his experiences while intoxicated being proverbially untrustworthy" – insufficient because the experiments had not been continued long enough. Hammond himself continued to address medical meetings around the country in support of cocaine. Speaking at the meeting of the Medical Society of Virginia in November 1887 he revealed that he had been using the drug intranasally for acute rhinitis for six months in different strengths in a total of about 600 grains a month, but of course nothing like this amount had entered his system. Its only effects had been slight mental exhilaration.

In the discussion which followed, Dr Hugh M. Taylor expressed his surprise to hear Dr Hammond deny the existence of a cocaine habit. He cited one of his own patients, a young physician who had been using cocaine hypodermically for nearly two years. His use of the drug had increased from a small to a large dose, from longer to shorter intervals until he found himself addicted to its use. He had left his practice in the country and come to Richmond where his conduct was so strange that his friends were telegraphed to come and take care of him. Placed under restraint he pleaded for the drug, insisting that he could not live without it, threatening his own and other lives if it was denied to him. It took six months to cure him of his addiction. This case had convinced Taylor that there was indeed a cocaine habit.

In 1893 Mattison, now medical director of the Brooklyn Home for Habitués, a newly-opened institution for the victims of the opium, chloral and cocaine habits, wrote from his by now considerable experience in the New York *Medical Record* of January 14, giving detailed notes of seventeen cases of cocainism under his care. Of these seventeen, ten were physicians. One of these physicians had become addicted from curiosity, having originally taken the drug experimentally. Five of the seventeen had used cocaine for hay fever in the form of a nasal spray or snuff; three had commenced its use for trivial complaints such as catarrh or sore throat, three as a tonic. On the advice of another physician, one used it for headaches and another for renal disease. Only one had got the habit from morphine. Those of the seventeen who were not doctors had taken the drug on the advice of their physicians. Thus Mattison was able to statistically refute the allegation still being made that only morphinists become addicted to cocaine; all his cases had had their origin in legitimate use of the drug. By this time there was little doubt that cocaine was capable of producing mania; few voices were now raised against Mattison. Demands for legislation restricting its sale became clamorous and by 1902 state after state had passed such laws. But for many these laws had come too late. Perhaps one of the most horrifying cases in the literature was that reported by J. W. Springthorpe in the *Scientific American* of 1897. The case was that of a friend and patient, an anonymous medical man "of great mental endowments". He had first used cocaine in 1885 while an army doctor in Germany and must have been one of the casualties of the experiments of Aschenbrandt. He took it orally in doses of one grain and remembered very well the marvellous effect when, after a forced march of over eight hours, he found himself arriving back at his quarters fresh, untired, neither thirsty nor hungry – but with bleeding feet. Returning to his medical studies he had nothing further to do with cocaine for over four years. In 1889, however, he was sent to relieve a country physician whom he found in bed unconscious with a syringe sticking into his breast. Never in his life had he seen a more startling effect than that which followed the injection of a twenty per cent solution of cocaine. "Nearly instantaneously he sat up in bed, with perfectly clear eyes, and received me, a total stranger, in the most cordial manner." The occurrence haunted him but it was not until summoned to a late confinement some weeks later when stiff with lumbago, that he was weak enough to follow suit. "That night in the month of November 1889 settled my future," he wrote. Remembering well the effect of cocaine he gave himself an injection combined with some morphia and five minutes later was ready to travel a couple of miles in a snowstorm. He repeated the performance before driving home again. From that time on he took cocaine regularly until he was taking eighty to one hundred grains daily.

His first symptom was enormously increased acuity of hearing, so that he claimed to hear flies walking over paper. But soon every sound began to be a remark about himself. Every passer-by seemed to be talking about him, and he began to stop strangers in the streets ordering the police to arrest them. He suffered badly from the "cocaine bug". The extraordinary thing in his case was that the worms seemed to be projected only on to his own person or clothing. He saw them in his washing, on his skin, creeping along his penholder, but not on other people or things and not on clothes brought clean from the laundry.

As his addiction progressed, he sat up in his rooms all night injecting himself with cocaine till morning when he would fall asleep in a coma. This occurred to such an extent that he had to hire a hospital warder to come in the morning and revive him with about ten syringes of a five per cent solution so that he was able to drive (not walk, as he feared someone might garrot him). Objects seemed to come alive and stare threateningly from every corner. Yet as soon as the effect of the injection had worn off he laughed at his fears and willingly produced the same terrors by a new injection. For protection he bought three St Bernard dogs but:

> "One night I found they were talking about me – how they could get rid of me – so I stood up and shot one of them with a revolver, which I always used to carry. I think this was the most dreadful night of my life, I standing on the table, with an Indian dagger and a syringe on the ground; one three-feet high dog going to die, and two other rather dangerous dogs roaring and groaning aloud, reproachfully looking at me, who always fancied, 'Now comes the moment when they will tear you in pieces'".

He stood the whole of that dreadful night on the table until the arrival next morning of the warder, who hardly dared enter the room.

This was an extreme case. The German doctor had, however, been deliberately injecting himself with cocaine entirely for its stimulatory mental effects. To achieve the maximum peak of these effects he would have had to repeat the injection at short intervals, intervals that grew shorter as time went on. But most of the patients in Mattison's series had begun using cocaine solely for its decongestant properties, to relieve their hay fever or allay the effects of a severe cold. Yet they had become addicted. How had this happened?

The effects of cocaine on the nasal mucous membranes were in these cases almost miraculous. They were closely observed by Andrew Fullerton and described in his article in the *Lancet* of September 19, 1891. Examination of the nose in cases presenting with acute coryza (the common cold) usually revealed red, congested and swollen membranes so that those covering the turbinate bones met those over the septum, rendering nasal breathing impossible. "If now a spray used as a solution of hydrochlorate of cocaine (2%) be applied to the membranes the latter will be seen to shrink, the discharge cease, the surface become pale and dry and the cavity restored," he wrote. Breathing through the nose was again possible, with considerable comfort to the patient.

Fullerton does not mention the "rebound phenomenon" but it must inevitably have followed with the heavy dosages then in use. The phenomenon has already been described when eye surgeons, if the operation was lengthy, faced a risk of haemorrhage supervening on the clear bloodless field of operation they had achieved by the vasoconstrictive properties of cocaine. When the effects of the drug wore off, a rebound dilatation of the vessels occurred with a consequent gush of blood to the site of the incision which could be difficult to control. In the intranasal use of the drug for conditions such as hay fever and coryza, the same rebound dilatation of the blood vessels would obtain, leading to engorgement and swelling of the membranes and leaving the patient in a worse state of discomfort than before. A fresh application of cocaine would now be an urgent necessity. Thus a vicious circle was set in motion. Almost without realising it, patients became addicted to the drug. It will have been noticed that Hammond, who began the nasal use of cocaine for an *acute* rhinitis, was still using it six months later. In due time impairment of the nutrition to the tissues such as had occasionally been encountered after eye operations, would have led to sloughing and infection, the patient being left with a constantly running, inflamed nose. The final outcome is suggested by a Dr E. Fletcher Ingals writing in the *Journal of the American Medical Association* in 1886. Advising caution in the use of cocaine in hay fever, he stated, "The continued use of the drug renders it necessary for the patient to take more and more of it for relief, and finally the constant stimulation of the sympathetic nerves in the nasal tract causes paresis, with resulting swelling of the turbinated bodies, which may at length permanently obstruct the naris."

Personal accounts by doctors in the medical journals of the time confirm the inevitable progression to dosages of greater strength in more frequent applications. A Dr Windle, recording his own experience of the use of cocaine in hay fever, reported in the *Birmingham Medical Review* of 1889 that during the first fortnight or three weeks of its use there was little physical reaction to the drug and it relieved his symptoms within a minute or two. But after a short time he found that the drug acted less powerfully, requiring a stronger solution and more frequent applications and then a strong reaction was experienced, with anorexia, insomnia and a rapid and irregular action of the heart. Many other physicians reported similar experiences. In one case reported in the 1886 *Journal of the American Medical Association* by a Dr

Brower, a physician under his care had used cocaine for *only ten days* before becoming firmly addicted. It was the same *rebound phenomenon* described above that was the mechanism which led Freud to an increasing spiral of cocaine usage, with its inevitable consequences. Freud and Fliess did not initially use the drug for hay fever or any other nasal condition, but for the relief of the migraine they both suffered from. But the same rebound mechanism would have obtained. The severe pain of migraine is caused by the dilatation of blood vessels in and around the head. Through its vasoconstrictive properties, cocaine would have dramatically relieved this symptom. But inevitably this effect would have been succeeded by a rebound dilatation of the vessels, rendering the pain more acute than before and calling urgently for renewed applications of the drug. These applications would have had to be repeated in solutions of ever increasing strength and at ever shorter intervals. But there would also have been a rebound dilatation of the vessels of the *nose*, leading to the swelling of the membranes. Because of Fliess' theory of the nasal aetiology of migraine, it would have been important to attack the cause of the headaches at their source in the nasal membranes. The rebound swelling of these membranes would have been an indication for the further use of cocaine even when the migraine attack itself was at an end. The use of cocaine would soon have become practically continuous.

Tucked away in *The Interpretation of Dreams*, unnoticed in the eighty years since it was written, is a short passage demonstrating conclusively that this, in fact, is what had occurred. Recalling a dream he had in 1895, Freud relates that he dreamed that he had found scabs on the turbinate bones of his patient "Irma", though in actual fact, this patient did not have these symptoms. "The scabs on the turbinal bones recalled a worry about my own state of health," he wrote. "I was making frequent use of cocaine at that time to reduce some troublesome nasal swellings, and I had heard a few days earlier that one of my women patients who had followed my example had developed an extensive necrosis of the nasal mucous membrane." Thus Freud's use of cocaine was not merely for the relief of an occasional attack of migraine. He was trapped in a vicious circle of using it to reduce nasal swellings which had actually been caused by the drug itself and which would inevitably recur more intensely as its effects wore off. Almost continuous usage would be the result.

Freud's misgivings about the state of his own nose suggest that he himself was developing similar pathology to that of his patient. Such extensive necrosis implies chronic cocaine usage over a considerable period of time, and in her use of cocaine the patient had "followed my example". Chronic cocaine usage, as we have seen, leads to crusting and ulceration with frequent nose-bleeds. Infection of the ulcerated tissues leads to chronic nasal and sinus infections. In severe cases the septum is perforated due to necrosis of the cartilage and the round puncture is considered very characteristic of the cocaine effect. This was the kind of pathology probably present in his patient and which Freud feared for himself. Subsequent events prove that Freud's nose, if not actually in this condition, was at least in a very unhealthy state. Fliess too was undergoing much the same experience with his own nose. When this *real* pathology developed it was regarded as confirmation of the truth of the theory of the "nasal reflex neurosis."

So by 1895 Freud must have been using cocaine regularly for well over two years. What would the systemic effects of this usage have been? Physically they would have corresponded in every way to the catalogue of symptoms tabled by Fliess as those of the "nasal reflex neurosis". Identical symptoms were noted by Mattison in the series of patients reported by him in 1893. Listing the effects of the drug on the organism, he described the toxic action of the drug on heart and respiration, the cold clammy perspiration, the gastrointestinal disturbances. More marked, however, were the effects on the nervous system. Restlessness and overactivity were prominent symptoms – "a peculiar unrest, almost constant movement", Mattison described it. He wrote of a physician-patient as living in a state of constant unrest, unable to remain quiet for five minutes to read, write or talk. Insomnia was a frequent feature; addicts passed nights and days without sleep. When it finally came it was robbed of its restfulness by "horrid dreams". Mattison describes the fugitive pains in the limbs, the brilliant eyeballs, the dilated pupils, light intolerance, distortions and hallucinations. In advanced cases the patient, tormented with the sensation that something was crawling around under the skin, would dig into it with a knife or needle until it was raw. There is ample documentation that Freud suffered some, at least, of these effects. His cardiac condition which has never yet been adequately explained, is characteristic of that produced by cocaine. The gastrointestinal complaints which ensued were also typical. We have no information on its effect on his appetite or whether or not it caused insomnia, but this tells us little, as many of the doctors mentioned who took cocaine for hay fever learnt to curtail its use before a meal or before going to bed at night and so avoided these symptoms. There is one other physical symptom, however, which is highly revealing. It will be remembered that dislike of and intolerance of alcohol was one of the symptoms listed by Fliess as part of the "nasal reflex neurosis", in other words, cocaine usage, and that aversion to alcohol was also reported in the American case studies just described. There is an allusion to alcohol in the *Origins* which suggests such a symptom. "You know how limited my pleasures are," Freud wrote to Fliess on March 11, 1900, "I must not smoke heavy cigars, alcohol does not mean anything to me . . ." Some years later, however, in 1912, in a letter to Ludwig Binswanger on the subject of recent attacks of loss of consciousness he is more explicit: "I had several such attacks," he wrote. "In each case there were similar contributary causes, often a bit of alcohol for which I have no tolerance."

But it is obviously the mental symptoms of the two men which must interest us most. Mattison, by then the foremost authority in the USA, listed a revealing catalogue of the most prominent of these symptoms in the series reported in his *Lancet* paper of 1893. A common feature was *mental excitement alternating with depression*. Equally common was the extreme loquacity which, "if noted after a supposed cocaine quitting, might well excite distrust". A greatly increased prolixity in correspondence was also present – "Under the lashing effect of the drug ideas were evolved rapidly, finding expression in surprising volubility", Mattison wrote. But this "brain spurt" soon expended itself on doggerel verse and "trashy prose". When coupled with a weakened memory this could lead to the greatest embarrassment and confusion. This symptom is interesting in view of Freud's phenomenal output of correspondence and a corpus of written works estimated to amount to three million words. We have already encountered the manifestation in Hammond's experiments when he experienced a strong compulsion to write, filling page after page, flinging the sheets to the ground in his impatience to produce more. Boastful and extravagant conduct with expansive delusions were common, as were visionary schemes, absurd business ventures and wasteful extravagances. A special feature among his physician patients, marked even in incipient cases, was what Mattison described as "a peculiar mania as to the panaceal powers of cocaine". So striking was this that in some cases this "mania" might sway the balance towards certainty in cases of suspected cocaine taking. The increased self-esteem reported in addicts was confirmed by Mattison. Typically, one physician of thirty-five thought himself a superior being and that the only link between himself and the world was tobacco. He had become violent and had assaulted patients. Another physician of twenty-five began to have absurd business ventures, trying to sell property not his own and performing "other crazy acts". He eventually became violent, suicidal and homicidal.

The progression to violence was a disturbing feature of cocaine addiction. In the other drug manias, Mattison declared, the impulses to kill were largely suicidal. "Not so with cocaine, but homicidal, distinctly and almost without exception." Often these patients would rush out of their houses onto the street, firing indiscriminately into the air. These acts of violence were often the result of the paranoid delusions of persecution which were so frequently encountered in the later stages of addiction. One patient, a "young professional man", attacked strangers in the street whom he believed were talking about him and accusing him of crime. A young physician of thirty dared not venture out after dark, believing himself about to be arrested for some imaginary crime. He had had hallucinations of sight and sound, saw ghosts and grinning devils and heard millions of voices. A physician of thirty-four had changed his hotel three times in one night to escape imaginary pursuers. Another roused the household every night to search for robbers.

It is not suggested that either Freud or Fliess was ever as severely affected as these advanced cases. Any homicidal inclinations in Freud were expended in death wishes. But even when paranoid delusions, hallucinations and violence were not present in Mattison's series, even the least affected showed a considerable *personality change*. A young doctor, formerly reticent and dignified, became "loquacious and boyish". Another, usually reserved, made a "confidant of everyone". His "moral sensibilities and social responsibilities were obtunded". He began *to regard intimate friends as persecutors*.

By now other physicians were contributing observations from advanced cases of their own. They warned of the treacherous and insidious nature of the action of cocaine in that the mental effects were at first minimal. There was nothing but a slight feeling of exaltation and well-being, general satisfaction and good humour, without any of the mental confusion attendant on – for instance – alcohol. In fact, an increased desire for mental and bodily activity was present. In this it was probably the most agreeable of all narcotics. It was only later that the more distressing symptoms appeared. Dr Conolly Norman of the Richmond Asylum, Dublin, speaking at a medical meeting reported in the *Journal of Mental Science* of 1892, described a case under his observation in which the mental symptoms had appeared after about a year and a half of use of the drug. The most prominent of these were hallucinations of hearing with persecutory ideas. The patient constantly heard voices making "vile and indecent" charges against him. Sometimes he accused those around him of giving utterance to these abominations, but at others he fully recognised their subjective and morbid nature. He was now in the asylum with advanced paranoia. Another patient came to him when he had been addicted to cocaine for an unknown period. Pale, emaciated, with dilated pupils, muscularly feeble, mentally depressed, he was suspicious and restless. His memory was failing, he was furtive and shifty in manner and unable to tell the truth. He was convinced he was dying and that everyone saw his vice in his face.

Dr Conolly Norman also reported *trance-like* conditions as a feature of the later stages of cocaine intoxication. These trance-like conditions were reported in varying terms by many other authors. Dr Frank Wing, mentioned earlier, wrote of passing his nights in a "*fanciful and visionary wakefulness*". Dr R. P. Smith of Bethlem Hospital wrote in the *Journal of Mental Science* of 1892 of the "*waking dreams*" experienced by an addicted nurse in which hallucinations of sight and hearing appeared , when friends and acquaintances seemed to be in her room and talking to her. She carried on conversations with these visitors and laughed at their jokes. The act of laughing would rouse her and she would come to herself again. She recognised them as hallucinations by the fact, for instance, that her landlady appeared to be talking to her in French and German, though she did not know these languages, leading the patient to infer that the conversations themselves were imaginary. From this she deduced that the other visitations were also imaginary, though she experienced considerable difficulty in making out *what was real and what fancy.*

With their growing experience of the drug, the natural history of addiction to cocaine was becoming clearer to asylum doctors and others caring for such patients. One effect, above all, emerged into prominence by the nineties – its action on the sexual function. Like opium, Mattison claimed in 1893, cocaine first stimulated this function but excess soon had its effect and "sooner than with the poppy salt comes loss of desire and power and impotence complete". Conolly Norman considered that "undue sexual excitement, abnormal voluptuous sensations and the like" were early features of the condition but that in severe chronic cases impotence was the rule. He cited a case of a "modest married woman" who exhibited violent "erotic delirium" (unspecified) after the application to the nasal cavity of a small quantity of a ten per cent solution of cocaine. The three cases under his care reported in the *Journal of Mental Science* of 1892 displayed similar symptoms. An elderly businessman is described as being "tormented by sexual excitement" with sometimes *sexual hallucinations* occupying his mind in his half dreamy state. In another case where the "sexual passions seem to have always been urgent" cocaine, though at first very much exciting their activity, finally had the effect of depressing them.

Sexual hallucinations appear to have been a prominent feature of the intoxication and are perhaps most candidly described by the anonymous German doctor described earlier, whose horrific experience with cocaine was reported by Springthorpe in the *Scientific American* of 1897. Describing the "new kind of illusion" which supervened at a later stage in his addiction, he said:

> "I mean the revolting, dirty, sensuous illusions. The remembrance of it is for me so awful that I can only tell you that one day every person I saw, near or far, appeared to be naked, and in the most lascivious positions, alone or with others. I remember on entering the surgical theatre to have seen everybody – operator, assistant, students – naked."

This was the end of his cocaine habit. In terror he fled to a medical friend at a lunatic asylum and was placed under restraint. So ended an experience that had "embraced the whole gamut of wretchedness and shame, and included both hospital and gaol".

Finally, from the men who were by now emerging as authorities on the subject of cocaine addiction comes the assertion that this increased sexuality often took forms verging on the *perverse and aberrational*. Conolly Norman, for instance, described a patient who under the drug developed "sexual excitement of a depraved nature leading, though the patient was no longer young, to frequent, very irregular modes of gratification". All were agreed, however, that the final outcome was complete impotence. All these symptoms have a bearing on Freud's case and on the development of the sexual content of his theories.

Freud's abrupt conversion to the sexual hypothesis was not caused by any chance remark of Charcot or any other such influence. It was caused by cocaine. It was cocaine too which induced the early cessation of sexual activity in both Freud and Fliess which they called the "male menopause".

XI

Early Patients and Theories

Many commentators have questioned the calibre of Freud's patients during this time. Feeling instinctively that they were an unrepresentative group such as would not be found in the waiting room of the average neurologist, some critics have claimed that a more libertine climate of opinion must have prevailed in Vienna than in other cities. Others, including Freud himself, have denied this. Freud's patients were certainly a *small* group. When his psychoanalysis had settled down to a regular pattern, a pattern which was to last all his life, every patient was seen for an hour each day, six days a week. Many patients attended for years, and the total numbers must have been small indeed.

But apart from the paucity of the numbers, there *was* a factor which made them a different and unrepresentative body – a high proportion of them must, on Freud's recommendations, have been *making use of intranasal applications of cocaine*. There are several clues in the Fliess correspondence which point conclusively to this fact. We have already encountered one such patient, the unnamed woman mentioned in *The Interpretation of Dreams*.

The Fliess correspondence confirms that Freud's conversion to the theory of the sexual origin of the neuroses was a sudden one. Before 1892 letters between the two men were sparse and, though friendly, matter of fact and unremarkable. Out of the blue, at the end of 1892, we find Freud submitting for Fliess' approval a draft of the first announcement of the thesis that "No neurasthenia or analogous neurosis can exist without a disturbance of the sexual function". No clinical material or other evidence is put forward in support of the theory. Another draft, that of February 8, 1893, calls for the complete overthrow of established sexual morality. "Free sexual intercourse between young males and respectable girls" was urgently necessary, he said. If this were not implemented, society was "doomed to fall a victim to incurable neuroses which reduce the enjoyment of life to a minimum, destroy the marriage relation and bring hereditary ruin on the whole coming generation". This is a remarkable piece of writing coming from a man hitherto a believer in the conventional morality of his time.

During the summer of 1892, when Fliess was paying frequent visits to Vienna on his engagement to the heiress Ida Bondy, he was deeply involved in his theory of the "nasal reflex neurosis". During these visits he had not only introduced Freud to the treatment of his migraine with cocaine, but he had also evidently made him thoroughly acquainted with his beliefs. Freud unreservedly accepted Fliess's theory of the "nasal reflex neurosis" – the evidence for this is irrefutable. He was the "friendly colleague" who advised Fliess to publish the theory (draft C, *Origins*). In the same communication, he hoped that the "nasal reflex neurosis" would "soon be generally known as Fliess's disease". Commenting on a proposed paper by Fliess on the theory, he urges him not to avoid mentioning the sexual aetiology of the neuroses which would be "tearing the finest leaf out of the wreath".

There were therefore three components in Freud's sudden conversion to his sexual theories: his cocaine use and its effect on his own sexuality; his belief in his friend's theory which linked the aetiology of the neuroses to sexuality; and lastly, the evidence from those of his patients whom, on the advice of Fliess, he was treating with cocaine.

Believing unreservedly in his friend's theories, Freud had evidently lost no time in applying them in his own practice. His letter of May 30, 1893 (*Origins*) specifically states:

> "I am curious to know whether you will accept my diagnosis of the cases I have sent you. I make it often now, and entirely agree with you that the nasal reflex neurosis is one of the commonest disorders."

So from quite early in 1893 he was diagnosing the "neurosis" by the use of cocaine and, since by this method he would assuredly have found patients in whom the symptoms would have been dramatically relieved by the drug, many patients must by then have been started on regular treatment with it. Quite early on he was referring patients to Fliess in Berlin for examination as to possible nasal pathology and presumably also for treatment. "Wasn't M.D. a jewel?" he asked Fliess on May 21, 1894. "She will not be included in the collection of case histories [the *Studies*] with Breuer, since the second level, that of the sexual motives, will not be disclosed there."

Fliess' treatment, in addition to cocaine, included also cauterisation of the "genital spots" and other surgery – probably when the progression of nasal cocainisation outlined in the previous chapter had resulted in permanent swelling of the turbinate bodies through injury to the nerves, and cocaine failed to reduce them. Fliess' ministrations on one patient, "Emma", resulted in near disaster, as is narrated by Schur (1972). "Freud had asked Fliess (as he had also done in the case of many other patients) to examine her for any pathology of the turbinate bones and the sinuses which might be a factor contributing to her hysterical abdominal symptoms." Upon the insistence of Freud, Fliess came from Berlin in February 1895 to operate on Emma, though he was unable to stay in Vienna long enough to undertake her aftercare. Following surgery the patient had persistent pain, foul secretions and haemorrhage. Freud initially attributed these to her "hysteria" but finally had to call in a specialist who found that Fliess had inadvertently left a half-metre strip of iodoform gauze in the wound. On removal of the gauze, the patient had a severe haemorrhage and went into shock. She subsequently had to undergo further surgery and had repeated haemorrhages so severe that at one time ligation of the carotid artery was considered. Sending Fliess the news, Freud made a solemn protestation of his unshaken trust in his friend. "Emma" also continued to have implicit trust in Fliess, such was the confidence he appears to have inspired in his patients.

Emma's repeated haemorrhages were given a psychogenic interpretation by Freud. His letter to Fliess of March 8, 1895 (quoted in Schur, 1966) says:

> "Then in the sanatorium, during the night, she began to feel restless out of unconscious longing and the intention of drawing me to her side. And since I did not come during the night, she renewed the haemorrhage as an unfailing means of reawakening my affections."

The true explanation, however, probably lay in the unhealthy state of the membranes resulting from chronic cocaine usage. Fliess' involvement with the case points to the likelihood of her having been originally diagnosed as having some elements at least of the "nasal reflex neurosis" and hence introduced to long term use of the drug. Haemorrhage, as we have seen, is not infrequent in chronic cocaine usage as a result of the increased blood pressure and the corrosive action of the drug on the Schneiderian membrane.

Freud's belief in the diagnostic efficacy of cocaine in the nose was evidently still strong as late as 1905 when the "Dora analysis" was published. Discussing his patient's gastric pains which he believed to be hysterical, he wrote:

"According to a personal communication made to me by Wilhelm Fliess, it is precisely gastralgies of this character which can be interrupted by an application of cocaine to the 'gastric spot' discovered by him in the nose, and which can be cured by cauterisation of the same spot."

Significantly, when Freud's heart condition, one very character-istic of cocaine intoxication, developed early in 1894, he wrote to Fliess that he had begun to see a great deal of the same thing in his practice.

Thus Freud's patients must indeed have been an unrepresenta-tive body and many of his more bizarre theories probably origin-ated with them. But the fact that these theories seemed entirely reasonable to him probably stemmed from his own involvement with the drug. To Freud, the experiences of his patients must have seemed a duplication of his own. A heightening of his own sexuality is implicit in his remark to Fliess when discussing his health in his letter of April 19, 1894, quoted by Schur. "The libido has long since been subdued," he wrote, a remark pointing to initial hypersexuality by then brought under control. Freud had evidently not experienced any increase in libido in his use of cocaine in the years 1884 to 1887. During his earlier experiments he had taken it by mouth. Used orally, cocaine is hydrolysed in the stomach with variable absorption, and reaches the circulation in a vitiated form, with only mild effects on the central nervous system. By the nasal route, however, the drug would have entered the bloodstream practically unchanged. Hence his failure to recognise his increased sexuality and other effects as being due to the systemic action of cocaine.

Coupled with the increased libido produced by the drug, characteristic messianic traits appeared early. Examples of this have already been mentioned. They seem to have attracted some attention from his Viennese colleagues. "They regard me rather as a monomaniac," he wrote to Fliess on May 21, 1894, "while I have the distinct feeling that I have touched on one of the great secrets of nature." These messianic traits are reflected in what psychiatrists term "monotony of interpretation" expressed in his letters to Fliess during this period, though they had not as yet appeared in so unrestrained a fashion in his published papers. Melancholia was "mourning over loss of libido" (Draft G, *Ori-gins*); *anorexia nervosa* – "Loss of appetite – in sexual terms, loss of libido . . . She had felt a longing for her husband, i.e. for sexual relations with him." The peculiar inverted reasoning common in drug users appeared with his equation of migraine as "a fantastic parallel which equates the head with the other end of the body (hair in both places – cheeks and buttocks, lips and labia)" etc., from which it followed that "a migraine can be used to represent a forcible defloration, the illness thus again standing for a wish fulfilment". The phobic fear of "throwing oneself out of the window" he saw as an unconscious idea of "going to the window to beckon to a man as prostitutes do" (letter of December 17, 1896, *Origins*); agoraphobia, "repression of the impulse to take the first comer on the streets – envy of the prostitute and identification with her". No clinical evidence was quoted in support of these pronouncements which were baldly stated as fact. Nor were they apparently accepted by every patient. Freud's letter of November 17, 1893, reports "an unusual shortage of patients". One of his case reports sent to Fliess about this time (Draft J, *Origins*) ends with the laconic phrase, "Interrupted by the patient's flight".

The characteristic physical symptoms of cocaine intoxication appeared in Freud himself in the autumn of 1893. Schur mentions "headaches, which he described as 'migraine attacks' (an affliction which he had in common with Fliess); nasal symptoms, which may or may not be due to a chronic sinus infection; some rather vague gastrointestinal symptoms. However, the most important by far were his cardiac symptoms". Schur found the first allusion to the latter in an unpublished letter of October 18, 1893, indicating that the subject had been discussed at a recent meeting. Fliess had by now become Freud's trusted physician, examining him and treating him during their frequent "congresses" or giving him advice by letter. He had by this time discovered ever more frequent confirmation of his theory of the "nasal reflex neurosis", finding a point for the origin of "nervous cardialgia" in the anterior third of the middle turbinate bone, for the abdominal pains of dysmenorrhoea in the lower turbinate bodies, and for pains in the small of the back in the *tuberculum septi*. Not surprisingly he linked Freud's cardiac condition to nasal pathology which was augmented by his inordinately heavy smoking, and for the latter prescribed abstinence, a severe penance for Freud. Treatment for the nose was, of course, cocaine in ever increasing strengths and dosages.

The interdiction on smoking did not help, however. For a few days of abstinence Freud felt moderately well when:

"suddenly there came a severe cardiac oppression greater than I had before giving up smoking. I had violent arrythmia, with constant tension, pressure and burning in the heart region, burning pains down the left arm, some dyspnoea – suspiciously moderate as though organic – all occurring in attacks lasting continuously for two thirds of the day, accompanied by depression which took the form of visions of death and departure in place of the normal frenzy of activity." (Letter of April 19, 1894, *Origins*)

Significantly, in the same letter he writes, "last time you explained it as being nasal, saying that the percussive signs of a nicotinic heart were missing". Breuer too had failed to find anything serious on examination. Freud's alarm over his condition was great and he begged Fliess not to hide the truth from him as he would "endure with dignity the uncertainty and shortened life expectancy connected with a diagnosis of myocarditis".

Freud's heart condition which gradually subsided over the course of the decade has never been adequately explained. It was undoubtedly a cocaine effect. The arrythmia, oppression and dyspnoea are characteristic and were documented in many reports of self-experimentation by physicians around this time in the United States. A typical experience was reported by a Dr Amory Chapin in the *Medical Record* of 1887. Using a four per cent solution he made several applications on cotton wool in both nostrils until he had finally used up seven grains. He was restless and unable to sleep, but finally he fell asleep at 1.00 a.m. He woke with a start half an hour later with impeded respiration and a slowing heart rate. The typical "oppression" was vividly described. Chapin felt unable to turn over on his left side because of fear that his heart would stop if he did so. He ended the attack with bromide which he had at hand.

Inconsistencies, mis-spellings and other errors become apparent in Freud's letters and drafts sent to Fliess from about 1893. In the letter of April 19, 1894 the character of his writing changed markedly. In contrast with Freud's usual "mastery and elegance in the use of the German language," Schur found distorted or at least quite uncommon versions of several words, somehow suggestive of neologisms with an awkward sentence structure. These changes could not be detected in the English translation of the *Origins*, and Schur quotes the original German to demonstrate·Freud's use of non-existent words and distorted sentences. Schur attributes these aberrations to mental stress, but they are typical of the kind of dysphasia we have already encountered in the nitrous oxide experiments of William James and which occur in many drug intoxications.

About this time also, Freud began having attacks of severe

depression with "visions of death and departure". It was the start of the "very considerable psychoneurosis" described by Jones. This "psychoneurosis" has been interpreted by Jones and others as a "creative neurosis" – "The neurotic symptoms must have been one of the ways in which the unconscious material was trying to emerge," explained Jones. The "neurosis", consisting chiefly in extreme changes of mood with occasional dread of dying, is very characteristic of chronic cocaine usage. "The alterations of mood were between periods of elation, excitement and self-confidence on the one hand, and periods of severe depression, doubts and inhibitions on the other," Jones commented. Added to the mood changes were what Jones described as a state of "restless paralysis" and sometimes "periods where consciousness was narrowed, producing an almost twilight condition of the mind". We have already encountered these conditions in the previous chapter, in the "waking" dreams experienced by Dr Smith's patient for instance, and Dr Wing's "fanciful and visionary wakefulness". Or the "kind of nightmare" described by Fullerton (1891), "a condition between waking and sleeping in which objects could be recognised and sounds distinguished."

The "lashing effects" of cocaine referred to by Mattison become increasingly evident in Freud's letters to Fliess around this time. Ideas put forward at one point are never alluded to again, e.g. the "pleasure pump", "boundary ideas" and so on. Statements made in one sentence are rejected in the next. The letters become increasingly lengthy and meandering, often confused and inconsistent, with many non-sequiturs and arguments in a circle, making his theories difficult to follow and presenting many problems later for his translators as evidenced by their many footnotes. A typical non-sequitur occurs in Draft H of January 24, 1895.

> "In psychiatry delusional ideas stand alongside obsessional ideas as purely intellectual disorders, and paranoia stands alongside obsessional insanity as an intellectual psychosis. If obsessions can be traced back to affective disturbances and their strength can be shown to be due to a conflict, the same view must be applicable to delusions, and they too must be the consequences of affective disturbances and their strength to a psychological process."

All these efforts appear to have met with unmitigated praise from Fliess. "Your praise is nectar and ambrosia to me," Freud wrote on July 14, 1894 (unpublished letter quoted by Jones, 1953).

For his part, Freud was lavish in his praise of Fliess, encouraging him to publish ideas which as time went on took on an increasingly bizarre quality. Commenting on some of Fliess' papers sent to him for approval, he wrote on October 31, 1895, "My first impression was one of amazement at the existence of someone who was an even greater visionary than I, and that he should be my friend Wilhelm." In his letter of June 30, 1896, he referred to "looking forward to our congress as to a slaking of hunger and thirst". The same letter reveals his dependence on Fliess for ideas and material for his own theories. "I expect great things – so self-centred am I – for my own purposes. I have run into some doubts about my repression theory which a suggestion from you, like the one about male and female menstruation in the same individual, may resolve. Anxiety, chemical factors, etc. – perhaps you may supply me with the solid ground on which I shall be able to give up explaining things psychologically and start finding a firm base in physiology!"

Meanwhile, Fliess' health too had begun to suffer. He evidently never experienced such severe heart symptoms as had Freud. With him the effects of the drug appear to have been mainly in the form of intractable headaches likely to have been caused initially by the rebound phenomenon, later by the same exhaustion of the autonomic nerves as occurred in the nose. Fliess naturally regarded the headaches as nasal in origin. His writing evidently began to show the same cocaine effects as did Freud's. "It was not written on an entirely headache-free day," Freud comments on one of Fliess' drafts, "because it lacks the pregnancy and succinctness with which you can write." It is unfortunate that Fliess' letters to Freud covering this period have never been found. They would have documented more fully the interesting phase he was evidently going through. Some day they may even now turn up; Freud may indeed have only "hidden them ingeniously" (see page 154) and they may yet see the light of day as Freud's own letters to Fliess have done.

It is an arresting thought that if it had not been for the discovery of the Fliess correspondence and its subsequent publication in the *Origins*, no hint of the part played by cocaine in Freud's theories would have come down to us. His published works dating from this period contain only two brief allusions to the "nasal reflex neurosis" and no hint of its important role in the formation of these theories. By the time of the publication of the *Origins* sixty years later, Freud's teachings had long been accepted as fact and the references to the neurosis were overlooked or misinterpreted.

Why was there no discussion in any of Freud's published papers of the "nasal reflex neurosis" and its diagnosis and treatment by cocaine which the *Origins* reveal to have played such a large part in his practice? The answer is simple. Nearly all the papers dating from this decade were concerned with hysteria, which differed in symptomatology from the "nasal reflex neurosis" and in which the cocaine test on the nose had probably proved negative, not surprisingly in view of the known convulsant effects of the drug. It was in the other "neuroses" – the wide range of conditions subsumed under the all-embracing title of "neurasthenia" – that the nasal reflex neurosis played the greatest part. But Freud actually published very little on neurasthenia. Presumably he had never managed to collect the hundred cases which was his stated aim in his Draft B of the *Origins*. In contrast, however, in the Fliess correspondence, neurasthenia is seen to occupy an important place in his ideas and in his practice. In fact, in his Draft C he refers to the "neurasthenic nasal neuroses". But some of the actual *symptoms* of hysteria such as the abdominal pains which we have already encountered in two of Freud's patients, "Emma" and "Dora", *were* deemed to be of nasal origin as they probably responded to cocaine. These were cases of the "mixed neuroses", i.e. of hysteria *and* neurasthenia, which he mentions in his published papers. But in "pure hysteria", though his own growing messianic traits and obsession with the subject of sex led him to assign its causation to sexual factors along with the other neuroses, he was still heavily under the influence of Charcot's teaching on "traumatic hysteria", and this he made the starting point of his investigations. But whereas before he had accepted *any* emotionally traumatic event such as illness and death in a family as the main aetiological factor, he now asserted that the trauma in question was *always* a sexual one, a theory that eventually led to the ill-fated seduction hypothesis.

The term neurasthenia is now obsolete. It was coined by the American neurologist George Beard in 1881 and embraced a wide variety of conditions thought to be caused by "nervous exhaustion" but which like "hysteria" reflected the diagnostic poverty of the time. The occasional case histories referred to in the Fliess correspondence emphasise this poverty. It is obvious that a man of thirty-four with decreased appetite and dyspepsia for three years with loss of 20 kilogrammes in weight is suffering from something more than a neurosis. No mention is made of a physical examination or of any relevant investigations. Those that would have been most helpful in this situation were not yet in use. It was two years before Röntgen's discovery of the X-ray and many years before that of the barium meal. It was cases such as this, however, which would have seemed to respond most favourably to nasal applications of cocaine and it is probably these cases that furnished the material for Freud's dogmatic statement in his Draft A of the *Origins* that "No neurasthenia or analogous neurosis can exist without a disturbance of the sexual function". These "neurasthenics" Freud tells us in his *Autobiographical Study* (1925) "used to visit me in numbers during my consultation hours". "I went beyond the domain of hysteria and began to investigate the sexual life of the so-called neurasthenics," he states. This was apparently successful. "The sexual business attracts people," he wrote to Fliess on October 6, 1893, "they all go away impressed and convinced, after exclaiming 'No one has ever asked me that before!'." The "disturbances of the sexual function" responsible were, he maintained, sexual abstinence, *coitus interruptus, coitus reservatus* (use of a condom), and masturbation. In the case of one patient Freud claimed, "this strong man, who was subjected to no more than the stock noxae had *never* been properly potent (never from the age of seventeen to thirty); so he could never perform

19 Bergasse, where Freud lived and had his consulting rooms.

coitus more than once at a time!" (letter of May 21, 1894). This latter "noxa" is the normal condition, and Freud's higher expectations were probably based on his own early cocaine experience and those of some of his patients. Fritz Wittels, a contemporary and early follower of Freud, though later a deviant, denied the influence of these so-called *noxae*. From his intimate knowledge of Vienna gained from his practice as a family doctor he stated in 1924 that both *coitus interruptus* and *coitus reservatus* were practised far too frequently for them to cause neuroses, which affected only a small number of people. Masturbation, of course, was many years later shown to be harmless by Havelock Ellis and others.

The harmful effects of the noxae, Freud asserted, were the result of the damming up or accumulation of "sexual excitation". Here he was allotting the same humoral quality to sexual excitation as he had done with other emotions in hysteria. The actual mechanism whereby this damming up caused neurosis led him into a complicated, tortuous and involved system of hypothetical (but dogmatically asserted as fact) pathways, diversions, blockages and even holes through which the sexual excitation "dropped out". He described this excitation as sometimes physical, sometimes mental. None of these alleged pathways, blockages, diversions or holes exist in the nervous or any other system. As time went on and Freud appeared to depart more and more from reality, there was less mention of patients and more of the "schematic picture" he had formed of the various pathways for the dammed up excitation, arbitrarily inventing outlets, substitutions and transformations. An example from Draft G is characteristic.

> "Here there is a similarity to neurasthenia. In neurasthenia a very similar impoverishment arises owing to the excitation running out, as it were, through a hole. But in that case, what is pumped empty is somatic sexual excitation . . . in melancholia the hole is in the psyche."

Though Freud, in spite of all this work, published little on neurasthenia, he did, in 1895, write a paper *On the Grounds for Detaching a Particular Syndrome from Neurasthenia under the Description 'Anxiety Neurosis'*. In this paper he singles out a syndrome that, because its principal symptoms were those of anxiety, did not fit into the general neurasthenic picture. The division was necessary, he said, because "We shall then be in a position to differentiate from genuine neurasthenia more sharply than has hitherto been possible various pseudo-neurasthenias (such as the clinical picture of the organically determined nasal reflex neurosis, the disorders of the cachexias and arterio-sclerosis, the preliminary stages of general paralysis of the insane, and of some psychoses)." There is a suggestion here of another paper that is to follow in which presumably neurasthenia and the nasal reflex neuroses would appear, but this paper never materialised. He was by then off on another tangent. So we have to rely on such of the Fliess correspondence as has been published for information on this important part of his work.

The conditions Freud subsumed under the diagnosis "anxiety neurosis" were diverse and included agoraphobia, vertigo, chronic "anxiety states" resembling, from his descriptions, thyrotoxicosis, and acute "anxiety attacks", some of which sound suspiciously like hypoglycaemia (low blood sugar); others resembled the epileptic attacks described by Hughlings Jackson which probably arise in the limbic system in which sudden intense and unprovoked feelings of fear, panic or anxiety occur. Recently the syndrome of prolapsed mitral valve has been implicated in cases of so-called anxiety neurosis. It is a common and benign condition and its symptoms include many of those described by Freud. No physical examination or investigations to exclude these disorders are described. But for all these conditions, the aetiological agent was the same — the sexual noxae described above. The symptoms of the anxiety neurosis, he claimed, were "surrogates of the omitted specific action following on sexual excitation". In support of this, he pointed out that "in normal copulation too, the excitation expends itself, among other things, in accelerated breathing, palpitation, sweating, congestion and so on. In the corresponding anxiety attacks of our neurosis we have before us the dyspnoea, palpitations, etc. of copulation in an isolated and exaggerated form."

The paper was strongly criticised on grounds which Freud was forced to concede in a paper published soon after, *A Reply to Criticisms of my paper on Anxiety Neurosis* (1895). "I was under no illusion as to its power to carry conviction," he said. "In the first place, I was aware that the account I had given was only a brief and incomplete one, and even in places hard to understand – just enough, perhaps, to arouse the reader's expectations. Then, too, I had scarcely brought forward any examples and given no figures." In reply to the criticism that he had produced no evidence for his contention that "the aetiology of the neuroses lies in sexuality", he merely reiterates what was to become his stock formula – "my observations had led me to . . ." etc., repeating the long and tedious theorising in the paper under criticism – but again without producing the required evidence.

Here, however, for the first time Freud employed what was to become a devastating defence used to good effect by all future generations of psychoanalysts to silence all but the most intrepid of critics, the famous "resistance" argument. Accusing official academic medicine of ignoring the sexual factors in the neuroses, he said, "Such behaviour must have a deep-seated cause, originating perhaps in a kind of reluctance to look squarely at sexual matters." That this argument was sufficient to silence reasonable scientific criticism and rational debate is an ironic commentary on human nature. Many people regard being accused of having sexual inhibitions as one of the worse insults that can be given them. In fact, contrary to Freud's teaching, some degree or other of inhibition is *natural* to the human race, and this probably subserves necessary eugenic factors. Paradoxical as it may seem, *dis*inhibition is actually an *abnormal* condition produced by pathological processes. Drug and alcohol toxicity can produce it temporarily, disease of the frontal lobes permanently. It occurs frequently in cases of tumour and neurosyphilis, in which it is one of the most prominent and early symptoms. It was, of course, a symptom of cocaine intoxication. (It is interesting that James Joyce, who suffered from neurosyphilis, wrote the celebrated reverie in *Ulysses* under the influence of cocaine.) A second line of argument which Freud also used to good effect was that those who rejected his theories were too old to accept new ideas and that psychoanalysis was for the young. This argument has been used in every age to defend every otherwise indefensible form of quackery and non-science. Such is human vanity that it is nearly always successful. These arguments have been used by psychoanalysts ever since to bludgeon their critics into silence. That the "resistance" argument was not always fairly employed is evident from Freud's rejoinder on hearing that Havelock Ellis had said he (Freud) was a writer rather than a scientist – "a highly sublimated form of resistance" was Freud's comment. Since Ellis had spent many years pioneering the scientific study of sex, it was hardly a fair accusation.

The criticisms of his paper were not directed to their sexual content, but to their methodology. Freud had supplied no case histories or statistics – in short, no proof. But even so, the critics were in the minority. Contrary to legend, Freud's contemporary, Wittels (1924), relates that "Freud's work on the actual neuroses was generally acclaimed . . . the paper found favour as having at length given due place to the neglected sexual factors of disease. People were delighted at the direct transformation of a noxious influence (masturbation or coitus interruptus) into a morbid entity" (Wittels, 1924). But those critics who had looked for evidence in the form of case history material had to wait a very long time.

XII

Hysteria and Psychoanalysis

It was in Freud's investigations in "hysteria" that the theories that were to become the basis of psychoanalysis gradually emerged, and it is in his writings on the subject that we follow the gradual development of "free association" from the "cathartic" method of his earlier days.

Faced with the exigencies of his practice and his therapeutic impotence, Freud had begun to use Breuer's cathartic method at the end of the eighties. His first documented use of the method took place in 1889 when a rich widow of forty years, reported in the *Studies* six years later, was referred to him by Breuer. A recent writer, M. B. MacMillan (1979), has convincingly suggested that his immediate impetus was the fact that both Janet and Delboeuf had recently claimed cures by using hypnosis to trace the origins of their patients' symptoms to mental traumas experienced some years previously. MacMillan's contention is an interesting one in view of the later dispute over priority that was to ensue between Janet and Freud. Interesting too, is Freud's claim in his *Autobiographical Study* written nearly thirty years later that he had *from the very first* made use of hypnosis for questioning his patients on the origins of their symptoms. If this had been true it would have established his priority over Janet. But here his memory had played him false. He had definitely stated in the *Studies* that his first use of the cathartic method was in the case of "Frau Emmy" which began on May 1, 1889, a date since unequivocally confirmed from contemporary sources by the researches of D. Andersson and H. F. Ellenberger cited in MacMillan's paper.

Described as a case of hysteria, Frau Emmy's condition was almost certainly a variant of Gilles de la Tourette's disease, described by Tourette in the same year as Freud's visit to Paris. (He mentioned on his return in his report to the College of Professors that the disease was receiving "special attention" while he was there.) Gilles de la Tourette's disease is a chronic condition characterised by multiple tics and involuntary movements, most frequently involving the head, face and shoulders and upper limbs. Involuntary utterances taking the form of barks, grunts, yelps, screams, hisses, or formed words and phrases are prominent features of the disease. A famous case in the past identified by Tourette was the Prince Condé who was compelled to stuff his mouth with any nearby object, including a curtain, to suppress an involuntary bark in the presence of Louis XIV. Nearer our own time is the case of Samuel Johnson, whose tics, grunts, clicks, whistles and other vocalisations, so well documented by the faithful Boswell and other contemporaries, as well as the compulsive gesticulations evocatively captured by the brush of Reynolds, have recently been identified as manifestations of Gilles de la Tourette's disease (Murray, 1979).

In about half the cases, the symptom of coprolalia (the utterance of profane or obscene words or phrases, often in the most inappropriate surroundings) is a distressing development. As the involuntary curses frequently occurred during church services or other solemn occasions, the disease in the past was deemed "the work of the devil" and as with so many other brain diseases consigned to the priest rather than to the physician. It was 1825 before the first known report in a medical context was published. This was the celebrated case of the Marquise of Dampierre, reported by the French physician, Itard. The Marquise had suffered from the age of seven from convulsive spasms, contortions and grimaces, bizarre noises and involuntary utterances of words that "made no sense" and some which were definitely obscene. The symptoms remitted in her teens but then reappeared, becoming progressively worse and persisting until her death at the age of eighty-five. In the middle of a conversation she would suddenly interrupt her words by "bizarre cries, rude oaths and obscene adjectives", described by Itard, who saw her when she was twenty-six, as being "in deplorable contrast to her customary distinguished manner". In her eighties she was seen by Charcot, her symptoms then having lasted for seventy-nine years. It was with Charcot's encouragement that his pupil Gilles de la Tourette published her case along with eight others in 1885. La Tourette's own life came to an untimely end at the age of forty-five when, believing she was under his hypnotic influence, a deranged young woman patient shot him as he sat in his consulting room.

The pathological basis and anatomical localisation of Gilles de la Tourette's disease have not yet been established. The condition is a classic example of the retrogressive effect of psychoanalysis on the investigation of brain disease. La Tourette had attributed the disease to a degenerative process of the brain. After Freud's theories became fashionable in the early decades of the present century, attention in such conditions was deflected from the brain and the trend fostered by the pioneering work of Meynert, Krafft-Ebing and other psychiatrists of the Vienna school was reversed. The consequence of this retrograde movement was that patients tended to be referred to psychiatrists (usually of a psychoanalytical persuasion) rather than to neurologists, so that physical examinations and investigations were not performed. A difficulty was encountered by these psychiatrists who found that, contrary to Freudian theory, the patient did not symbolise the forbidden words or phrases but came right out with them!

The occurrence of tics and involuntary vocalisations as late sequelae of encephalitis, and the remarkable response to Haloperidol and other drugs introduced in the nineteen-sixties, which alter the catecholamine receptors in the brain, indicated an organic cause. This was confirmed when the patients were submitted to *neurological* examination and investigation, when subtle neurological deficits, abnormal EEG studies, a higher than expected percentage of left-handed or ambidextrous patients, and three-fold incidence in boys as compared with girls were found. The uncovering of family histories showing a high incidence of tic and minor neurological abnormalities in other family members has implicated a genetic component. But the years wasted by psychoanalysis had taken their toll. Professor Arthur Shapiro writing in 1978 was only able to find four post-mortem reports in the literature, so the nature and site of the brain pathology has not yet been identified.

Meanwhile, the victims of the disease underwent long and fruitless sessions of psychoanalysis and psychotherapy, their hopes raised by the spontaneously occurring remissions which are characteristic of the disease, only to have them dashed by the relentless onset of the subsequent relapses. It is significant that Professor Shapiro reports that eighty per cent of his patients came to him, not referred by their own physicians or psychiatrists who had evidently failed to make the diagnosis, but from having recognised their own signs and symptoms from television broadcasts and other media presentations that followed the interest aroused by the dramatic response to the drug Haloperidol.

Frau Emmy is described in the *Studies* as still youthful looking with finely cut features, full of character. Her speech was interrupted from time to time by "spastic interpolations amounting to a stammer". A ceaseless agitation affected her fingers and there were frequent convulsive tic-like movements of the muscles of her face and neck, during which some of them, especially the right sternocleido-mastoid stood out prominently (a fact which by itself would rule out psychogenesis, as such movement of individual muscles could not be voluntarily produced). Furthermore, her remarks were frequently interrupted by a curious clacking sound which defied imitation and was compared by Freud to "the sound of a capercaillie" – a ticking noise with a pop and a hiss. It appears to have been very similar to that produced by a palatal myoclonus which produces many strange clicks and other noises often impossible to describe. Indeed Gilles de la Tourette's disease has many features in common with myoclonic epilepsy, and in the course of time may come to be recognised as a sub-group of this condition. Lennox (1960), who reminds us that "a curse can be a fit", actually subsumes the case described by Michael in 1957 as Gilles de la Tourette's disease under the classification "myoclonic epilepsy". Many features are common to both conditions, for instance, myoclonic spasm of the diaphragm produces the typical "wood-choppers' grunt" frequent in the former disease. Frau Emmy had "fainting fits" and spasms from the age of five which would lend support to the diagnosis in her case.

Frau Emmy proved amenable to hypnosis and, though Freud combined the cathartic method with that of the "suggestion" method of Bernheim and Liébeault as well as the rest-cure methods lately introduced by the American neurologist S. Weir Mitchell, it was to the first that he attributed her improvement. Under hypnosis he traced the onset of her distressing symptom of involuntary utterances to times in her life when, for one reason or another, she had had to keep silence. The clacking sound, for instance, was attributed to an occasion when she was sitting beside her daughter who was very ill and she had wanted to keep completely quiet, obviously a rationalisation. Patients afflicted with Gilles de la Tourette's disease are apt to rationalise their symptoms, attributing for instance, headshaking tics to a habit of tossing their hair out of their eyes as children. Samuel Johnson, when asked by a child why he made such strange gestures replied, "From bad habit. Do you, my dear, take care to guard against bad habits." Frau Emmy was also apt to rationalise what were probably mild tonic seizures describing to Freud how she "went stiff all over and was rooted to the spot" after a hallucinatory experience.

It was probably occurrences such as these which inspired Freud's theory of "abreaction", though no exact date is given for its inception in the *Studies*. Abreaction in psychoanalytic theory is defined as the energetic working off of a repressed disagreeable experience by reliving it through in speech and action. During a session under hypnosis, Frau Emmy had been relating a series of events judged to be "traumatic precipitating causes" of her symptoms.

"At the end of each separate story she twitched all over and took on a look of fear and horror. At the end of the last one she opened her mouth wide and panted for breath. The words in which she described the terrifying subject-matter of her experience were pronounced with difficulty and between gasps. Afterwards, her features became peaceful."

This slight fit, unrecognised by Freud, was deemed the result of the cathartic method and regarded as confirmation of its efficacy.

Like Bertha Pappenheim, Frau Emmy was not cured. Though she left Freud temporarily symptom free, she later relapsed, this being attributed to a "fresh psychic shock" caused by the illness of a daughter and, as described by Freud, "she undid the effects of my treatment and promptly relapsed into the states from which I had freed her". A few years later at a scientific congress, Freud met a prominent physician from Frau Emmy's part of the country. "She had gone through the same performance with him – and with many other doctors – as she had with me."

Though Frau Emmy had proved amenable to hypnosis, subsequent patients did not. As Freud relates in the *Studies*, he soon found that contrary to Bernheim's teaching, his own powers in this direction were severely limited. "The percentage of cases amenable to somnambulism was very much lower in my experience than what Bernheim reported," he wrote. It was no use telling the patients they *were* hypnotised as had been done with the simple and superstitious peasants at Nancy. "I soon began to tire of issuing assurances and commands such as: 'You are going to sleep ... sleep!' and of hearing the patient, as so often happened when the degree of hypnosis was light, remonstrate with me: 'But doctor I'm not asleep', and of then having to make the highly ticklish distinctions: 'I don't mean ordinary sleep; I mean hypnosis. As you see you are hypnotised, you can't open your eyes' etc., 'and in any case, there's no need for you to go to sleep', and so on."

At first it seemed as if he would have to abandon the cathartic method, dependent as it was on the enhanced memory often exhibited during hypnosis, of which there were many striking instances in the literature. He then remembered an experiment he had seen at Nancy which seemed to show a way out of the dilemma. Bernheim had given a woman in a state of somnambulism a negative hallucination of his own presence and then tried to draw her attention to himself in a variety of ways, including "some of a decidedly aggressive kind", all without success. (A similar experiment has been described in Chapter VIII.) After she had been woken he asked her to tell him what had been done to her but she was unable to do so.

"But he did not accept this. He insisted that she could remember everything and laid his hand on her forehead to help her recall it. And lo and behold! she ended by describing everything that she had ostensibly not perceived during her somnambulism and ostensibly not remembered in her waking state."

This "astonishing and instructive experiment" served as Freud's model. He decided to start from the assumption that his patients knew everything that was of any pathogenic significance and it was only a question of obliging them to communicate it. Thus, when questioning a patient on the origins of her symptom and being met with the answer "I really don't know", he used the following method.

"I placed my hands on the patient's forehead or took her head between my hands and said: 'You will think of it under the pressure of my hand. At the moment at which I relax my pressure you will see something in front of you or something will come into your head. Catch hold of it. It will be what we are looking for.'"

There is an inconsistency here. Bernheim's method induced the patient to recall the events of the trance, normally veiled by the amnesia which customarily followed the induction of hypnosis. This amnesia would have been caused by the passage of the epileptic discharge through the temporal lobes, the regions of the brain demonstrated by the work of Penfield to be the sites for the deposition of permanent memory records. Patients who have psychomotor attacks usually have complete amnesia for the events of the trance but in a few cases with a good deal of prompting, the events were eventually recalled, though dimly, "as if in a dream", suggesting that in such cases the memories have been recorded. It is therefore the recall process which has been impaired. Bernheim's method of pressure on the forehead was a standard procedure in hypnosis at the time, designed to bring about a lightening of the trance, thus rendering the patient in the "lethargic" state of hypnosis able to communicate. It probably achieved its effect by reflexly inducing a shift in the abnormal discharge. But in the normal *unhypnotised* state the manoeuvre would have had no effect. The patient would have been recalling events perfectly

accessible to consciousness. There was no "enlargement of consciousness" as Freud suggested, no dredging up of long forgotten
or repressed memories from "the unconscious".

In abandoning hypnotism for a derivative, Freud was following
the example of a number of erstwhile enthusiasts who found that,
contrary to Bernheim's claim, they were unable to hypnotise the
great majority of their patients. But, since suggestion was deemed
the most important aspect of the procedure and the greatest
adjunct to healing, many turned to other means, among the most
important of which was suggestion in the *état de veille*, and the
words "autosuggestion" and "psychotherapy" began to be used.
Miss Lucy, the first case reported in the *Studies* on whom the
pressure method was used, came under Freud's care in the autumn
of 1892, four years after his treatment of Frau Emmy. An English
governess with a Viennese family, she had come to him because of
troublesome olfactory hallucinations of which the smell of burnt
pudding and of cigar smoke were the most prominent. She appears
to have been a classic case of "uncinate epilepsy", a variety of
temporal lobe epilepsy described by Hughlings Jackson (1874),
who maintained that "a sudden and temporary stench in the nose
with transient unconsciousness" was an epileptic event, a statement amply confirmed since.

The temporal lobes are more vulnerable to infection than other
parts of the brain, the pathogenic organisms travelling up the
olfactory nerves from the nose. Miss Lucy had a chronic nasal
infection, and in fact, during Freud's treatment it had been
discovered (evidently not by Freud) that she had caries of the
ethmoid bone, the sieve-like structure between the nose and the
skull. One of her initial symptoms had been loss of the sense of
smell and absence of sensation in the nose, indicating involvement
of the olfactory nerves. These obvious pointers were, however,
ignored by Freud.

Under the pressure method (Miss Lucy was refractory to
hypnotism) Freud traced her hallucinations of burnt puddings and
cigar smoke to a rebuff from her employer, a widower with two
little girls, with whom she had fallen in love. The slight had dashed
her hopes of eventually replacing his dead wife. This explanation
calls for some criticism. Miss Lucy's situation must have been a
not unusual one at a time of high maternal mortality in childbirth
when governesses were frequently required to take charge of the
motherless families. Many must have entertained similar hopes,
later to be disappointed, but did *not* develop the unusual symptom
of olfactory hallucinations. Moreover, the memory of Miss Lucy's
recent rebuff and its consequences must have been only too

painfully present in her mind. There was no dredging up of long-forgotten memories from the "unconscious" or "enlargement of consciousness", as Freud later described it in the *Studies*. It was the simple elicitation of a recent traumatic event and attribution of the illness to this event, *post hoc, ergo propter hoc* reasoning of the most naive variety. Yet she was under his care for nine weeks, no doubt at some expense, to discover this.

Freud's abrupt reorientation towards the sexual theory of the neuroses made little difference in practice to the cathartic theory. Whereas before he had aimed to trace the patient's symptoms back to some mental trauma, whether it was a bereavement, shock or fright, he now sought specifically such a mental trauma in the sexual sphere.

He began to publish in 1893, and it is in the series of papers on hysteria from this time on that the fundamental postulates of psychoanalysis emerge. The first herald of his new orientation, however, was probably contained in the additions he made to his translation of the first volume of Charcot's *Leçons du Mardi de la Salpêtrière*. This appeared in instalments from 1892 onwards and the editors of Freud's Standard Edition are thus unable to date it precisely. For reasons given below, however, the bulk of it must have appeared by early 1893. In addition to his translation of the text, Freud also contributed a foreword and footnotes. These footnotes amounted to gratuitous interpolations giving his own views on the subject under discussion. He availed himself, for instance, "of the opportunity offered in the text in order to lay before the reader an independent view of hysterical attacks". A long exposition of his own cathartic theory followed. Later, on page 224, he has begun to interpolate flat contradictions to Charcot's statements in the text.

> "I venture upon a contradiction here. The more frequent cause of agoraphobia as well as of most other phobias lies not in heredity, but in abnormalities of sexual life. It is even possible to specify the form of abuse of the sexual function involved."

Such brash interpolations by a then little known neurologist in the work of a man of Charcot's eminence were undoubtedly the result of a cocaine effect. The dogmatic affirmation of his own views without explanation or proof, a mere "I have spoken" being apparently considered sufficient, demonstrates the increased self-esteem and self-confidence reported by so many users of the drug. Charcot, however, was understandably displeased, as Freud himself later relates in *The Psychopathology of Everyday Life*. Discussing a chain of memories involved in one of his "parapraxes" he mentions "an even earlier occasion involving a translation from the French, in which I really did infringe the rights of property that apply to publications. I added notes to the text which I translated, without asking the author's permission, and some years later I had reason to suspect that the author was displeased with my arbitrary action." This dates the footnotes in question to well before Charcot's death on August 16, 1893.

However, in his first paper on "hysteria" in this period, *On the physical mechanism of hysterical phenomena* (1893), Freud gives due acknowledgement to Charcot, declaring his own work to be a continuation of the former's on "the traumatic paralyses which appear in hysteria". He reiterates Charcot's teaching that the *mental* suffering, the shock and fright attendant on a trauma, could produce a paralysis without any physical injury and this doctrine is illustrated by an example almost certainly remembered from his translation of Volume III of Charcot's lectures.

> "Let us suppose that a heavy billet of wood falls on a workman's shoulder. The blow knocks him down, but he soon realises that nothing has happened and goes home with a slight contusion. After a few weeks or after some months, he wakes up one morning and notices that the arm that was subjected to the trauma is hanging down limp and paralysed, though in the interval, in what might be called the incubation period, he has made perfectly good use of it. If the case is a typical one, it may happen that peculiar attacks set in – that, after an aura the subject suddenly collapses, raves and becomes delirious."

How is this phenomenon to be explained, Freud asks.

> "Charcot explains the process by reproducing it, by inducing the paralysis in a patient artificially. In order to bring this about, he needs a patient who is already in a hysterical state; he further requires the condition of hypnosis and the method of suggestion. He puts a patient of this kind into deep hypnosis and gives him a light blow on the arm. The arm drops; it is paralysed . . ."

Freud was describing a favourite experiment of Charcot's which we have already briefly encountered. As we have seen, he would juxtapose a man diagnosed as a case of traumatic hysteria alongside one of his *hystériques* in a state of hypnosis and demonstrate that the paralysis he produced in her by suggestion was identical to that produced by trauma in the man. From experiments such as these Freud drew the simple deduction that mental suggestion alone could induce symptoms of the severity of paralysis or contracture. As he was fond of relating to his followers in later years, Charcot had *proved experimentally* that the mind could cause bodily disease.

But it was not actually so simple. Firstly, Charcot could not just take *any* subject and suggest to him or her that a limb was paralysed. It had to be a "hysterical" subject and that subject had to be in a state of hypnosis. Secondly, the latter state could by no means be considered normal, as the reader will have learnt from Chapter VI. Thirdly, the patients were diagnosed as hysterical on invalid criteria.

Three cases of isolated paralysis of an arm appear in Volume III of Charcot's published lectures which Freud translated on his return from Paris in 1886. It was a relatively uncommon condition and Charcot made a special presentation of the three cases he had treated, without mention of any others, so it is highly probable that it was one of these cases to which Freud referred. But the only one of the three whose paralysis followed a blow from a heavy billet of wood on the shoulder was Deb— who in fact was the only patient of the three deemed by Charcot to have actually sustained a *real*, organically determined, paralysis of the arm, presumed due to injury to the brachial plexus. It was the other two, Porcz— and Pin—, who were diagnosed as hysterical, though in both cases the trauma to the shoulder was sustained *in a fall* and not by a blow from a billet of wood. Freud's hypothetical case is evidently a composite of all three cases.

Porcz—, a twenty-five-year-old cab driver, sustained his monoplegia consequent to a fall from the driving seat of his cab – "the horse which Porcz— was driving became restive, and our patient was pitched from his seat on to the pavement, falling upon his right side, the posterior part of his shoulder receiving the first impulse. There was no loss of consciousness, no intense emotion." The monoplegia did not actually supervene until six days after the accident, when, "after a restless night" he woke to find his right arm hanging limp and motionless.

Pin—, an eighteen-year-old mason's apprentice, had fallen from a height of about six and a half feet and had remained for some minutes unconscious on the spot where he fell. He had suffered slight contusions of the shoulder, knee and left ankle, but was otherwise unhurt. Paresis of the left arm developed on the third day after the accident. Pin—'s paralysis was most probably cortical in origin, sustained as a result of a head injury in a man with a strong family history of epilepsy, such patients being more liable to develop epilepsy after head trauma than patients with a normal family history. In fact, soon after his admission to the Salpêtrière, Charcot was able to produce in him an epileptic fit reflexly, by excitation of a "hysterogenic zone" under the left breast. Slight pressure of this zone produced the characteristic aura – "a sensation of constriction of the thorax, and then of the neck, beating in the temples, and buzzing sounds, especially in the left ear." On repeating the pressure the patient suddenly lost consciousness, threw himself backwards, stiffening his limbs and went into a violent fit which Charcot called "a classic attack of hystero-epilepsy". The paralysed left arm did not move in the convulsions. From then on the fits returned spontaneously. His paralysis began to resolve when, during one of these seizures the left arm was agitated with the other limbs in the clonic phase. On recovery, the patient discovered he was able to move the arm.

Porcz—'s monoplegia was probably a true injury to the brachial plexus, a ganglion, or subsidiary nerve centre, forming a great network of nerves of neck and armpit which supply the whole arm. But in his case the injury was probably *preganglionic*, i.e. caused by traction with avulsion of the sensory and motor nerve roots from the spinal cord. The growing popularity of motorcycles in recent years and the typical accidents that can occur with their use have greatly increased medical knowledge of brachial plexus injury which frequently occurs when the rider is thrown from his machine. With a *pre*-ganglionic lesion, as in the case of upper motor neurone lesions caused by head injury, muscle wasting and degeneration of the electrical reactions do not occur. The reverse is true of *post*-ganglionic lesions. Combinations of the two can occur, however, and are frequent in this type of accident. Porcz— and Pin— were diagnosed by Charcot as cases of traumatic hysteria because, though by the time they came under his care their paralyses had been present for some months, in neither man were the muscles in any way atrophied. Nor were the electrical reactions modified.

In contrast, Charcot demonstrated Deb— who had *really* had a heavy billet of wood fall on his shoulder and who Charcot considered to be a case of *true* brachial monoplegia. In Deb— the paralysed muscles were extremely atrophied. On electrical examination they presented the "reaction of degeneration" in its "most aggravated form". The tendon-reflexes were abolished; the skin was cold and its surface marked by violet spots, especially in the fingers, and the subcutaneous tissue was slightly oedematous. The sharp contrast he presented with the other two was brought out by Charcot with all his flair for medical showmanship. Deb – was probably a case of *post*-ganglionic brachial paralysis and as such would have exhibited these typical signs of a *lower* motor neurone lesion. Porcz— on the contrary was most probably a case of *pre*-

ganglionic injury and would therefore have shown no muscle wasting or electrical signs. Thus we have now arrived at the conclusion that the two cases which started Freud off on his long journey were not cases of hysteria at all but true organic conditions.

To further emphasise his point, Charcot introduced one of his *hystériques*, Greuz—. By means of a light pressure on the eyeballs, he quickly induced a state of somnambulism in which, by a series of light touches, he was able to produce a "peculiar rigidity" of the limbs, e.g. a tonic spasm of the muscle. While she was in this condition, Charcot stated in a loud voice, "Your right hand is paralysed". At first there was little result, but after Charcot had repeated the statement a number of times, her right arm hung motionless by her side, all motion and sensation abolished. There was no deception as some critics have since alleged. Sensation was tested by violent torsion of the joints and faradisation of the nerve trunks severe enough to bring about violent contraction of the muscles without causing the slightest facial expression of pain. He had produced this effect by suggestion *using speech*, Charcot claimed: but in the cases of Porcz— and Pin— the cause had actually been a blow on the shoulder. It was also possible, he claimed, to obtain the same effect by a blow on the shoulder in the hypnotised girl, Greuz— and he proceeded to demonstrate this by sharply striking this region in the girl with the palm of his hand.

> "Immediately the patient starts, emits a cry, and being interrogated as to what she feels, she states that she experiences in the whole extent of the extremity a sensation of enervation, of weight and feebleness; it seems, she says, as if the member struck did not belong to her, that it had become strange to her. And then we find that the paralysis is really established. It attains its maximum at the very outset, and presents all the clinical features with which you are familiar."

If this experiment had been valid, Charcot would indeed have demonstrated that the mind alone could produce paralysis. But it contained serious flaws. Under hypnosis, the patient Greuz— would have been in an epileptiform condition. In this state it was a simple matter to produce spread of the abnormal discharge by any reflex method, as Charcot demonstrated. A mere touch on the limbs made them instantly rigid. That spread of the discharge from the temporal lobes to the adjacent parietal lobes had already occurred was evidenced by the fact that severe faradisation evoked no sign of pain. Spread to the motor cortex – in fact to the "arm" area of this cortex – would have been reflexly achieved by either of the processes used by Charcot. Repeated assertions in a loud voice that she could not move her arm would result in the patient's attempt to test this out by doing so, thus bringing into play the motor pathway for willed movements, the pyramidal tract that descends from the motor cortex to the limbs, and in particular, that part of it subserving the region of the arm, with consequent spread of the discharge to this region. A light blow on the arm would have achieved the same result via sensory-motor connections.

Experiments such as these were apparently entirely convincing to Freud; "in my opinion," he stated in *On the psychical mechanisms of hysterical phenomena*, "there is scarcely any point at which he (Charcot) has penetrated into the understanding of hysteria more deeply than here." This was the legend that passed down into psychoanalysis – that Charcot had proved experimentally that the mind could cause disease. As Fritz Wittels said later, "This man maintained, and could prove, that mere ideas were able to cause disease." Thus from the very beginning Freud's premises were based on error.

XIII

Repression and Conversion Hysteria

On December 18, 1892 Freud wrote to Fliess, "I am delighted to be able to tell you that our theory of hysteria (reminiscence, abreaction, etc.) is going to appear in the *Neurologisches Centralblatt* on January 1, 1893, in the form of a detailed preliminary communication. It has meant a long battle with my partner" (*Origins*). Recalling this period in later life, Freud was accustomed to attribute the reluctance of his collaborator to Breuer's unwillingness to face the sexual implications of his work. In fact the cases reported in the *Studies* had been completed in the earlier phase before his "sexual revolution" and sexual factors play little part. A more probable explanation is Breuer's awareness that, in the main case which was to open the series, the patient, Bertha Pappenheim, had *not* been cured. Somehow Freud must have overridden these scruples, for the *Preliminary Communication* which appeared under their joint authorship in January, 1893, contained the following passage:

> "For we found, to our great surprise at first, that *each individual hysterical symptom immediately and permanently disappeared when we had succeeded in bringing clearly to light* the memory of the event by which it was provoked and in arousing its accompanying affect [emotional excitation], and when the patient had described that event in the greatest possible detail and had put the affect into words."

Freud's next paper published the following year, *The Neuro-Psychoses of Defence* (1894), was an important event in psychoanalytical history. It contained two fundamental post-ulates – conversion and repression – on which all his later work was based.

Contrary to the assertions of Freud's biographers, the term "conversion" is not a new one. It appears in early nineteenth-century texts, used in essentially the same context. It was a concept of the old neurophysiology and depended on theories of nervous function inherited from previous centuries still extant though destined to be overthrown by the establishment of the neurone theory at the end of the century.

As we have seen, ideas of nervous function had, since the days of the ancients, involved notions of the "animal spirits", the messengers and handmaidens of the soul, travelling back and forth in either direction through nerves believed hollow, taking motion and sensation to whatever parts they visited. By the end of the eighteenth century the spirits had been replaced by a hypothetical substance called "nervous energy" or "nervous force" vaguely presumed electrical in nature, but in all other respects the system had not changed. The identification of separate nervous pathways for motion and sensation by Bell and Magendie, improved microscopy which demonstrated that the nerves were not hollow, and other anatomical findings had hinted at a far more complex arrangement. But confusion resulted from the many discoveries as yet unexplained, such as that of Helmholtz who had demonstrated that the speed of nervous conduction was far slower than that of an electric current passing along a wire. In the absence of any adequate explanation for these findings, men continued to think in the old ways of a comparatively simple system forming a communicating network in which every part of the body was in direct nervous contact with every other part, and in which nervous energy travelled at will back and forth in either direction. The consequence of such an arrangement, which if true would cause the brain to be bombarded by electrical signals from all parts of the body, was evidently not appreciated.

In their progression through the nerves at the behest of the soul, the animal spirits could find their path blocked by, for instance, "cold phlegm" or some other "morbific humour". When this occurred, they could be forced into another direction, into the *wrong channel*, and thus give rise to untoward bodily symptoms. In this theory there was no anatomical difficulty in an emotion being *converted* into a *bodily* symptom. It also provided a plausible explanation for the idea that a strong emotion could cause a lesion as localised as, for instance, a "hysterical club foot" or a "hysterical contracture" at wrist or elbow.

By the latter part of the nineteenth century a few critical voices were beginning to be raised against the diagnosis of hysteria as existing in one particular site of the body. If the symptoms were caused by the mind, why did they stop at one half of the body, was a question asked in 1870 by Hughlings Jackson in criticism of the diagnoses of "hysterical hemi-chorea" then so frequently being made.

The old theories of "conversion" into the "wrong channels" which had adequately explained these local manifestations of "hysteria" were gradually becoming insufficient. Already the great Spanish pathologist Ramon y Cajal was engaged on the work that was to finally render them obsolete, work that was to culminate in the enunciation of the neurone theory in 1891. From painstaking microscopic studies using his own modification of the Golgi stain, Cajal had arrived at the conclusion that each neurone or nerve cell, with its long nerve fibre or axon, and the shorter dendrites, was a separate, distinct, and independent structure which did not communicate directly with its neighbour and that its conduction was in one direction only. Publishing in obscure Spanish journals, Cajal's findings had not reached the ears of the main scientific world. It was only when his conclusions were welded together by Waldeyer in 1891 as the first announcement of the "neurone theory" that his views became known worldwide.

But even then his conclusions were disputed till the end of the century and beyond and many men of standing and repute still adhered to the network theory. The new neuronal system completely precluded the "conversion" mechanism postulated in the old theories. But they explained many findings which had tended to invite a diagnosis of hysteria, such as the fact that the distal portion of a limb could be less affected than the proximal part for instance. But it was many years before the full implications of the theory were recognised and translated into clinical terms.

The problem of how a mental trauma could cause a specifically localised symptom was raised by Freud in the case of a Frau Cäcilie briefly mentioned in the *Studies*, whose painful trigeminal neuralgia he had traced to a quarrel with her husband when he had made a remark regarded by her as "a slap in the face".

> "Everyone will immediately ask how it was that the sensation of a 'slap in the face' came to take on the outward forms of a trigeminal neuralgia, why it was restricted to the second and third branches and why it was made worse by opening the mouth and chewing – though, incidentally, not by talking."

The conversion theory solved these problems for Freud as they had done for previous generations. Hysterical symptoms were, he maintained, the result of emotional excitations (affects) caused by mental trauma which had not been discharged by abreaction or otherwise disposed of. These were then *converted* into the physical innervation of the body, causing *bodily* symptoms in parts as localised as Frau Cäcilie's cheek. The process played an essential part in the defences of the ego in fending off unwelcome ideas or memories. As expressed in *The Neuro-Psychoses of Defence*, "In hysteria, the incompatible idea is rendered innocuous by its *sum of excitation being transformed into something somatic*. For this I should like to propose the name of *conversion*." Much space is devoted in these early papers and in the *Studies* which appeared the following year (1895) to the alleged activities of the "excitation".

> "The distribution of excitation thus brought about in hysteria usually turns out to be an unstable one. The excitation which is forced into a wrong channel (into somatic innervation) now and then finds its way back to the idea from which it has been detached, and it then compels the subject either to work over the idea associatively or to get rid of it in hysterical attacks – as we see in the familiar contrast between attacks and chronic symptoms."

Phrases such as "a quota of affect or sum of excitation", liberally used throughout the paper, betray the humoral origin of Freud's thinking. Though accepting the neurone theory in principle, he continued to think in terms of the old neurophysiology as if nothing had changed. The strictures levelled at Freud's contemporary, the neurologist C. E. Brown-Séquard, by his biographer J. B. S. Olmstead, could equally well have been applied to Freud:

> "He continued to think in vague terms of the "nervous energy" of his youth, as if a certain quantity of this commodity were released and had to flow somewhere – if it were not allowed to take one channel it would take another" (Olmstead, 1948).

In the old physiology there was no dichotomy between mind and body or mind and brain. The animal spirits conveying sense and motion to the body were the "handmaidens of the soul". Their channels were the nerves, and the consequent equation of nerves with mind is evident in words such as "nervous" or "neurotic" that have survived from those times. This explains the seeming inconsistency of Freud's practice of jumping back and forth from a physical to a psychological standpoint. In his *Project for a Scientific Psychology* found among the Fliess letters and published in the *Origins*, he wrote of a "cathected neurone filled with a certain quantity, though at other times it may be empty", using purely neurological terms. The same model was described in purely *psychological* terms in the theoretical seventh chapter of *The Interpretation of Dreams*, an inconsistency that has worried subsequent Freud scholars. Similarly the "principle of constancy" so often referred to in the Fliess correspondence was enunciated first in neurological terms in the *Project* as "the principle of neuronal inertia, which asserts that neurones tend to divest themselves in quantity"; later it appears in *psychological* terms in *Beyond the Pleasure Principle* (1920) where it is given the name of the "Nirvana principle" – "The mental apparatus endeavours to keep the quantity of excitation present in it as low as possible, or at least to keep it constant". In terms of the old neurophysiology, this was perfectly consistent.

No experimental evidence was offered for this edifice of theoretical constructs. Nor would Freud have been able to supply it. Neurones do not contain "a quota of affect or sum of excitation . . . capable of increase, diminution, displacement and discharge"; nor do they "strive to keep this excitation constant". They are not "sometimes empty". It was not until well into the present century that the actual mode of transmission in the nervous system was discovered. Cajal's assertion that each neurone had a separate existence and was not connected to its neighbours presupposed that the energy for the nerve impulse was generated in the nerve itself but how this was done remained unexplained. The insuperable barrier to closer investigation was the microscopic size of the nerve fibre, the largest axon of the human, for instance, having a diameter of only .003937 of an inch. The matter therefore remained in abeyance until 1936 when the biologist J. Z. Young discovered that the giant Atlantic squid possesses enormous axons as much as one millimetre in diameter, the fibres being part of the mechanism that allows the creature to propel itself backwards at high speed by taking in water into a large cavity and then squirting it out under pressure through a funnel in front. The fibres conveying the nerve impulses capable of generating these powerful movements were found large enough to admit an extremely fine electrode and from 1939 onwards the physiologists A. L. Hodgkin and A. L. Huxley, working from the Laboratory of the Marine Biological Association, Plymouth, England, performed a series of experiments that unequivocally established the membrane theory of nerve conduction, for which they were awarded the Nobel Prize in 1963. Their findings showed that the nerve impulse is generated within the neurone by the movement of electrically charged sodium and potassium ions across the cell membrane, movements which result in a change of polarity at the site of the transition which in turn alters polarity further along the nerve fibre, and so on down the nerve. The nerve impulse is thus a wave of depolarisation resembling the chain reaction of nuclear fission or the slow combustion of a gunpowder trail, quite unlike the passage of an electric current along a wire. Helmholtz' findings were thus explained. But the new discoveries, had anyone made the correlation, also completely invalidated Freud's theory of "conversion hysteria". There is no quota of affect, no sum of excitation, and no principle of constancy.

But Freud's theories gave yet another rationale to the myth of hysteria. With the gradual infiltration of his theories into psychiatry and medicine, a process accelerated after the "Freud revolution" of the nineteen-sixties, the term "conversion hysteria" passed into medical nomenclature, along with another Freudian concept introduced in this paper – the "flight into illness". In fact, in recent years the term "conversion reaction" has come to be employed in place of "hysteria" as being considered more appropriate to twentieth-century medicine than the older term, with its connotations of the uterine theory, an example of the uncritical acceptance of Freud's theories in modern psychiatry.

The same paper (*The Neuro-Psychoses of Defence*, 1894) contained the first detailed exposition of another of Freud's fundamental hypotheses – that of "repression". Years later he declared in his *History of the Psycho-analytical Movement* (1914) that the theory of repression (or to give it its other name "defence") was the "corner-stone on which the whole structure of psychoanalysis rests". It had been referred to briefly in the *Preliminary Communication* but is fully discussed in this paper. Stated as proven fact, the theory of repression is described as part of the process of "conversion" by which the ego fends off unwelcome ideas by "*turning this powerful idea into a weak one, in robbing it of the affect – the sum of excitation – with which it is loaded*". This was achieved by the process of "conversion".

> "The conversion may be either total or partial. It proceeds along the line of the motor or sensory innervation which is related – whether intimately or more loosely – to the traumatic experience. By this means the ego succeeds in freeing itself from the contradiction; but instead it has burdened itself with a mnemic symbol which finds a lodgement in consciousness, like a sort of parasite, either in the form of an unresolvable motor innervation or as a constantly recurring hallucinatory sensation, and which persists until a conversion in the opposite direction takes place. Consequently the memory-trace of the repressed idea has, after all, not been dissolved; from now on, it forms the nucleus of a second psychical group."

This flight of ideas is presented dogmatically as fact. Again no experimental or pathological evidence is offered in support. Nor does Freud provide any corroborative clinical case material apart from a brief reference to the patients described in the *Studies*.

> "I will give some examples, which I could easily multiply, from my own observation: the case of a girl, who blamed herself because, while she was nursing her sick father, she had thought about a young man who had made a slight erotic impression on her; the case of a governess who had fallen in love with her employer and had resolved to drive this inclination out of her mind because it seemed to her incompatible with her pride; and so on."

So this paper gives no real indication of the source of the repression theory. However, Freud's *Autobiographical Study* written over thirty years later in 1925, is more explicit. We learn from this that it was from the aberrations of memory in the hypnotic trance that the theory was derived. Describing his use of hypnosis as an aid to the cathartic method and his later abandonment of it, he writes:

> "But hypnotism had been of immense help in the cathartic treatment, by widening the field of the patient's consciousness and putting within his reach knowledge which he did not possess in his waking life. It seemed no easy task to find a substitute for it."

While in this perplexity he recalled Bernheim's experiments and his method of applying pressure to the patient's forehead to induce him to remember the events of the trance. He describes his own adaptation of the method for use on patients who had not been hypnotised. This method was, he claimed, completely successful – "I was set free from hypnotism". He was, he alleged, able to obtain long-forgotten memories in this way. The validity of the claim has already been discussed. These memories, he maintained, were in some way distressing, either alarming, painful, or shameful. It was impossible not to conclude that that was precisely why they had been forgotten, why they had not remained conscious. Moreover, the effort expended by the physician in extracting the memories signified the measure of *resistance* on the part of the patient. "It was only necessary to translate into words what I myself had observed, and I was in possession of the theory of *repression*." The theory was a novelty, he continues, "nothing like it had ever before been recognised in mental life".

The theory was, like "conversion hysteria", neither new nor true. In 1914 the Polish psychologist Luise von Karpinska had pointed out·the striking resemblance of Freud's theories to those propagated seventy years before by Johann Friedrich Herbart (1776–1841). The system he taught was almost identical to that of Freud. He wrote of unconscious mental processes, of ideas being repressed from consciousness by opposing ideas and of the same kind of "forces" possessing specific quantities as had Freud. In his biography, Ernest Jones discusses these similarities, but rejects the idea that Freud derived his theories from Herbart; it was hardly likely, he objected, that Freud would ever have had reason to read Herbart's writings, though it was, of course, possible. Then came this revealing passage:

> "After this paragraph was written, Dr and Mrs Bernfeld, thus increasing my great debt to them, have communicated the remarkably interesting fact that in Freud's last year at the Gymnasium the following text-book was in use: Gustaf Adolf Lindner, *Lehrbuch der empirischen Psychologie nach genetischer Methode*, 1858 . . . the book may be described as a compendium of the Herbartian psychology. It contains, among other things, this passage: 'A result of the fusion of ideas proves that ideas which were once in consciousness and for any reason have been repressed (*Verdrängt*) out of it are not lost, but in certain circumstances may return'" (Jones 1953, 407).

The process has been continued by other authors, notably by H. F. Ellenberger, who traced Freud's fundamental hypotheses to the "Romantic" phase of German medicine when the Philosophy of Nature was the dominant force in medicine and psychiatry. "As we shall see in the following page", he wrote in his *Discovery of the Unconscious* (1970), "there is hardly a single concept of Freud or Jung that had not been anticipated by the Philosophy of Nature and Romantic medicine."

Thus Freud's fundamental hypotheses are actually a concept of the early decades of the nineteenth century when "animal magnetism", the forerunner of hypnotism, was taken more seriously in Germany than anywhere in Europe. Chairs were established in the universities for its study; it permeated all aspects of intellectual life and played an important role in the establishment of the Philosophy of Nature. Strange aberrations of memory had been encountered in magnetism; from these the early concepts of repression arose. Apart from the well known amnesia, it sometimes happened that a patient would remember an event or person from very early childhood, long forgotten in the normal waking state. Similar reports were published later in the century when magnetism was replaced by hypnosis. A striking example occurs in the book by Binet and Féré, two of Charcot's assistants at the Salpêtrière.

"A young girl was in M. Charcot's consulting room at the Salpêtrière. Unexpectedly, M. Parrot, the orphanage doctor arrived. On asking the somnambule the name of the stranger, she replied without hesitation, to the great astonishment of all: M. Parrot. On awakening, she affirmed that she did not know him but after having examined him for some time she finally said, 'I believe this is a doctor of the orphanage.' She had been admitted to the orphanage at the age of two." (Binet and Féré, 1887).

Occasionally a patient under hypnosis would be subject to a flood of such childhood memories, all in pristine state as if they had occurred only the day before. Such "panoramas" have been described by patients resuscitated after near-drowning episodes or by patients suffering from epilepsy.

Wilder Penfield's discovery of the physical substrate of memory in the temporal lobes of the human brain is the common denominator between all three types of panoramic memory described above. The temporal lobes are primarily affected in states of drowning and suffocation because their structure and peculiar vascular supply renders them more susceptible than other parts of the brain to states of anoxia (absence of oxygen), hypoglycaemia, and drugs. They have the lowest seizure threshold of all parts of the brain with more rapid spread of the epileptic discharge. Hence the aberrations of memory so prominent in such states. S. A. K. Wilson (1928) quotes a personal account from Admiral Sir Francis Beaufort who fell into the sea from a small boat he was trying to tie alongside his ship. Beaufort estimated that "two minutes could not have elapsed from the moment of suffocation to that of my being hauled up". Though his senses were deadened, not so the mind – "its activity seemed to be invigorated in a ratio which defies all description, for thought rose after thought with a rapidity of succession that is not only indescribable but probably inconceivable, by anyone who had not himself been in a similar situation". The recent events and the effects of his accident on home and family were the first series of reflections that occurred.

"They then took a wider range – our last cruise – a former voyage – my school – and even all my boyish pursuits and adventures. Thus travelling backwards, every past incident of my life seemed to glance across my recollection in retrograde succession, not, however, in mere outline, but the picture filled up with every minute and collateral feature; in short, the whole period of my existence seemed to be placed before me in a kind of panoramic review; indeed, many trifling events which had been long forgotten then crowded into my imagination, and with the character of recent familiarity."

Wilson describes the case of another patient who had tried to commit suicide by hanging while depressed, estimating that he had been suspended for a matter of minutes or even seconds only.

"The scenes of his early life were, in their minutest particulars, revived. Incidents connected with the school in which he received his early instruction were reproduced to his mind. The remembrance of faces (known when a child) that had been (as he supposed) entirely obliterated from his memory was restored to his recollection in a most remarkably truthful and vivid manner. During that critical second of time (when it may be reasonably presumed he was struggling with death) every trifling and minute circumstance connected with his past life was presented to his mind like so many pictorial sketches and drawings."

A colleague's son who had choked on a piece of meat in a restaurant provided Wilson with a personally observed instance of panoramic memory. The time that had elapsed since the son had become semi-asphyxiated till his father extracted the meat impacted in the upper larynx was one minute at the most. In that brief period the boy had "gone back in thought, in the most pleasant way in the world, to scenes and incidents of his earliest childhood. Trifling events of his nursery life, his childhood and schooldays passed before him in a succession of vivid pictures. He saw again the furniture of his nursery, its paper and carpet, his nurse and so on." He later told Wilson of his astonishment that these things could all thus rise in clear outline before him.

Panoramic memories occur as the aura of an epileptic attack, the patients reporting that their seizures are ushered in by "a string of old memories". One of Wilson's patients described his attacks:

"I then seem to wander back many years of my life to things that happened when I was an absolute child. Trifling things, childish things, come back to me, and I wonder how it is I could remember them . . . It is like a vision. It seems as if I had gone right back and become part of the scene again."

Another patient described her auras:

"I go into a curious state in which I suddenly remember all sorts of things that happened when I was a child. They are stupid, silly old-fashioned things of my childhood. They are things that I have done in years gone by, in other places. I remember silly things like swinging, playing with toys with other girls, and then I go off."

The events recalled by Penfield's patients under the stimulating electrode were more recent memories, though were of a similarly unremarkable nature. One patient, for instance, said while the electrode was being held in place, "Something brings back a memory. I see Seven-up Bottling Company . . . Harrison Bakery." Stimulation of a point on the cortex of another patient caused him to see a man and a dog walking along a road near his home in the country. A young secretary exclaimed with surprise, "Oh, I had a very, very familiar memory, in an office somewhere. I could see the desks. I was there and someone was calling me, a man leaning on a desk with a pencil in his hand." R.M. said, "A guy coming through the fence at the baseball game, I see the whole thing." Another patient heard a telephone conversation between his mother and his aunt – "my mother telling my aunt to come up and visit us tonight".

The evocation of memories under hypnosis is achieved by an analogous mechanism. There is no enlargement of the field of consciousness. It is a random process and the memories recalled are generally of a trivial nature. They are not repressed memories "brought to the surface". There is in fact no known mechanism by which memories can be repressed by the ego. Painful and distressing events are, as common sense tells us, those which most clearly stand out in our memory. We may "put them out of our head" – i.e. turn our attention to something else, but they will return unbidden when some chance association recalls them to mind. Moreover the recovery of memories under any of the above conditions is essentially an involuntary process. Individual memories cannot be recalled to order. Occasionally the memories recalled under hypnosis may have been of greater significance than the trivia mentioned above. This probably occurred often enough to credit the process with the power of widening the field of consciousness to reveal *all* forgotten material. But for the most part "hypnotic regressions" are merely the products of the ingenious use of the subject's imagination. Alleged regression to the first years of life and even to birth itself are especially suspect. The brain in early life has not yet matured; large tracts of nervous pathways are still unmyelinated; the mechanisms for the laying down of long-term memory have not yet developed. (For this reason, contrary to psychoanalytic theory, the first years of life are probably the *least* important for the development of future character.)

In recent decades some experimenters have claimed to have taken their hypnotised subjects still further back to before their birth and still further to alleged previous existences. The famous case of "Bridey Murphy" in 1952 signalled the start of numerous similar experiments in "hypnotic regression". It began in Pueblo, Colorado, when a local businessman, whose hobby was hypnosis, operated on a Mrs Virginia Tighe, a housewife. Under hypnosis she began to talk in an Irish accent and assume the personality of an Irish girl, Bridey Murphy, who had lived in Ireland in the eighteenth century and claimed to be a previous incarnation of Mrs Tighe. The book subsequently published by her hypnotist was a world-wide success. Less widely reported was the exposé in the *Chicago American* and *Time* magazine in June 1956 by a group of reporters who had visited the home town of Mrs Tighe and investigated her background. Across the road from the family home where she grew up lived a widow, a Mrs Anthony Corkell. As a child Virginia had been fascinated by Mrs Corkell's stories from her Irish background. The similarity of the names Corkell and Cork, where Bridey was supposed to have lived, and the fact that one of the Corkell boys was named Kevin (the name of one of "Bridey's" friends) roused the reporters' suspicions, finally confirmed when it was revealed that the maiden name of Mrs Corkell was none other than *Bridey Murphy*.

His claim of originality for the repression theory tells us not a little about Freud himself at this time. To have forgotten its source in a school textbook signifies a considerable deterioration of memory.

Additionally, the fact that Freud was definitely acquainted with the literature of the Romantic period is evidenced by his championship of the medieval physician and alchemist Paracelsus, one of the heroes of *Naturphilosophie*, and his claim expressed to Theodore Reik that he had been an early exponent of something akin to psychoanalysis. Freud's entire theoretical edifice was simply a regurgitation of old theories he had read many years before. That they flashed into his brain as new and original concepts is, of course, completely compatible with his cocaine usage.

In *The Neuro-Psychoses of Defence*, all the old concepts of the Romantic period, repression, resistance, transference, sublimation, which Brücke and his generation had devoted their lives to replacing with scientific principles, Freud brought back as new discoveries. Even the famous "flight into illness" concept was a product of Romantic medicine though still extant in the popular imagination. This was the background to the epithet "horrible old wives' psychiatry" levelled by one critic. Yet Freud must have heard a hundred times from Brücke's own lips the story of the old battles and the reason they had to be fought.

XIV

The Ill-fated Seduction Theory

Meanwhile, Freud's cardiac irregularity was still continuing but now caused less alarm in view of Fliess' diagnosis of a nasal aetiology. This, less sinister, diagnosis was reinforced when, during the winter of 1895, Freud eventually developed *real* nasal pathology, at first taking the form of chronic suppurative rhinitis leading to frequent sinus infections, which, by a strange coincidence, his friend Fliess also suffered from. Both men, in fact, were experiencing the frequent infections which so often followed the sloughing and ulceration caused by the drug. When Fliess came to Vienna to operate on "Emma" in February 1895, he performed a cauterisation operation on Freud's nose, the first of many such procedures. Sinus operations are mentioned in the letter to Fliess on August 16, 1895 (*Origins*) and in addition surgery to the turbinate bones was performed more than once. Both men were greatly preoccupied with the states of their noses, not unnaturally in view of their symptoms and the more serious pathology they believed dependent on nasal reflexes.

Freud welcomed the nasal symptoms as confirmation of the validity of Fliess' diagnosis, though still having misgivings as to the possibility of a more serious heart condition. "I would like you to be right," he wrote to Fliess on April 20, 1895, "in thinking that the nose has a large share in it, and the heart a small one. Only a very strict judge would take it amiss that with this kind of pulse and the insufficiency I often believe the opposite." On April 26 he wrote, "A great deal of pus is coming out. I evidently have an empyema of the sphenoidal bone, which naturally makes me very happy" (this because it confirmed Fliess' diagnosis and refuted a more sinister aetiology). Significantly the letter contained a reference to putting an end to "the last horrible attack with cocaine" On May 25 he reported, "I secreted abundant masses of pus and throughout it felt splendid" (Schur, 1972).

It was in this year, 1895, that the first neurological symptoms emerged. He had the first of several "fainting attacks" gleaned by

Schur from the unpublished Fliess correspondence as occurring during the haemorrhaging episodes of his patient Emma. It was attributed by Schur to the sight of blood but Freud who had spent several months in the surgical wards of the Vienna General Hospital was no stranger to blood. The "faint" was the herald of many later attacks of loss of consciousness in circumstances which would indicate that these "faints" were actually seizures. Significantly too, he tells Fliess in his letter of April 27, 1895 that he is suffering from Bernhardt's disease (*meralgia paraesthetica*), a condition characterised by a disturbance of sensation in the outer surface of the thigh in the distribution of the external cutaneous femoral nerve.

In his turn Fliess was undergoing a similar progression. His headaches under his cocaine treatment were understandably worsening and his attribution of these to nasal pathology led to ever more frequent surgical onslaughts on his nose. We learn from Schur that Fliess consulted many prominent nose and throat specialists and underwent several operations, some of them extensive and hazardous in view of the serious post-operative complications at the time and – though Schur does not mention this – the unhealthy state of the nasal tissues and their tendency to haemorrhage.

It was in this phase that Freud began to compose his *Project for a Scientific Psychology*, an attempt to correlate psychology with the neurone theory and the other new findings in neurophysiology. It began as a pencilled scrawl dashed off in the train returning from a visit to Fliess in Berlin in September 1895 and rapidly became, in his own words, his "consuming passion", a "tyrant", and "incubus". "I have never been so intensely preoccupied by anything," he wrote to Fliess on April 27, 1895 (*Origins*). Every free moment was devoted to the work.

> "The hours of the night from eleven to two have been occupied with imagining, transpositions and guesses, only abandoned when I arrived at some absurdity, or had so truly and seriously overworked that I had no interest left for the day's medical work."

The whole essay, Jones tells us, "a brochure of some hundred pages, was written feverishly in a couple of weeks, with a few necessary intervals and despatched to Fliess on October 8."

The "obsessive feverishness" with which he wrote the essay, Jones believed, hinted at "some deep underground activity". But the episode is highly suggestive of "the lashing effects" of cocaine described by Mattison. It was in connection with this essay that

Freud wrote the letter of October 20, 1895, already quoted on page 164, containing unmistakable signs of drug writing – the barriers lifted – the veil drawn aside – the clear vision. The essay represents a series of flights of ideas, unsupported by any foundation in anatomy or physiology, of the alleged activities of the neurones, their "flight from excitation" and their "tendency to divest themselves of quantity". In one such incomprehensible flight Freud arrives at the "basis of consciousness":

> "But my hypothesis goes further, and asserts that the perceptual neurones are incapable of receiving quantities $(Q\dot{\eta})$, but that they assimilate the *period* of an excitation and that this condition of theirs of being affected by a period, while being filled with only a minimum of quantity $(Q\dot{\eta})$, *is the fundamental basis of consciousness.*"

As we have already seen, Freud later realised that he had perpetuated an aberration. He never asked Fliess for the return of the manuscript and it was found with the rest of the correspondence after his death, since when it has taxed in vain the utmost ingenuity of a succession of Freud scholars.

He was meanwhile continuing his work at the Kassowitz clinic, yet there is no mention of it in the published letters. No interesting cases are discussed – and they must have been many. He published several papers from the institute – mainly reviews of the literature, but these he dismissed with scorn – "my book on the diplegias which I knocked together almost casually with a minimum of effort," he writes on May 21, 1894, "has been a huge success." He contrasted its reception with the bad one he forecast for the "really good things" – for the coming aetiology and theory of the neuroses he could "expect no more than a respectable flop". As time went on there were more complaints about the "uninteresting work on children's paralyses". He had now to put all work on psychology out of his thoughts and concentrate on the commitment to contribute a treatise on children's palsies for Nothnagel's great encyclopaedia of medicine. He evidently completed the work with difficulty when it was long overdue. He was finding the work increasingly uncongenial, as his comment to Fliess (November 2, 1896) – "Pegasus yoked to the plough" – testifies. The work involved, sifting and summarising the extant literature on the subject, must have been greatly at variance with the racing thoughts and flights of ideas he was now experiencing, which had found free expression in psychological speculation.

By the beginning of the following year (1896) Freud had begun to exhibit a very characteristic trait. It will be remembered from

Chapter X that chronic cocaine users showed a marked propensity to breaches with former friends, in most cases because of suspicion and delusions of persecution. The Dr Brower previously mentioned (1886) considered that "besides the perversion of the affections and disturbances of the moral emotions, there was a tendency to quarrel with friends and former associates and to form alliances with persons formerly regarded as inferiors". In Freud's case the breach was with his friend of many years, Breuer, and the "alliance" was the greater intensification of his friendship with Fliess.

The famous *Studies in Hysteria* dealt with in Chapters VIII and XII, published jointly by Breuer and Freud, had appeared the previous year. Freud inadvertently provided a fair summing up of the work:

> "I have not always been a psychotherapist. Like other neuro-pathologists, I was trained to employ local diagnoses and electro-prognosis and it still strikes me myself as strange that the case histories I write should read like short stories and that, as one might say, they lack the serious stamp of science."

Jones tells us that after the summer of 1894, i.e. *before* the publication of the *Studies*, Freud and Breuer never collaborated again. This would imply that Breuer no longer sent Freud patients, as their previous professional association had centred on their mutual cases. No satisfactory explanation for this is given by Jones. In his *Autobiographical Study* Freud infers that the main reason for Breuer's withdrawal was that he had been affected by the bad reception the book received in Austria and Germany and that the "severe rebuff" from the German neurologist Strümpell caused him to feel hurt and discouraged. He himself was "able to laugh at the lack of comprehension which his criticism showed". But Strümpell's criticisms, as has been emphasised by Ellenberger and Sulloway, were mild and reasonable. Moreover, the collaboration had ceased in 1894 *before* the publication of the *Studies*.

Jones ascribes the differences between the two men to Freud's sexual theories. But "The scientific differences alone cannot account for the bitterness with which Freud wrote about Breuer in the unpublished Fliess correspondence of the nineties," he writes, recalling what Breuer had meant to Freud in the previous decade, his generosity and the understanding sympathy and intellectual stimulation he had given to Freud. "Where previously no word of criticism for the perfect Breuer could be found, now one hears no more of his good qualities." Jones dates the main reversal of Freud's sentiments towards Breuer to the spring of 1896, "a date which coincided with the onset of the more passionate phase of his relationship with Fliess". Freud's antipathy rapidly increased from this time. In an unpublished letter of March 29, 1897 cited by Jones he declared he was glad he saw no more of Breuer: the very sight of him would make him inclined to emigrate. "These are strong words," comments Jones, "and there are stronger ones which need not be reproduced. They go much beyond the actual complaints Freud formulates."

These omissions from the published letters have led to much speculation. As Frank Sulloway (1979) describes it, "the editors of the Fliess correspondence felt compelled to omit from publication most of the vitriolic and unattractive side of Freud revealed by his bitter remarks about Breuer." This process of expurgation has continued, he noticed. In the abridged edition of Jones' biography by Trilling and Marcus, Jones' remarks are minimised. Sulloway's quick eye detected still further deletions in the volume of letters edited by Freud's son Ernst (1961) in which vindictive remarks by Freud are omitted but *without* the customary punctuation which would indicate that an omission had been made. There is no doubt that the very intensity of Freud's antipathy towards his former friend has perplexed Freud's biographers, especially those who had access to the whole of the Fliess correspondence. We shall probably only discover its whole extent when the embargo on the remainder of the correspondence is removed.

The tendency of cocaine users to quarrel and break with former well-liked friends was, as we have seen, based on fear of some imaginary threat or danger from the friend in question. We do know that Breuer was understandably critical about the length of time his patients were in analysis with Freud – in one case nearly five years (Schur, 1972). In the American cases mentioned in Chapter X this paranoia was manifested in extreme cases by actual homicidal threats but in milder forms by a great repugnance for the former friends and avoidance of their society. Many of these patients, as we have seen, went to extreme lengths to avoid the threatening person or situation, making frequent changes of hotel rooms and taking wide detours and adopting similar strategems to do so. Freud's aversion for Breuer took a remarkably similar turn.

Two episodes document the paranoiac elements of his anti-pathy. In his *Psychopathology of Everyday Life* (1901) Freud, illustrating his theory of unconscious motivation in forgetting, relates his efforts to find a certain shop selling safe-boxes with which he had previously been familiar. Though he had forgotten the address he had in his mind's eye an unusually vivid picture of the shop window in the centre of Vienna and felt sure he could find the shop if he walked through the town, since his memory told him he had passed it on countless occasions. To his chagrin he was unable to do so, though he walked all over the Inner Town in every direction. The name of the street was eventually found in a trade directory and Freud immediately remembered the shop.

> '"It was true that I had passed the shop window innumerable times, every time, in fact, that I had visited the M. family [Breuer appears as "M" in writings of this kind] who have lived for many years in the same building. Our intimate friendship later gave place to a total estrangement; after that, I fell into the habit – the reasons for which I never considered – of also avoiding the neighbourhood and the house."

Another revealing incident is disclosed in a letter dated April 21, 1954, now in the Jones' Archives, sent to Jones by Breuer's daughter-in-law. Walking in the streets of Vienna many years after the break with Breuer, now an old man, they one day saw Freud coming towards them. Breuer instinctively opened his arms but Freud, head down, walked briskly by, pretending not to see them.

Freud's gradual withdrawal from the society of his medical colleagues after 1897 which he describes as his "splendid isolation" has elements of the same causation. Withdrawal from the society of former friends and colleagues is a characteristic effect of heavy cocaine usage documented by the German pharmacologist Lewin and many others. Freud's often avowed aversion to his native city of Vienna, of which Jones gives many instances, was probably also a cocaine effect; "bitterness towards his environment" is asserted by Lewin to be a prominent characteristic of the cocainist.

The lack of Breuer's restraining influence soon made itself felt. From now on Fliess was the only sounding board for Freud's proposed publications and lectures. From that quarter he evidently received nothing but unstinted praise. So there was nobody to advise against the publication of the disastrous seduction papers in 1896.

Freud had already introduced in the paper discussed in the previous chapter his conviction that the "incompatible ideas" whose repression led to hysteria and other "defence neuroses" were invariably of a sexual nature – in all the cases he had analysed it was the subject's sexual life that had given rise to the distressing effect. He now took the theme further – this process had arisen as a result of a sexual assault or seduction in infancy – he had invariably found this to be the case. He first announced the theory in a contribution to a French journal – *Heredity and the*

Aetiology of the Neuroses (1896) and especially addressed his words to the disciples of Charcot, dead now for three years. In this paper he expressly rejected Charcot's contention that a hereditary predisposition underlay the propensity of psychic events to precipitate hysterical attacks. Here Freud, who never used statistical methods himself and always denied their application to psychoanalysis, criticised Charcot's lack of statistics. "Our opinion of the aetiological role of heredity in nervous illnesses ought decidedly to be based on an impartial statistical examination" he declared, "and not on a *petitio principii.*"

Basing his claim on all the thirteen cases he had analysed he declared that the traumatic precipitating event was either a brutal sexual assault by an adult, or a seduction less rapid and less repulsive, but reaching the same conclusion. In seven out of the thirteen cases the intercourse was between children on both sides, sexual relations between a little girl and a boy slightly older (most often her brother) who had himself been the victim of an earlier seduction by some female servant or governess, and on account of their origin, often of a disgusting sort. It was this kind of situation which gave a false impression of hereditary factors, he believed. The commonest age for these seductions was the fourth or fifth year but in two cases they had occurred in the second year of life. "One sometimes comes across a pair of neurotic patients who were a pair of little lovers in their earliest childhood – the man suffering from obsessions and the woman from hysteria. If they are brother and sister, one might mistake for a result of nervous heredity what is, in fact, the consequence of precocious sexual experiences." The theory was elaborated in his next paper, *The Neuro-psychoses of Defence (II)* published in 1896. Citing the same thirteen cases he admitted the astonishing nature of his statements, justifying them in one of the circular arguments that had become increasingly evident in his writings at this time. "I should not lend credence to these extraordinary findings myself," he added, "if their complete reliability were not proved by the development of the subsequent neurosis." However, "it would be useless to try to elicit these childhood traumas outside psychoanalysis; their traces are never present in conscious memory, only in the symptoms of the illness".

In neither of the two papers is any evidence in the form of case history material offered. The thirteen cases are not described. "But this is not the place in which to present the documents and the experiences which have forced me to my conviction", he had said in the French paper. "I must postpone entering into any more far-reaching psychological discussion till another occasion," he said in

The Neuro-psychoses of Defence (II). The occasion was never to arise. Nor were the psychoanalytic methods he had used to arrive at his conclusions described. In fact, his readers had to wait nine years before learning of these methods or for any detailed case history until the publication of the "Dora analysis" in 1905. Meanwhile in this paper he forestalled any criticisms of these deficiencies, asking "that no one should form too certain judgements in this obscure field until he has made use of the only method which can throw light on it – of psychoanalysis for the purpose of making conscious what has so far been unconscious." He declared that "In this kind of communication it is not possible to bring forward the evidence needful to support my assertions, but I hope to be able to fulfil this obligation in a detailed presentation."

On April 21, 1896 before the assembled members of the Society for Psychiatry and Neurology, Freud repeated confidently his infantile seduction theory. It was a distinguished audience, composed of the élite of the profession and chaired by the eminent professor of psychiatry, Richard von Krafft-Ebing. To this gathering he expounded his conviction that nursemaids, governesses, tutors, or "all too often a close relative" were the chief culprits; a little boy thus prematurely initiated into sexual practices repeated the seduction on a little sister. He warned his audience of the sexual practices carried out by nurses and nurserymaids even on infants in arms. Moreover, the abuses, he informed his audience, frequently took the form of sexual perversions – "they include all the abuses known to debauched and impotent persons, among whom the buccal cavity and the rectum are misused for sexual purposes." These pronouncements were evidently communicated to his distinguished audience with messianic fervour. "I believe this to be a momentous revelation," he declared, "the discovery of a *caput Nili* of neuropathology." But this neurological "source of the Nile" was evidently received by his distinguished audience in stunned silence. "The donkeys gave it an icy reception," he wrote to Fliess (unpublished letter of April 26, quoted by Schur, 1972). "Krafft-Ebing, who was in the chair, said it sounded like a scientific fairy tale." Years later he recounted the incident in his *History of the Psychoanalytic Movement*:

"Unsuspectingly, I spoke before the Vienna Neurological Society, then under the presidency of Krafft- Ebing, expecting to be compensated by the interest and recognition of my colleagues for the material losses I had willingly undergone. I treated my discoveries as ordinary contributions to science and hoped to be met in the same spirit. But the silence with which my addresses were received, the void which formed itself about me, the insinuations that found their way to me, caused me gradually to realise that one cannot count upon views about the part played by sexuality in the aetiology of the neuroses meeting with the same reception as other communications."

Here Freud was using the famous "resistance" argument to good effect. He failed to mention that the content of his address to the society was the bizarre seduction theory which he himself was forced to retract a year later. He also failed to indicate that the Krafft-Ebing in question was the author of the famous *Psychopathia Sexualis* who with this book had many years before pioneered the investigation of the sexual aberrations and as such would have been the last to cavil at the discussion of sexual matters *per se* at a medical gathering. Ellenberger, Roazen and Sulloway have refuted the allegations made by Freud and his followers that the discussion of sexual matters in those days was taboo and that Freud had had to break a formidable barrier of silence to ventilate his ideas. In fact, sexuality was by this time a widely discussed subject in medical circles and Sachs tells us that there were in addition many books for the enlightenment of the lay public. The Victorian era was over. In any case the much cited extreme prudery of that time was largely a myth, much of it generated by the psychoanalysts and other would-be breakers of the conventions. The often repeated tale that the Victorians even screened the legs of their pianos out of prudery is an example of the legends that have grown around the era. (It was actually to shield the legs from the kicks of children practising their scales.) With his sure touch for the dramatic, Freud continued, quoting Hebbel, "I understood that from now onward I belonged to those who have 'troubled the sleep of the world'." He could no longer count on objectivity and tolerance, he declared.

Apart from its content the paper (published later under the title *Aetiology of Hysteria* (1896)) had deficiencies which probably did not escape his experienced audience. He again failed to give details of the methods of psychoanalysis by which he had arrived at his thesis and, though claiming his theory was based on eighteen cases, failed to give any clinical details of these cases. Again the issue of providing hard evidence was evaded. "Shall I put before you the actual material I have obtained from my analyses?" he asked, "Or shall I rather try first to meet the mass of objections and doubts which, as I am surely correct in supposing, have now taken possession of your attention? I shall choose the latter course." The use of the word "first" here implies that the necessary material was to follow but for this his audience waited in vain. Neither statistical nor clinical evidence was given.

Leaving the issue, Freud then proceeded to furnish a variety of "proofs". Discarding the objection that the patients might have deliberately invented their stories of infantile seduction, he cited as "conclusive proof" their repugnance and distress when "reproducing these infantile experiences" and their strong objections that they had no feeling of remembering the scenes. "Why should patients assure me so emphatically of their unbelief, if what they want to discredit is something which – from whatever motive – they themselves invented?" he asked. A further proof was "the uniformity which they exhibit in certain details", as if there were "secret understandings" between the patients. "Another and stronger proof" was "the relationship of the infantile scenes to the content of the whole of the rest of the case history," he said, comparing it to the fitting together of a jigsaw puzzle when "we become absolutely certain in the end which piece belongs to the empty gap". However, as he had given no case histories his audience was unable to judge the quality of this proof for itself. A final "proof" is even less clear. "Lastly, the findings of my analysis are in a position to speak for themselves. In all eighteen cases (cases of pure hysteria and hysteria combined with obsessions, and comprising six men and twelve women) I have, as I have said, come to learn of the sexual experiences of this kind in childhood." This was only one of the circular arguments in the paper. Earlier, he asks, "since infantile experience with sexual content could after all only exert a psychical effect through their *memory-traces*, would not this view be a welcome amplification of the finding of psychoanalysis which tells *us that hysterical symptoms can only arise with the cooperation of memories?*" Finally, the statement that the infantile events often involved perverse practices was "proved" by the fact that the patients' symptoms – choking, vomiting, anal sensations, etc. – were related to the mouth and rectum – another circular argument.

There were some perhaps less obvious discrepancies. The number of cases had, in this paper, risen to eighteen whereas in the two previous papers there had only been thirteen, implying that in the intervening four months Freud would have finished a further five cases. Yet in his letter to Fliess of May 4, 1896, i.e., two weeks after the meeting, he complained that he was getting no new cases for treatment and that "not one of the old ones is finished yet". In another letter of December 17, 1896 he wrote, "Not a single case is finished yet: I feel an essential piece is still missing. So long as I have not seen to the bottom of a single case I cannot feel happy. When I have once got to the bottom of a single case I shall be in a state to enjoy a good day between two night journeys." Writing to Fliess on January 3, 1897 about a proposed "congress" at Easter, he said, "Perhaps I shall have got a case finished by then." We know that psychoanalysis as practised by Freud and by most analysts subsequently lasted a very long time and we have already seen that Breuer had been concerned about a patient he had referred to Freud whose analysis had already lasted for nearly five years and was not yet completed.

A further discrepancy is that in the paper the guilty parties were cited as nursemaids, tutors, governesses, older brothers and lastly, "a close relative". In contrast, in his letter to Fliess of September 21, 1897 he stated that *fathers* were the chief culprits. In fact the many discrepancies, non-sequiturs and circular arguments in the paper point to a considerable diminution in Freud's critical faculties at this time.

It was a little more than a year later when the truth gradually dawned on Freud. On September 21, 1897 he confided in Fliess the "great secret" that he no longer believed in the seduction theory. Firstly, there was "the continual disappointment of my attempts to bring my analyses to a real conclusion" – this after he had presented his eighteen cases to the Neurological Society as completed and by implication, cured, cases! Then there was "the running away of people who for a time had seemed my most favourably inclined patients, the lack of the complete success on which I had counted, and the possibility of explaining my partial successes in other, familiar ways". Secondly, there was the astonishing fact that in every case "blame was laid on perverse acts by the father": Jones reveals from the unpublished Fliess correspondence that Freud had inferred from the existence of some hysterical symptoms in his brother and several sisters that even his own father had to be thus incriminated (letter of February 11, 1897, quoted by Jones, 1953). Doubts about the theory arose but were always repelled by fresh "evidence"; a letter to Fliess of May 31, 1897 (*Origins*) describes a dream which had reinforced his belief in the theory. "Not long ago I dreamt that I was feeling over-affectionately towards Mathilde [his eldest daughter] – but her name was Hella" (actually the name of an American niece whose photograph they had been sent). "The dream of course fulfils my wish to pin down a father as the originator of neurosis and put an end to my persistent doubts."

The collapse of the seduction theory was a devastating blow for Freud. "I do not know where I am, as I have failed to reach theoretical understanding of repression and its play of forces," he wrote to Fliess. Dreams of fame and fortune vanished. "The hope of eternal fame was so beautiful and so was that of certain wealth, complete independence, travel and removing the children from the sphere of the worries which spoiled my youth." Years later he recalled in his *History of the Psychoanalytic Movement* (1914) his "helpless bewilderment". "Analysis had led by the right paths back to these sexual traumas and yet they were untrue. Reality was lost under one's feet." He would have gladly given up the whole thing. "Perhaps I persevered only because I had no choice and could not then begin again at anything else," he added. In his *Autobiographical Study* (1925) by way of excuse for his admitted credulity, he pleads "this was at a time when I was intentionally keeping my critical faculty in abeyance so as to preserve an unprejudiced and receptive attitude towards the many novelties which were coming to my notice every day".

At last, however, he was obliged to recognise that the scenes of seduction had never taken place. He was completely at a loss. When he had pulled himself together, however, he was able to draw the "right conclusions", namely that the neurotic symptoms were not related directly to actual events but to wishful fantasies. "I do not believe even now that I forced the seduction-phantasies on my patients, that I 'suggested' them. I had in fact stumbled for the first time upon the *Oedipus complex*, which was later to assume such an overwhelming importance, but which I did not recognise as yet in its disguise of phantasy" (*Autobiographical Study*, 1925). Thus by a skilful *trompe l'oeil* exercise, Freud was able to present the whole affair not as the effects of some mental aberration, but as one of the many false trails and wrong turnings taken by all men of genius on their way to their ultimate goal, in this case the discovery of infantile sexuality and the Oedipus complex.

XV

The Unconscious Mind and The Oedipus Complex

Did Freud force the "seduction phantasies" on his patients or did they actually occur? In the paper read to the Society for Psychiatry and Neurology (*Aetiology of Hysteria*, 1896) there are passages which suggest that Freud did indeed impose the theory on his patients. In accordance with his theory that hysteria originated with a mental trauma of a sexual nature, his patients were urged to search their memories for such trauma as would prove "a suitable determinant" – i.e. a sexual one.

> "If the first-discovered scene is unsatisfactory, we tell our patient that this experience explains nothing, but that behind it there must be hidden a more significant earlier experience."

Pursuing these memories further and further back through many different chains of memories and their associations, *"in the end we infallibly come to the field of sexual experience"*. In doing so, the period of earliest childhood was reached, a period before the development of sexual life. This would seem to invalidate a sexual aetiology of the neuroses, but it was not so.

> "If we have the perseverance to press on with the analysis into early childhood, as far back as a human memory is capable of reaching, we invariably bring the patient to reproduce experiences which, on account both of their peculiar features and of their relations to the symptoms of his later illness, must be regarded as the aetiology of his neurosis for which we have been looking."

But the experiences were *not remembered* by the patients.

> "They are indignant as a rule if we warn them that such scenes are going to emerge. Only the strongest compulsion of the treatment can induce them to embark on a reproduction of them. While they are recalling these infantile experiences to consciousness, they suffer under the most violent sensations, of

which they are ashamed and which they try to conceal; and even after they have gone through them once more in such a convincing manner, they still attempt to withhold belief from them, by emphasising the fact that, unlike what happens in the case of other forgotten material, they have no feeling of remembering the scenes."

This suggests that the patients did not confess to remembering the childhood experiences – they only "reproduced them". What probably happened was that, as in the case of Frau Emmy, Freud misinterpreted some facial spasm or minor epileptic attack for a sign that the forbidden memory was emerging. Such physical manifestations would have implied confirmation of his theories. An example of Freud's circular reasoning from his patients' symptoms is contained in his letter to Fliess of January 11, 1897. Describing the events of a patient's illness, he said: "These attacks regularly started either with diarrhoea or with catarrh and hoarseness (n.b. the oral sexual system!) – that is, with a reproduction of his own passive experiences." In other words, the fact that his patient's symptoms involved the oral and anal regions proved to Freud's satisfaction that his alleged seducer must have used these areas for irregular modes of sexual gratification.

In fact, Freud was showing an increasing preoccupation with the more deviant aspects of sexuality; this would have been the expected course of events arising from his chronic cocaine usage. It will be remembered from Chapter X that many physicians who had the care of addicts found that the increased sexuality with cocaine usage frequently took the form of perverse and deviant practices. His preoccupation, however, went far beyond any clinical interest and was undoubtedly his alone. In his Draft N for example, of May 31, 1897 (*Origins*), he states that "saintliness" was based on the fact that, "for the sake of the larger community, human beings have sacrificed some of their freedom to indulge in sexual perversions". In pursuit of his interest in perversion we find a morbid preoccupation with excrement, with which he associated money, though the association is not altogether clear. It may have arisen from the literature on witchcraft he was avidly reading in pursuance of this interest. "I read one day that the gold which the devil gave his victims regularly turned into excrement," he wrote to Fliess on January 24, 1897 (*Origins*), "and the next day Herr E [a patient] who reports that his nurse had money deliria, suddenly told me (by way of Cagliostro – alchemist – Dukatenscheisser) [literally one who excretes ducats] that Louise's money was always excrement." (Louise was his patient's nurse and alleged seducer.)

When he writes that Herr E told him this, Freud obviously means that he himself derived this from the associations he had made from Cagliostro, which casts some doubt on his other claims. In a foretaste of his infantile sexuality theory only published eight years later, his letter to Fliess of January 17, 1897 (*Origins*) states that the perversions "are not to be explained by the functioning of erotogenic zones which have later been abandoned, but by the operation of erotogenic sensations which have subsequently lost their force".

The first reference to "bisexuality" occurs about this time – his letter of December 6, 1896 refers to "the universal bisexuality of human beings". This was a concept of Fliess, which Freud enthusiastically embraced. It had followed from Fliess's 28 and 23 day periods; there was of course no biological basis for the theory and the discovery of the sex chromosomes was far away in the future. But there was another factor. Schur refers to the "sexualisation" of the relationship between the two men. Freud himself gives some confirmation of this. Jones, writing of a "fainting attack" Freud suffered in a hotel in Munich in 1912, says that Freud connected the episode to a previous attack he had had in that very hotel room when he had been visiting Fliess during an illness and the town seemed to have acquired "a strong connection with my relation to that man". "There is some piece of unruly homosexual feeling at the root of the matter," he added. A homosexual element appearing in the friendship around this time would be consistent with the other symptoms of cocaine usage.

Fliess himself had already taken off into the flight from reality with his preoccupation with the 28 and 23 day sexual periods to which people of all ages and both sexes were supposed to be subject. From these premises he had already embarked on far-flung hypotheses which found expression in a peculiar numbers mystique and by now he was finding a deeper connection between astronomical relations and the creation of organisms. Such writing is practically pathognomonic of drug usage.

Not only did Freud lavish praise on the theory but he looked to it for solving problems in his work. "I have run into some doubts about my repression theory," he wrote on June 30, 1896 (*Origins*), "which a suggestion from you, like the one about male and female menstruation in the same individual may resolve." He constantly furnished Fliess with mathematical formulae concerning the dates of his family's illnesses and other events – "Martin took to bed with an acute onset of illness on January 14 $(5 \times 28^2 - 10 \times 23)^3$, he wrote on February 1, 1900 (quoted by Schur, 1972). This data Fliess used in his published works. When Freud's father died on his expected period day, Fliess included in his works *Der Ablauf des Lebens* the formula:

$$\left.\begin{array}{l}\text{Herr Freud sen. 1 April 1815}\\ \text{24 Oktober 1896}\end{array}\right\} 29792$$
$$= 38.28^2 \quad 2.38^3 - 2.23^2 = 28^3 + 2.28^2 \triangle$$

Both Freud and Fliess kept periodic calendars, and Freud frequently wrote to his friend about having had bad period days. "A critical day prevented me from going on", he wrote on December 3, 1897 (*Origins*). His letter of December 22, 1897 looked forward to a forthcoming "congress" when he would hear "the fine new things you will have to tell me about life and its dependence on the world process".

Conclusive proof that Freud fully accepted his friend's hypothesis is shown by the incident which occurred after the publication of Fliess' 1897 monograph. A highly unfavourable review had appeared in the *Wiener Klinische Rundschau*, which effectively exposed the many absurdities in Fliess' theories. Freud was on the editorial board of this journal and the editor-in-chief, Paschkis, was a personal friend. Immediately on reading the review Freud wrote to him demanding an explanation. When this produced no satisfactory result he resigned from the editorial board in protest. Three years later, in his monograph *On Dreams*, Freud wrote, "The unfavourable reception of my friend's work had made a profound impression on me. It contained, in my opinion, a fundamental biological discovery, which is only now – many years later – beginning to find favour with the experts" (1901, *Standard Edition V*).

This was the solution to the "unsolved enigma" of the friendship between the two men which his biographers have been at so much pains to explain – the need for a sympathetic listener in his "isolation" – the supposition that Fliess had become for him a "transference-figure" and so on. The secret was that the critical faculties of both men had been so much diminished by drug usage that they were completely receptive to each other's most fantastic ideas and so ready listeners – a very necessary requirement in view of the heightened prolixity engendered by cocaine.

About this time the two men were experiencing another expected cocaine effect. It will be remembered from Chapter X that the increase in sexuality which was an initial feature of cocaine usage was succeeded by the reverse effect and a partial or complete loss of potency occurred. A Dr C. L. Gregory, for instance, was reported in the *New York Medical Record* of 1892 as calling attention in *The American Therapist* to the "loss of virility amounting even to impotence which he had observed in a number of cases to follow repeated application of cocaine to the nasal mucous membranes". Many other reports confirmed this. Some suggested that the loss of potency was often accompanied by unimpaired libido. Something very like this evidently occurred with Freud. On October 31, 1897 he wrote to Fliess about the lack of pleasures in his life . . . "Also sexual excitation is of no more use to a person like me," he said. He was then only 41. Three years later on March 11, 1900 he was writing to Fliess, "You know how limited my pleasures are ... I have finished with begetting children." Jones confirms this. "While it is likely that the passionate side of married life subsided with him earlier than it does with many men," he wrote, " – indeed we know this in so many words – it was replaced by an unshakable devotion and a perfect harmony of understanding" (Jones, II, 386). We have no direct evidence that Fliess experienced the same symptom. But it is interesting that about this time he developed his concept of the "male menopause". Freud wrote to him on March 1, 1896 (*Origins*): "I was also delighted with the idea of the male menopause; in my 'Anxiety Neurosis' I boldly stated that it might turn out to be the final conditioning factor for men." In this work he had written, "There are men who have a climacteric like women and who develop anxiety neurosis at the time of their waning potency and increased libido."

The medical profession has always had doubts about the reality of the "male menopause", a concept popularised by psychoanalysis. It was finally laid to rest at the Second International Congress on the Menopause held in Jerusalem in 1979. On the basis of 10,000 male out-patients claiming to be suffering from this symptom, Dr E. Nieschlag was able to state categorically, "The syndrome 'male climacteric' does not exist as a pathological entity." There was an age-related increase in sexual disturbances as there was with insomnia and memory dysfunction. But these alterations occurred slowly over a long period. There was no abrupt change during a distinct phase of life, as occurred in women.

Freud's increasingly depressive moods and preoccupation with death and dying had by this time become inextricably bound up with Fliess' periodic theory. The theory had predicted that he would die at the age of 51 (28×23) and he awaited this date with mingled trepidation and fatalistic resignation. As the critical date passed, the periodic calculations pointed to a new date, so that Freud must have spent a large part of his life in anxious expectation of a premature demise. (He actually lived till the age of 83.)

The theme recurred constantly in his letters and other writings. Telephone numbers, hotel room numbers and various dates assumed for him a sinister significance. An extreme instance of Freud's obsession occurs in his letter to Jung of April 16, 1911. "A few years ago I discovered in myself the conviction that I would die between the ages of 61 and 62," he wrote. He had gone on a trip to Greece with his brother in 1904 and

> "it was absolutely uncanny how the numbers 61 or 60 in conjunction with 1 or 2, kept cropping up under all kinds of circumstances involving the naming of common objects, especially in connection with means of transportation, all of which I conscientiously noted down. Being in low spirits, I hoped to breathe again when in our Athens hotel a room on the first floor was assigned to us; there could be no 61."

But the room number was 31, half of 61-62 and this number proved to be "more persistent in its persecution than the first one". Long after his break with Fliess he was still working out new dates for his death. His interest in the American President Wilson which led to his "psychoanalytic study" of the President, written in the latter part of his life and published posthumously, was activated by the fact that both men were born in the same year, 1856.

It is against the background of a deepening drug psychosis that we must view Freud's theory of the "unconscious mind" which was now beginning to assume its own very characteristic shape and pattern. Gradually during the mid-nineties Freud had progressed from references to "unconscious mental processes". In other words he had progressed from using the word "unconscious" as an adjective, to using it as a noun, with connotations of a definite region, a dark and forbidding territory to be apprehensively but courageously explored.

The concept of an "unconscious mind" was not a new one and Freud claimed for it no originality. It had, in fact, enjoyed a considerable vogue earlier in the century and Edward von Hartmann had written an influential book, *The Philosophy of the Unconscious* (1869). Ideas of an "unconscious mind" had persisted since the ancients who, ignorant of the autonomic nervous system, had explained the continuation of breathing and other vital functions during sleep, by claiming for the soul an unconscious faculty. Robert Whytt's treatise, *An Essay on the Vital and other Involuntary Motions of Animals* (1763) which is often cited as one of the first works on the reflex functions of the nervous system, is actually a plea for the presence of the soul in even such seemingly automatic and involuntary acts as blinking when the eyes are threatened. The easy solution of a problem in the morning that had defeated them the previous night was cited by some writers as evidence for unconscious mental functioning, which, of course, could be equally attributed to the restorative effects of sleep. Loose terminology accounts for many uses of the word "unconscious" where the word "unnoticed" should be used.

But the great impetus towards the adoption of the concept of an unconscious mind stemmed from the rise of animal magnetism in the early decades of the century and its re-emergence under the name of "hypnotism" in the last three decades. In both these periods the hypnotised subject was thought to be sleepwalking and therefore unconscious. Numerous demonstrations during these epochs had presented hypnotised subjects capable of speech and of performing comparatively complex mental activities for which, on awakening, they had no memory. It was understandable that some concept of unconscious mental functioning should arise.

This feeling was augmented by the reports of "double consciousness" or "double personality" which accompanied each phase. It was the phenomena of hypnotism, and cases of "double personality" which convinced psychoanalysts of the existence of an unconscious mind and provided for them the ultimate "proof" of Freud's concept. As Fritz Wittels (1924) described it, "Cases of double consciousness had been elaborately described, and it was necessary to assume that the mind has a bipartite character, for there was no other way of explaining these cases". Jones discussed the existence of the "unconscious mind" in almost indentical fashion:

> "The cases of multiple personality, and the beautiful experimental work carried out on patients in a state of deep hypnosis, seemed to furnish convincing proof that the mind was not coextensive with consciousness and that complicated mental processes could be going on without the subject being in the least aware of them. The concept of an unconscious mind was therefore perfectly familiar to us, though we knew nothing about what it contained" (*Free Associations*).

The "proof" provided by hypnotism is easily disposed of. In the trance state, whether occurring in spontaneous attacks of temporal lobe epilepsy or in those induced, as in "hypnotism", the subject *is not unconscious*, a fact demonstrated by numerous EEG studies in recent decades which show a waking record in either case. There is often a clouding of consciousness, but the degree of mental activity as manifested in speech, etc., will be commensurate with the extent of this clouding.

The first of these "proofs" is more complicated. The existence of double personalities had been tentatively postulated earlier in the century, when the phenomena of animal magnetism had generated a renewed interest in the strange cases of spontaneous "somnambulism" that were being increasingly reported: veiled in mystery throughout the centuries and associated with prophecy and divination or even demonic possession, these cases were now being subjected to the more critical scrutiny of medical observation. It was noticed that though a subject might appear to have no memory for the events of the trance condition, these events could be recalled in *subsequent* trances, leading to the conjecture that the subject in question was possessed of two souls.

The classic case of double personality most widely quoted in nineteenth-century literature is that of Mary Reynolds, daughter of a clergyman living at Titusville, Pennsylvania. Her strange condition began in 1811, when she was aged eighteen. After a protracted coma she remained blind and deaf for five or six weeks. Recovery took place, gradually as far as vision was concerned, suddenly with respect to her hearing. After a second episode of loss of consciousness lasting for eighteen to twenty hours she woke, this time in possession of all her senses, but totally without remembrance of her former life and unable to speak, read or write. All of these skills she had to be retaught, though her education was rapid and after a few weeks she could again do all these things. In this second existence her character was transformed; formerly intelligent, calm and rather reserved and melancholy, she was now lively, cheerful and independent. She was completely oblivious to danger, wandering alone in the wild forest land near her home, then roamed by bears and wolves, and playing unconcernedly with deadly rattlesnakes. After ten weeks of this existence she again had one of her comatose attacks and on awakening found herself back in her previous existence with full recovery of her previous knowledge and memories, though seeming slower and more melancholy than ever. No memory for the events of her secondary existence survived and she expressed surprise at the change of seasons. From that time on these states alternated. In each state she had no memory for the events of the other, but on passing into the secondary state, remembered the events in previous such states. Interestingly in her *dreams* in the secondary state she remembered things from the normal state, recalling, for instance, her dead sister and episodes from the Bible which had been completely erased from her memory. For many years she lived two separate existences, each complete in itself though separated by intervening phases of the other life which would be taken up again at the exact point at which it had been left off.

When hypnotism became widely used later in the century it was found in such cases that though the patient had no memory for the events of the secondary state in normal life, they could be recalled *under hypnosis*. The curious case of Anselm Bourne which occurred in 1887, and evoked a good deal of notoriety, was cited in most of the articles published around this time as a proven instance of double personality. Subject in childhood to fits of deep depression and said to present in later life "symptoms suggestive of epilepsy" (unspecified), he was, in his thirty-first year, struck down by what was called "severe sunstroke" associated with which were circumstances leading to a profound religious conversion, though specific details are lacking. At the age of sixty-one, he was an itinerant preacher living in the small town of Greene, in Rhode Island; on the morning of January 17, 1887 he disappeared and was not heard of again until March 13 when he woke one morning in a house in the strange town of Norristown, Pennsylvania, without the slightest idea of how he had got there. Failing to recognise his surroundings, he was further mystified by being accosted by the landlord with the greeting, "Good morning, Mr Brown". Bourne declared he had never seen him before and knew nothing of the town or of the people in the house where he had been living. Having arrived at Norristown six weeks earlier, he had opened a store for the sale of confectionery and stationery, and had conducted the business efficiently. On returning to his normal state, Bourne had had no recollection of the period spent in Norristown; however, when hypnotised by William James in 1898 he was able to give a complete account of the intervening period.

These cases had *mutually exclusive* memories. In the famous case of Félida X., quoted in every review of "double personality", the patient, while in the normal state, had no memory of events of the secondary state; in the latter she had access to memories of *both*. She was the patient of the professor of surgery at Bordeaux Medical School, Eugène Azam, who followed her up for several years and spoke on her case at many medical meetings, publishing a full account in 1887. Born in 1843, Félida had, at the age of thirteen, developed "severe hysterical symptoms" by which one may assume that she had epileptic fits. Soon after she began to have brief attacks of loss of consciousness, following which she would suddenly wake, and, in place of her usual reserved, melancholy and timid manner, appeared to assume a new personality, gay and carefree and untroubled by the headaches and neuralgias previously habitual to her. But this state was vastly different from that of Mary Reynolds. Félida had preserved all knowledge of her previous life. There was no necessity for re-education in reading or writing, for instance; she retained full possession of these skills. After a few hours she had another attack of loss of consciousness and then reverted to her usual state. But in this phase, she had forgotten everything that had happened in the secondary state.

At first this secondary state occurred only occasionally and lasted at the most for an hour or two, but little by little its length and frequency increased. During one of these phases she had "given herself up to a young man who was to be her husband". Lapsing into the normal state shortly after, she had no remembrance of the incident. When unmistakable symptoms of pregnancy later developed, she told Azam that this was impossible. "The pregnancy was evident," said Azam, "but I dared not make it known to her." She reverted to the secondary state soon after, realised what had happened and arranged for her marriage. Later the secondary state occupied the greater part of her consciousness, and because in the normal state she had amnesia for the events of the former, this caused considerable embarrassment. Thus, while returning from a funeral on one occasion she felt her *crise* come on. She became unconscious for a few seconds without her companions noticing it, waking in the primary state absolutely ignorant of the reasons why she was in the funeral cortège. She had become accustomed to handling such incidents and by skilful questioning was able to grasp the situation and no one present realised what had happened. Later, her sister-in-law, after a long illness, had died, and soon after, lapsing into the normal state, Félida knew nothing of the death but only surmised the fact from seeing that she was dressed in mourning. The periods of unconsciousness which had marked the transition between one state and the other had now grown so brief that she was able to conceal them altogether and few beside Azam and her family knew of her disability.

Similar observations were made when a new generation of physicians, following Charcot's lead, began to explore the more exotic phenomena of hypnotism. Many of their subjects, experimented on constantly and hypnotised daily, often for long periods of time, ultimately began to show the expected effects of such experimentation; their spontaneous somnambulistic or trance states became longer in duration and more coherent in content until they presented the complete spectacle of "double consciousness" or "double personality" and as a result this once rare condition became reported with increasing frequency. The best known accounts from this period are probably those of Pierre Janet of his subjects Lucie, Léonie and Rose, and Morton Prince's study of his patient Christine Beauchamp.

Interesting details abound in these reports. A patient who was a good linguist, for instance, might speak in a foreign language in the secondary state under the impression that it was the native one, having forgotten all knowledge of the latter. Contractures and transitory paralyses not present in the normal condition often accompanied the secondary state (revealing its epileptic nature) though these were at that time diagnosed as hysterical. But for the most part the accounts emanating from this period are concerned with slight differences between the various "sub-personalities" that were now being discovered, and these were reported in tedious detail. The "sub-personalities" had been "created" by some manipulation of the hypnotic process, by increasing or lightening the depth of trance, for instance. It was Pierre Janet who started the practice of giving these "sub-personalities" names and thus postulating for them separate identities. "Once baptised, the unconscious personality is more clear and definite; it shows its psychological traits more clearly," he wrote. Accordingly for his famous subject Léonie's two other "personalities" he invented the names Léontine and Léonore, a practice with which his patient evidently complied and which led to a rash of imitators with similar and often colourful names for their own subject's sub-personalities which probably owed more to the imagination of the physicians than the reality of the situation. After 1910 there was a reaction against the concept of multiple personality with the realisation that in many cases the different personalities had been shaped by the physicians themselves who had undoubtedly allowed enthusiasm to outrun caution.

There was a hard core of cases, however, that could not be disregarded: Mary Reynolds, Félida, Anselm Bourne and others like them. But when these cases are examined, it becomes evident that the only *constant* phenomena common to all were the aberrations of *memory* and the fact that the events occurring in the trance state were not remembered in the normal state but were recalled in subsequent trances or under hypnosis. The other phenomena were probably coloured by the imagination of the observers. A cheerful mood in place of a melancholy one does not necessarily imply that a different personality has taken over the patient's consciousness. Without one's memories one is without one's cares and prohibitions. Moreover, the apparently different personality sometimes arose because the patient had regressed in memory to a younger, more carefree existence, as in the case of a minister's wife reported by Benjamin Rush in 1812.

"Sometimes every thing is forgotten in the interval of a parox-ysm, but recollected in a succeeding paroxysm. I once attended the daughter of a British officer, who had been educated in the habits of gay life, who was married to a Methodist minister. In her paroxysms of madness she resumed her gay habits, spoke French, and ridiculed the tenets and practices of the sect to which she belonged. In the intervals of her fits she renounced her gay habits, became zealously devoted to the religious principles and ceremonies of the Methodists, and forgot every thing she did and said during the fits of her insanity" (Rush, 1812).

These cases were probably those of temporal lobe *status epilepticus* lasting for hours and days instead of the much shorter period of the usual attack. The reason why the events of the previous trances were recalled only in subsequent ones was most probably the facilitatory effect of previous seizures in breaking down resistance to the spread of the discharge. The fact that the events of the previous trance states could still be recalled indicated that it was not the recording process that had been interrupted in the previous attack but that mechanism, as yet unknown, by which access to memories is gained.

But whatever the exact pathology, it is obvious that the nineteenth-century observers were confusing what were phe-nomena of *memory* alone with the entire phenomena of con-sciousness. This was, of course, consistent with the philosophy of the day in which memory was regarded as a function of mind alone without physical substrate in the brain, and as such a faculty of the immaterial indivisible soul.

In fact, *some* part of the function of memory – some aspects of the recall system, for instance, may be governed by something higher than the brain itself. Towards the end of his life, looking back on his brain operations and his experiences in evoking memories from the cortex of the temporal lobe, Wilder Penfield affirmed his belief in something higher than the highest functions of the brain. He described his operation on the patient C. H. in whom the focus of brain-irritation in the temporal lobe that seemed to be producing his fits was alarmingly near to where the major speech area should be. So, in order to avoid the danger of producing permanent aphasia, Penfield used his stimulating electrode to map out the exact position of this patient's speech area. The gentle electric current produced was enough to interfere with the function of the speech mechanism and as the brain is not sensitive the patient did not realise that this had made him aphasic until he tried to speak and was unable to do so.

Tested for speech by being asked to name pictures, at first C. H. named each one correctly. Then, before the picture of a butterfly was shown to him, the electrode was applied to the presumptive speech area. The patient remained silent. Then he snapped his fingers as though in exasperation. The electrode was withdrawn and C. H. spoke at once: "Now I can talk," he said. "Butterfly. I couldn't *get* that word 'butterfly' so I tried to *get* the word 'moth'!" It was clear to Penfield that while the speech mechanism was temporarily blocked the patient could perceive the meaning of the picture of a butterfly. He had made a conscious effort to remember the corresponding word. Then, not understanding why he could not do so, he turned back for a second time to the interpretative mechanism, which was well away from the interfering effect of the electric current, and found a second concept that he considered the closest thing to a butterfly. He must then have presented that to the speech centre, i.e. the memory stores of the names of objects, only to draw another blank. "The patient's simple statement startled me", Penfield wrote (*The Mystery of the Mind*). "He was calling on two brain-mechanisms alternately and at will . . . I can only say the decision came from his mind."

But Penfield's discovery of the physical substrate of memory was half a century away in the future; separate areas of the brain subserving memory were as yet unthought of. So the loose terms "double personality" and "double consciousness" came to be attributed to patients who, in reality, possessed only double sets of *memory*. The nineteenth-century concept of an unconscious mind derived from hypnotism and "double personality" was therefore based on premature theorising from imperfectly understood facts. Can there be such a thing as an "unconscious mind"? The mind is not a substantive entity; it cannot have deeper levels, layers, depths, or any other dimensions. What man calls his mind is a concept, a convenient abstract term encompassing his conscious awareness of himself and his environment and the cognitive activities involved in their interactions, perceiving, thinking, remembering, feeling. All these functions are coexistent with consciousness. The term "unconscious mind" is therefore a contradiction in terms.

But by the middle of the eighteen-nineties, the "unconscious" had for Freud assumed a much greater significance, going far beyond the then current ideas of a relatively benign subconscious mind working in close conjunction with the conscious. For him it was a definite topographical region, a hostile and forbidden territory to be explored with trepidation. Irrational and contradictory in its working, it was often in direct conflict with the sober dictates of the conscious mind. Sinister forces emerged from its depths, homicidal impulses and incestuous desires, repressed with danger and difficulty by the conscious mind. Freud's concept of the "unconscious" must be attributed to his cocaine usage; death wishes, infantile incestuous desires and perversion and excrement are not the preoccupations of a normal mind. Constantly recurring throughout the drug literature are the same words and phrases used by Freud and his followers to describe his concept of the unconscious mind, all the varieties of the word "phantasy" and "phantasmagoria" for instance. Lewin's classic work on addiction is entitled *Phantastica*. In both psychoanalysis and this literature the same metaphors of "looking down into an abyss" occur.

That Freud's concept of the "unconscious mind" arose from his cocaine usage is substantiated by the fact that according to Jones it was between 1897 and 1900 that Freud's "neurosis" reached its height. This was the period of Freud's self-analysis. Essentially the "neurosis" consisted of extreme changes of mood, which is a classic symptom of cocaine usage.

> "The alternations of mood were between periods of elation, excitement and self-confidence and severe depression and doubt. In the depressed moods he could not write or concentrate on anything and spent his leisure hours turning from one thing to another, cutting open books, looking at maps of ancient Pompeii, playing patience or chess, but being unable to continue at anything for long – a state of restless paralysis. Sometimes there were spells where consciousness would be greatly narrowed: states difficult to describe, with a veil that produced almost a twilight condition of mind" (Jones, 1953).

Jones relates that Freud's son Ernst remembered of this period that "his father used to come into meals, from the arbour where he had been writing 'as if sleep-walking', and altogether gave the impression of 'being in a dream'". Freud himself in his letter to Fliess dated June 20, 1898 (*Origins*) wrote, "The psychology is going curiously; it is nearly finished, was written as if in a dream." His letter to Fliess of June 12, 1897 (*Origins*) states, "Incidentally, I have been through some kind of neurotic experience, with odd states of mind not intelligible to consciousness – cloudy thoughts and veiled doubts, with barely here and there a ray of light . . ." Unfortunately the remainder of the paragraph has been expunged.

Jones gave these episodes a psychoanalytical interpretation – "it is as if he divined all along that the path he was treading would sooner or later lead to terrible secrets, the revealing of which he dreaded but on which he was nevertheless as determined as Oedipus himself". But for all this, Freud's cocainism was obviously following a classic course. It was against this background that he began his legendary self-analysis in the summer of 1897. "My recovery can only come about through work in the unconscious," he wrote to Fliess, "I cannot manage with conscious efforts alone" (unpublished letter quoted by Jones, 1953, 357). It was from this analysis that the remainder of Freud's basic concepts emerged – the Oedipus complex and infantile sexuality.

Freud's self-analysis occupies an important place in the folklore of psychoanalysis. Jones describes it as Freud's most heroic feat, a long and painful struggle of Herculean labour. "What indomitable courage, both intellectual and moral, must have been needed!" (Jones, 1953, 351). In terms of the dangers involved the analysis was compared by Schur to Benjamin Franklin's flying a kite in a thunderstorm to discover the laws of electricity.

Freud's major instruments in self-analysis were the interpretation of his own dreams and – significantly – his own "phantasies". His letter to Fliess of October 27, 1897 (*Origins*) reveals that he was now experiencing himself "all the things that as a third party I have witnessed going on in my patients", and he complained of "days when I slink about depressed because I have understood nothing of the day's dreams, phantasies or moods . . ." So Freud as well as some of his patients was experiencing phantasies. Here one must question the word "Phantasie" and what was meant by it. Was it just a daydream? If so would he not have just used the word *Wachtraum*, or *Luftschlösser*? Or was it more akin to the "waking visions" so often reported in the drug literature. The frequency with which all the varieties of the word appear in this literature had already been remarked on. The dictionary definition would seem to rule out ordinary day-dreaming and convey rather a definite element of imagery. The drug literature gives this imagery a definite hallucinatory quality. As we have seen, hallucinatory episodes are a frequent late manifestation of cocaine intoxication. We have already encountered them in Chapter X together with a glimpse of the difficulty experienced by the patients in distinguishing between what was real and what was fancy. The nights passed by Dr Frank Wing in "a state of fanciful and visionary wakefulness" were probably similar to those that Freud now experienced. It was in this period and probably from these "phantasies" that the theories that follow were evolved.

At the start of his self-analysis Freud was still in the grip of his seduction theory though having increasing doubts on its validity.

These he endeavoured to quell by fresh dream interpretations – his dream about his niece Hella, for instance, which he had interpreted as implying a seduction wish towards his eldest daughter. In the end, he had to admit his error. There had been no seductions.

The way in which Freud resolved his difficulty and salvaged part of his theory by a simple reversal of roles is told by Ernest Jones:

"Four months after this, however, [the Hella dream] Freud had discovered the truth of the matter: that irrespective of incest wishes of parents towards their children and even of occasional acts of the kind, what he had to concern himself with was the general occurrence of incest wishes towards their parents, characteristically towards the parent of the opposite sex. This other side of the picture had been quite concealed from him. The first two months of his self-analysis had disclosed it" (Jones, 1953, 354).

Thus Freud did not "stumble upon" the Oedipus theory as he had asserted in his *Autobiographical Study* (by implication in his clinical work); the theory was the product of his own self-analysis – the self-analysis of a man with the distorted perceptions and sense data produced by a powerful drug. Jones continues:

"He had now recognised that his father was innocent and that he had projected on to him ideas of his own. Memories had come back of sexual wishes about his mother on the occasion of seeing her naked."

The Fliess letters included in the *Origins* that decribe these events leave no doubt as to the subjective nature of the so-called discovery of the Oedipus complex. "I can only say that in my case my father played no active role, though I certainly projected on to him an analogy from myself," he wrote on October 13, 1897. Then followed the passage which documents the origin of the "Oedipus complex": after describing his old nurse as his "primary originator" (his seductress) he continues, "later (between the ages of two and two-and-a-half) libido towards *matrem* was aroused; the occasion must have been the journey with her from Leipzig to Vienna, during which we spent a night together and I must have had the opportunity of seeing her *nudam*." There was a discrepancy here which Jones picked up – the journey from Leipzig to Vienna had actually taken place when Freud was four years old, not two-and-a-half, and it is remarkable how well this accords with Freud's own statement in *The Psychopathology of Everyday Life*, "Any such statement by the subjects of the enquiry as that their first recollection comes from about their second year is clearly not to be trusted". The unlikelihood of the episode is also suggestive. A woman of the nineteenth century would not have undressed completely on a night train journey. On an earlier train journey one year before, when the family had left Freiberg for Leipzig, the train passed through Breslau where Freud saw gas jets for the first time; according to his letter to Fliess of December 13, 1897 (*Origins*) they "reminded me of souls burning in hell". Such an association with what were probably ordinary gas jets is not that of a normal three-year-old child. Were these episodes true memories, or were they the hallucinatory events of a cocaine psychosis? During his earlier involvement with cocaine, while in Paris, Freud had experienced *auditory* hallucinations. He reveals this in a discussion on paranormal phenomena in his book *The Psychopathology of Everyday Life* (1901, S. E. VI, 261).

> "During the days when I was living alone in a foreign city – I was a young man at the time – I quite often heard my name suddenly called by an unmistakable and beloved voice; I then noted down the exact moment of the hallucination and made anxious enquiries of those at home about what had happened at that time. Nothing had happened."

Auditory hallucinations are common in cocaine intoxication. More significantly, as we have seen, visual hallucinations *of a sexual nature* were also frequently described, as exemplified in the personal account of the German doctor addict already quoted. Such hallucinatory events were the probable origin of his avowal of having had sexual desires towards his mother in infancy.

In a typical flight of ideas, Freud now made the characteristic generalisation to the whole population, normal and abnormal. Writing to Fliess of his analysis (October 27, 1897, *Origins*) he said, "One single thought of general value has been revealed to me. I have found, in my own case too, falling in love with the mother and jealousy of the father, and I now regard it as a universal event of early childhood . . ." This, he thought, explained the gripping power of *Oedipus Rex* – "the Greek legend seizes on a compulsion which everyone recognises because he feels its existence within himself. Each member of the audience was once, in germ and in phantasy, just such an Oedipus, and each one recoils in horror from the dream-fulfilment here transplanted into reality, with the whole quota of repression which separates his infantile state from his present one." Drawing an analogy with Shakespeare's tragedy *Hamlet*, he continues, "How better could he justify himself than by the torment he suffers from the obscure memory that he himself had meditated the same deed against his father from passion for his mother and – 'use every man after his desert, and who should 'scape whipping'?"

Oedipus in Greek legend was the son of Laius, king of Thebes, and Jocasta, daughter of Creon, king of Corinth. He had been abandoned in the open as a baby because an oracle had warned Laius that the as yet unborn child would be his father's murderer. The child was rescued and grew up as a prince in a foreign court until he too questioned the oracle about his origin and was warned to avoid his home since he was destined to murder his father and marry his mother. On the road leading away from what he believed to be his home, Oedipus met King Laius and killed him in a sudden quarrel. He then went to Thebes and solved the riddle posed by the Sphinx who barred his way. Out of gratitude the people made him their king and gave him Jocasta's hand in marriage. He reigned peacefully for many years, four children being born to the marriage. But then a plague broke out and the oracle predicted that it would only cease when the murderer of Laius had been driven from the country. When it was finally revealed to Oedipus that he had killed his father and married his mother he put out his own eyes in horror at his deeds and left his native land. Jocasta, his mother, hanged herself.

Freud had studied Sophocles' tragedy *Oedipus Rex* at the gymnasium and had to translate a passage from it for his final examinations. He had also seen a performance of the tragedy in Paris. It was not a piece from which any universal generalisations could be made, as it embodied the true elements of drama by recounting events as far removed from ordinary human experience as possible. Why the tragedy held such special significance for Freud is impossible to discover. On the other hand a common effect of drug intoxication is that its victims see some special significance in whatever attracts their attention at the time. There is often no logical reason for their choice. Sometimes they will stare enraptured for hours at a blade of grass as if it held all the secrets of the universe.

The Oedipus complex now became the central point of Freud's theories. The first published mention of Oedipal motivation occurs in *The Interpretation of Dreams* published three years later. "It is the fate of all of us, perhaps, to direct our first sexual impulse towards our mother and our first hatred and our first murderous wish against our father. Our dreams convince us that this is so." The story of Oedipus and his destiny "moves us only because it might have been ours – because the oracle laid the same curse upon us before our birth as upon him," he declared. Oedipal conflicts now replaced seduction as the origin of the neuroses.

Wittels tells us that when Freud had brought an analysis to a successful conclusion, he used to show the patient an engraving after a painting by Ingres, "Oedipus solves the riddle of the Sphinx".

Many years later Freud enlarged on the Oedipus theory with an excursion into anthropology in *Totem and Taboo* (1912–1913), when he traced the beginnings of religion to the "father of the primal horde" who, "since he was an unlimited despot, had seized all the women for himself; his sons, being dangerous to him as rivals, had been killed or driven away. One day, however, the sons came together and united to overwhelm, kill and devour their father, who had been their enemy but also their ideal. After the deed they were unable to take over their heritage since they stood in one another's way. Under the influence of failure and remorse they learned to come to an agreement among themselves; they banded themselves into a clan of brothers by the help of the ordinances of totemism, which aimed at preventing a repetition of such a deed, and they jointly undertook to forgo the possession of the women on whose account they had killed their father. They were then driven to finding strange women, and this was the origin of the exogamy which is so closely bound up with totemism" (Freud, *Autobiographical Study*, 1925). The horror of incest dated from this time, Freud maintained. In the same work Freud stated that the chief sources of his anthropological studies were the books of J. G. Fraser (*Totemism and Exogamy* and *The Golden Bough*), "a mine of valuable facts and opinions".

Fraser was a typical nineteenth-century "armchair" anthropologist. He was, according to his biographer R. Angus Downie (1970), the prototype of the unworldly professor who lived his life largely in libraries. A fellow of Trinity College, Cambridge, he seldom left his rooms there and his only contact with a member of a primitive tribe was when he was taken as a child to see the Wild Man of Borneo at a fairground. The sight of the "wild man" dashing from his tent sent the young Fraser running from the scene howling in terror. His anthropological works were composed largely from collections of travellers' tales and the exercise of a vivid imagination but they nevertheless exerted a great influence over many literary figures including D. H. Lawrence, T. S. Eliot, Ezra Pound and Edith Sitwell, and had a significant effect on classical studies. Anthropologists themselves have discarded his theories long ago and Fraser is now read in this discipline only for antiquarian interest.

Supporting the Oedipus theory was the whole edifice of "infantile sexuality" built up around this time. Though not published until 1905 in *Three Essays on the Theory of Sexuality*, the Fliess correspondence shows that these theories were actually formulated as early as 1897. The *Three Essays* contained the core of Freud's infantile sexuality theory, describing the stages allegedly passed through by the infant in its development towards full genital sexuality culminating in the Oedipal stage at the age of four to five years.

The earlier stages centred around the "erotogenic zones" (an obvious derivative from Charcot's hysterogenic zones) of the mouth and anus. The first stage was "the oral or, as it might be called, cannibalistic pregenital sexual organisation". The infant imbibing nourishment from its mother's breast was performing a sexual as well as a nutrient activity;

> "No one who has seen a baby sinking back satiated from the breast and falling asleep with flushed cheeks and a blissful smile can escape the reflection that this picture persists as a prototype of the expression of sexual satisfaction in later life . . ."

The mother's breast was, in fact, the child's first sexual object. A later substitute was thumb-sucking, "in which the sexual activity, detached from the nutritive activity, has substituted for the extraneous object one situated in the subject's own body".

This stage was succeeded by the anal phase.

> "Children who are making use of susceptibility to erotogenic stimulation of the anal zone betray themselves by holding back their stool till its accumulation brings about violent muscular contractions and, as it passes through the anus, is able to produce powerful stimulation of the mucous membrane. In so doing it must no doubt cause not only painful, but also highly pleasurable sensations."

A 1915 footnote adds that the contents of the bowels "behave like forerunners of another organ, which is destined to come into action after the phase of childhood". But the contents of the bowel had other meanings. They were clearly treated as part of the infant's own body and represented his first "gift" – "by producing them he can express his active compliance with his environment and, by withholding them, his disobedience," he wrote. This theory, whether derived from his patients or himself, is highly pathological, reminiscent of the many strange fancies held by the insane about their own excretions. Guy de Maupassant, for instance, dying of advanced neurosyphilis, deliberately practised retention, saying his urine was "all diamonds . . . all jewels".

From being a gift, the contents of the bowel came to acquire the meaning of "baby" – "for babies, according to one of the sexual theories of children, are acquired by eating and are born through the bowels". This retention was the root of the constipation which was so common in neuropaths and though forgotten in later life, it left behind "the deepest (unconscious) impressions in the subject's memory" determining the development of his character if he was to remain healthy and the symptomatology of his neurosis if he was to fall ill after puberty. The character traits arising from these pregenital phases of sexual activity were outlined in a later paper, *Character and Anal Erotism* (1908). Orderliness, parsimony and obstinacy "which are so often prominent in people who were formerly anal erotics," he wrote, "are to be regarded as the first and most constant results of the sublimation of anal erotism." Sadism was later added to the catalogue of anal traits. He believed other character-complexes, too, might show a connection with the excitations of particular erotogenic zones. "At present I only know of the intense 'burning' ambition of people who earlier suffered from enuresis [bed-wetting]", he wrote, with somewhat obscure reasoning.

Thus in early childhood sexuality was "polymorphously perverse". Sexual aberrations in adult life resulted from fixations occurring at the oral or anal stages of development. These earlier stages then gave way to the genital phase, when the child's sexual impulses were first directed to the parent of the opposite sex.

Discussion of the Oedipus complex was muted in the *Three Essays*, a comparatively early text. In later editions Freud was more explicit. In the 1920 edition he inserted a footnote referring to the Oedipus complex as the "nuclear complex of the neuroses", claiming it to represent the peak of infantile sexuality. Its universal prevalence was insisted upon: "Every new arrival on this planet is faced by the task of mastering the Oedipus complex," he declared, "anyone who fails to do so falls a victim to neurosis." "Recognition of the Oedipus complex," he continued, "has become the shibboleth that distinguishes the adherents of psychoanalysis from its opponents." A 1915 footnote also refers to the barrier against incest – "Psychoanalytic investigation shows, however, how intensely the individual struggles with the temptation to incest during his period of growth and how frequently the barrier is transgressed in phantasies and even in reality."

The subject of "bisexuality" was also ventilated in the *Three Essays*. With somewhat obscure reasoning he declared, "we might lay it down that the sexuality of little girls is of a wholly masculine character" and that "libido is invariably and necessarily of a masculine nature, whether it occurs in men or in women and irrespectively of whether its object is a man or a woman." The decisive factor was bisexuality – "without taking bisexuality into account I think it would scarcely be possible to arrive at an understanding of the sexual manifestations that are actually to be observed in men and women."

Infantile sexuality is one of those things which can be neither proved nor disproved. The infant himself is too young to comprehend questions on the subject and we ourselves do not remember the years of our infancy. Freud in fact, in *Three Essays*, refers to the "peculiar amnesia" of early childhood, implying that the memories of early life are repressed precisely for the reason of their sexual content. He returned to the theme in his *Autobiographical Study*, claiming that the reason why infantile sexuality remained for so long undiscovered "must be connected with the amnesia which, with the majority of adults, hides their own infancy". The true, if less dramatic, reason for the amnesia of infancy does not lie in repression of sexuality, but in the fact of the immature development of the neonatal brain. Between birth and the age of six, the brain approximately quintuples in size and weight; between birth and maturity, it adds to its weight by roughly 1000 grammes. Most, though not all, the increment is due to the myelinisation of the nerve fibres without which efficient conduction cannot occur. Myelination and maturation occur gradually in a manner commensurate with the developmental progress of the child. This had been one of Meynert's chief interests with which Freud must have been well acquainted but which he had now evidently forgotten.

Freud never actually analysed children. His theories were based on "reconstructions" from his analyses of adult patients and his own self-analysis. "My surprising discoveries as to the sexuality of children were made in the first instance through the analysis of adults", he wrote in his *Autobiographical Study*. "But later from about 1908 onwards, it became possible to confirm them fully and in every detail by direct observation upon children." He was referring to the famous "Little Hans" case published as *Analysis of a phobia in a five year old boy* in 1909. In the introduction to this monograph Freud states that after the publicàtion of the *Three Essays* he had for many years been urging his pupils and friends "to collect observations of the sexual life of children – the existence of which has as a rule been cleverly overlooked or deliberately denied". Thus encouraged, his disciples vied with each other in detecting evidence of sexual activity in the random movements of even babes in arms. Jung wrote a paper on alleged sexual activity in his little daughter. Only a few years later he was confessing to Freud that he no longer believed in infantile sexuality (Jones, 1959). The "Little Hans" analysis was another product of such efforts. It was carried out by proxy by the boy's father, a staunch adherent of Freud's; Freud himself saw the child briefly on one occasion only. He even anticipated the objections he felt would be aroused by the publication of the case:

> "According to the second and more uncompromising objection, an analysis of a child conducted by his father, who went to work instilled with *my* theoretical views and infected with *my* prejudices, must be entirely devoid of any objective worth."

Another objection is even more appropriate:

> "It is true that during the analysis Hans had to be told many things that he could not say himself, that he had to be presented with thoughts which he had so far shown no signs of possessing, and that his attention had to be turned in the direction from which his father was expecting something to come. This detracts from the evidential value of the analysis: but the procedure is the same in every case."

Freud's efforts to seek confirmation from his own children had evidently been frustrated by Martha. "I wanted to ask you," he wrote to Fliess on February 8, 1897 (*Origins*) "in connection with excrement-eating . . . and animals, when disgust first appears in small children and whether there is a period in early infancy when no disgust is felt. Why do I not go to the nursery and experiment? Because with twelve and a half hours' work, I have no time, and because the womenfolk do not back me in my investigations." "Psychoanalysis stops at the nursery door," Martha is reported to have said on another occasion.

It is clear from the *Three Essays* that Freud took as confirmation of his theory the reports that from time to time appeared in the lay and medical press of "the remarkably frequent reports of what are described as irregular and exceptional sexual impulses in childhood". In fact, much interest had been aroused in medical circles by recent reports of sexual activity in children of very tender years and the whole subject was coming under scrutiny at this time. The birth of stillborn twins to a seven-year-old girl in Brazil in 1884 had created widespread interest. The girl, Inacia da Silva, had menstruated regularly each month from the age of *eight days*. A little earlier in 1878, Mobiter had reported the case of a girl actually born with pubic hair. She began to menstruate when she was four, becoming pregnant at the age of eight, though later miscarrying. Pregnancy has occurred even earlier; the youngest

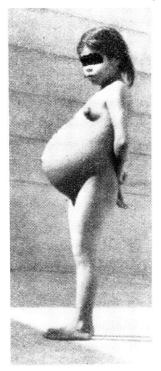

The youngest mother in the world at the age of five and a half.

mother in the world was a Peruvian girl named Lina. Her fully authenticated case was reported by Escomel in the *Presse Medicale* in 1939. Born in 1933, Lina developed secondary sex characters in the first year of life and her first period occurred at the age of eight months. She became pregnant shortly before her fifth birthday and on May 14, 1939 was delivered by Caesarean section of a baby weighing 2,700 grammes (5lb 13oz). An ovarian biopsy performed at the time of the section showed all the characteristics of a mature organ. Published in the same year as Freud began to form his theories on infantile sexuality, the famous book *Anomalies and Curiosities of Medicine* by Gould and Pyke contained many further instances from the older literature though these cases were often lacking in medical detail. The interest aroused by the two recent cases and the publication of this book were no doubt what Freud had in mind when he mentioned "the remarkably frequent reports of what are described as irregular and exceptional sexual impulses in childhood". But, as he said, these reports were always quoted as exceptional events, or as oddities. "So far as I know, not a single author has clearly recognised the regular existence of a sexual instinct in childhood," he declared. In fact, these cases *were* exceptional, *were* oddities. They were examples of what is now known as "precocious puberty".

The events which regulate the onset of puberty are still not completely known, but there is now much more information available than existed in Freud's time. It is known that the sex hormones, androgen, oestrogen and the gonadotrophins are secreted at a low level during infancy and childhood. The onset of puberty is signalled by a sharp rise in these hormones which brings about the physical changes of puberty. Precocious puberty is caused by a variety of factors such as tumour, or metabolic conditions such as the inability to secrete cortisol, all of which lead to excess secretion of the sex hormones. None of these hormones were known at the time Freud wrote his monograph.

Freud had postulated a latency period between the emergence of the "Oedipal situation" and genital sexuality at the age of four or five and the onset of puberty. If this were the case, there would be a pattern of rising hormonal secretion till the age of four or five and then a fall, succeeded by a second rise at puberty. No such hormonal pattern has been established. No major increase occurs until the onset of puberty. There is, therefore, no support in modern physiology for Freud's theories of infantile sexuality.

XVI

The Interpretation of Dreams

Drugs and dreaming have always gone hand in hand. Dreams feature prominently in the literature of addiction and in the reminiscences of addicts. Coleridge wrote of the "distempered dreams" of his opium period, "in which things and forms in themselves common and harmless, inflict a terror of anguish" (quoted in Hayter, 1968). Crabbe in his poem significantly entitled *The World of Dreams* described dreams peopled with "sad emigrants from hell". De Quincey's opium dreams, at first pleasant, later contained such horrors that he grew afraid to sleep, fighting its onset until eventually overpowered.

Freud began to experience unusually vivid dreams in 1894. He had from boyhood a keen, if somewhat superstitious interest in dreams and dreaming. He had written to Martha on July 19, 1883 mentioning a blissful dream of a landscape, "which, according to the private note-book on dreams which I have composed from my experience indicates travelling" (Jones, 1953). But though he related a good number of dreams to Martha, it was mostly without comment and his remarks were more conventional. An exception was one, however, which Jones thought "specially worth recording on account of its exceedingly unusual structure. It was what he called a 'sharp dream', quite different from the usual confused ones." Freud had just taken some ecgnonin, a new alkaloid recently isolated from cocaine, to compare its action with that of cocaine itself. This was at the invitation of Merck who had sent him 100 grammes of the substance. His dream was of a walk that lasted so long that he finally reached Lübeck where he met Fleischl and Exner. When they heard of his great walk they insisted on his going to bed. "Once there it occurred to me that the whole thing might be a dream, but then I laughed at the idea and was quite convinced it was reality – after which I woke up."

Freud's first published reference to his interest in dreams occurs in the *Studies* where he reports unusually vivid dreams, beginning in late 1894. "For several weeks I found myself obliged to exchange my usual bed for a harder one," he said, "in which I had more numerous or vivid dreams, or in which, it may be, I was unable to reach the normal depth of sleep. In the first quarter of an hour after waking I remembered all the dreams I had had during the night; and I took the trouble to write them down and try to solve them." Significantly, at about this time some of his patients began to relate their dreams, which they often interpolated in their associations.

Freud's unusually vivid dreams, which he had no difficulty in remembering are explained by the peculiar properties of cocaine which he was then using so freely. In common with many other drugs of addiction, cocaine significantly reduces or even suppresses both total sleep and REM (rapid eye movement) sleep in which dreaming occurs. However, as the effects of the drug wear off, there is a compensatory rebound effect so that REM sleep becomes more prolonged and more intensified, accounting for the vividness and hallucinatory quality of the dreams and the fact that on waking there is no difficulty in recalling them. The first complete analysis of one of Freud's own dreams was the "Irma dream" of July 24, 1895 mentioned in Chapter X; as we have seen, he admitted in *The Interpretation of Dreams* that he was making frequent use of cocaine at this time. This fact explains the vividness of the dream and the ease with which he was able to recall its details. The date of the "Irma dream" and its interpreta-

The Belle Vue, where Freud had his first inception of the dream theory.

tion, July 24, 1895 is regarded by psychoanalysts and by Freud himself as "an historic moment". It occurred when Freud and his family were holidaying in the Vienna suburb of Bellevue. Five years later he wrote to Fliess (July 12, 1900, *Origins*), "Do you suppose that some day a marble tablet will be placed on the house . . .?" The "Irma dream" later became the "specimen dream of psychoanalysis" taking up the entire second chapter of *The Interpretation of Dreams*.

At about the time of the "Irma dream" some of Freud's patients who, on his advice, were using cocaine intranasally, must have experienced the same phenomenon of rebound compensatory REM sleep. They began to tell Freud their dreams and interpolate them in their associations *because* of the resulting vivid and hallucinatory quality of these dreams. Thus it was that dream interpretation came to assume a major role in psychoanalysis. Probably the more bizarre of Freud's own dreams were withheld from publication. But from a letter of January 4, 1898 (not included in the *Origins* but published by Schur in 1972) we can infer that they were indeed of this quality. "I am sending you today No. 2 of the *Drekkologikat* reports," he wrote, "a very interesting periodical, published by me for a single reader. No. 1, which I have retained, contains wild dreams which would hardly be of interest to you; they are part of my self-analysis which is still very much in the dark. I would appreciate your returning this to me for future examination, but by no means right away." Thus Freud's "*Drekkologikat*" must have been returned by Fliess and has consequently not survived. "*Drekkologikat*", according to Schur, is a "witty neologism, partly deprecatory, partly indicative of the abundance of anal material then emerging in his self-analysis. The German word *Dreck* (mud, dirt, filth, feces) is written in Greek letters." During this period Freud had remarked that his cardiac symptoms were now frequently replaced by gastrointestinal ones. In later years he maintained that the appearance of "anal" material in analysis was frequently preceded or was accompanied by functional or even organic gastrointestinal pathology. Freud's state of health had not improved. Deeply depressed moods still oppressed him. He was preoccupied with death and dying and his nose continued to give trouble. "I have gone through a desolate and foggy period and am now suffering quite painfully from [nasal] suppuration and occlusion," he wrote to his friend on December 12, 1897, adding that he would have to ask Fliess to cauterise him again in Breslau if he did not improve (quoted in Schur, 1972). He continued to lavish praise on Fliess' fantastic hypotheses which by now were in the phase of generalisation to the whole planet and the cosmos beyond. Their content and Freud's reception of them can be gauged from his letter of March 29, 1897. "Many thanks for your lecture," he told Fliess, "it reveals an incredible power of condensing ideas and takes one in twenty minutes through the universe . . ." Freud's remarks indicate that he was actually describing a typical piece of drug writing. Soon after their meeting on July 30, 1898, he bestowed on Fliess the title of the "Kepler of Biology". Freud not only admired his friend's theories extravagently, but suited his life's events to Fliess' periodic calendar and furnished him with numerical data for every item of family news he sent him.

In his self-analysis Freud was discovering further elements of the Oedipus complex – a deep hostility to his father and death wishes to his baby brother who had died in infancy. His paper *Screen Memories* (1899) was a major product of his self-analysis. The anonymous patient of the paper was none other than Freud himself and the memories analysed in it his own. The title "Screen Memories" came from Freud's belief that an early memory is used as a screen for a later event. Significantly, Freud claimed that his memories dating from his second and third years were "very well preserved and furnished with every detail of sense perception, in complete contrast to my memories of adult years, which are entirely lacking in the visual element". One of these vivid memories is described as a country scene when Freud is playing with two little "cousins" picking flowers (actually, his nephew and niece by his older half-brother whom we met in Chapter I.)

> "We are picking the yellow flowers and each of us is holding a bunch of flowers we have already picked. The little girl has the best bunch; and as though by mutual agreement, we – the two boys – fall on her and snatch away her flowers."

This scene of seemingly innocent childhood was naturally given a sexual interpretation by Freud – "Taking flowers away from a girl means to deflower her" – and illustrates his single-mindedness in the search for sexual undertones in the most commonplace events and his early use of symbolism in pursuit of this end.

Bound up in his self-analysis was the investigation of his errors, slips of tongue, "symptomatic actions" and other "parapraxes". These later formed the basis of his *The Psychopathology of Everyday Life* published in 1901. Intended as a popular book for general readership, the book avoids theoretical considerations, merely listing series of examples of the way in which Freud believed "*unconscious yet operative* mental processes" lay beneath apparently unmotivated mistakes. It is a revealing book, giving a glimpse of Freud's mental state at the time of its composition and the distorted upside-down reasoning which suddenly breaks in amid a number of comparatively innocuous examples. Thus the act of a fond father swinging his favourite child in the air and on one occasion swinging him so high that the boy almost hit a heavy chandelier was interpreted by Freud as being an unconscious wish for the death of the boy so that the way would be cleared for a divorce from his wife. A young father registering the birth of his second daughter gave her name as "Hanna" and had to be told by the official that he already had a child of that name. "We may conclude that the second daughter was not quite so welcome as the first had been," was Freud's comment.

The Interpretation of Dreams appeared on November 4, 1899. Over thirty years later Freud wrote of the book in his preface to the third English edition:

> "It contains, even according to my present day judgement, the most valuable of all the discoveries it has been my good fortune to make. Insight such as this falls to one's lot but once in a lifetime."

Freud's main theory of the dream was that it represented "the disguised fulfilment of a repressed wish" – the brief summary in his *Autobiographical Study* describes how an unconscious impulse "often of a very repellent kind" uses the nocturnal relaxation of repression to push its way into consciousness with the dream. "But the repressive resistance of the ego is not abolished in sleep but merely reduced. Some of it remains in the shape of a *censorship of dreams* and forbids the unconscious impulse to express itself in the forms which it would properly assume." Thus the repressed wishes were disguised by symbolisation, distortion, or other similar mechanisms. The unconscious "wishful" impulses requiring such treatment were defined in a later paper (Freud, 1925): "They are an expression of immoral, incestuous and perverse impulses or of murderous and sadistic lusts. The dreamer reacts to many of these dreams by waking up in a fright." The dreams that caused this reaction were those that had escaped the censorship; the purpose of dreaming was therefore to safeguard sleep. There is an obvious discrepancy in the above; though defining the dream as the disguised fulfilment of a repressed wish, the material that broke through undisguised he called dreams also. The nature of the material specified, too, tells us not a little about Freud's own dreams.

Dreams had an additional interest for him in that they had "access" to the forgotten material of childhood, thereby affording "knowledge alike of the patient's conscious and of his unconscious processes" (*Autobiographical Study*). The dream, therefore, was for Freud the "royal road to the unconscious". As Ellenberger and others have pointed out, none of this was original – almost identical theories had been extant in the Philosophy of Nature era and stemmed from the same source – interest in "unconscious mental processes" derived in this case from "animal magnetism". Had Freud but known it, the first observations in sleep physiology that approached the recent discoveries on dreaming had already been made in 1892 by the psychologist George Trumbull Ladd, who had noticed periods during sleep when the eyeballs of the sleeper were seen beneath the closed lids to be perceptibly performing series of movements. These movements he associated with periods of dreaming. He did not pursue the matter further, however, and neither at the time did his observations arouse any interest. They had been completely forgotten when a postgraduate physiologist, Eugene Aserinsky, working with Nathanial Kleitman at the University of Chicago in 1952, noticed that episodes of rapid eye movement occurred periodically during the night. When the sleeper was roused and interrogated during these episodes he invariably reported detailed dreams. It had previously been re-vealed by the electroencephalogram that sleep occurred in regular cycles, going in orderly sequence from Stage I to Stage IV and then back to Stage I, every ninety minutes or so, these stages having definite EEG correlates. Kleitman found that dreaming occurred almost exclusively in Stage I sleep. These and other experiments have established that throughout the night, regular periods of REM sleep and hence of dreaming occur in orderly sequence and the proportion of REM sleep to non-dreaming sleep is constant throughout the night. If the subject is deprived of sleep for a considerable time, the length of the periods of REM sleep in proportion to non-dreaming sleep is extended in compensation but the pattern remains regular and constant.

These findings do, of course, disprove Freud's theory that the dream is a mechanism to safeguard sleep. It would be difficult to conceive of forbidden wishes arising in orderly sequence at regular intervals throughout the night. It has also been found that infants have a much larger proportion of REM sleep to non-dreaming sleep. As observed by Professor Madow (1970), "Here it would appear as though there may be some conflict with psychodynamic concepts since it is difficult to believe that newborn infants need to dream to disguise their instinctual wishes." Current research implicates some definite physiological purpose for the events that take place while we believe we are "dreaming". Recent studies indicate that this purpose is related to the processing of short-term into long-term memory traces. If confirmed, this research would validate the intuitive statement of Wilder Penfield, who deduced that the temporal lobes, with their immense stores of memory records, were in some way involved in the production of dreams.

Many of our dreams appear fairly coherent, having apparently some logical connections and even elements of crude reasoning. This would seem to negate the ideas of the dream being simply the result of random activation of some neurons while others remain inactive. This is not the case, however. What probably occurs in the dreams we actually remember and which appear to have coherence and evidence of rudimentary thought processes are those which occur just before waking. If this waking process is *gradual* some parts of the brain are already becoming activated while others are still dormant. But not all associations become available at the same time; though superficially resembling mental functioning, the product, the remembered dream, is more like the "confabulation" with which patients with, for instance, Alzheimer's disease, supplement the deficient information supplied by their diseased brains by the interpolation of seemingly appropriate (but untrue) material. Laboratory studies in which patients are woken more abruptly during REM sleep report series of quick flash-like pictures rather than coherent sequences.

When compensating for loss of REM sleep, not only does the sleeper spend more of the night in REM or dreaming sleep, but the dreams become more intense, with greater vividness and with a greater bizarre element. This is the reason for the peculiar quality of the dreams of addicts, the "terrifying abysses of darkness and despair" and the "cosmic flights and vast precarious constructions" (Hayter, 1968) so evocatively described in their literature. Freud and those of his patients who were using cocaine must have experienced many such dreams. In *The Interpretation of Dreams*, unfortunately Freud decided not to use his patients' dreams, so depriving us of an interesting source of material. The dreams related in the first edition were mainly his own and those of a few acquaintances who knew of his interest and told him of their dreams.

But Freud was not completely frank in recounting his own dreams, confessing to "some natural hesitation about revealing so many intimate facts about one's mental life". He felt it was possible to overcome such hesitation, but he nevertheless in a footnote qualified this by adding that "in scarcely any instance have I put forward the *complete* interpretation of one of my own dreams as it is known to me. I have probably been wise in not putting too much faith in my readers' discretion." Schur (1966a) reveals from the unpublished Fliess correspondence that some of his dreams had actually been suppressed. In an unpublished part of Letter 90 (June 9, 1898) Freud acknowledged Fliess' critical help in censoring a dream he had proposed to include in *The Interpretation of Dreams* "because in this instance I myself have lost the feeling of shame required of an author". He asked Fliess to tell him which part of the dream he took exception to, and where he feared an attack by a malicious critic, so that he could omit the offending topic in a substitute dream, "because I can have dreams like that to order". In later life, in a letter dated December 13, 1932 to the surrealist André Breton he said, "I think that if I have not pursued the analysis of my own dreams as far as that of others, the cause is only rarely due to timidity towards sexual matters. The fact is that very often I would have had to discover that the secret basis of all the series of dreams had to do with my relations to my father who had just died. I maintain that I had the right to set a limit to the inevitable exhibition (also to the childhood tendency which I have surmounted)" (F. B. Davis, 1973). So *The Interpretation of Dreams* is less informative about both Freud's cocaine dreams and those of his patients than they might have been. We know from the *Origins* that at least one patient must have been having quite bizarre dreams – Freud refers in the letter of March 4, 1895 to "D's dream psychosis", but apart from that there is little information. Nor does *The Interpretation of Dreams* give much information on how dream interpretation was used with patients under analysis. For this we have to turn to the "Dora analysis" or, to give it its full title, *Fragment of an analysis of a case of hysteria* (1905). This analysis is also a valuable specimen of the "free association" method which had by now replaced that of direct questioning of patients as to the origin of their symptoms. Patients were invited to make associations from their dreams or other material which were then *interpreted* by Freud, as we shall see in the Dora analysis, in a highly subjective manner. A relic of his excursion into hypnosis, the famous couch was retained, with Freud sitting behind the patient's head where he was able to see him without being seen himself. He later spoke to Joseph Wortis of the importance of the couch to assure relaxation and freedom from restraint. "Besides," he added, "I don't like to have people stare me in the face" (Wortis, 1954).

The case of "Dora" was the first to be published giving details of what Freud in the 1895 paper had described as "the laborious but completely reliable method of psychoanalysis" but which he did not further elaborate. Any enquiring minds desiring more explicit information had to wait until its publication in 1905 for enlightenment as to his methods or for any case history in support of his theories. The paper that eventually met the demands of these critics was actually written in January 1901. Reporting its despatch to the *Monatsschrift für Psychiatrie und Neurologie*, Freud wrote to Fliess that it would "meet the gaze of an astonished public in the autumn". In the event, Freud withheld the paper from publication for a further four years. Did he have some dim recognition that in this paper he had perpetrated an aberration as he had with the ill-fated *Project*? (see page 164). Though published in 1905, the "Dora analysis" is considered by the editors of Freud's *Standard Edition* "to be a fair representative of his technical methods and theoretical views in 1901". Freud's own appraisal of the paper is contained in his letter to Fliess of January 25, 1901: "It is the most subtle thing I have yet written" he says, "and will produce an even more horrifying effect than usual. One does one's duty, however, and what one writes is not for the passing day." Evidently sensitive to the criticisms of his publications of 1895 and 1896, Freud wrote, "No doubt it was awkward that I was obliged to publish the results of my enquiries without there being any possibility of other workers in the field testing and checking them, particularly as those results were of a surprising and by no means gratifying character." But whereas before he had been accused of giving no information about his patients, now he would be accused, he believed, of giving too much. However, he anticipated the "ill-will of narrow-minded critics" by what was to become the standard (and highly effective) riposte of psychoanalysts to criticism – "What is new has always aroused bewilderment and resistance," he declared.

In the autumn of 1900 a young girl – the "Dora" of the analysis – was sent to Freud for treatment. An intelligent girl of eighteen, with "engaging looks" she suffered from attacks of loss of consciousness accompanied by convulsions and "delirious states" – in other words, epilepsy, an interpretation further substantiated by an intermittent tendency to drag one leg and her complaint of nocturnal enuresis. In addition she had recurrent attacks of an illness accompanied by cough and loss of voice lasting for several months at a time. Her father suffered from tuberculosis and had, moreover, contracted syphilis before his marriage, sufficient grounds, one would have thought, to indicate an organic aetiology. There is in the case history, however, no record of either ordinary physical or special neurological examination and the facts of her past and family medical history are badly documented and mentioned mostly incidentally. In contrast, the emotional aspects of Dora's life receive a disproportionate amount of space.

Dora had been the subject of unwelcome attentions from a friend of the family, Herr K. To complicate the situation, Dora's father had shown signs of having an illicit love affair with Herr K's wife. The two families lived in close contact and Dora had formerly been on good terms with Frau K., but since her suspicions of her father's attachment, this friendship had ceased. So distressed was she by the situation that she had even threatened suicide. It was in these circumstances that Freud began his analysis. This revolved around two dreams and is a good illustration of Freud's use of symbolism in their interpretation, a subject which had received little attention in the first edition of *The Interpretation of Dreams*. The analysis also illustrates Freud's theory of *symptomatic actions* and other methodological innovations.

Dora's first dream was a recurrent one. The house was on fire. Her father was standing beside her bed and woke her up. She dressed quickly. Her mother wanted to stop and save her jewel-case; but her father said he refused to let himself and his two children be burnt for the sake of the jewel-case. They hurried downstairs and as soon as they were outside, Dora awoke. A further detail added by Dora was that each time when she woke she distinctly smelt smoke. The fact that it was a *recurrent* dream and that it was associated with olfactory hallucinations of smoke points to the dream being an epileptic phenomenon.

Asked by Freud to make associations from this dream, Dora produced the information that her parents had been arguing about her mother's practice of locking the dining room at night, from which her brother's room had its sole exit. This led *Freud* to associate – with a very characteristic flight of ideas. The word *"Zimmer"* [room] he said, "in dreams stands very frequently for *'Frauenzimmer'*" [literally 'women's apartments']. "The question whether a woman is 'open' or 'shut' can naturally not be a matter of indifference" he continued. "It is well known too, what sort of 'key' effects the opening in such a case."

The fact of her mother wanting to save her jewel-case caused Dora to mention that Herr K. had made her a present of an expensive jewel-case a little while before. This led to the following exchange:

"Then a return present would have been very appropriate. Perhaps you do not know that 'jewel-case' is a favourite expression for the same thing that you alluded to not long ago by means of the reticule you were wearing – for the female genitals, I mean."

"I knew you would say that."

"That is to say, you knew that it *was* so. – The meaning of the dream is now becoming even clearer."

By a somewhat tendentious argument, Freud deduced from the smell of smoke still present on awakening from the dream, that Dora had developed a "transference" to himself. "Smoke, of course, fitted in well with fire, but it also showed that the dream had a special relation to myself; for when she used to assert that there was nothing concealed behind this or that, I would often say by way of rejoinder: 'There can be no smoke without fire!' Dora objected, however, to such a purely personal interpretation, saying that Herr K. and her father were passionate smokers – as I am too, for the matter of that." The fact that the smell of smoke had only come up as an addendum told Freud that it must therefore have had to overcome a particularly strong effort on the part of repression. Accordingly, it was probably related to

> "the thoughts which were the most obscurely presented and the most successfully repressed in the dream, to the thoughts, that is, concerned with the temptation to show herself willing to yield to the man. If that were so, the addendum to the dream would scarcely mean anything else than the longing for a kiss, which, with a smoker, would necessarily smell of smoke . . . Taking into consideration, finally, the indications which seemed to point to there having been a transference on to me – since I am a smoker too – I came to the conclusion that the idea had probably occurred to her one day during a session that she would like to have a kiss from me."

The allusion to the reticule was as follows. Having been invited to confess that she had masturbated in childhood, Dora denied flatly that she had ever done so.

> "But a few days later she did something which I could not help regarding as a further step towards the confession. For on that day she wore at her waist – a thing she never did on any other occasion before or after – a small reticule of a shape which had just come into fashion; and, as she lay on the sofa and talked, she kept playing with it – opening it, putting a finger into it, shutting it again, and so on. I looked on for some time and then explained to her the nature of a 'symptomatic act'."

Dora's reticule, he declared, was "nothing but a representation of the genitals" and her fiddling with it a "fantasy of masturbation". He had, he continued, begun to suspect masturbation after Dora had complained of gastric pains. "It is well known that gastric pains occur especially often in those who masturbate," he declared. "According to a personal communication made to me by Wilhelm Fliess, it is precisely gastralgias of this character which can be interrupted by an application of cocaine to the 'gastric spot' discovered by him in the nose, and which can be cured by cauterisation of the same spot."

The patient's attack of asthma produced another flight of ideas. "Dora's symptomatic acts and certain other signs gave me a good reason for supposing that the child, whose bedroom had been next door to her parents', had overheard her father in his wife's room at night and had heard him (for he was always short of breath) breathing hard while they had intercourse," he declared. "I maintained years ago that the dyspnoea and palpitations that occur in hysteria and anxiety neurosis are only detached fragments of the act of copulation," he continued, "and in many cases, as in Dora's, I have been able to trace back the symptom of dyspnoea or nervous asthma to the same exciting cause – to the patient's having overheard sexual intercourse taking place between adults." Somewhat obscurely, he continues, the asthma "formed the boundary between two phases of her sexual life, of which the first was masculine in character and the second, feminine".

The interpretation of his patient's second dream shows Freud making free use of symbolism in straining after sexual associations. Dora dreamt she was walking about in a town which she did not know, with streets and squares strange to her. Then she came to the house where she lived, went up to her room and found a letter from her mother lying there. Her mother had written to say that as Dora had left home without her parents' knowledge, she had not wished to write to tell her her father was ill. "Now he is dead, and if you like you can come." She went to the railway station which she had difficulty in finding, going through a thick wood to reach it. Then she reached her home, to be told that her mother and others were already at the cemetery. She went upstairs to her room and began reading a big book that lay on her writing table.

The patient had seen precisely the same thick wood the day before, in a picture at the Secessionist exhibition. In the background of the picture there were nymphs. This last item played an important part in Freud's interpretation:

"At this point a certain suspicion of mine became a certainty. The use of 'Bahnhof' [station, literally 'railway court'] and 'Friedhof' [cemetery, literally 'peace court'] to represent the female genitals was striking enough in itself, but it also served to direct my awakened curiosity to the similarly formed 'Vorhof' ["vestibulum"; literally "fore-court"] – an anatomical term for a particular region of the female genitals. This might have been no more than mistaken ingenuity. But now, with the addition of 'nymphs' visible in the background of a 'thick wood', no further doubts could be entertained. Here was a symbolic geography of sex! 'Nymphae', as is known to physicians though not to laymen (and even by the former the term is not very commonly used), is the name given to the labia minora, which lie in the background of the 'thick wood' of the pubic hair. But any one who employed such technical names as 'vestibulum' and 'nymphae' must have derived his knowledge from books, and not from popular ones either, but from anatomical text-books or an encyclopaedia – the common refuge of youth when it is de-voured by sexual curiosity. If this interpretation were correct, therefore, there lay concealed behind the first situation in the dream of a fantasy of defloration, the fantasy of a man seeking to force an entrance into the female genitals."

The big book which Dora had started reading on her return home was therefore arbitrarily declared to have been an encyclo-paedia from which the use of the anatomical terms emanated. (Even Freud could not have claimed that "the unconscious" knew the correct medical terminology.) But the patient *had not used these words* – they had been associated not by her but by Freud himself from the ordinary everyday words "station" and "cemet-ery". And Freud *had* a medical training and *did* know the anatomical terms. In addition, there was a significant selection in the association to the word *vestibulum* and hence to the female genitals. In anatomy the term simply means the space at the entrance to a canal. It is applied to several other organs in the body, but especially to the oval cavity of the internal ear forming the approach to the cochlea. This is the more usual application of the term.

The "defloration fantasy" had a sequel. Dora declared that she had only ever consulted an encyclopaedia once, when an aunt had developed appendicitis. Freud remembered that shortly after the aunt's death Dora herself had had an attack of appendicitis. On hearing that the attack had occurred *nine* months after the occasion when Herr K. forced his unwelcome attentions on her, he declared her appendicitis to be a fantasy of childbirth. The dragging of her leg which first appeared after this illness was now given a symbolic significance: "That is how people walk when they have a twisted foot. So she had made a 'false step': which was true indeed if she could give birth to a child nine months after the scene by the lake."

The "sexual symbols" used in the interpretation of these dreams were only a few of the many postulated by Freud and his followers in the succeeding years – anything cylindrical was a male or "phallic symbol" and anything hollow was a female symbol. Such objects are very common and by their use as "symbols" any dream of any nature whatever could be and was deemed to have a sexual significance. Moreover, in both dreams the "associations" were not those of the patient. They were made by Freud. It was *he* who associated from "*Bahnhof*" and "*Friedhof*" to "*Vorhof*" and from the nymphs in the painting to the "nymphae". It was *he* who decided that the "big book" of the dream must have been an encyclopaedia consulted for the enlightenment of sexual curiosity. Moreover, the associations break down by reason of their obvious inconsistencies. The smell of smoke from the fire in the first dream would have been quite different from that of tobacco, and this association is a particularly interesting one as the inconsistency it displays points to a subtle form of receptive dysphasia.

Freud's final interpretation of his patient's throat symptoms illustrate his current preoccupations with incest and the perversions. Dora had insisted that Frau K. only loved her father because he was a "man of means". This led Freud to infer that "behind this phrase its opposite was concealed" and that her father, as a man, was without means, was, in fact, impotent (this might have been a fact known to Freud as the father had also been his patient). From there, he deduced that Dora, knowing her father's impotence, had pictured his affair with Frau K. in "scenes of sexual gratification *per os*": moreover, in that fantasy she must have been putting herself in Frau K.'s place and "identifying" with her, thus revealing an unconscious wish to indulge in the same perverse practices with her father.

The analysis came to abrupt conclusion when after three months the patient announced her firm intention of discontinuing the sessions. Freud consoled himself with the thought that Dora's defection was due to the fact that she had formed a "transference" to himself which he had failed to notice in time. But it had evidently been a bitter blow. "No one who, like me, conjures up the most evil of those half-tamed demons that inhabit the human breast, and seeks to wrestle with them, can expect to come through the struggle unscathed," he said. A more plausible explanation will probably occur to the reader. This brief summary of the analysis conveys only a small part of the pathological nature of the paper which should be read in full by anyone with any remaining doubts on the subject.

XVII

Freud the Scientist?

The Dora analysis is a valuable specimen of Freud's analytical methods and theoretical approach at the turn of the century, by that time already crystallised into a pattern from which there was to be little divergence for the rest of his life. The paper already contained a number of what were to become standard Freudian expressions: "somatic compliance", "sublimation", "bisexuality", "erotogenic zones", "acting out", "identifying with" and many others which had been used for some years in the Fliess correspondence and which were to become the catchwords of the analytic movement in the ensuing years. The Dora analysis can therefore be regarded as the final and peak stage of Freud's work on "hysteria" and other "neuroses" demonstrating the interpretation of dreams and the roles allegedly played by the Oedipus complex and "infantile sexuality".

Freud's work in "hysteria" turned the wheel full circle back to the naive theories of the ancients. Ignorant of the history of his subject, he learned only later that his theories went back to this era; but under the impression that antiquity confers validity, this pleased him. "Nor was I then aware," he wrote in his *Autobiographical Study*, "that in deriving hysteria from sexuality I was going back to the very beginnings of medicine and following up a thought of Plato's." He had learnt this only later from an essay by Havelock Ellis. Plato's actual words were:

> "The womb is an animal which longs to generate children. When it remains barren too long after puberty, it is distressed and sorely disturbed, and straying about in the body and cutting off the passages of breath, it impedes respiration and brings the sufferer into the extremest anguish and provokes all manner of diseases besides" (Timaeus).

Not only did Freud's work revive the old corollary of the uterine theory – sexual repression as the cause of "hysteria" – it also revived the old theories of the influence of the mind on the body and its ability to cause disease. Medicine had been moving away from these theories in the latter decades of the nineteenth century. The new discoveries in medicine and the development of methods of scientific investigation had tended to diminish the importance of the psychogenesis theory of disease.

Another important influence during these years was the work of Joseph Babinski. His years at the Salpêtrière had convinced him that bodily disease could not originate in the mind and after his appointment to an independent post at the Pitié hospital in 1890 he began to investigate this problem intensively. It was in this period that he discovered the plantar reflex that now bears his name – the fanning out of the toes in disease of the pyramidal or voluntary motor tract when the sole of the foot is stroked, in contrast to the normal flexion of non-diseased subjects. In a series of papers from 1893 onwards Babinski took issue with the traditional concept of hysteria. Though not dispensing altogether with the concept, he restricted its application to conditions capable of being voluntarily simulated, thus excluding the many absurdities such as the use of this diagnosis in cases of hemiplegia with exaggerated reflexes and ankle clonus, and in ulceration, haemorrhage and even gangrene, examples of which, thanks to Charcot, had proliferated in the previous decades. The erroneous *post hoc ergo propter hoc* reasoning behind these diagnoses was stressed – "if there is a history of an emotion, it is regarded as being the cause of the symptoms in question," he said.

To establish this point, he began to investigate the effects of natural disasters "under the circumstances [when] emotion must have reached its utmost intensity". The experience of his contemporary Neri after the earthquake of Messina confirmed his suspicions. "Although he examined more than 2,000 persons immediately after the catastrophe he did not see a single case of paralysis, contracture or convulsive attacks. Studies carried out later, in the weeks following the disaster, at a time when suggestion might have entered into play and accentuated the phenomena caused by the psychical shock, gave the same results."

Babinski personally carried out a study in which he questioned all the mortuary attendants in the various Paris hospitals on the reactions of relatives on confrontation with the dead bodies of their loved ones.

"Among these enquiries, all of which led to the same result, I will specially mention that which I made in company with my colleague Richardière at the Hospital for Sick Children. During a period of eighteen years, in which more than 20,000 deaths had been entered in the register, the mortuary attendant had seen about 10,000 women come to identify their child's body and be present when it was put in a coffin; there can be no doubt that he witnessed sincere emotions. Now this man, in his very full replies to our questions, declared that he had never observed a single manifestation of undoubtedly hysterical character; he remembers that only five or six times in his long experience women had a sort of faint and remained unconscious for a few moments, but he had never witnessed a convulsive attack, and he declares that he had never seen a single case of paralysis or contracture. Enquiries of the same kind were made of medical men, sisters and nurses who had several times had occasion to observe the effects of the most violent moral shocks, and all had the same result."

The belief of Charcot and his contemporaries that the vasomotor nerves were under the control of the mind was now being challenged in another direction by the work of the Cambridge physiologists W. H. Gaskell and J. N. Langley on what they were later to name "the autonomic nervous system". The anatomical features of this system had been observed for centuries and fanciful names given to the nerves and ganglia – "the solar plexus" due to its resemblance to the rays of the sun, "the semi-lunar ganglia" – "the vagus (wandering) nerve" etc. But the function of the system, its separateness from the central nervous system and the manner in which it exerted control over the involuntary functions of the body were only being delineated around the turn of the century. Almost simultaneously with this research, investigation of the function of the "ductless glands" had led to the isolation of the active principle of the extract from the adrenal gland – adrenaline. Injecting their newly extracted substance into various animals, Oliver and Schäffer found it resulted in a great rise in blood pressure, acceleration of the heart rate, contraction of the small peripheral arteries, dilation of the bronchioles, increase of blood sugar, inhibition of activity of the digestive organs, sweating, widening of the pupils and erection of hairs. It was later found that injection of adrenaline markedly shortened the clotting time of the blood and caused a release of red blood corpuscles from the spleen.

The final synthesis of all these data comprising ingredients, as disparate as the hairs on a cat's tail to the centres for the physical expression of the emotions in the brain, was performed by Walter B. Cannon of Harvard in the years from 1897 onwards. He had been working with the newly discovered roëntgen rays and had devised the bismuth meal, a forerunner of today's barium meal which rendered the gastrointestinal tract opaque to X-rays. His subjects were a goose fitted with a box and a collar to hold the neck straight which gave it a "most absurd and pompous air", a medical student who had developed the art of regurgitation of his gastric contents at will, and a second Alexis St Martin (see page 000) with a fistula through which it was possible to make studies of the gastric digestive processes quite as Beaumont had done many years before. In studying the movements of the stomach Cannon was disconcerted to find occasional interference with his observations. Although some animals displayed the rolling waves of the stomach wall during the digestive process with the utmost definiteness, others showed no movements whatever. Only after some time did he notice that the absence of activity was accompanied by signs of perturbation in the animal and that when serenity was restored the waves promptly reappeared. Beaumont had observed the same phenomenon in his investigations on St Martin on the Canadian frontier a century before. The observation led to a long series of studies on the effects of strong emotion on the body and instigated a closer investigation of the autonomic nervous system. The enigma posed by the disparate and seemingly unrelated facts so far collected was finally solved by a brilliant flash of inspiration when Cannon conceived his "flight or fight" hypothesis. All the changes produced by the action of adrenaline on the sympathetic nerves were, he realised, designed to prepare the organism for the instant action that often followed the intense emotions of fear or anger. The raised blood pressure, the accelerated action of the heart, the contraction of the peripheral blood vessels (which caused the pallor attendant on fear) and the release of red blood cells from the spleen made more blood available for brain and muscles. The release of glucose from the liver into the bloodstream made more energy accessible to them. The dilation of the pupils gave maximum use of light to aid vision and the shortening of the period of time necessary for the blood to coagulate protected against excessive bleeding should injury occur. The reactions produced by the action of adrenaline were, Cannon realised, adaptive mechanisms designed to render the organism ready for instant and vigorous action.

But all the somatic effects mentioned above are produced by the action of adrenaline on the sympathetic nerves leading to the viscera and blood vessels involved in the reactions. These nerves are affected *simultaneously and automatically*. There is no control by mind or will. The ancients who had witnessed the pallor and acceleration of the pulse attendant on fear or other strong emotion had drawn the simple conclusion that the mind could directly influence bodily functions. This belief persisted down the centuries. The clinicopathological methods of the Vienna school and the new discoveries in medicine had done much to dispel these old fallacies. Now Freud was bringing them back. Growing further away from orthodox medicine as the new century progressed, he ignored the later developments in neurology and in the growing science of endocrinology. The researches of Babinski passed him by. The teaching that the mind could cause bodily disease was handed on to his disciples as a novel and revolutionary precept. Many of these disciples were later to outdo even Freud himself in the application of this teaching. The apotheosis was probably reached with Georg Groddeck, who sought the purpose of every symptom in the "unconscious" – a sore throat was developed to force the whispering of secrets, pain in the arm to ward off a tendency to forcefulness or thievery, halitosis to keep the suitor at a distance, cold hands to hide hot emotions and so on. Groddeck's most startling claim was that visual difficulties *always* expressed emotional conflicts and that even retinal bleeding and other organic changes in the eye were efforts to defend the patient against forbidden wishes. Thus did Freud and his followers amuse themselves with their patients' often grave conditions in need of urgent medical care. Thus too did the later generation of physicians who embraced the theories of psychoanalysis during the Freud revival of recent decades amuse themselves when the concept of hysteria and the old theories of the power of the mind over the body once more became fashionable. These theories were now designated by the sophisticated term "psychosomatic medicine." But they were still the same theories. The medical advances in the intervening years since they were first postulated were ignored. Even the contagious diseases were implicated, as though the discoveries in microbiology and immunology had never been made.

Hysteria is, of course, never usually diagnosed today on the same criteria as in Freud's time. It is not, for instance, applied to an upper motor neurone lesion because of the absence of muscle wasting or because of normal electrical reactions. The progress of medicine has overtaken these fundamental errors. In fact, some psychiatrists discuss what they call "the changing symptomatology of hysteria". There is, of course, no changing symptomatology. Hysteria is now being *diagnosed* for different conditions – rare diseases of obscure aetiology that the physician is either ignorant of or has forgotten. The usefulness of the diagnosis in this respect was recognised by Sydenham who wrote,

"As often as females consult me concerning such, or such bodily ailments as are difficult to be determined by the usual rules for diagnosis, I never fail to carefully inquire whether they are not worse sufferers when trouble, low spirits, or any mental perturbation takes hold of them. If so, I put down the symptoms for hysterical . . ."

One of his contemporary physicians, Thomas Willis, shrewdly put his finger on the weak spot in the diagnosis of hysteria.

". . . for when at any time a sickness happens in a woman's body, of an unusual manner, or more occult origin, so that its causes lie hid, and Curatory indication is altogether uncertain, presently we accuse the evil influence of the Womb (which for the most part is innocent) and in every unusual symptom, we declare it to be something hysterical, and so to this scope, which oftentimes is only the subterfuge of ignorance, the medical intentions and the use of Remedies are directed".

A century later Guy's Hospital magazine contained the following advice in *A Guide to Medicine*:

A group of symptoms unexplained you label a neurosis,
And this is rather clever, for you've made a diagnosis.

The role of ignorance in the diagnosis of hysteria is emphasised by the testimony of physicians specializing in those rare diseases so often misdiagnosed as neurotic or hysterical. Dr Raymond Greene, the eminent endocrinologist who specialises in *myasthenia gravis*, a rare disease in which failure of the neurotransmitter between the nerve ends and the muscles leads to transient bouts of weakness and paralysis, found that many of his patients had had their condition for *twenty years* or more before being correctly diagnosed. *Myasthenia gravis* is an eminently treatable condition and the diagnosis of patients with the disease as neurotic or hysterical does them grave injustice.

The eminent American neurosurgeon Irving Cooper tells a similar story of his patients with *dystonia musculorum deformans*, a genetically determined disease of the basal ganglia of the brain giving rise to dystonic postures and involuntary movements. Untreated it follows a progressive course until a stage of almost total incapacity is reached. By the placing of stereotactic lesions in the part of the brain where the symptoms originated Cooper has been able to effect a complete cure in some of the worst cases that have come to him. Virtually all the patients in this series had been diagnosed as hysterical at some time during their illness.

"Moreover, many of the children, while the symptoms progressed and their incapacity increased, were subjected to long-range, futile, psychoananalytic investigations. This invariably multiplied the burden that the child and parents were forced to assume and aggravated the social and practical disabilities produced by the hyperkinetic disorder."

In one of the cases cited in Cooper's book *Involuntary Movement Disorders*, a 24-year-old man had at the age of seventeen been diagnosed as a case of conversion hysteria, based on the observation that his symptoms had "an exhibitionist quality", and that his manner of walking caused people to notice him. He had had a hundred and forty-six psychotherapeutic sessions before being discharged, by now totally disabled. After surgery by Cooper a complete cure was effected. At follow-up after ten years he was working as the driver of a heavy truck at an airport, and had received his able-bodied seaman certification from the coast-guard medical authorities.

Other treatable medical conditions that often invite a diagnosis of "hysteria" are acute intermittent porphyria, systemic lupus erythematosus and temporal lobe epilepsy. Emphasising the dangers of the diagnosis, Eliot Slater, in a famous follow-up study in the *British Medical Journal* of 1965, published the results of an investigation of eighty-five patients diagnosed as suffering from hysteria at the National Hospital for Nervous Diseases, London. The patients were young or middle-aged. In the nine-year follow-up period twelve had died, fourteen had become totally disabled and only nineteen were well at the time of follow-up. Other studies have produced similar results. A legacy from the Charcot era, the diagnosis of "*globus hystericus*" is now wrongly applied to *any* sensation of a lump in the throat for which no obvious cause can be found. A series reported by K. G. Malcomson in the *Journal of Laryngology and Otology* in 1968 showed organic lesions in a total of seventy-nine per cent of three hundred and seven patients previously diagnosed as having "*globus hystericus*". The published studies probably represent only a small fraction of the cases of *treatable* organic disease diagnosed as hysteria, often with tragic results. A recent hospital case presented with a massive brain tumour causing total blindness. She had first experienced visual disorders six years before but had been diagnosed as a case of hysteria because the eyes themselves were normal on examination and because she had recently left her husband. Had her complaints been taken seriously at that time, her sight could have been saved. In recent years the popularity of the diagnosis has spread to family doctors by way of the fashionable Balint seminars, named after a disciple of Freud who introduced psychoanalytic theories into general practice. The end result has been a vast overprescription of tranquillisers and a serious *underdiagnosis* of major *treatable* conditions. A recent article in the *British Medical Journal* (Watkins, 1982) stated that, "Of the 15 new patients with diabetes presenting in our diabetic ward for the first time in ketoacidosis [a serious and avoidable complication of diabetes] 14 had had no urine test after a total of 41 visits to their doctors. Almost all these serious cases could have been prevented."

Children diagnosed as hysterical had been harshly treated in the nineteenth century. When, after the Freud revival, psychoanalytic theory was introduced into paediatrics by David Winnicott the diagnosis began to reappear in the children's wards and clinics. Parents were told to ignore their children's fits and render no assistance; the children themselves were inevitably made to feel that in some way they did not understand, they themselves were responsible for bringing about the attacks that caused so much anxiety to their parents and so much disruption in school and family. A little girl of seven was recently brought into hospital for reassessment of her epilepsy. Her major seizures were not in doubt but she also had other attacks which instead of ending in convulsions, culminated in vomiting. These, because they were atypical, had been diagnosed as hysterical fits. They were later demonstrated by EEG recordings to be epileptic variants. But the diagnosis of hysteria had filtered through to the special school she attended and whenever she had one of these fits this little girl of seven, who probably had more than enough to contend with in her epilepsy, was made to clear up the vomited material as a punishment.

And yet the diagnosis persists. Ten years after Slater published his warning, Aubrey Lewis (1975) in an article on *The Survival of Hysteria* stated, "Hysteria is a tough subject, unlikely to be killed so long as clinicians find it useful, if not indispensable." Will it ever become obsolete? Most lay people are unaware that such a medical diagnosis exists. The movement campaigning for allowing patients access to their case-notes should never have become necessary; that it *is* now necessary stems from the growing number of physicians wedded to the concept of hysteria and *continuing to diagnose it* even after one of their patients so diagnosed has died. Slater cited a tragic instance – a nurse with a cerebral abscess who surely deserved better of her medical colleagues. Freud himself in *The Psychopathology of Everyday Life* described such a case of his own. He gave it as an example of "motivated forgetting" – he was unable to remember any details of the patient whose name appeared in his appointment book when he was sending out his accounts, but this was probably an example of his own memory deterioration consequent on his drug use.

> "M—l was a fourteen-year-old girl, the most remarkable case I had had in recent years, one which taught me a lesson I am not likely ever to forget and whose outcome cost me moments of the greatest distress. The child fell ill of an unmistakable hysteria, which did in fact clear up quickly and radically under my care. After this improvement the child was taken away from me by her parents. She still complained of abdominal pains which had played the chief part in the clinical picture of her hysteria. Two months later she died of sarcoma of the abdominal glands. The hysteria, to which she was at the same time predisposed, used the tumour as a provoking cause, and I, with my attention held by the noisy but harmless manifestations of the hysteria, had perhaps overlooked the first signs of the insidious and incurable disease."

Unfortunately this self-justifying attitude still exists. Freud at least admitted distress. All too often there is now a complacent shrugging of the shoulders and the claim that "hysteria" can co-exist with organic disease. A growing number of physicians find the pursuit of Freudian "flight into illness" and "secondary gain" motivation far more fascinating than the painstaking and more pedestrian investigations needed to exclude treatable organic disease.

Freud must take a large share of the blame for the lack of progress in psychiatry since his theories became fashionable. In all his psychoanalytic works there is scarcely an indication that the brain had been established as the organ of the mind in the century of his birth. There is now a growing body of evidence from genetic studies, from the effects of drug therapy and latterly from the findings of biochemistry and the evidence from the newly disco-vered brain scanners that in so-called mental disease we are, in fact, dealing with *brain* disease. As with hypnosis, the large physical component in these diseases is, as a result of the psychogenic interpretation, usually ignored. A case in point is agoraphobia, always fertile ground for psychoanalytic specula-tion. The psychogenic interpretation that these patients are afraid of open spaces is incorrect. The main symptom is that the patients *become giddy* in open spaces, pointing to the organs of equilib-rium in the inner ear and their connections to the brain. This interpretation is supported by the fact that head injury is often followed by agoraphobia, and that patients with agoraphobia have been found to have a higher than normal incidence of physical disease which could involve these pathways. Equilibrium is a complex function, involving coordination with eyes, position in space, variations of body posture and so on. The complex nerve pathways involved in these interactions necessitate considerable adaptation in open spaces when the familiar visual cues are further away. Faulty functioning of the organs of equilibrium renders this difficult and giddiness with consequent insecurity and fear is the result. If the patient is encouraged to persevere in going into open spaces, adaptive and compensatory higher cerebral mechanisms come into play to correct the defect and this might seem to confirm the psychogenic theory. All too often, however, the disease is perpetuated by psychotherapy which seeks for the root of the condition in unconscious motivation.

Thanks to Freud, a patient coming under the care of a psychoanalytically orientated psychiatrist has an excellent chance of never receiving a single physical investigation in the whole course of his illness. An example of this approach is the Freudian psychiatrist who was invited to a children's ward and asked for his diagnosis of some of the patients there (Benda, 1960). He made various Freudian suggestions involving Oedipal motivation and so on. The children were actually suffering from phenylketonuria, a congenital disease in which metabolism of phenylalanine, one of the amino acids, is impaired.

The promising lines of research initiated by Meynert and other psychiatrists of the clinico-pathological school were largely abandoned when Freudian theory became popular; somehow over the years, Freud's florid and bizarre concepts achieved medical respectability and orthodoxy, while the organic approach became slightly disreputable, its adherents having to adopt an apologetic and deprecatory stance, while from the lofty heights of superior knowledge the psychoanalysts spoke patronisingly and disparagingly of the "medical model". The continued illogical separation of psychiatry and neurology, as if only part of the brain belonged to the central nervous system, is another legacy of Freudian dominance. The brain is part of the body, subject to the same virus infections, tumours, vitamin deficiencies and biochemical defects that afflict the body. All these can affect brain cells and lead to the impaired cognitive functioning and distorted sense perceptions we call mental disease. It is only common sense to exclude these conditions at the outset of an illness. Ideally a patient should never be sent to a mental hospital without a minimum number of physical investigations in a general hospital; if compulsory commital proceedings are used at all, it should be to such a hospital. Only this can remedy a source of great injustice to the patient; a pathologically low blood sugar level can give rise to extremely bizarre behaviour; someone in a temporal lobe attack can present all the appearances of mania.

Freudian psychiatry today is supported by large numbers of psychotherapists, counsellors, social workers, child guidance experts and others, and the numbers are steadily increasing. Even the familiar figure of the health visitor has been diverted from her former duties to counselling the patients on their "emotional problems". Large amounts of public money are swallowed up in these activities which have produced nothing but a proliferation of literature, case conferences, theorising and jargon. Meanwhile there has been no abatement of the growth of "mental disease". No progress in psychiatry can occur until the invalid and aberrational theories of Freud are eradicated and the way cleared for the incorporation of all the medical advances since Freud laid the foundations of psychoanalysis in the last decade of the nineteenth century.

The year of the publication of the Dora analysis also saw the appearance of the full exposition of Freud's theories of infantile sexuality in the *Three Essays* discussed on page 264. By 1905, therefore, the fundamental postulates of psychoanalysis, the unconscious mind, repression, conversion, infantile sexuality, the Oedipus situation and dream interpretation, had been published. On lesser issues Freud changed his position many times, but these fundamental principles remained unchanged in their essentials. During the years that followed, these concepts were systematised and elaborated. The alleged strata of the mind were in 1923 given new names, the ego, id and superego replacing the older terms. The only major innovation occurred in 1920 with the postulation of a "death instinct" in *Beyond the Pleasure Principle*. In association with the death instinct, where formerly he had treated aggression as a component of sexuality, Freud now assumed an independent aggressive or destructive instinct. Repression of this instinct carried the same dangers and difficulties as that of sexuality. "If civilisation" he wrote in *Civilization and its Discontents* (1927a) "imposes such great sacrifices not only on man's sexuality but on his aggressivity, we can understand better why it is hard for him to be happy in that civilisation." In *The Future of an Illusion* (1927b) he stated that among the instinctive wishes of mankind were "those of incest, cannibalism and lust for killing".

It would be unprofitable to follow Freud through the tortuous paths of the later elaboration of his theories. Since their basis was the fundamental errors discussed in previous chapters and since they were coloured by his cocaine intoxication, further dicussion would be fruitless. We will therefore leave Freud's theoretical edifice at this stage. As we have seen the foundations of this edifice were presented in a series of papers characterised by inconsistencies and circular arguments, with a total lack of evidence for the postulates they contained.

Freud himself was not proud of these early papers. Writing in 1924, Fritz Wittels says, "Freud is not fond of discussing his earlier writings. When they are attacked, he will engage in savage rearguard skirmishes." And yet, though they contained no actual proof, only promises of future papers giving full case histories to support his theses that never appeared, it was to these early papers that Freud in subsequent publications refers the reader for the evidence of the truth of his fundamental theories. In the 1908 publication *'Civilized' Sexual Morality and Modern Nervous Illness* he wrote of his conviction that sexual repression in civilised society was harmful, "I have tried to bring forward the evidence for this assertion in a number of technical papers. I cannot repeat it here." The reference he gave is to the early papers we have been discussing. Few people go back to these texts which contain the original formulations of his theories. Even dedicated psychoanalysts prefer Freud's *Introductory Lectures* written many years later and which are easier to follow. Thus Freud's work seems to have acquired a miraculous dispensation from the requirements of science that the announcement of new findings should be supported by evidential proof and that adequate descriptions of the methods by which these findings were arrived at should be incorporated so that the quality of the proof can be assessed independently by competent colleagues in the field.

XVIII

The Psychoanalytic Movement

The Dora analysis shows Freud at the dawn of the new century as a man of pathological preoccupations. Associated with these traits were the characteristic paranoiac tendencies of cocaine usage. Paranoia had probably caused his break with Breuer. Now it led to a similar dissolution of his friendship with Fliess.

The break came in the summer of 1900 during their last "congress" at Achensee in Munich. Jones says of the event, "How the clash itself came about we do not know exactly. Fliess' subsequent (published) version was that Freud made a violent and unexpected attack on him, which sounds very unlikely." In fact, from what we know of Freud it would be entirely characteristic. "What is certain," continues Jones, "is that he responded, perhaps to some criticism of the periodic laws by Freud, by saying that Freud was only a 'thought-reader' and – more – that he 'read his own thoughts into his patients'." Fliess in 1906 revealed that the reason for the violence shown him by Freud was that he, Fliess, had claimed that periodic phenomena were responsible for the psychopathic problems of Freud's patients and that hence neither deterioration nor improvements could be attributed to psychoanalysis alone. "During the rest of the discussion" he continued, "I thought I detected a personal animosity against me on Freud's part which sprang from envy. Freud had earlier said to me in Vienna: 'It's just as well that we're friends. Otherwise I should burst with envy if I heard anyone was making such discoveries in Berlin!'." As a result, Fliess continues, he quietly withdrew from the friendship and dropped the regular correspondence (*Origins* p. 324). The two men never met again.

Four years later an unseemly public quarrel broke out between the two men, with acrimonious letters to journals and other publications. Freud had revealed one of Fliess' theories on bisexuality to a pupil, Otto Weininger. This theory alleged the fundamental bisexual nature of every living cell. Weininger later wrote a book outlining this theory as his own discovery and without acknowledgement to Fliess. Fliess thereupon wrote to Freud accusing him of having leaked the "secret" to Weininger. At first Freud denied the accusation, but later confessed that he must have been influenced by his wish to rob Fliess of his originality, a wish compounded of envy and hostility. But these psychoanalytical explanations failed to placate Fliess and two years later he published the whole of this private correspondence. Fliess' preoccupation with his priority for the "discovery" has now only an antiquarian interest. Discoveries in the new science of genetics which began in the present century have disclosed that each living cell contains the appropriate chromosomal pattern for the sex of the individual – XY in the case of males and XX in females. Genes and chromosomes were unknown in Fliess' day. His theory of bisexuality was, as we have seen, based on his 28-23 day hypothesis.

Freud himself reveals an interesting sidelight to the dispute in *The Psychopathology of Everyday Life*. As an example of "unconscious" forgetting to "fend off unpleasure" he reveals that at the "congress" in Breslau in 1897 Fliess had told him of his conviction that all human beings had a bisexual constitution derived from the periodic laws 28 and 23. At the last meeting in the summer of 1900 Freud had announced the theory as a new idea of his own, whereupon Fliess, astonished, replied, "But I told you about that on our evening walk in Breslau and then you refused to accept the idea." One week later Freud recalled the whole conversation. "It is painful to be requested in this way to surrender one's originality," he wrote. It was, as Jones remarks, a very severe case of amnesia. In at least two letters in the period in between, he had assured Fliess of his conversion to belief in his (Fliess') theory. Freud's "unconscious forgetting" was probably due to memory deterioration associated with his cocaine usage.

Psychoanalytic legend has it that after the herioc feat of his self-analysis, Freud emerged triumphant, free forever from his "neurosis". As Jones expresses it, "The end of all the labour and suffering was the last and final phase in the evolution of Freud's personality. There emerged the serene and benign Freud, henceforth free to pursue his work in imperturbable composure." The fact is that we do not know Freud's state of mind in the years that followed his break with Fliess. When that friendship ended, a correspondence of incomparable source material ceased also. Freud was never again on such intimate terms with any of his friends. From 1902 when he gained his titular professorship and at the same time began the weekly discussion meetings which inaugurated the Vienna Psychoanalytic Society, he became "Herr Professor" to his followers and there were few he conversed with or corresponded with on the "du" level. His role as head of a movement that rapidly became national and then international, required a mantle of detachment and authority which he easily assumed.

The legend of Freud's triumphal emergence from the ordeal of self-analysis is, as Frank Sulloway entertainingly points out, part of the "myth of the hero" centring on the common theme of the "perilous journey" undertaken by the archetypal hero, originally described by Joseph Campbell in 1968. "The dangerous journey itself has three common motifs," writes Sulloway, "isolation, initiation, and return, all of which appear prominently in the Freud legend" (Sulloway 1979, 446). "Having undergone his superhuman ordeal, the archetypal hero now emerges as a person transformed, possessing the power to bestow great benefits upon his fellow man." In Freud's case the myth probably originated, with his sure touch for the dramatic, from Freud himself. The subsequent vicissitudes of Freud's relations with his disciples, the quarrels and schisms that rent the psychoanalytic movement and dogged his path in later years, hardly give credence to Jones' idealised view of a serene and benign Freud imperturbably pursuing his researches into the human psyche.

The question is of interest as it is bound up with the problem of the date of the cessation of Freud's cocaine usage. As late as 1900 there were no signs of any amelioration of his depressive moods despite three years of self-analysis. They were, if anything, worse. His letter to Fliess of March 23, 1900 says, "You know I have been going through a deep inner crisis, and if we met you would see how it has aged me . . . No one can help me in what oppresses me, it is my cross, which I must bear, and heaven knows my back is getting noticeably bent under it" . . . On July 10 he writes in a characteristic piece of drug imagery, "The big problems are still unsettled. It is an intellectual hell, layer upon layer of it, with everything fitfully gleaming and pulsating; and the outline of Lucifer-Amor coming into sight at the darkest centre."

Did the break with Fliess signal also the end of the physician-patient relationship between the two men and the consequent cessation of the nasal therapy with cocaine? There is no mention of later use of cocaine by Schur, who became Freud's physician in 1928 and we have his testimony that Freud refused all analgesics during his terminal illness in 1939. So some time before then one assumes that Freud had ceased the medication. But there are reasons to suppose that this occurred later rather than earlier, and certainly not immediately after the break with Fliess.

Freud had four documented attacks of loss of consciousness,

two occurring in the years of his friendship with Fliess and two *after* the break; both these latter were witnessed by Jung and other disciples who described them as "faints" and postulated varying psychoanalytical explanations, as did Freud himself. But, as pointed out by S. A. K. Wilson, a faint can be a fit. The recurrent incidence of Freud's attacks rules out transient environmental factors. Moreover, four such episodes in public implies many more unrecorded, occurring in the privacy of his own home. This, as we shall see later, is confirmed by Freud himself.

The first attack described by Jung, was in 1909 when he, Freud and Sandor Ferenczi met in Bremen, where they were to embark for the United States on a lecture tour. The conversation turned on the recent discoveries of the 'peat-bog corpses' in pre-historic Copenhagen cemeteries, a topic which seemed to annoy Freud.

> " 'Why are you so concerned with these corpses?' he asked me several times. He was inordinately vexed by the whole thing and during one such conversation, while we were having dinner together, he suddenly fainted. Afterwards he said to me that he was convinced that all this chatter about corpses meant I had death wishes towards him. I was more than surprised by this interpretation . . ." (Jung, 1963).

Freud in 1909 in America with: back row left to right, Brill, Jones, Ferenczi and front row, Freud, Stanley Hall and Jung.

Again at a meeting in Munich in 1912, Jung describes a similar attack. Freud and Jung had been discussing Abraham's recent paper on the pharaoh Amenophis IV. Abraham had mentioned in passing that though not epileptic, he had had fits as a boy. The others had claimed that at the back of the pharaoh's creation of a monotheistic religion there lurked a father complex. This irritated Jung who argued against it. "At that moment," said Jung, "Freud slid off his chair in a faint" (Jung, 1963). Freud himself wrote of the incident (Binswanger, 1957):

"My fainting attack in Munich was surely provoked by psychogenic elements, which received strong somatic reinforcements (a week of troubles, a sleepless night, the equivalent of a migraine, the day's tasks). I had had several such attacks; in each case there were similar contributory causes, often a bit of alcohol for which I have no tolerance. Among the psychic elements there is the fact that I had had a quite similar seizure in the same place in Munich on two previous occasions, four and six years ago. In the light of a most careful diagnosis, it seems scarcely possibly to attribute my attacks to a more serious cause, for instance, a weak heart. Repressed feelings, this time directed against Jung, as previously against a predecessor of his, naturally play the main part."

Recurrent attacks of loss of consciousness in a man in his forties would strongly suggest a brain lesion, and this would be consistent with prolonged cocaine usage which, as we have seen, eventually causes structural damage to the nervous system.

Giving support to this interpretation are smaller, though significant neurological signs. Joseph Wortis, who was in analysis with Freud in the twenties, reports that Freud held his hand stiffly, "bent in at the wrist; whether a surgical contracture or mannerism, I did not know." R. R. Grinker (1940), describing a meeting with Freud in 1933, says he found him "extremely energetic . . . constantly moving about". Freud's extreme penchant for writing has also evoked comment, many people expressing astonishment at the sheer bulk of his writings – "almost beyond comprehension" (Ruitenbeck 1973, p. 18) when it was realised that he had no secretary and did not use a typewriter. Every letter was written by hand and deciphering his handwriting was "a challenging task". Martin Grotjahn in 1967 referred to his "writing passion", enumerating, for example, more than 2,000 letters to his disciple Ferenczi and almost 500 to Abraham. "Every free minute between patients was used for letter writing," reports Grotjahn. "In the

evening when the work was over, more letters would be written"
(Grotjahn, 1967).

After 1912 there are no more reports of overt attacks of loss of
consciousness, a fact which may have some bearing on the date
of the cessation of his cocaine therapy. But other epileptic
phenomena suggesting minor temporal lobe attacks lasted till
much later in life. In an addition to *The Psychopathology of
Everyday Life* made in 1907, Freud recalls a curious episode
which took place during the serious illness of his eldest daughter
in 1905. Hopes of her recovery had been given up, but that day
there had been an improvement and she was now expected to
live. As Freud was passing through a room in his dressing gown
with straw slippers on his feet, "I yielded to a sudden impulse
and hurled one of my slippers from my foot at the wall, causing a
beautiful little marble Venus to fall down from its bracket". His
explanation for his admittedly "wild conduct" was that the
attack represented a "sacrificial act" – "rather as I had made a
vow to sacrifice something or other as a thank-offering if she
recovered her health!" The choice of the Venus of Medici was
clearly only a gallant act of homage towards the convalescent,
but he was still mystified as to how he had made up his mind so
quickly, aimed so accurately and avoided hitting anything else
among the objects so close to it. The episode is highly reminiscent
of the characteristic automatisms that occur in minor temporal
lobe attacks.

Freud admits to at least one attack of "depersonalisation" – a
period when his surroundings became suddenly strange and
unfamiliar – in his paper *A Disturbance of Memory on the
Acropolis*. The incident occurred in 1904 in Greece. Such attacks
were recognised many years ago as epileptic phenomena by
Hughlings Jackson and are now categorised as temporal lobe
events. Similarly the "fleeting experiences of *déjà vu*" which
Freud admits to in *The Psychopathology of Everyday Life* are
now regarded as one of the aberrations of memory that can occur
in temporal lobe epilepsy, first described by Jackson in the doctor
patient we have already encountered. A case reported by S. A. K.
Wilson (1928) in a patient who had had epilepsy for eleven years
demonstrates this aberration in an extreme form. In Wilson's
consulting room he described his condition:

"I seem to be constantly in a state which is a panorama of my
past life. At this moment, I feel that I have said all this to you
before, exactly the same. I do my best to shake it off, it is so
uncomfortable. Everything that you are saying to me I feel you

have said before. It is exactly the same with my wife's sayings and doings – in fact, with everything."

Freud's own explanation for the *déjà vu* phenomenon was characteristic – "whenever a man dreams of a place or a country and says to himself, while he is still dreaming: 'this place is familiar to me, I've been here before', we may interpret the place as being his mother's genitals . . ." (*The Uncanny*, Standard Edition 17, 245).

In this same paper, Freud reports one of the strangest episodes in his life, that of seeing his own double.

> "I was sitting alone in my *wagon-lit* compartment when a more than usually violent jolt of the train swung back the door of the adjoining washing-cabinet, and an elderly gentleman in a dressing-gown and a travelling cap came in. I assumed that in leaving the washing-cabinet, which lay between the two compartments, he had taken the wrong direction and come into my compartment by mistake. Jumping up with the intention of putting him right, I at once realised to my dismay that the intruder was nothing but my own reflection in the looking glass on the open door. I can still recollect that I thoroughly disliked his appearance."

He compared his experience to those of Ernst Mach, who had had two such apparitions. He too had thoroughly disliked his double and formed a distinctly unfavourable opinion of the supposed stranger who entered the omnibus, thinking "what a shabby-looking school-master that man is".

The phenomenon of the double or *Doppelgänger* has been reported from the earliest days of written records. It has proved a fruitful theme for many a chilling tale of the macabre, used to good effect by Oscar Wilde, Edgar Allan Poe, Alfred de Musset, Gabriele d'Annunzio, Jean Paul Richter and Dostoievsky. Some of the accounts from these authors have a verisimilitude resulting from a personal acquaintance with the phenomenon. Legend portrays the *Doppelgänger* as the sinister harbinger of approaching death and the story goes that he who sees his own double is doomed to die. The prophecy would seem to have been uncannily fulfilled in the case of Guy de Maupassant, who died soon after the first appearance of his double. The occasion is recorded by Axel Munthe in his book *The Story of San Michele*:

> "One day he told me that while he was sitting at his writing table hard at work on his new novel he had been greatly surprised to see a stranger enter his study notwithstanding the severe vigilance of his valet. The stranger had sat down opposite

him at the writing table and begun to dictate to him what he was about to write. He was just going to ring for François to have him turned out when he saw to his horror that the stranger was himself."

Dostoievsky's story *The Double* also springs from his own auto-scopic experiences. In this story his double appears to the petty official Goliadkine, and thereafter becomes his constant compan-ion, finally accompanying him in the carriage taking him to the lunatic asylum, hanging on to the carriage door and poking his head in through the window.

It was the German physician Menninger-Lerchenthal, who, in 1935, solved the mystery of these strange events. The double, he postulated, was, in fact, one of those bizarre phenomena arising from disorders of the *body image* – that scheme of our own bodies that we possess in our brains which enables us to relate to our surroundings and our different positions in space. Of the many curious disorders of the "body image" perhaps the best known is the "phantom limb" which appears after amputation of an extremity. Other parts of the body besides limbs can have their phantoms – the most recent case reported being a phantom tongue which moved up and down on swallowing exactly as had the living one, and which actually attempted phonation. The location in the brain of the cortical lesion generating disorders of the body image is now known to lie somewhere in the temporo-parietal region. This site has been confirmed experimentally – artificial stimulation of these areas in conscious patients operated on under local anaesthesia has elicited the typical hallucinatory experiences of a distorted body image. This would accord with Freud's other signs and symptoms of temporal lobe pathology.

Freud's belief that his fainting attack was caused by Jung's death wishes towards him shows that his old paranoia was still active as late as 1909. A classic example of a paranoid reaction is given by Franz Alexander (1940) who reported that he had heard from one of the older Viennese psychoanalysts that on one occasion Freud, referring to a younger member of the Viennese group said, "I cannot stand the parricidal look in his eyes." Jung appears to have been especially prone to arouse this reaction. Freud had originally been delighted when in 1906 he received an appreciative letter from the young psychiatrist, then chief assistant to Eugen Bleuler at the renowned Burgölzli mental hospital in Zurich, and warmly welcomed him to the psychoanalytic circle. His early followers, gathered around him since 1902, had been of an inferior calibre, many having no medical or scientific background and later described by Jung as "a degenerate and bohemian crowd" who did him no credit. The acquisition of Jung was therefore an important event, winning for psychoanalysis a foothold in academic psychiatry.

However, the very day after Jung's first visit to Freud in 1907 Ludwig Binswanger, another Swiss psychiatrist who accompanied him, relates that Freud questioned both about their dreams. "I do not recall Jung's dream," said Binswanger, "but I do recall Freud's interpretation of it, namely, that Jung wished to dethrone him and take his place." When later Jung tried to diminish the importance of sexuality in psychoanalytic theory his fate was sealed. The final schism was marked by analyses of slips of the tongue, and "symptomatic actions" to which Jung appears to have been particularly prone. Eventually Freud's polemic *On the History of the Psychoanalytic Movement* (1914) denounced him in such terms as to force his resignation from the International Psychoanalytic Association and Jung formed a new psychoanalytical school of his own.

It was in defence of the libido theory that Freud's paranoia reached its height. As Fritz Wittels wrote in 1924, "He watches over this theory jealously, will not tolerate the smallest deviation from it, and fences it round with a palisade . . . It was on account of differences concerning this theory that breaches occurred between Freud and three of the most noted among his scientific collaborators: Jung, Adler and Stekel."

Psychiatrists know many cases where the patient is ostensibly sane, converses normally, carries on his daily work, performing his duties and obligations competently in fact, presenting a picture of complete normality until his particular monomania is touched upon. Jung, in his *Memories, Dreams, Reflections* (1963) relates a significant episode in his association with Freud.

"There was no mistaking the fact that Freud was emotionally involved in his sexual theory to an extraordinary degree. When he spoke of it, his tone became urgent, almost anxious, and all signs of his normally critical sceptical manner vanished. A strange, deeply moved expression came over his face, the cause of which I was at a loss to understand."

"I can still recall vividly how Freud said to me, 'My dear Jung, promise me never to abandon the sexual theory. That is the most essential thing of all. You see, we must make a dogma of it, an unshakable bulwark.' He said that to me with great emotion, in the tone of a father saying, 'And promise me this one thing, my dear son: that you will go to church every Sunday'."

Jung early queried Freud's attitude to culture which the latter regarded as nothing more than "repressed sexuality".

> "I protested that the hypothesis carried to its logical conclusion, would lead to an annihilating judgement upon culture. Culture would then appear as a mere farce, the morbid consequence of repressed sexuality. 'Yes', he assented, 'so it is, and that is just a curse of fate against which we are powerless to contend'."

"Freud never asked himself why he was compelled to talk continuously of sex, why this idea had taken possession of him" continued Jung. "He remained unaware that his 'monotony of interpretation' expressed a flight from himself."

Freud's messianic obsession was evidently still alive as late as 1919 when he was maintaining that "the theme of sexuality is our shibboleth" (Jones, Vol III). It was the messianic traits of its leader that gave the psychoanalytic movement its unique quality of a quasi-religious, quasi-political body. On the religious side there were the "heretics" (Freud's own term – *Autobiographical Study*), excommunications and schisms. As one of his followers, Max Graf (actually the father of "Little Hans") wrote (1942): "Freud – as the head of a church – banished Adler; he ejected him from the official church. Within the space of a few years, I lived through the whole development of a church history." Reminiscent of the more extreme political movements is Freud's remark in a letter to Abraham, "I have completed the purge of the society and sent Adler's seven followers packing after him." Adler's sin was that his theories had "departed too far from the right path . . . He has created for himself a world system without love, and I am in the process of carrying out on him the revenge of the offended goddess Libido" (Quoted in Roazen 1971, p. 199). There was, incidentally, an inconsistency here, as Freud had always declared that libido was masculine.

Many who knew him in those days referred to Freud's extreme bitterness. Jung considered it was his most outstanding characteristic, "every word being loaded with it . . . his attitude was the bitterness of the person who is entirely misunderstood, and his manners seemed to say: 'If they do not understand; they must be stamped into hell'." (Jung, 1925).

In later years Freud wrote bitterly of the reception that greeted the publication of his early works, implying that they were not reviewed at all or reviewed badly. In the *History of the Psychoanalytic Movement* he writes of his "splendid isolation", inferring complete ostracism by his medical colleagues during the nineties. He was prone to rally his disciples with accounts of this "isolation" writing to Jung, for example, on September 2, 1907, "I would like . . . to tell you . . . of my many years of honourable but painful isolation which started after I had had my first glimpse into the new world . . ." (*The Freud/Jung Letters*, McGuire, 1974).

Freud claims in his *Autobiographical Study* that when he entered the university he was expected to feel inferior and an alien because he was a Jew. This contention is the most difficult of all Freud's allegations to understand. A great many members of the medical faculty in the top rank were Jews. A nineteenth-century account by a visiting postgraduate student states,

> "It was interesting to find that in this famous Vienna School of Medicine the great majority of the Professors were Jews. There was Professor Nothnagel (Medicine), Professor Kaposi (Skin), Professors Chiari and Panzer (Ear, Nose and Throat), Professor Monti (Children), Professor Wertheim (Gynaecology) and probably many more whose clinics we didn't attend."

The researches of Alfred Schick (1968) have confirmed that, "During the Freudian era about a hundred and fifty of Vienna University's faculty members were of Jewish origin; some were heads of departments, many were highly honoured and esteemed professors in their fields. Jews contributed greatly to the renown of the Vienna Medical School, which was once foremost among the universities of the world. Three Viennese Nobel Laureates in Medicine were Jews." Hans Sachs, one of the founder members of the Psychoanalytic Association, though agreeing with Freud on most things, refutes his assertions that antisemitism played a part in the resistance to psychoanalysis in Vienna. Himself a Jew as were the greater number of Freud's circle in those days, Sachs pointed out that many of Freud's most vigorous opponents were themselves Jewish.

As for the allegations of ostracism, Ellenberger and others have pointed out that Freud *did* get quite respectable reviews during the period, many favourable to his ideas. The truth seems to be that Freud was no more isolated than any other physician with a demanding practice carried on from his home. But apart from his practice he attended the Kassowitz clinic twice weekly, and lectured weekly at the university. His work at the Kassowitz clinic received due recognition from colleagues who acknowledged him as one of Europe's leading experts on children's paralyses, the great Nothnagel, for instance, inviting him to contribute to his monumental encyclopaedia of medicine. As we have seen, Freud was on the editorial board of the influential journal *Wiener Klinische Rundschau*. He was co-editor of another publication which reviewed each year the advances in the different medical specialities and was responsible for the reviews on neurology and psychiatry. Scattered throughout the Fliess correspondence are entries which give a rather different picture from the isolated existence Freud described. On November 2, 1896, for instance, he records that the great Wernicke had sent him a patient. The letter of February 9, 1898 announces he has been in Hungary for a consultation. On May 16, 1897 he writes, "I now have several new listeners and a real pupil from Berlin, a Dr Gattl who came to learn from me."

In spite of his disastrous presentation of the seduction theory to the Society of Neurologists and Psychiatrists and the void he sensed had formed around him, the episode was evidently soon forgotten as the letter of February 8, 1897 records,

"When I called on Nothnagel the other day to give him a complimentary copy, he told me spontaneously, and as a secret for the time being, that he and Krafft-Ebing were going to propose me for a professorship . . ."

That Freud had to wait till 1902 before receiving the title of professor was not, as pointed out by Varea (1966) due to prejudice, but to a long-standing disagreement between the ministry who preferred the title to be awarded to those more actively engaged in teaching, and the faculty, who rejected such narrow interpretations. So the picture Freud drew of himself as the spurned outcast was quite untrue. But Freud, as Roazen points out, knew the power of the legend and exploited to the utmost the popular concept of the lonely and misunderstood hero, the martyr of science, in the tradition of Galileo.

So we have good evidence that Freud's paranoiac tendencies and his "bitterness with the environment" were still strong well into the second decade of the twentieth century. Coupled with these traits, as is so often the case, was a certain shrewdness which enabled him to turn every situation to his own advantage and to conceal his psychotic tendencies from others. His attacks associated with loss of consciousness lasted until about 1912. Thereafter these attacks were succeeded by minor seizures of the temporal lobe variety. As we have seen, epileptiform seizures were a frequent concomitant of cocaine usage. There is in this pattern the tentative suggestion of continued use of cocaine up until 1912, after which the major effects of its use were no longer seen, pointing to cessation about this time, but leaving residual brain damage leading to minor attacks till well into his later years.

How was it that Freud's psychosis was not detected by colleagues and disciples at the time? In cases like this it is the borderline patients that are the most difficult to assess. If Freud had rushed around firing pistols in the air or picking off non-existent insects from his skin, there would have been little difficulty. But his psychosis was of a more subtle and circumscribed variety; the homicidal impulses which affected the doctor addicts in a previous chapter were, with him, expended in death wishes. He was, as far as we know, able to lead a reasonably normal life and carry on his work in his practice (he had by now left the Kassowitz clinic) and there would have been little to indicate his psychosis until his particular monomania was touched on. The disciples who surrounded him in the early years seem to have been unusually uncritical. Many had no medical or scientific background. Prominent among the group from the first were Viennese intellectuals and we have the testimony of Max Graf (himself a music critic) that it had from the first been Freud's intention to recruit such disciples.

"One day he startled me by announcing that he would like to have a meeting in his house once a week; he wanted there not only a number of his pupils [from his university lectures], but also some personalities from other fields of intellectual endeavour. He mentioned to me Hermann Bahr, the writer who was then the leader of modern artists in Vienna, who had a keen feeling for all new intellectual trends."

It was this intellectual coterie who gave the major impetus to the spread of Freud's ideas, propagating his theories as proven fact to a lay public, over the heads of the medical profession. Freud's messianic fervour must have played no small part in misleading these disciples into thinking that this man indeed possessed the truth, an attitude Freud carefully fostered. Jung plainly had his suspicions. He had been exposed to many days of Freud's company on the trip to the United States and was a psychiatrist with years of experience in a mental hospital behind him. But Freud's other followers plainly had no idea that their leader was anything other than the misunderstood genius he claimed to be. Many of these disciples too had their own problems, as the high suicide rate among the early circle, testifies (Wittels names Schrotter, Weininger, Tausk and Silberer). Stekel, also one of the early circle committed suicide after the completion of Wittels' book. There were to be many more among the later analysts. Their motives were given the customary psychoanalytical attributions. According to Wittels, Otto Weininger did a fragmentary self-analysis, and "the glimpse into his unconscious drove him to suicide".

But what they lacked in discrimination the intellectuals made up for in service to the "cause", many being in a position to sway public opinion in its favour. From Freud they learnt the shrewd and calculating methods of crushing opposition by the "resistance" and "youth" arguments, and, with direct access to the news media, used them to good effect. If Jung and a few others rebelled against the sexual theory, many early disciples became more orthodox than the master, more Freudian than Freud, happy to worship at the shrine of the goddess Libido. Let loose on unsuspecting patients they must have done considerable harm. Some examples from Fritz Wittels (1924) illustrate their methods.

"If a man is impotent because, in the unconscious, he detests his wife, we shall not help him much by convincing him that, long years ago, he was in love with his mother. He believes that he is devoted to his wife; he loads her with presents; he fancies he could not live without her. The analyst's 'cruel' duty is to drag him out of his 'heaven'."

"The owner-superintendent of an Austrian home for nervous diseases had read Stekel without fully understanding that author's drift. A young man who was one of his resident patients, and who later came to me for treatment, had been given the following prescription: 'You must masturbate! At least twice a week!' This amazing neurologist knew nothing of the evil spirits that dwell in the unconscious. The lad was affected with an unconscious longing to kill his father and all his brothers and sisters in order that he might be left alone with his mother. The doctor's prescription meant that he was, in fancy, to commit murder, to wade through slaughter, at least twice a week. By following the advice, he had been brought to the verge of lunacy."

Truly, as Macdonald Critchley described psychoanalysis, "the treatment of the id by the odd".

Young men were told they were really homosexual, husbands were advised to divorce their wives and wives were told to take a lover. Freud himself records his embarrassment when later confronted with one of the recipients of such counsels. One of his disciples had been treating a respectable middle-aged lady recently divorced from her husband and had traced her "anxiety state" to this event. She was told that to recover her health she must either return to her husband or take a lover or obtain satisfaction for herself. Since then she had been convinced she was incurable since she would not return to her husband and the other alternatives were repugnant to her. She was accompanied by another woman who implored Freud to assure the patient that the doctor was mistaken; it could not possibly be true, for she herself had been a widow for many years and had nevertheless remained respectable without suffering from anxiety. "I will not dwell on the awkward predicament in which I was placed by this visit," he wrote (Freud, 1910).

The persecuted few of the early psychoanalytic movement was largely a figment of Freud's imagination. From the early days when in 1902 an informal group gathered at Freud's consulting rooms on Wednesday evenings to the first international congress was only six years, by which time there was an International Psychoanalytical Association with its own journal, soon to have its own publishing house. By the end of the First World War Freud and his movement were world famous. The catch-phrases of psychoanalysis were on all lips and already passing into the common language of everyday use. The climate of opinion by the twenties is illustrated by the report in the *Oxford Times* of 1922 of the visit of a Dr Emil Busch, announced as a friend of Professor Freud from Vienna. A large and distinguished audience of towns-

Freud with the leaders of the psychoanalytic movement: back row left to right, Otto Rank, Abraham, Carl Eitingon, Ernest Jones and front row, Freud, Ferenczi and Hans Sachs.

people, undergraduates and dons, including at least two college heads, were present at his lecture on the new psychological theories of Sigmund Freud. Busch's paper, consisting of eleven folios of closely written manuscript, was received with rapt attention. At its conclusion the usual vote of thanks was moved and the doctor retired to the enthusiastic applause of his listeners. A few days later, the distinguished audience read in the *Oxford Times* that they had been victims of a hoax. "Professor Busch" had, in reality, been an undergraduate of Balliol in disguise. To a reporter, the "professor" admitted that the paper had been complete nonsense. He and his accomplice, he added, were still laughing at the applause which greeted the chairman's remark that "Dr Busch's works were well known". A "palpable hit in the field of psychological experiment" was the verdict of *Isis*, the university journal.

Freud himself was devoting more of his time to didactic analyses of aspiring psychoanalysts. In 1922 he wrote to Eduardo Weiss, an Italian analyst, that he was kept busy with a stream of students from abroad: out of nine people under analysis with him there was only one actual patient. He only published a few more case histories, that of a female homosexual, the "Wolf-Man" and the "Rat-Man". His major works were devoted to analyses of literary, historical and biblical figures, to myths and fairy stories, and to excursions into anthropology, education and religion. He thus grew further and further away from any actual clinical material and had almost completely lost touch with orthodox medicine. Freud's later works suffered from many of the deficiencies of the earlier papers. His book on Leonardo da Vinci (1910), claiming that he was a homosexual, relied for its thesis on an early memory of the artist when he was attacked in his cradle by a bird. Freud had used a translation which had erroneously given the name of the bird in question as a vulture. This led Freud to an elaborate excursion into the theme of the vulture in Egyptian mythology in search of support for his thesis. He even professed to see the outlines of a vulture in the drapery clothing the figures in some of da Vinci's paintings. The bird in fact was a kite and so the whole edifice of Freud's thesis falls to the ground. Similarly his study *Moses and Monotheism* (1923) claiming that Moses was an Egyptian murdered by the Hebrews and replaced by an imposter was derived from a Professor Sellin, who had, in 1923, formed the murder hypothesis on the strength of an erroneous interpretation of a passage in the Bible. Ten years later he admitted his error. Professor H. S. Yahuda, a scholar of biblical history, told E. Ludwig that in 1938 he had advised Freud to recall his words as

Freud in Vienna awaiting his exit permit.

Sellin had done. "Freud did not argue," Yahuda relates, "but replied quite calmly, 'And yet it might be true, for it fits so well into the frame of my thesis'."

Freud's cancer of the mouth which appeared in 1923 necessitated a series of operations and pain and discomfort borne with courage and fortitude. Though limiting his appearances at meetings and congresses, the cancer never interrupted his analytical work. The rise of Hitler and the subsequent war scattered the movement. Freud himself, one of the last to leave Vienna, sought refuge in London in 1938. He had been fighting a losing battle with the recurrent cancer of the mouth for several years and finally succumbed on September 23, 1939, after a terminal illness borne with unflinching courage.

Freud's death left the movement leaderless, though in time the reins were taken over by his youngest daughter Anna. Most analysts fleeing the Nazis settled in the United States, where they eventually became the psychiatric establishment, exerting considerable power of patronage over university appointments and, it has been alleged, the allocation of grants from public and charitable funds. During these years they began to exercise a great deal of influence over theories of child rearing, education and social work, disciplines still heavily dependent on Freudian theory today. Spock's famous book on baby care introducing the application of

Freudian methods to child-raising dates from this era. It was in this period too that Freudian theory became adopted by social workers to such an extent that, according to one commentator, "American social workers confused Freud with the Declaration of Independence." These attitudes crossed the Atlantic and Freudian theory is still at the centre of social casework in Britain, a fact which explains many of the incomprehensible decisions reached by social workers in recent years.

The appearance of the Jones definitive biography in three volumes from 1953 to 1957 spanned the centenary celebrations in 1956 of Freud's birth. The centenary was marked by lectures, broadcasts and newspaper articles by prominent psychoanalysts in which his theories were given the status of established fact. Jones' work with its eulogistic and uncritical treatment of Freud satisfied a growing curiosity. A new generation was introduced to the Freud legend and the popular revival of Freudian theory dates from this time. Freud's theories rapidly became an intellectual cult and he himself was elevated to the status of a genius with, according to one writer, "no equal in the history of the world except Aristotle." This place he still occupies in the intellectual and academic world of today when it could truthfully be said that his theories have left their imprint on almost every facet of human existence.

There have been false prophets in the past, but surely none which have had the undivided following of an entire generation of intellectuals. The lessons of the Freud story must be many – that the loudest and most confident voices do not offer the best counsels and that a grave bearded countenance does not signify wisdom are ones that could be learnt with profit by the young. The readiness of many intellectuals to accept wide-ranging philosophical systems on the sole authority of a single individual must raise questions of the status of philosophy in current thought. Are we too preoccupied with philosophies, cults and "isms"? Do we over-revere their creators whom we set up as "great thinkers" and can any one person always be a "great thinker"? A little healthy scepticism might be beneficial. Perhaps we take life and its problems too seriously. The Viennese had a motto, "The situation is desperate but not serious". It is a maxim worth following today when Freud's gloomy and pessimistic determinism still dominates our thinking and culture. By demonstrating its subjective origins it is hoped that this book will open the door for many people to a more hopeful and optimistic way of life.

Epilogue

The Freudian revolution of the early sixties which saw the widespread adoption of Freud's theories and the appearance of the "permissive society" that followed, make the last two decades an ideal period for the assessment of these theories as applied in actual practice.

In many ways, the Freudian revival resembled the first upsurge of the psychoanalytic movement in the early part of the century. As in the twenties, writers, philosophers, educators, social workers and clerics, the latter evidently undismayed by the fact that Freud had called religion a "universal obsessional neurosis" (1907), became the most enthusiastic protagonists. The newspapers of the years covering the Freud revival convey some of the enthusiasm with which his theories were greeted by the new generation of converts. They will probably astonish the historians of the future and delight the satirists. Even now the London *Observer's* leading article "Birth and Death" (dated December 20, 1964) deploring the lack of study of the "immeasurable, illogical depths" of the unconscious mind in academic psychology make quaint reading: "Can it be that this is the frontier where man's heart fails him . . .? Is it that his undignified inner feelings concerning sex and violence disturb him too deeply, so that he prefers to study almost anything rather than this?" Quaint too are the utterances of the fashionable clerics who jumped on the Freud bandwagon ("Freud recaptures the intuitions of the Bible"). Who but *The Guardian* would have called the sputnik a phallic symbol? – (a question asked by an advertisement to demonstrate that paper's progressive views appearing about this time.)

By the early sixties, a group of writers and academics had emerged, working actively for the implementation of Freud's theories and dedicated to the urgent modification of existing social attitudes to sexual morality "in time to prevent a breakdown of civilisation". As in the early days of the century many enthusiasts became "more Freudian than Freud", crusading for the complete abolition of all sexual "taboos" including those against incest and the more unusual of the sexual deviations. They campaigned for the overthrow of "fig-leaf and four-letter-word-fixated censorship" and deplored the lack of the vocabulary of sexuality and excretion in middle-class language. For the married they advocated "therapeutic adultery" ("wife-swapping") and for the enlightenment of the young, recommended family nudity and a form of sex education in the schools that would fit the child for the full expression of Freudian sexuality and with none of the deviations excluded. Zealots in Sweden asserted that children should be exposed to pornography from the age of three. The neo-Freudians believed in bisexuality and claimed that gender roles were learnt from parents in childhood rather than being inherent elements of the personality. Nor was "Thanatos" neglected. A mystique arose based on Freud's teachings on the death instinct and its components in which the obsessive portrayal of cruelty and aggression on stage and in the media was deemed cathartic and healthy. The works of de Sade moved from the Soho bookshops to the libraries of academia.

The neo-Freudians were reinforced by recruits from the clergy who argued the merits of "charity before chastity" and became important co-workers in the pressure for social change. The politicisation of Freud that followed the revival brought other allies. Already reconciled with the fashionable existentialist philosophy by Sartre, Freudian theory was also amalgamated with Marxism by the philosopher Herbert Marcuse. Freud himself had always rejected any political application of his theories and the Russians had long ago declared his teachings to be counter-revolutionary. But the two philosophies had actually much in common. Marx too had believed in the overthrow of conventional sexual morality, though for different reasons. Marriage to him was "incontestably a form of private property" and he contrasted it with the situation under communism "in which women become communal and common property" (*Das Kapital*). Marcuse, who became a central figure in the Freudian revolution, is said to have inspired the student risings of 1968; the marchers' slogan "The riot is the social extension of the orgasm" demonstrates the extent of the Marcusean influence. Marcuse's teaching became the philosophy of the New Left and a major influence in left-wing thinking generally, a factor that was to play an important part in easing the passage of legislation in the spheres of divorce and abortion that were to pave the way for the social changes necessary for the implementation of Freud's theories. The New Left influenced psychiatry and a school arose led by T. S. Szasz and R. D. Laing known as "Radical Psychiatry" which named a "guilty society" as the chief culprit in the causation of mental disorders.

The drug cult of the sixties was an early result of the "quest for instant mental health" which followed the Freud revolution. LSD had originally been introduced into psychiatry by psychoanalysts who claimed that its use in analysis rapidly brought results which had formerly taken months or even years of conventional psychoanalysis to achieve. Use of the "psychedelic" (named from the Greek – "mind revealing") drugs spread to become an intellectual cult. They were called "consciousness expanders" because it was believed that their use could reveal the "hidden depths of the unconscious mind". The messianic traits induced by these drugs ensured the rapid spread of the cult and the call of the ex-Harvard academic, Timothy Leary, to "Turn on, tune in, and drop out" echoed all around the campuses. Other forms of "instant mental health" had appeared by the seventies – "primal scream" therapy, encounter groups and "psychodrama", all based on or derived from Freudian theory and all designed to fulfil the needs of a generation obsessed with its own mental health – "the ME generation of the seventies", as it has been described.

In the days of the first impact of Freudian theory in the twenties, the actual implementation of his philosophy was confined to small circles of intellectuals and bohemians. There were important differences in the social climate of the sixties which led to a far wider dissemination of Freud's teaching. The most important factor was the appearance, "almost on cue", of the oral contraceptive, "the pill" of popular journalism, a development which Freud had sought in vain from Fliess's researches. In the euphoria that greeted its arrival the early reports of the pill's adverse effects were largely disregarded. The grim consequences of venereal disease that had haunted those of Freud's generation had, with the advent of antibiotics, long receded into the background. There were no longer any medical prohibitions to the full implementation of Freud's social philosophy. Another important difference between the twenties and the sixties was the growth of the news media, radio and television providing channels for the far wider dissemination of the new social philosophy, outlets which the neo-Freudians exploited to the full. The "New Morality" which inaugurated the permissive society is said to have originated from famous television broadcasts in the early sixties.

In retrospect, the "permissive society" can be seen as a spontaneous experimental situation almost made to order for the assessment of Freudian theory in actual practice. By the end of the sixties, all the original goals set by the standard-bearers of the New Morality had been achieved. Neither social taboos nor legal restraints remained to frustrate the full implementation of Freud's social philosophy. Did the newly liberated generation achieve the optimal mental health he had promised? The hard data available, the rates for attempted suicide, for instance, or the occupancy rates for mental hospital beds, would suggest that the expected lack of mental illness has failed to materialise and rather that the reverse has occurred. Suicide, for example, had, by the seventies, become the most frequent cause of death in American universities; crime rates were soaring and the numbers of children in care had multiplied. The figures hardly give credence to a picture of a happy society. Less tangible, but still discernible, is the impoverishment of art and literature long under the domination of Freud's pessimistic determinism. The emphasis on "significance" and symbolism had proved a gift for the pretentious but the impact of such artistic offerings as blank canvasses scrawled with four-letter words or symbolic trays of manure had inevitably to pall with the passage of time. When the Freudian inspiration in literature had been exhausted there was nothing new to say. The sterile vein was empty.

By the end of the seventies the neo-Freudians had moved on from Eros to Thanatos. A rash of books and articles on the subject of death and dying (the "last taboo") illustrated the mood of the day, symptomatic, perhaps, of the mortal sickness of the movement. The beginning of the eighties saw the emergence of a joyless society, its horizons narrowed and its vision dimmed, a society weighted down with the social problems left in the wake of the permissive society. The promised land had proved to be stony desert and Freud, who had pointed the way, a false and faithless prophet.

Glossary

ACROMEGALY: A condition characterised by overgrowth of the extremities of the skeleton, especially the nose, jaw, fingers and toes. It is caused by excessive secretion of growth hormone.

ALBUMINURIA: The presence of albumin in the urine, usually due to impaired functioning of the kidneys.

ANEURISM: Local dilatation of a blood vessel due to a defect in its wall.

ANOREXIA: Loss or lack of appetite for food.

ANOREXIA NERVOSA: Chronic loss of appetite or distate for food, leading to gradual emaciation. It has been attributed to psychiatric causes but recent research has shown delayed emptying of the stomach contents in a series of anorexic patients, which would indicate impairment of feed-back or other mechanisms governing the regulation of food intake by the appetite control centre in the hypothalamus, an important organ in the mid brain.

ANURIA: Absence of excretion of urine.

APHASIA: Loss of the power of speech or of understanding speech due to injury or disease of the brain centres for speech.

AURA: The subjective sensations or phenomena that appear at the onset of an epileptic attack. There are many different varieties of the aura depending on the part of the brain first affected. Abnormal sensations of heat or cold, or tingling, an abnormal smell, a feeling of *déjà vu* (that the present events have happened before) are examples of the phenomena that can warn a patient that an attack is under way. In some patients the aura never proceeds to an overt seizure so that their symptoms are not recognised as being epileptic in nature. Many so-called "panic attacks" which occur unexpectedly and without provocation, are probably of this variety.

CATECHOLAMINE: One of a group of compounds involved in the biochemical transmission of nerve impulses.

CHOREA: A condition characterised by involuntary movements of an irregular and spasmodic type. Now rare, it was once much more common as a late result of rheumatic fever and was familiarly known as St Vitus' dance.

CLONIC MOVEMENTS: Irregular jerking caused by spasm in which rigidity and relaxation of the muscles alternate in rapid succession.

CYANOSIS: Bluish discoloration, especially that due to breathing obstruction.

DYSPNOEA: Distressed breathing.

ENCEPHALITIS: Inflammation of the brain.

ERYTHEMA: Redness of the skin.

GOLGI STAIN: A method of staining nerve cells invented by the Italian pathologist Camillo Golgi. Such stains are used to make otherwise colourless tissues distinct from their neighbours and thus visible under the microscope.

HEMIPLEGIA: Paralysis of one side of the body.

INSULA: An important area of the cerebral cortex in which many nerve pathways converge.

IRRADIATION: The dispersion of a nervous impulse beyond the normal conduction pathway.

ISCHURIA: Suppression or retention of urine.

LIBIDO: Sexual desire. Though some authors have asserted that Freud used the term in a wider connection, we have the testimony of Ernest Jones that this latter interpretation is invalid.

MITRAL VALVE: The mitre-shaped valve between the two left-sided chambers of the heart.

MYELINATION: The formation of the white fatty substance (myelin) which forms the outer sheath-like covering of the nerve. Its insulating properties further the efficient conduction of the nerve impulses.

NECROSIS: Localised death of tissue.

NEURASTHENIA: A vague diagnosis popular in the nineteenth century to explain conditions in which weakness, lassitude, inertia, and irritability, etc. were prominent features.

OBNUBLIATION: Clouding of the vision.

OPISTHOTONOUS: Extreme extension and rigidity of the body occurring in some brain diseases in which the head and heels are bent backwards and the body arched upwards – the famous *arc-de-ciel* of the French authors.

PARESIS: Partial or slight paralysis or weakness.

PEMPHIGUS: A skin condition characterised by blister-like eruptions.

PONS: Mass of nerve tissue at the base of the brain.

RHINITIS: Inflammation of the mucous membranes of the nose.

SYLVIAN FISSURE/SYLVIAN FOSSA: A deep fissure on either side of the brain. Named after the French seventeenth-century anatomist François de la Boe (latinised Sylvius).

THYROTOXICOSIS: A toxic condition due to overproduction of the thyroid gland hormone (thyroxine).

TONIC: Continuous muscle tension in which the muscles are rigid and extended.

TONIC-CLONIC PHASE: Phase of epileptic attack characterised by rigid extension followed by rapid jerking.

TUSSIS NERVOSA: Nervous cough.

Bibliography

ALEXANDER, F. (1940) "Recollection of Bergasse 19." *Psychoanalytic Quarterly*, vol. 9, p. 195.

ANON. (1879) "Charcot on the somnambulic and cataleptic condition in hysteria". *The Medical Record*, New York, vol. 35, p. 82.

APRIL, R. S. & TSE, P. C. (1977) "Crossed aphasia in a Chinese bilingual dextral". *Archives of Neurology*, vol. 34, p. 766.

ASCHENBRANDT, T. (1883) "Die physiologische Wirkung und die Bedeutung des Cocains". *Deutsche medizinische Wochenshrift*, vol. 9, p. 730.

ASERINSKY, E. and KLEITMAN, N. (1955) "Two types of ocular motility occurring in sleep". *Journal of applied Physiology*, vol. 8, p. 11.

AZAM, E. E. (1887) *Hypnotisme, double conscience et altération de la personalité*. Preface de J. M. Charcot. Paris.

BABINSKI, J. & FROMENT, J. (1918) *Hysteria or pithiatism and reflex nervous disorders in the neurology of war*. Translated by J. D. Rolleston. University of London Press, London.

BAREA, I. (1966) *Vienna: Legend and Reality*. Secker & Warburg, London.

BECKER, H. K. (1963) "Carl Koller and Cocaine". *Psychoanalytic Quarterly*, vol. 32, p. 309.

BENDA, C. E. (1960) *The Child with Mongolism*. Grune and Stratton, New York and London.

BERNFELD, S. (1948) "Freud's Scientific Beginnings". *American Imago*, vol. 6, p. 163.

BERNHEIM, H. (1888) *Hypnosis and Suggestion in Psychotherapy; A Treatise on the Nature and Uses of Hypnotism*. Translated from the Second Revised Edition by C. A. Herter, M.D. New York.

BINET, A. & FERE, C. H. (1887) *Le Magnetisme Animal*. Paris.

BINSWANGER, L. (1959) *Sigmund Freud: Reminiscences of a Friendship*. Grune & Stratton, New York & London.

BLUMENBACK, J. F.: (1828) *The Elements of Physiology*. Translated with notes by John Elliotson, 4th edition. London.

BREUER, J. & FREUD, S. (1895) *Studies in hysteria. Standard Edition*, vol. 2.

BRIQUET, P. (1859) *Traité clinique et thérapeutique de l'Hystérie*. Paris.

BROWER, D. R. (1886) "The Effects of Cocaine on the Central Nervous System". *Journal of the American Medical Association*, vol. VI, p. 59.

CHARCOT, J. -M. (1877–1879) *Lectures on the Diseases of the Nervous System*. Translated by George Sigerson, 3 vols. New Sydenham Society, London.

CHARCOT, J. -M. (1887) *Leçons du Mardi à la Salpêtrière: Policliniques 1887–1888*. Paris.

CHARCOT, J. -M. (1890) "L'oedème bleu des Hystériques". Leçon recueillie par Georges Guinon, chef de clinique. *Le Progrès Medical*, vol. 12, p. 259.

CHETWOOD, C. H. (1889) "The toxic effect of Cocaine Hydrochlorate with Report of a case." *The Medical Record*, New York. vol. 36, p. 144.

CLARK, R. W. (1980) *Freud: The Man and the Cause*. Jonathan Cape & Weidenfeld & Nicolson, London.

CONNOLLY, C. (1966) "Spare the rod and spoil the couch". *The Sunday Times*, 9 October 1966.

DAVIS, F. B. (1973) "Three Letters from Sigmund Freud to André Breton". *Journal of the American Psychoanalytical Association* vol. 21, p. 127.

318

DELAHUNTY, J. E. & ARDRAN, G. M. (1970) "Globus Hystericus – a Manifestation of Reflux Oesophagitis?" *Journal of Laryngology and Otology.* vol. 84, p. 1049.

DEWHURST, C. (1963) *Gynaecological Disorders of Infants and Children.* Cassell, London.

DOWNIE, R. A. (1970) *Frazer and the Golden Bough.* Victor Gollancz, London.

ELLENBERGER, H. F. (1970) *The Discovery of the Unconscious.* Allen Lane, London.

ELLENBERGER, H. F. (1972) "The Story of 'Anna O': a Critical Review with new Data". *History of the Behavioural Sciences.* vol. 8, p. 279.

ELLIOTSON, J. (1937) "On the Ignorance of the Discoveries of Gall Evinced by Recent Physiological Writers". *Lancet*, vol. 1, p. 295.

ENGEL, J., LUDWIG, B. I. & FETALL, M. (1978) "Prolonged Partial Complex Status Epilepticus: EEG and behavioural observations". *Neurology*, vol. 28, p. 863.

FALCONER, M. (1954) "Clinical Manifestations of Temporal Lobe Epilepsy and their Recognition in Relation to Surgical Treatment". *British Medical Journal*, vol. 2, p. 939.

FELDBERG, W. (1963) *A Pharmacological Approach to the Brain from its Inner and Outer Surfaces: Evarts Graham Memorial Lecture, 1961.* Edward Arnold, London.

FLIESS, W. (1893) *Neue Beiträge zur Klinik und Therapie der Nasalen Reflexneurose.* Leipzig and Vienna.

FLIESS, W. (1897) *Die Beziehungen zwischen Nase und weibliche Geschlechtsorganen in ihrer biologischen Bedeutungen dargestellt.* Vienna. English translation from *The Origins of Psychoanalysis*, (Freud 1954).

FOX, G. H. (1926) *Reminiscences.* Froben Press, New York.

*FREUD, S. (1884) "Über coca". *Centralblatt für die gesammte Therapie*, vol. 2, 289.

*FREUD, S. (1885a) "Beitrag zur Kenntniss der Cocawirkung". *Wiener medizinische Wochenschrift*, vol. 35, 129.

*FREUD, S. (1885b) "Über die Allgemeinwirkung des Cocains". *Medicinisch-chirurgisches Centralblatt*, vol. 20, p. 374.

FREUD, S. (1886) "Report on my Studies in Paris and Berlin". In *Standard Edition* vol. I., p. 3.

FREUD, S. "Observation of a Severe Case of Hemi-Anaesthesia in a Hysterical Male". *Standard Edition* vol. I: 24–31.

*FREUD, S. (1887) "Beiträge über die Anwendung des Cocaïn. Zweite Serie I Bemerkungen über Cocaïnsucht und Cocaïn-furcht mit Beziehung auf einem Vortreg W. A. Hammond's". *Wiener medizinische Wochenschrift*, vol. 37, p. 929.

FREUD, S. (1892–4) "Preface and Footnotes to the Translation of Charcot's *Tuesday Lectures*." *Standard Edition* vol. I, p. 131.

FREUD, S. (1893) With Breuer, J. "On the Psychical Mechanism of Hysterical Phenomena: Preliminary Communication". *Standard Edition*, vol. 2, p. 25.

FREUD, S. (1894) "The Neuro-Psychoses of Defence". *Standard Edition*, vol. 3, p. 43.

FREUD, S. (1895) "On the Grounds for Detaching a Particular Syndrome from Neurasthenia under the Description 'Anxiety Neurosis'". *Standard Edition*, vol. 3, p. 87.

FREUD, S. (1895) "A Reply to Criticism of my Paper on Anxiety Neurosis". *Standard Edition*, vol. 3, p. 123.

FREUD, S. (1895) With Breuer, J. *Studies on Hysteria. Standard Edition*, vol. 2.

FREUD, S. (1896) "The Aetiology of Hysteria". *Standard Edition*, vol. 3, p. 191.

FREUD, S. (1896) "Heredity and the Aetiology of the Neuroses". *Standard Edition*, vol. 3, p. 141.

FREUD, S. (1896) "Screen Memories". *Standard Edition*, vol. 3, p. 303.

FREUD, S. (1900) *The Interpretation of Dreams. Standard Edition*, vols. 4 and 5.

FREUD, S. (1901) *On Dreams. Standard Edition*, vol. 5, p. 631.

FREUD, S. (1901) *The Psychopathology of Everyday Life. Standard Edition*, vol. 6.

* English translation in *Freud's Cocaine Papers*. Edited and with an introduction by Robert Byck; notes by Anna Freud, Stonehill Publishing Company, New York.

320

FREUD, S. (1905) "Fragment of an Analysis of a Case of Hysteria". *Standard Edition*, vol. 7, p. 270.

FREUD, S. (1905) *Three Essays on the Theory of Sexuality.* In *Standard Edition* vol. 7, p. 125.

FREUD, S. (1908) "'Civilized' Sexual Morality and Modern Nervous Illness". *Standard Edition*, vol. 9, p. 179.

FREUD, S. (1909) "Analysis of a Phobia in a Five-Year-Old Boy". *Standard Edition*, vol. 10, p. 153.

FREUD, S. (1910) *Leonardo da Vinci and a memory of his childhood. Standard Edition*, vol. 9, p. 63.

FREUD, S. (1912–13) *Totem and Taboo. Standard Edition*, vol. 13, p. 1.

FREUD, S. (1914) "On the History of the Psycho-Analytic Movement". *Standard Edition*, vol. 14, p. 3.

FREUD, S. (1917) "Mourning and Melancholy". *Standard Edition*, vol. 14, p. 243.

FREUD, S. (1919) "The Uncanny" *Standard Edition*, vol. 17, p. 245.

FREUD, S. (1920) *Beyond the Pleasure Principle. Standard Edition*, vol. 18, p. 3.

FREUD, S. (1923) *The Ego and the Id. Standard Edition*, vol. 19, p. 3.

FREUD, S. (1925) *An autobiographical Study. Standard Edition*, vol. 20, p. 3.

FREUD, S. (1925) "Some Additional Notes on Dream-Interpretation as a Whole" *Standard Edition*, vol. 21, p. 131.

FREUD, S. (1926) "The Question of Lay Analysis". *Standard Edition*, vol. 20, p. 179.

FREUD, S. (1927) *The Future of an Illusion. Standard Edition*, vol. 21, p. 3.

FREUD, S. (1930) *Civilization and Its Discontents. Standard Edition*, vol. 21, p. 59.

FREUD, S. (1939) *Moses and Monotheism. Standard Edition*, vol. 23, p. 3.

FREUD, S. (1954) *The Origins of Psycho-Analysis, Letters to Wilhelm Fliess, Drafts and Notes: 1887–1902.* Edited by Marie Bonaparte, Anna Freud and Ernst Kris. Translated by Eric Mosbacher and James Strachey. Basic Books, London and New York.

FREUD, S. (1961) *Letters of Sigmund Freud.* Edited by Ernst L. Freud. Translated by Tania and James Stern. Hogarth Press, London.

FREUD, S. (1974) *The Freud/Jung Letters: The Correspondence between Sigmund Freud and C. G. Jung.* Edited by William McGuire. Translated by Ralph Manheim and R. F. C. Hull. Routledge & Kegan Paul, London.

FULLERTON, A. (1891) "Toxic Effects of Cocaine and their Treatment". *Lancet*, vol. 2, p. 663.

GAERTNER, J. (1919) "Die Entdeckung der Lokalanasthesie". *Der Neue Tag.* Quoted in Becker (1963).

GAMGEE, A. (1878) "Demonstration on the Phenomena of Hystero-Epilepsy". *The British Medical Journal*, vol. 2, 545 and 561.

GASTAUT, H. (1954) *The Epilepsies: Electro-Clinical Correlations.* Thomas, Springfield.

GILBERT, D. D. (1898) "The Cocaine Habit from Snuff". *The Boston Medical and Surgical Journal*, vol. 38, p. 119.

GRAF, M. (1942) "Reminiscences of Professor Sigmund Freud". *Psychoanalytical Quarterly*, vol. 11, p. 465.

GRINKER, R. R. (1940) "Reminiscences of a Personal Contact with Freud". American Journal of Orthopsychiatry, vol. 10, p. 850.

GROSSMAN, C. & S. (1972) *The Wild Analyst: The Life and Work of Georg Groddeck.* Barrie and Rockliff, London.

GROTJAHN, M. (1967) "Sigmund Freud and the Art of Letter Writing". *Journal of The American Medical Association*, vol. 10, p. 850.

GUILLAIN, G. (1959) *J. -M. Charcot, 1825–1893: His Life and Work.* Edited and translated by Pearce Bailey. Pitman Medical Company, London.

HAMMOND, W. A. (1886) "Remarks on Cocaine and the so-called cocaine habit." *The Medical Record* New York, vol. 30, p. 583.

HAYTER, A. (1968) *Opium and the Romantic Imagination.* Faber, London.

HIRSCHMÜLLER, A. (1978) *Physiologie und Psychoanalyse in Leben und Werk Josef Breuers.* Jahrbuch der Psychoanalyse, Beiheft 4. Huber Bern.

HUTCHISON, R. (1950) "Medicine today and yesterday: a retrospect". In: *Fifty Years of Medicine: A Symposium from the British Medical Journal.* British Medical Association, London.

INGALS, E. F. (1886) "Cocaine in Hay Fever". *Journal of the American Medical Association*, vol. 6, p. 206.

JACKSON, J. H. (1931–1932) *Selected Writings of John Hughlings Jackson.* Edited for the Guarantors of *Brain* by James Taylor with the Advice and Assistance of Gordon Holmes and F. M. R. Walsh, 2 vols. Hodder and Stoughton, London.

JAMES, W. (1898) "Consciousness under Nitrous Oxide". *Psychological Review*, vol. 5, p. 194.

JANET, P. (1925) *Psychological healing: a historical and clinical study.* Translated from the French by Eden and Cedar Paul. London and New York.

JONES, E. (1953) *The Life and Work of Sigmund Freud. Vol. 1: The Formative Years and the Great Discoveries, 1856–1900.* Hogarth Press, London.

JONES, E. (1955) *The Life and Work of Sigmund Freud. Vol. 2: Years of Maturity, 1901–1919.* Hogarth Press, London.

JONES, E. (1957) *The Life and Work of Sigmund Freud. Vol. 3: The Last Phase, 1919–1939.* Hogarth Press, London.

JONES, E. (1959) *Free Associations: Memories of a Psycho-Analyst.* Hogarth Press, London.

JONG, H. H. de (1945) *Experimental Catatonia: A General Reaction form of the Central Nervous System and its implication for Human Pathology.* Johns Hopkins University Press, Baltimore.

KEVRAN, R. (1960) *Laënnec: His Life and Times*. Translated from the French by D. C. Abrahams-Curiel, Pergamon, Oxford.

LENNOX, W. G. (1960) *Epilepsy and Related Disorders*. 2 vols. Churchill, London.

LESKY, E. (1976) *The Vienna Medical School of the Nineteenth Century*. Translated by L. Williams and I. S. Levig. The Johns Hopkins University Press, Baltimore and London.

LEWIN, L. *Phantastica: Narcotic and Stimulating Drugs, their Use and Abuse*. E. P. Dutton, New York.

LEWIS, A. (1975) "The Survival of Hysteria". *Psychological Medicine*, vol. 5, p. 9.

LUDWIG, E. (1948) Doctor Freud: An analysis and a warning. Hellman, Williams & Co. New York.

MACMILLAN, M. B. (1979) "Delboeuf and Janet as influences in Freud's treatment of Emmy vol. N". *Journal of the History of the Behavioural Sciences*, vol. 15, p. 299.

MALCOMSON, K. G. (1968) "Globus Hystericus vel Pharyngis". *Journal of Laryngology and Otology*, vol. 82, p. 219.

MATTISON, J. B. (1887) "Cocaine Dosage and Cocaine Addiction. *Lancet*, vol. 1, p. 1024.

MATTISON, J. B. (1893) "Cocainism" *The Medical Record*, New York, vol. 43, p. 34.

MEYNERT, T. (1885) *Psychiatry: A Clinical Treatise on Diseases of the Fore-Brain Based upon a Study of its Structure, Function and Nutrition*. Vienna. Facsimile Reprint (1968) New York Academy of Medicine, Hafner, New York.

MORTON, W. J. (1880) "Hystero-epilepsy – its history, etc". *The Medical Record*, New York, vol. 33, p. 246.

MORTON, W. J. (1880) "Hystero-Epilepsy, or Hysteria Major". *The Medical Record*, New York, vol. 33, p. 388.

MORTON, W. J. (1880) "Induced Hysterical Somnambulism and Catalepsy". *Medical Record*, New York, vol. 33, p. 467.

MULE, S. J. Editor (1976) *Cocaine: Chemical, Biological, Social and Treatment Aspects*. CRC Press, Cleveland, Ohio.

MUNTHE, A. (1929) *The Story of San Michele*. John Murray, London.

MURRAY, T. J. (1979) "Dr Johnson's Movement Disorder". *British Medical Journal*, vol. 2, p. 1610.

MUSTO, D. (1968) "Sherlock Holmes and Sigmund Freud: A Study in Cocaine". *Journal of the American Medical Association*, vol. 203, p. 308.

NIESCHLAG, E. (1979) In: *Female and Male Climacteric: Current Opinion*. Edited by P. A. van Keep, D. M. Serr and R. B. Greenblatt. MTP Press, Boston.

NORMAN, C. (1892) "A note on cocainism". *Journal of Mental Science*, vol. 38, p. 95.

THE MEDICAL RECORD, New York (1885) "Cocaine in General Practice". vol. 27, p. 181.

THE MEDICAL RECORD, New York (1885) "*The Cocaine Habit*". vol. 28, p. 359.

THE MEDICAL RECORD, New York (1885) "The Dangers of the Cocaine Habit". vol. 28 p. 603 and 633.

OBSERVER The, Editorial, "Birth and Death", 20 December 1964.

OJEMANN, G. A. & WHITAKER, H. A. (1978) "The Bilingual Brain". *Archives of Neurology*, vol. 35, p. 409.

OLMSTEAD, J. M. D. (1946) *Charles-Edouard Brown-Séquard*. The Johns Hopkins University Press, Baltimore.

PENFIELD, W. & JASPER, H. (1954) *Epilepsy and the Functional Anatomy of the Human Brain*. Little Brown, Boston.

PENFIELD, W. (1975) with discussion by William Feindel, Charles Hendel and Charles Symonds. *The Mystery of the Mind: A Critical Study of Consciousness and the Human Brain*. Princeton University Press, Princeton.

PLATO *Timaeus*. Translated by R. G. Bury (1929). Heinemann, London.

PLESCH, J. (1947) *János, the Story of a Doctor*. Translated from the Hungarian by E. Fitzgerald. Gollancz, London.

PRINCE, M. (1906) *The Dissociation of a Personality*. Longmans, Green & Co. New York and London.

RAMON Y CAJAL, S. (1937) *Recollections of my Life.* Translated by E. Horne Craigie with the assistance of Juan Cano. The American Philosophical Society, Philadelphia.

REYNOLDS, J. R. (1869) "Paralysis and other disorders of motion and sensation, dependent on idea". *The British Medical Journal*, p. 483.

RICH, R. R. & McCORDOCK, H. A. (1933) "The Pathogenesis of Tuberculous Meningitis". *Bulletin of the Johns Hopkins Hospital*, vol. 52, p. 5.

RING, F. W. (1887) "Cocaine and its Fascinations, from a Personal experience." *The Medical Record*, New York, vol. 32, p. 274.

ROBERTSON, E. G. (1954) "Photogenic Epilepsy: Self-Precipitated Attacks". *Brain*, vol. 77, p. 232.

ROBERTSON, G. (1892) "Hypnotism at Paris and Nancy: Notes of a Visit." *The Journal of Mental Science*, vol. 38, p. 494.

ROBINSON, H. R. (1942) *A Modern de Quincey.* George G. Harrap, London.

ROBINSON, V. (1929)"Guillaume Benjamin Amant Duchenne". *Medical Life*, vol. 36, p. 28.

ROMBERG, M. H. (1853) *A Manual of the Nervous Diseases of Man.* Translated and edited by E. H. Sieveking. Sydenham Society, London.

RUITENBEEK, H. M. Editor (1973) *Freud as we knew him.* Wayne State University Press, Detroit.

RUSH, B. (1812) *Medical Inquiries and Observations upon the Diseases of the Mind.* New York.

SACHS, H. (1944) *Freud, Master and Friend.* Harvard University Press, Cambridge, Mass.

SAUNDBY, R. (1891) "Clinical Lectures on Toxic Hysteria". *Lancet*, vol. 1, p. 2.

SCHAPIRO, A. K., SHAPIRO, E. S., BRUUN, R. D. & SWEET, R. D. (1978) *Gilles de la Tourette Syndrome.* Raven Press, New York.

SCHICK, A. (1968) "The Vienna of Sigmund Freud". *The Psychoanalytic Review*, vol. 55, p. 529.

SCHUR, M. Editor (1965) *Drives, Affects, Behaviour, vol. 2. Essays in Memory of Marie Bonaparte*. International Universities Press, Inc. New York.

SCHUR, M. (1966) "Some Additional 'Day Residues' of the 'Specimen Dream'". In *Psychoanalysis – a General Psychology*, edited by R. M. Loewenstein, L. M. Newman, M. Schur & A. J. Solnit. International Universities Press, New York.

SCHUR, M. (1972) *Freud: Living and Dying*. The Hogarth Press, London.

SLATER, E. (1965) "Diagnosis of 'Hysteria'." *British Medical Journal*, vol. 1, p. 1395.

SMITH, R. P. (1892) "Case of Cocainism". *Journal of Mental Science*, vol. 38, p. 408.

SPRINGTHORPE, J. W. (1897) "The Confessions of a Cocainist". *The Scientific American*, Supplement 1107, p. 17695.

STORR, A. (1966) "The Concept of Cure". In *Psychoanalysis Observed*. Edited by C. Rycroft. Penguin, London.

SULLOWAY, F. J. (1979) *Freud, Biologist of the Mind: Beyond the Psychoanalytic Legend*. Basic Books, New York.

SUTHERLAND, J. M. & EADIE, M. J. (1980) *The Epilepsies: Modern Diagnosis and Treatment*. 3rd edition, Churchill Livingstone, London and Edinburgh.

SYDENHAM, T. (1850) "Epistolatory Dissertation". In *The Works of Thomas Sydenham*, M. D. Vol. II. Translated from the Latin Edition of Dr Greenhill by R. C. Latham, M. D. London.

THORNTON, E. M. (1976) *Hypnotism, Hysteria and Epilepsy: An Historical Synthesis*. Heinemann Medical Books, London.

TREVES, F. (1928) *The Elephant Man and Other Reminiscences*. 2nd edition. Cassell, London.

TUKE, D. H. (1881) "Hypnosis Redivivus". *Journal of Mental Science*, vol. 26, p. 531.

WHYTT, R. (1751) *An Essay on the Vital and Other Involuntary Motions of Animals*. Edinburgh.

WILSON, J. R. (1971) "Perspective". *World Medicine*, July 28th.

WILSON, S. A. K. (1928) *Modern Problems in Neurology.* Edward Arnold, London.

WITTELS, F. (1924) *Sigmund Freud: His Personality, his Teaching and his School.* Translated from the German by Eden and Cedar Paul, Allen and Unwin, London.

WORTIS, J. (1940) "Fragments of a Freudian Analysis". *American Journal of Orthopsychiatry.* vol. 10, p. 843.

YELLOWLEES, D. (1880) "Notes of a Visit to Professor Charcot's Wards". *Journal of Mental Science*, vol. 26, p. 131.

Index

340